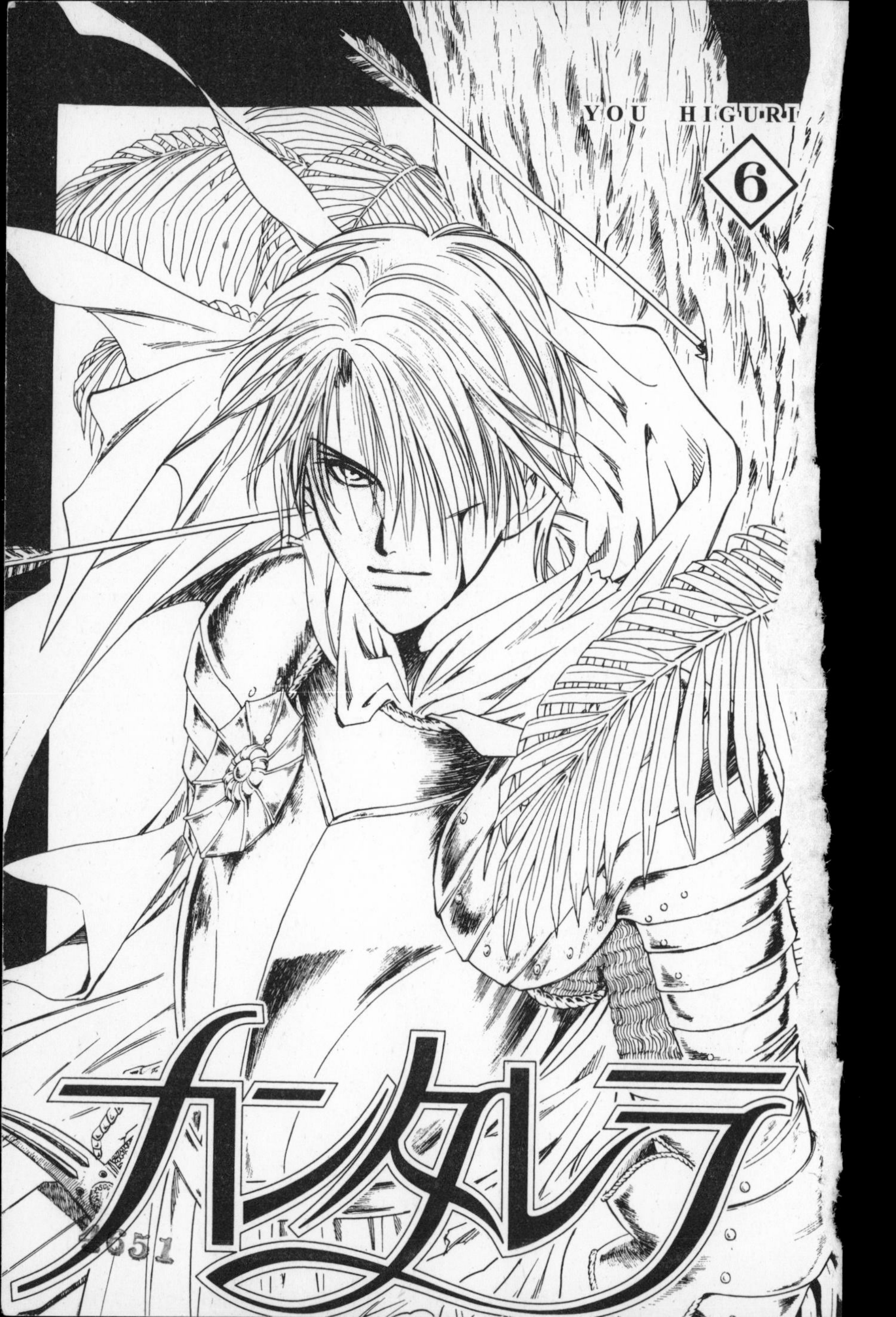
YOU HIGURI
6

Translation – Christine Schilling
Adaptation – Audry Taylor
Production Assistant – Mallory Reaves
Lettering & Design– Fawn Lau
Production Manager – James Dashiell
Editor – Audry Taylor

A Go! Comi manga

Published by Go! Media Entertainment, LLC

Cantarella Volume 6
© YOU HIGURI 2003
Originally published in Japan in 2003 by Akita Publishing Co., Ltd., Tokyo.
English translation rights arranged with Akita Publishing Co., Ltd.
through TOHAN CORPORATION, Tokyo.

English Text © 2007 Go! Media Entertainment, LLC. All rights reserved.

Visit us online at www.gocomi.com
e-mail: info@gocomi.com

ISBN 978-1-933617-09-1

First printed in March 2007

1   2   3   4   5   6   7   8   9

Manufactured in the United States of America

Cantarella

STORY AND ART BY
YOU HIGURI

VOLUME 6

go!comi

& Cast of Characters

Table of Contents

It is a poison that leaves not a trace, working in secret...

Cesare Borgia

The hero of our story. His father sold his soul to the devil in exchange for gaining the Papal throne. Constantly on the brink of being devoured by the demonic power within in, he is driven by the all-consuming desire to unify Italy.

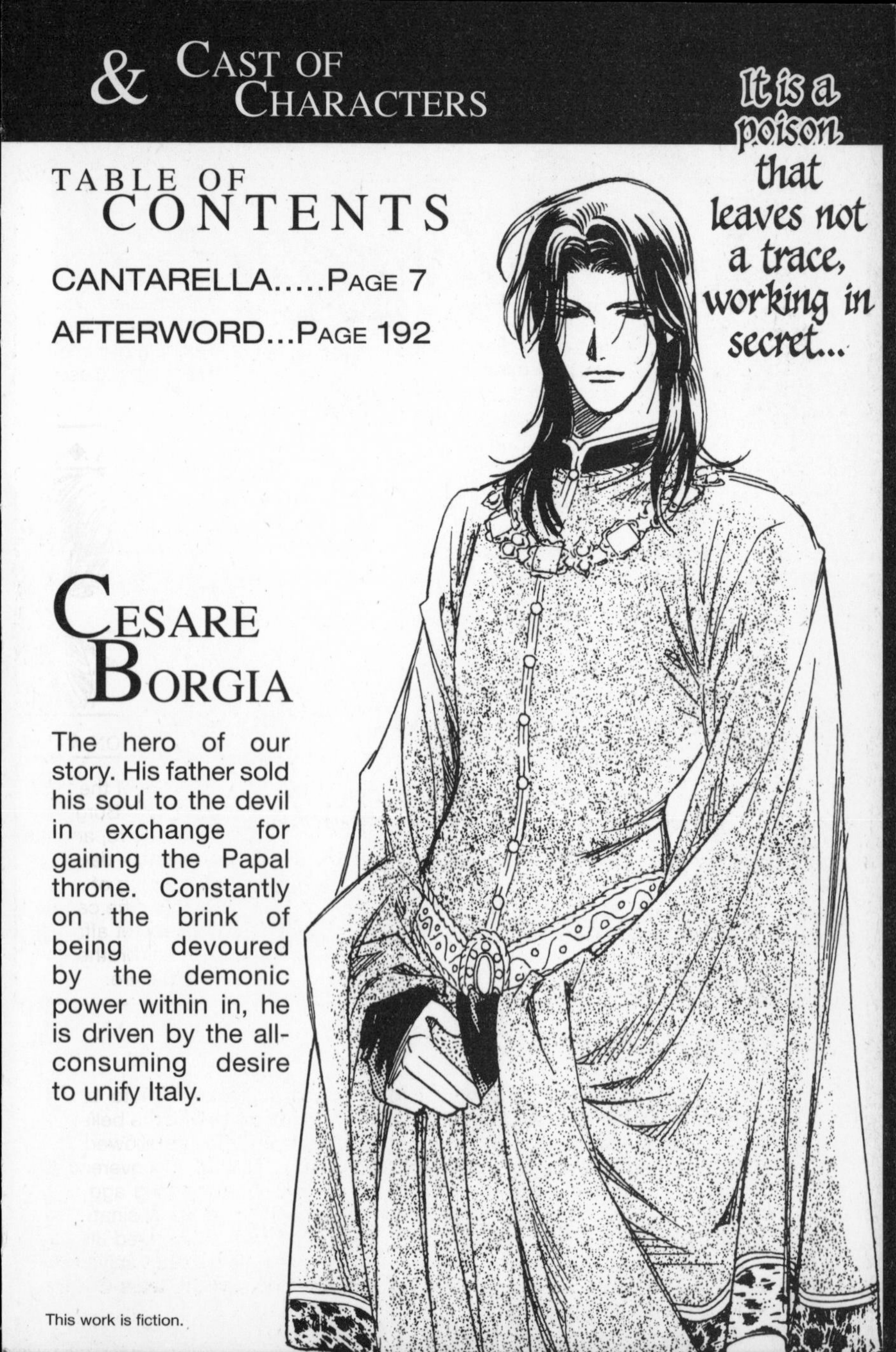

Cantarella 6 TABLE OF CONTENTS

◆ POPE ALEXANDER VI ◆

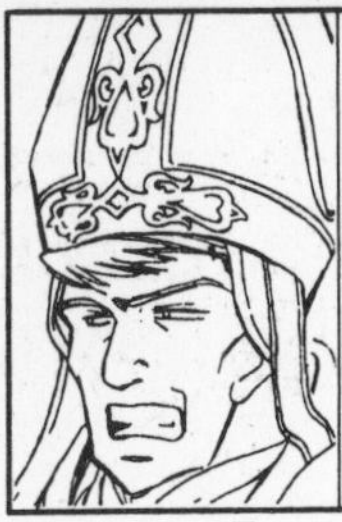

An ambitious man who sold his own son's soul to the devil in exchange for the Papal throne. He has solidified his authority through nepotism.

◆ MICHELOTTO (CHIARO) ◆

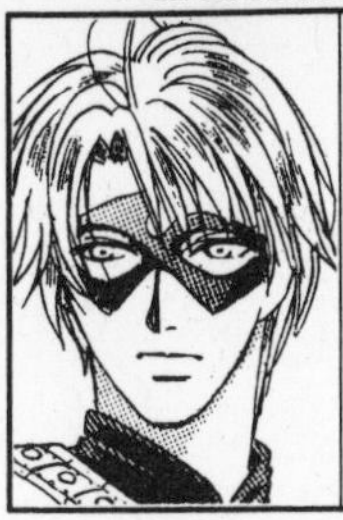

A legendary assassin who wears the mask of "Michelotto." He holds the power to repel the evil spirits possessing Cesare.

◆ JUAN BORGIA ◆

Cesare's little brother. Favored by his father, he led a blessed life.

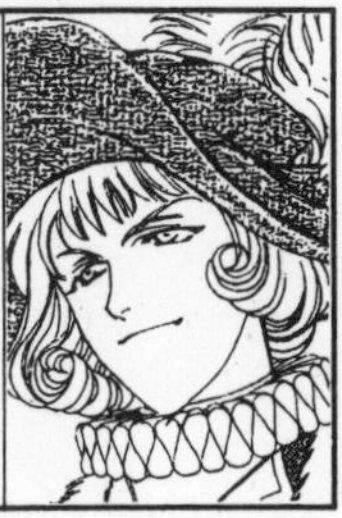

◆ LUCREZIA BORGIA ◆

A sweet girl who adores her older brother, Cesare. She was forced to wed the Lord of Pesaro but she has been called home and now resides in a monastery.

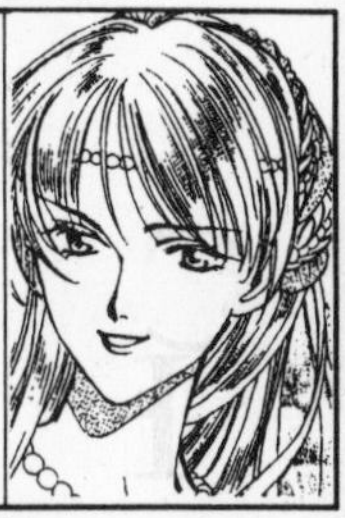

◆DELLA VOLPE◆

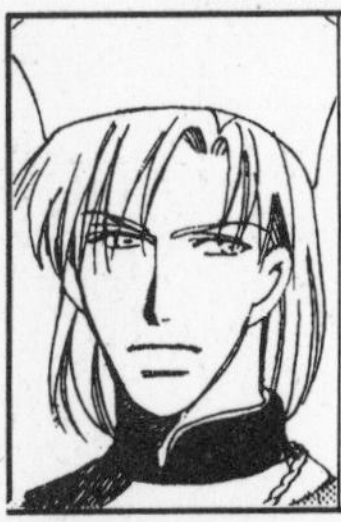

Cesare's loyal retainer. He looks up to Cesare because of his tyrannical nature.

◆ SANCIA D'ARAGON ◆

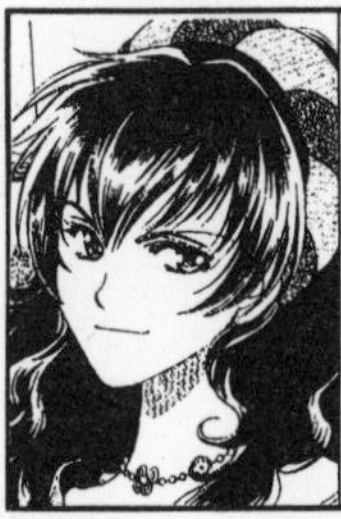

The wife of the third son in the Borgia family, Jofre, and the illegitimate daughter of the King of Naples. She carried on a secret affair with her brother-in-law, Cesare.

STORY SO FAR

In the last volume, Juan abducted Chiaro and subjected him to brutal torture. Cesare rushed to Chiaro's rescue, only to discover what he believed was Chiaro's dead body. Shattered by the discovery, Cesare allowed the demons within to take over his body. When Chiaro, still alive, discovered his friend's transformation, he vowed to do as he had promised long ago and kill the now inhuman Cesare. Meanwhile, Juan plotted to assassinate his older brother, a scheme that backfired when his brother slaughtered Juan's assassins and then went after him. Juan's death became Cesare's salvation, as Chiaro withdrew his vow to kill his friend when he saw the tears Cesare shed upon his brother's death...

Various cities and territories of Italy during *Cantarella* period

(end of the 15th century)

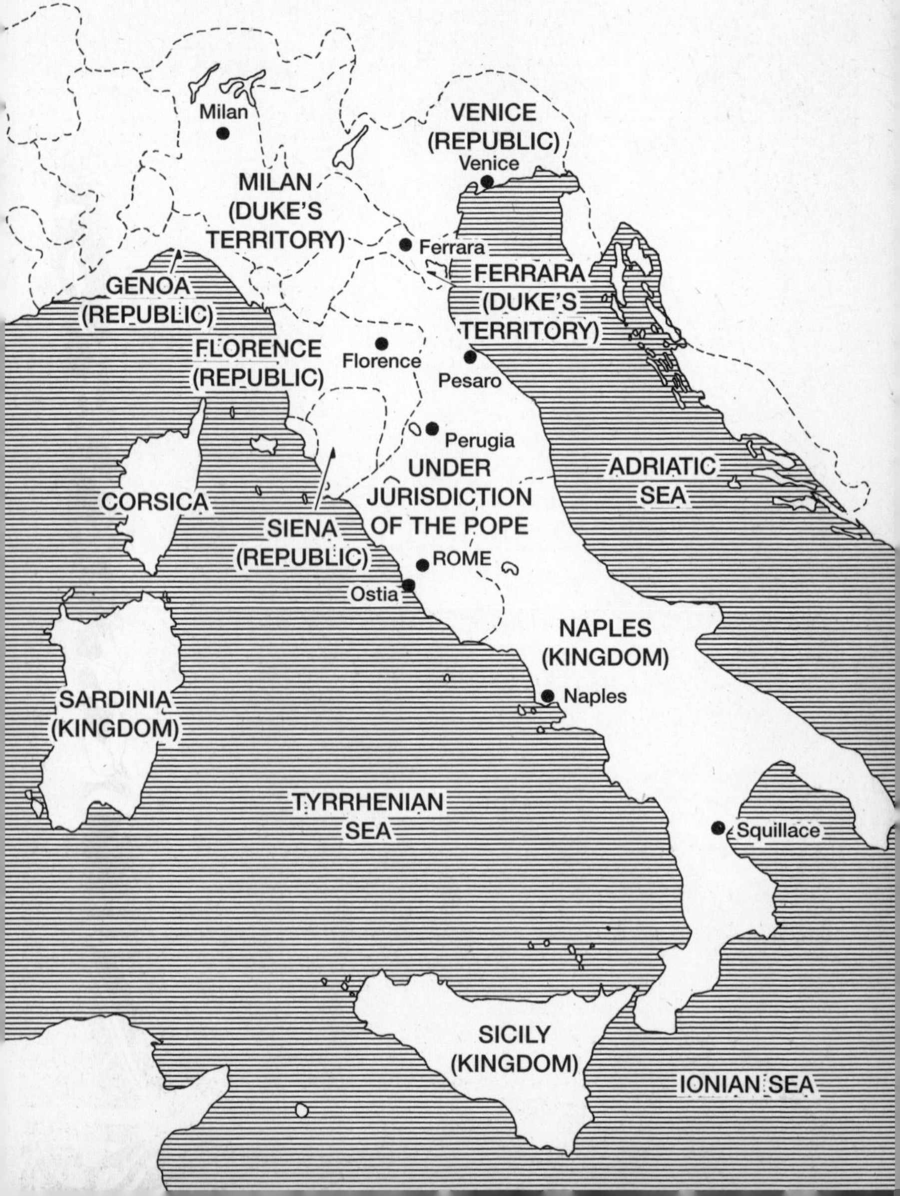
Milan
VENICE (REPUBLIC)
Venice
MILAN (DUKE'S TERRITORY)
Ferrara
FERRARA (DUKE'S TERRITORY)
GENOA (REPUBLIC)
FLORENCE (REPUBLIC)
Florence
Pesaro
Perugia
UNDER JURISDICTION OF THE POPE
ADRIATIC SEA
CORSICA
SIENA (REPUBLIC)
ROME
Ostia
NAPLES (KINGDOM)
Naples
SARDINIA (KINGDOM)
TYRRHENIAN SEA
Squillace
SICILY (KINGDOM)
IONIAN SEA

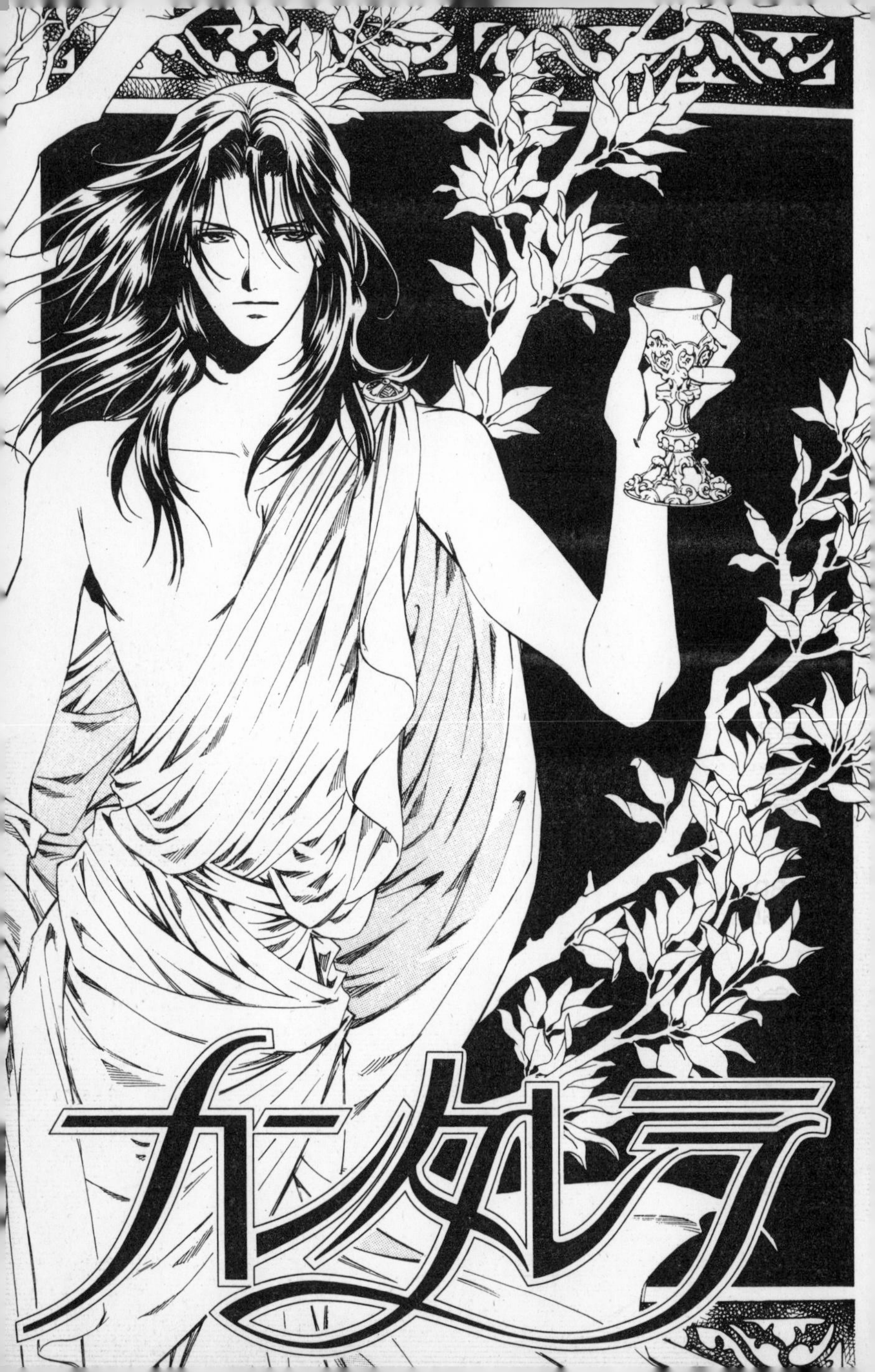
カンタレラ

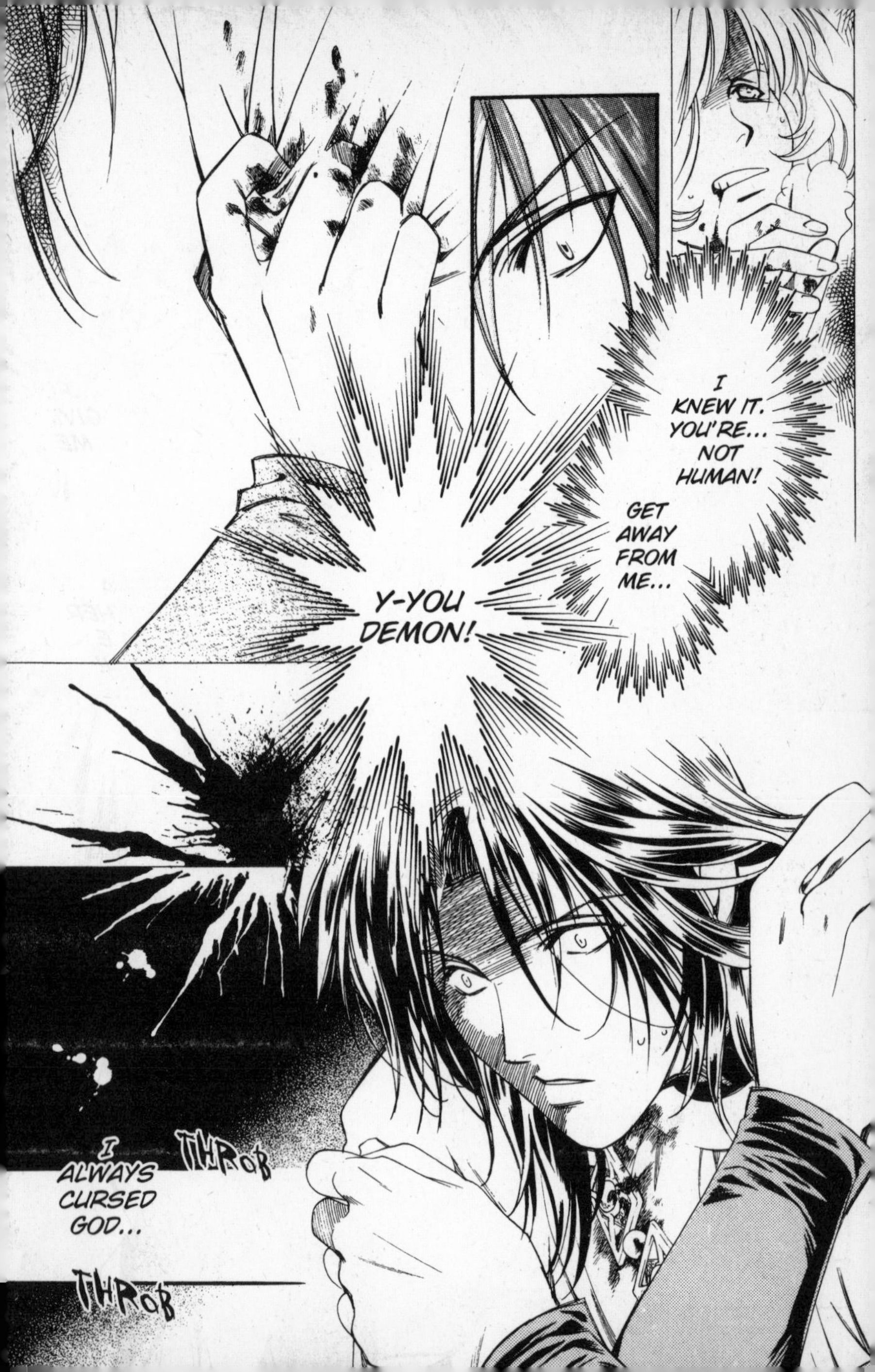
I KNEW IT. YOU'RE... NOT HUMAN!
GET AWAY FROM ME...
Y-YOU DEMON!
THROB
I ALWAYS CURSED GOD...
THROB

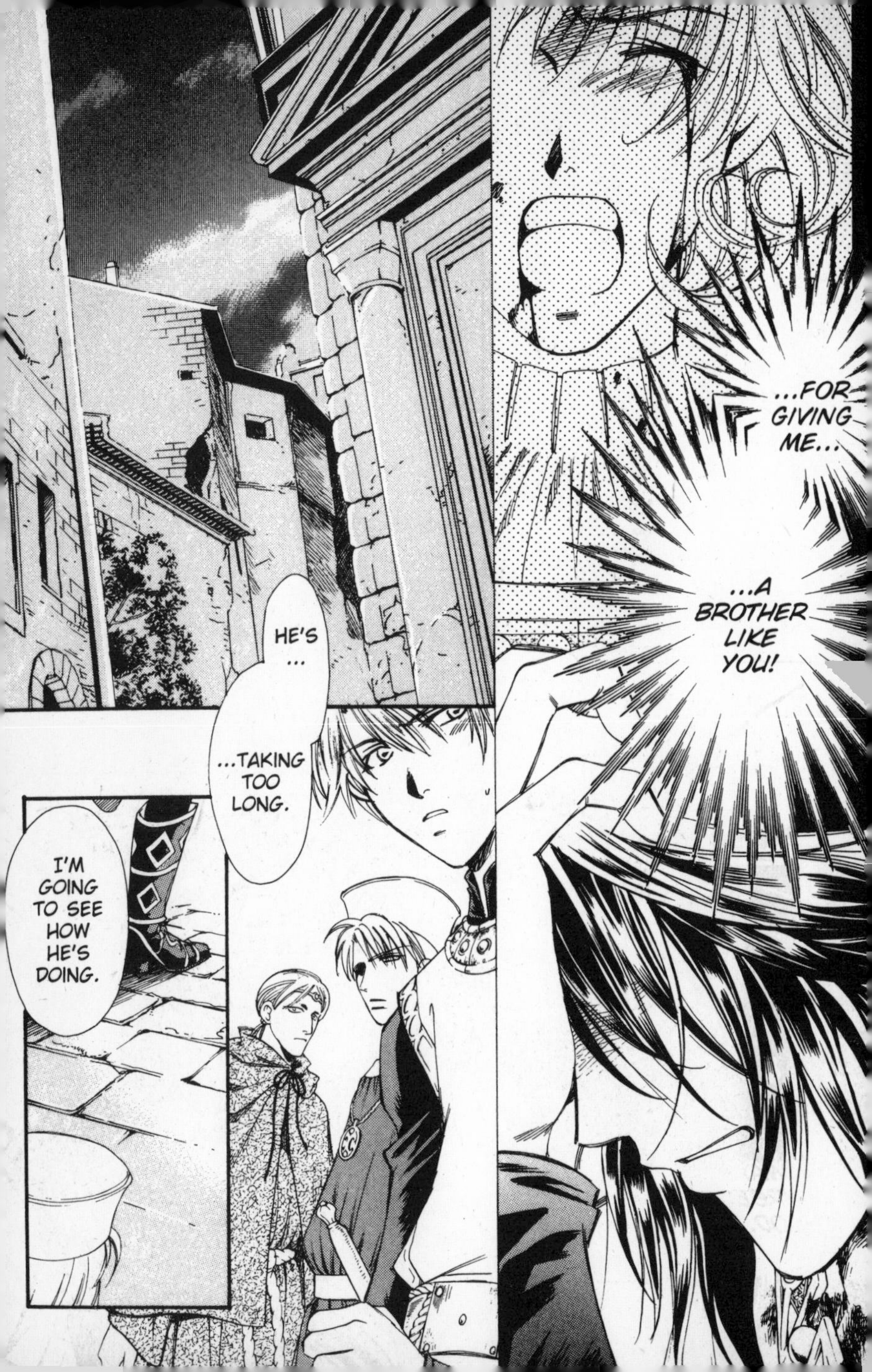
...FOR GIVING ME...
...A BROTHER LIKE YOU!
HE'S ...
...TAKING TOO LONG.
I'M GOING TO SEE HOW HE'S DOING.

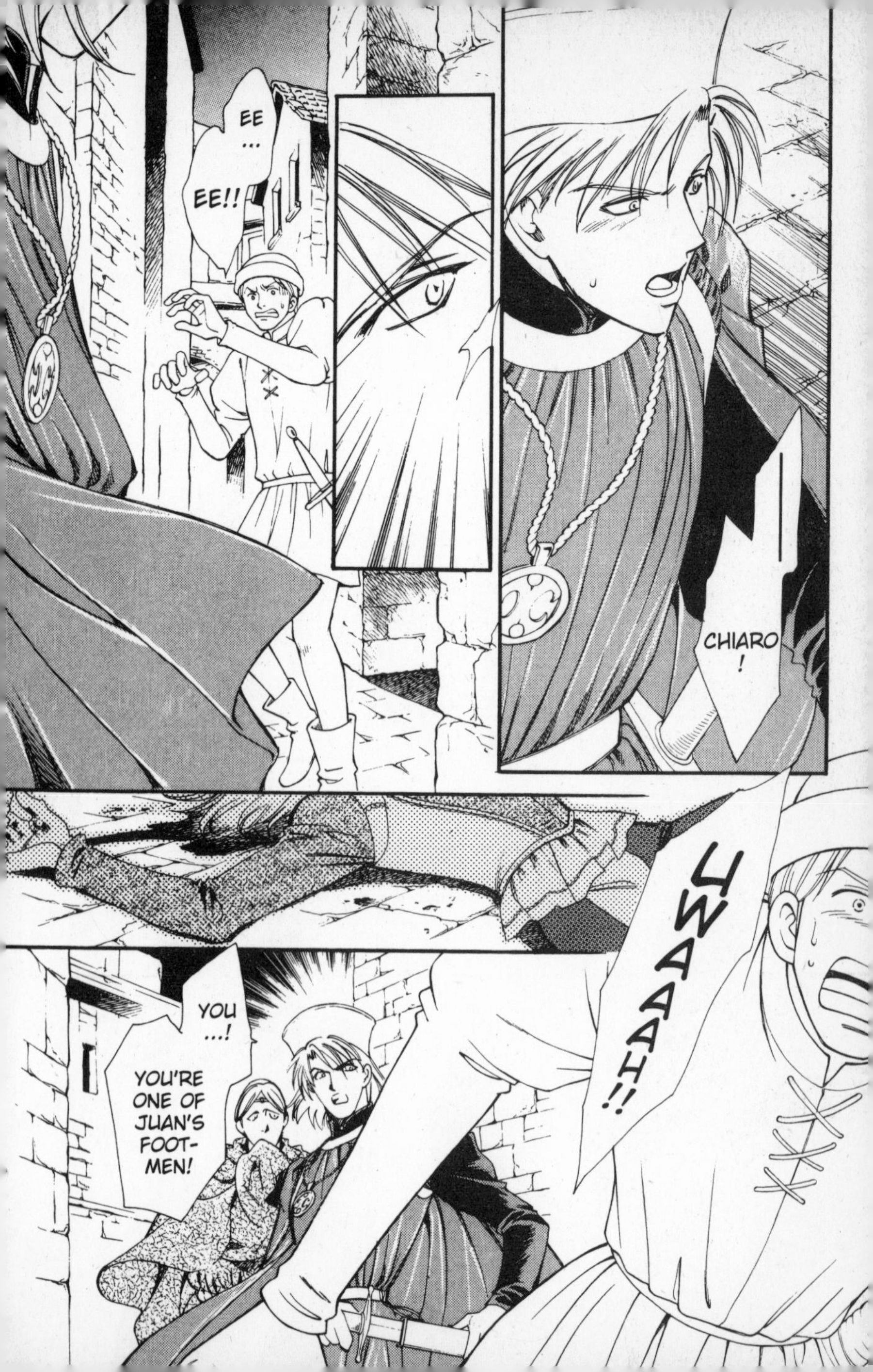
CHIARO!
EE... EE!!
UWAAAAH!!
YOU...!
YOU'RE ONE OF JUAN'S FOOT-MEN!

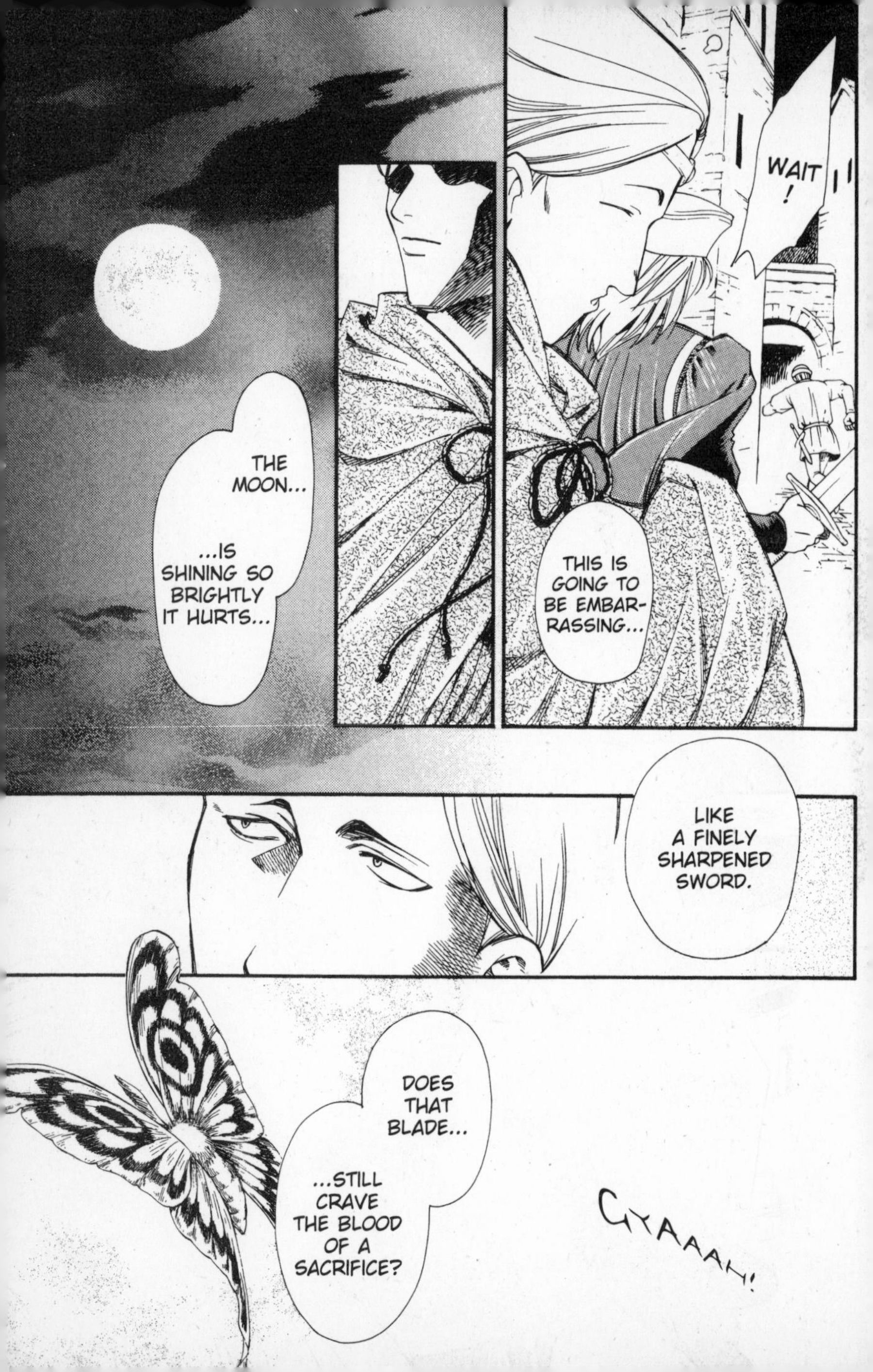
WAIT!
THIS IS GOING TO BE EMBARRASSING...
THE MOON...
...IS SHINING SO BRIGHTLY IT HURTS...
LIKE A FINELY SHARPENED SWORD.
DOES THAT BLADE...
...STILL CRAVE THE BLOOD OF A SACRIFICE?
GYAAAAH!

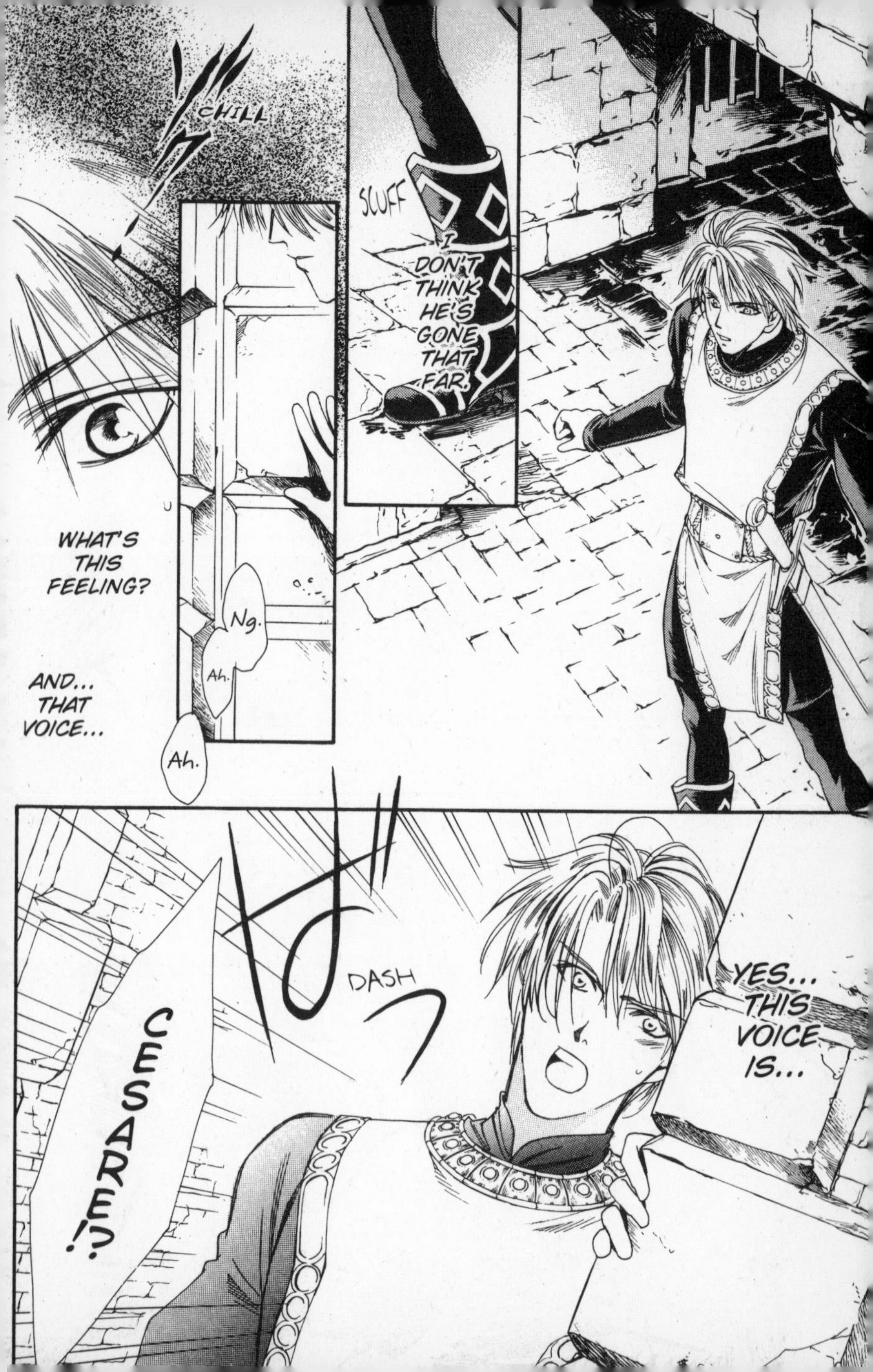
I DON'T THINK HE'S GONE THAT FAR.
SCUFF
CHILL
Ng.
Ah.
Ah.
WHAT'S THIS FEELING?
AND... THAT VOICE...
YES... THIS VOICE IS...
DASH
CESARE!?

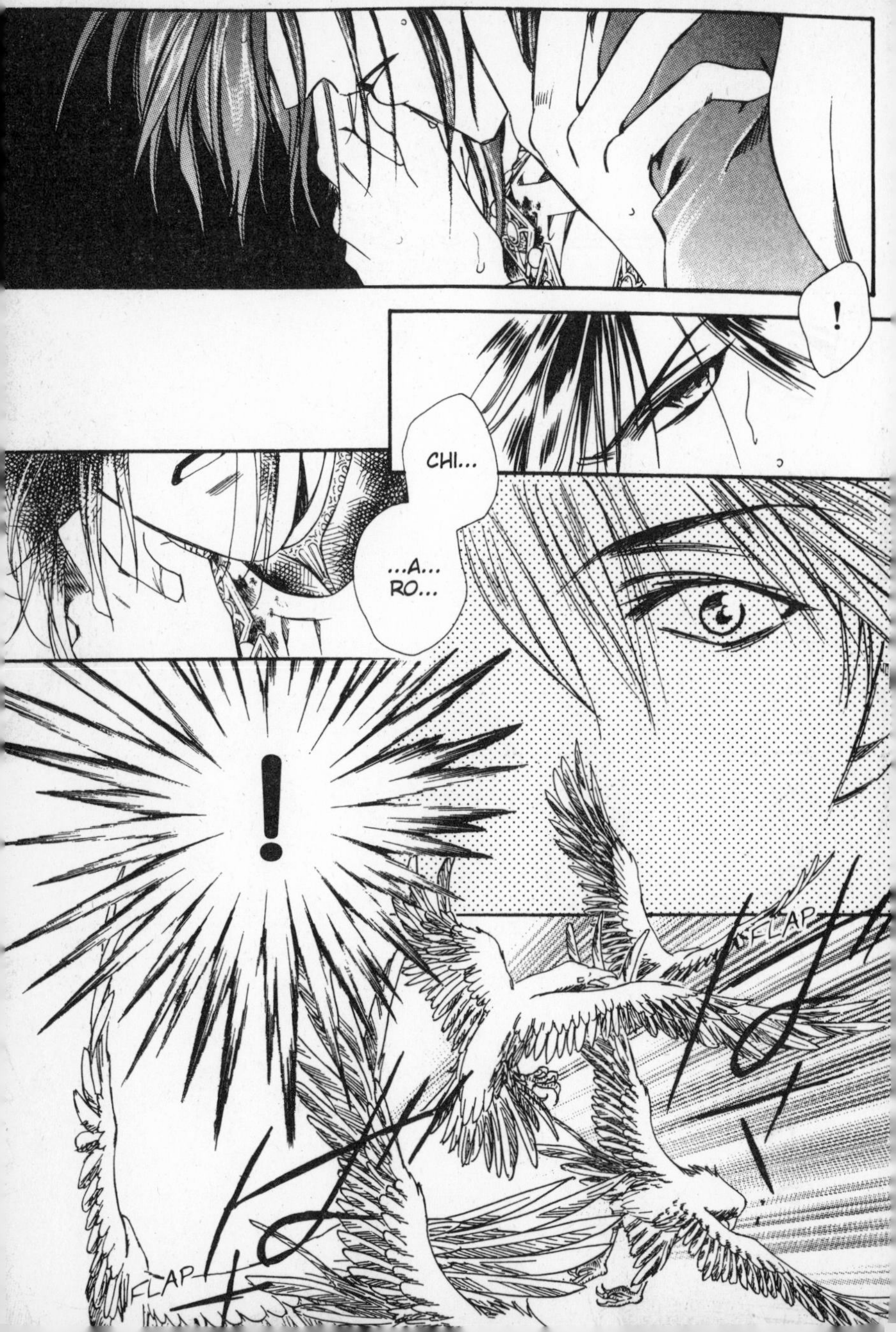
!
CHI...
...A...
RO...
!
FLAP
FLAP

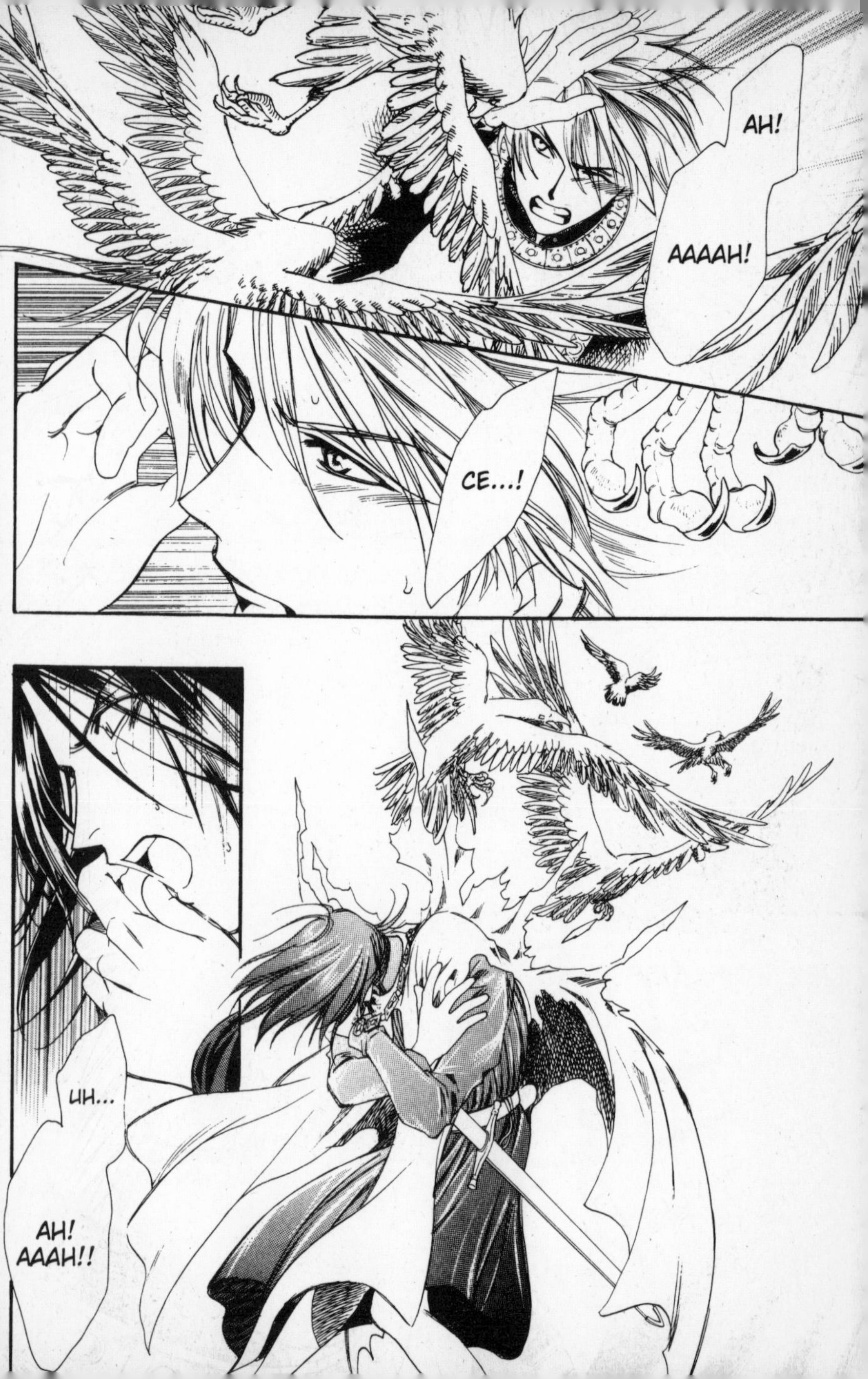
AH!
AAAAH!
CE...!
UH...
AH! AAAH!!

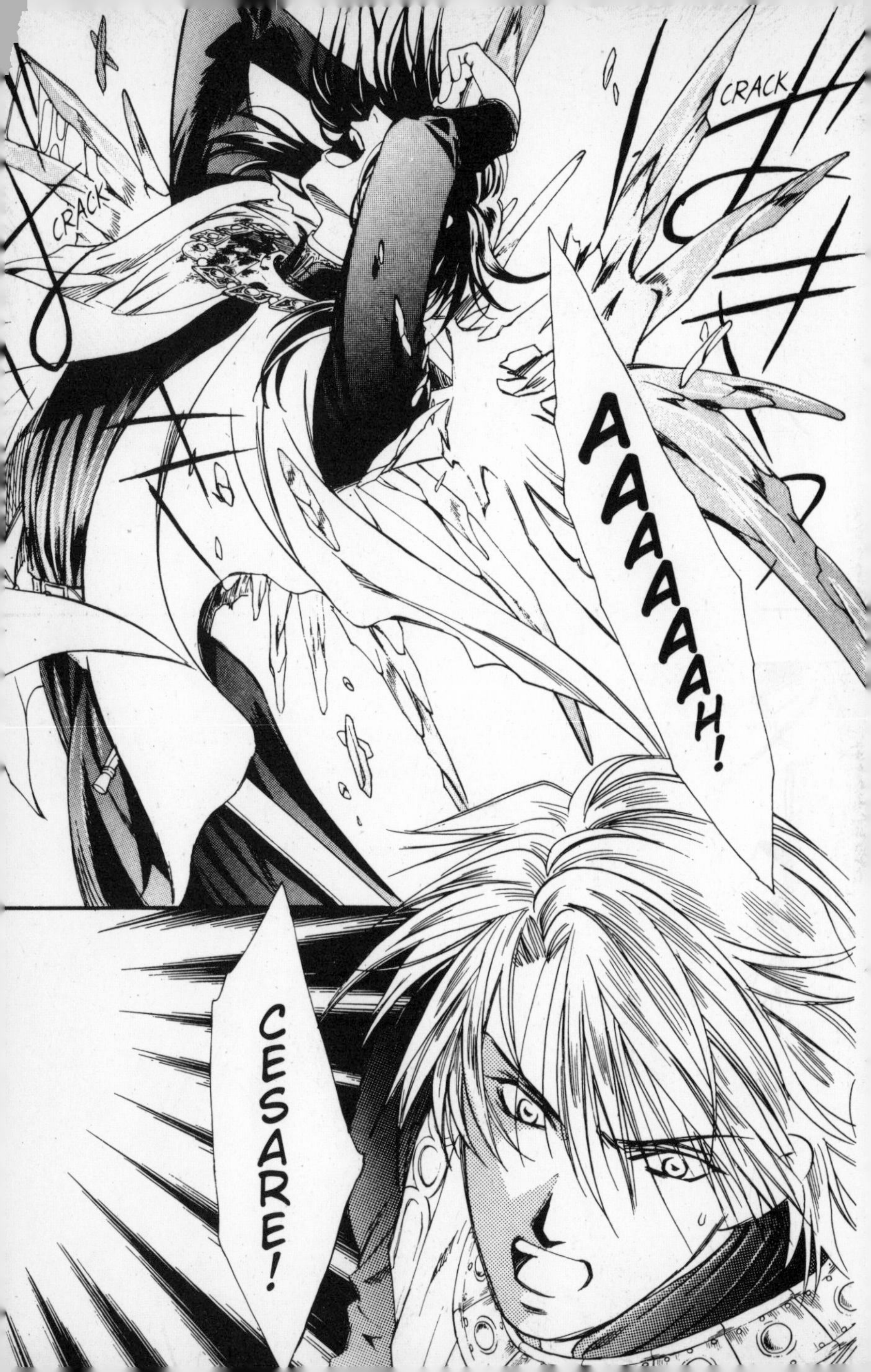
CRACK
CRACK
AAAAAAH!
CESARE!

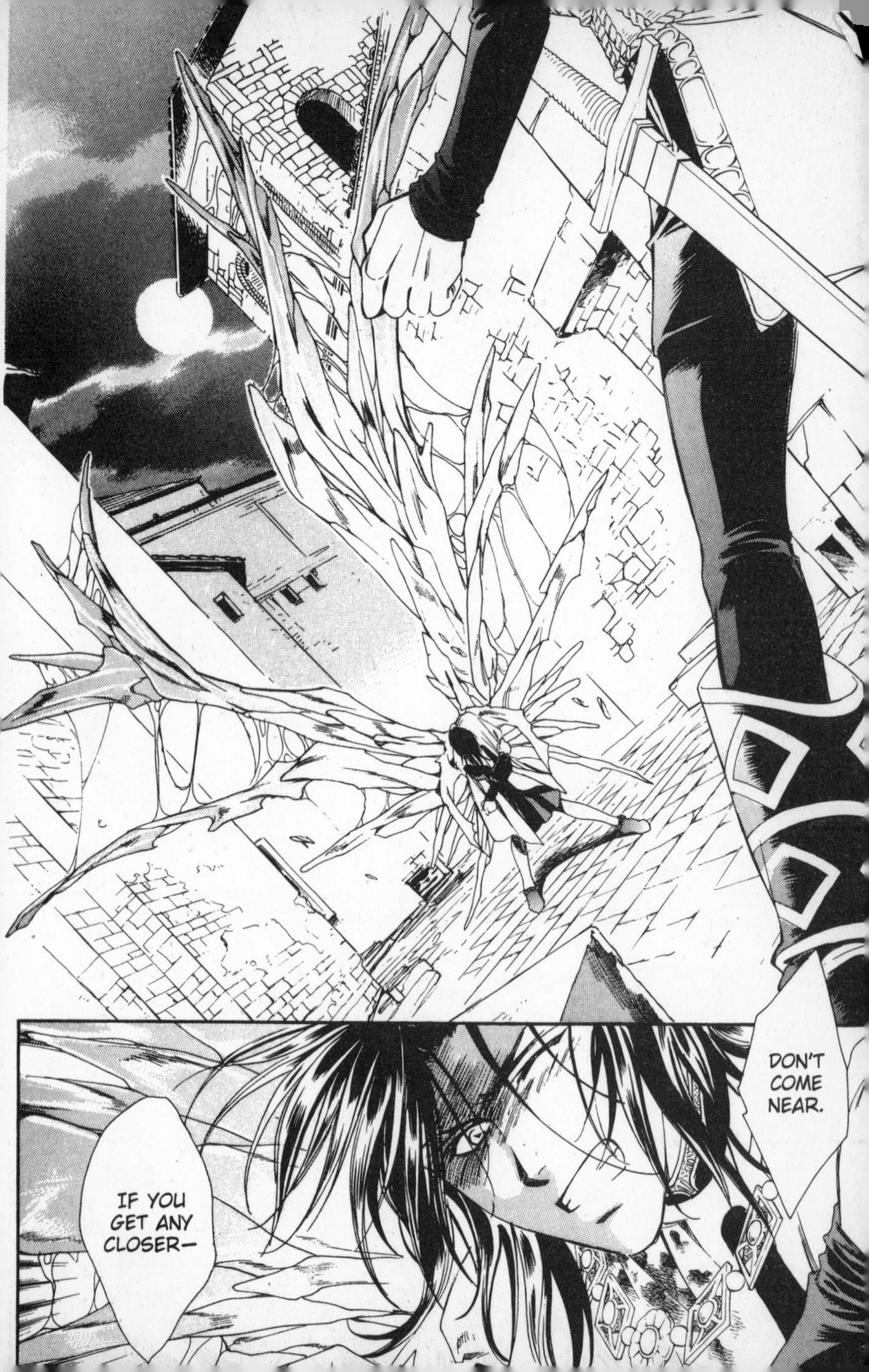
DON'T COME NEAR.
IF YOU GET ANY CLOSER—

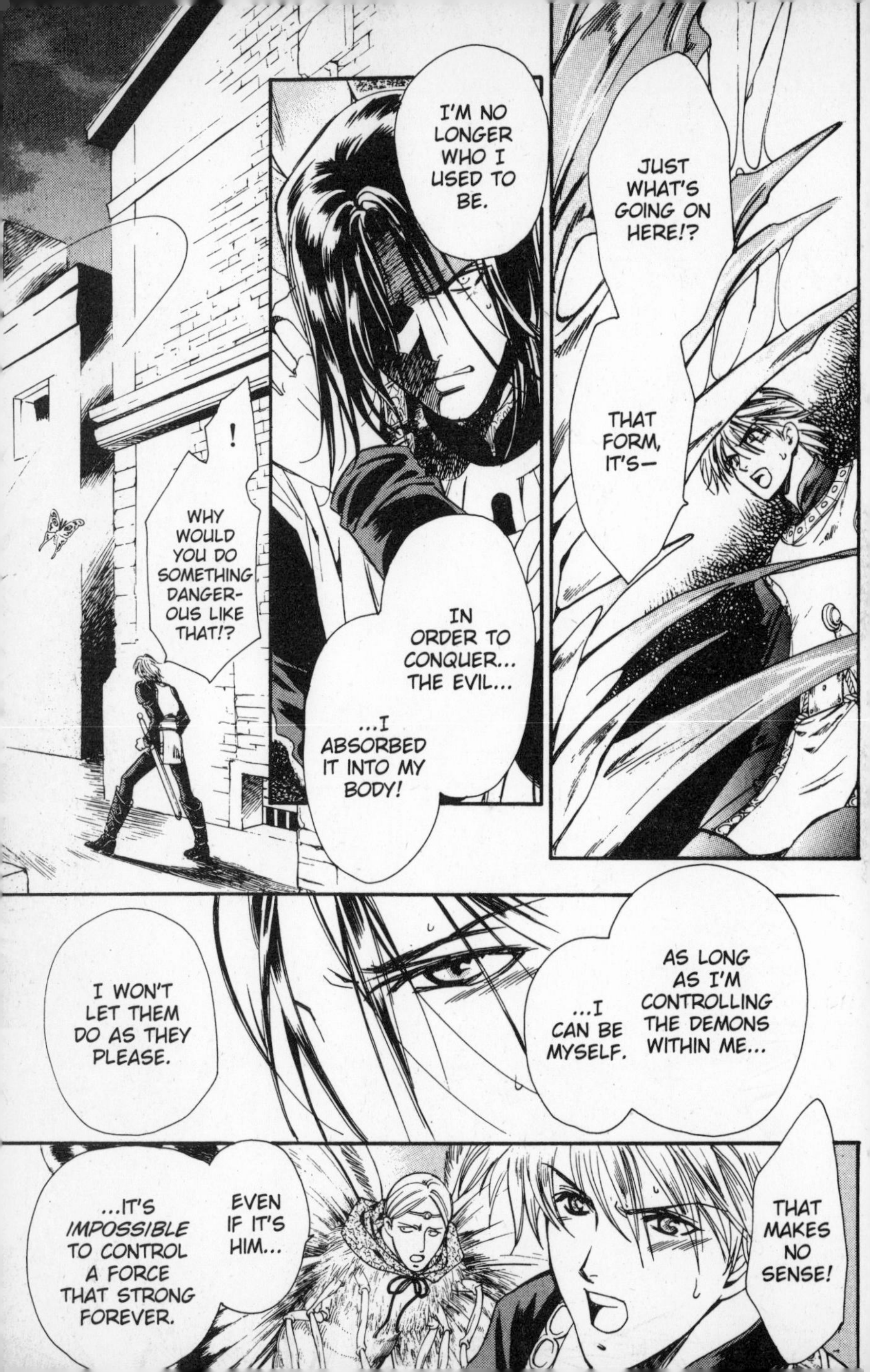
JUST WHAT'S GOING ON HERE!?
THAT FORM, IT'S—
I'M NO LONGER WHO I USED TO BE.
IN ORDER TO CONQUER... THE EVIL...
...I ABSORBED IT INTO MY BODY!
!
WHY WOULD YOU DO SOMETHING DANGER-OUS LIKE THAT!?
AS LONG AS I'M CONTROLLING THE DEMONS WITHIN ME...
...I CAN BE MYSELF.
I WON'T LET THEM DO AS THEY PLEASE.
THAT MAKES NO SENSE!
EVEN IF IT'S HIM...
...IT'S *IMPOSSIBLE* TO CONTROL A FORCE THAT STRONG FOREVER.

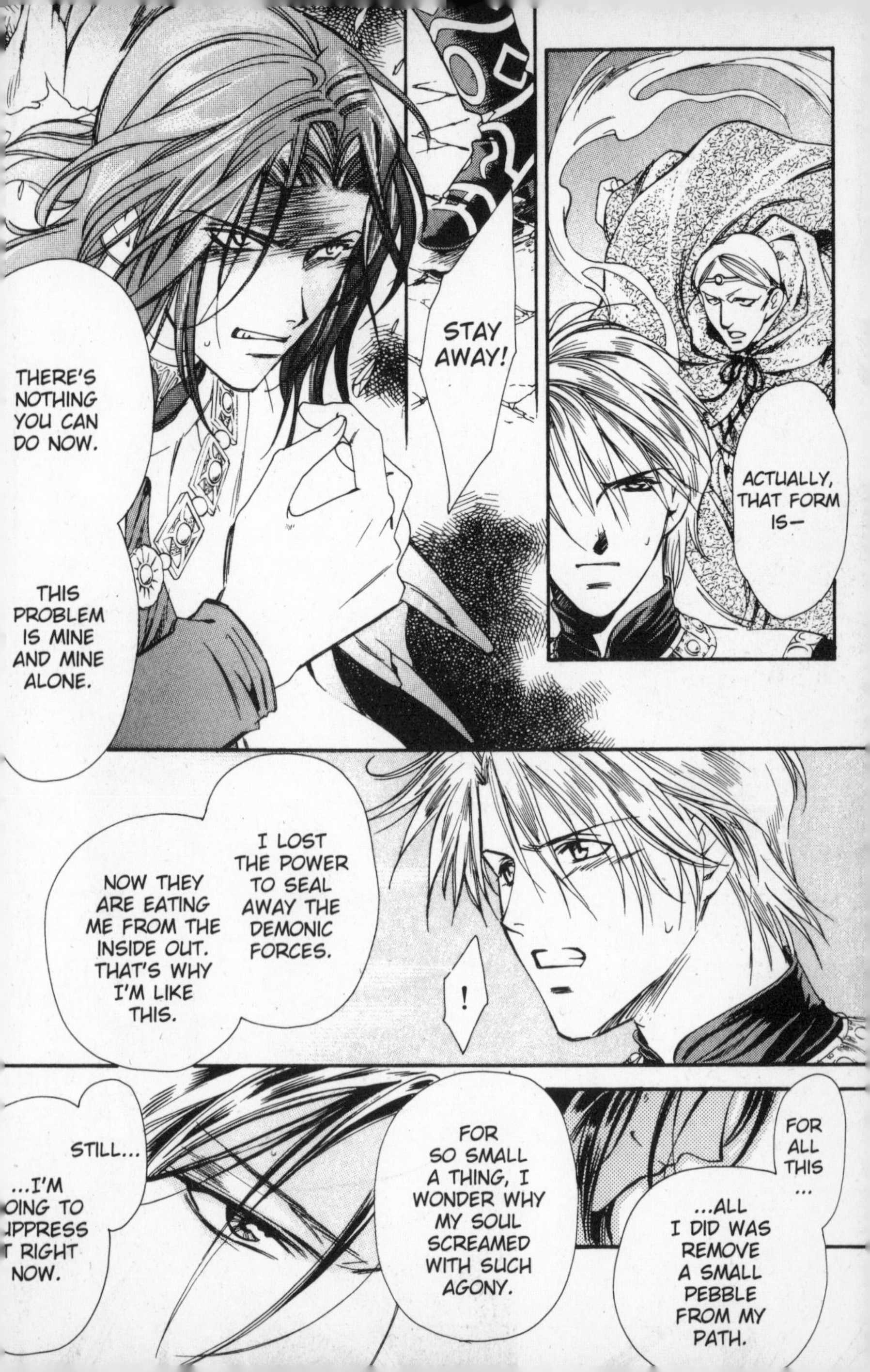
ACTUALLY, THAT FORM IS—
STAY AWAY!
THERE'S NOTHING YOU CAN DO NOW.
THIS PROBLEM IS MINE AND MINE ALONE.
!
I LOST THE POWER TO SEAL AWAY THE DEMONIC FORCES.
NOW THEY ARE EATING ME FROM THE INSIDE OUT. THAT'S WHY I'M LIKE THIS.
FOR ALL THIS ...
...ALL I DID WAS REMOVE A SMALL PEBBLE FROM MY PATH.
FOR SO SMALL A THING, I WONDER WHY MY SOUL SCREAMED WITH SUCH AGONY.
STILL...
...I'M OING TO UPPRESS T RIGHT NOW.

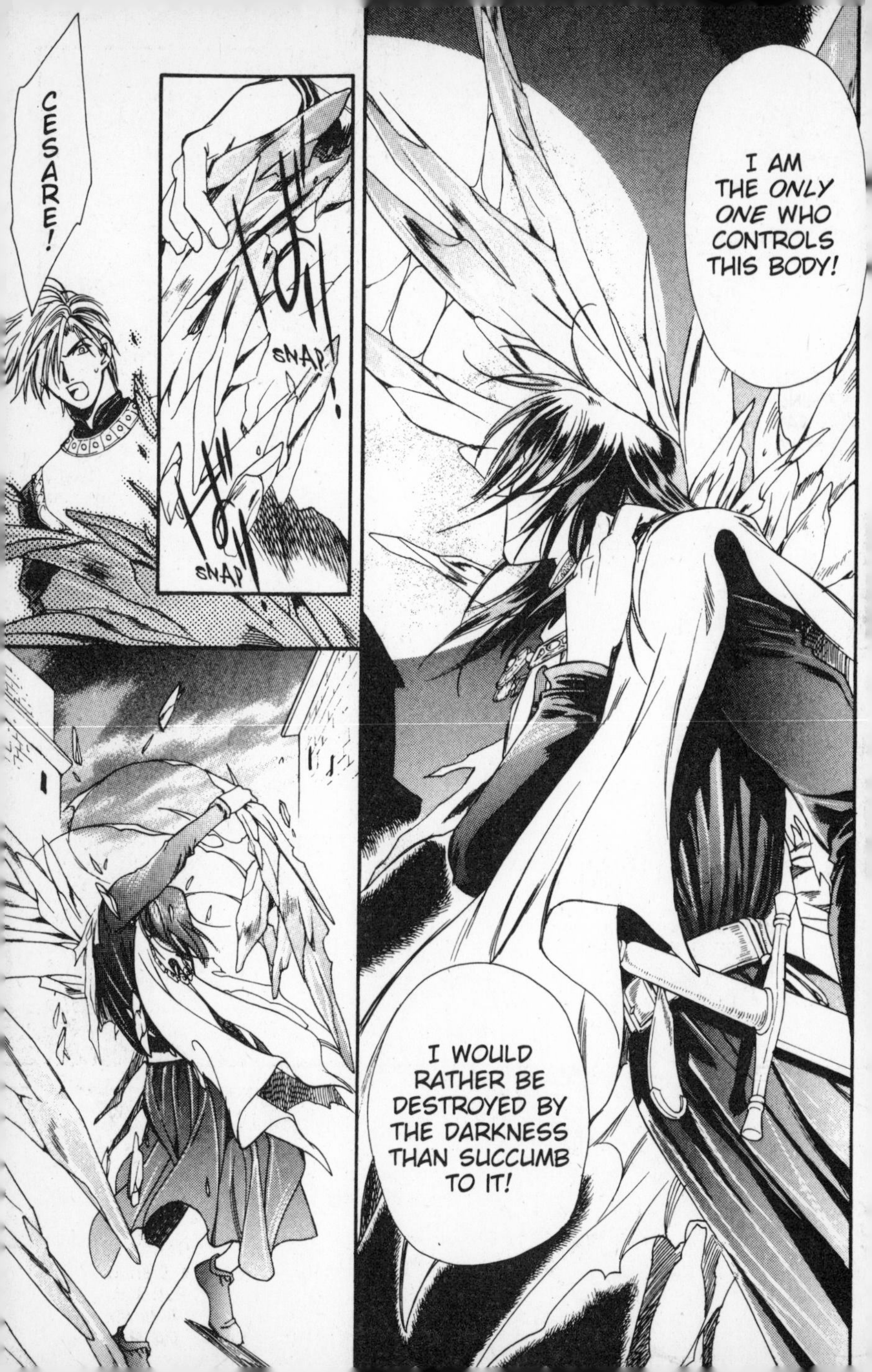
I AM THE *ONLY ONE* WHO CONTROLS THIS BODY!
I WOULD RATHER BE DESTROYED BY THE DARKNESS THAN SUCCUMB TO IT!
SNAP
SNAP
CESARE!

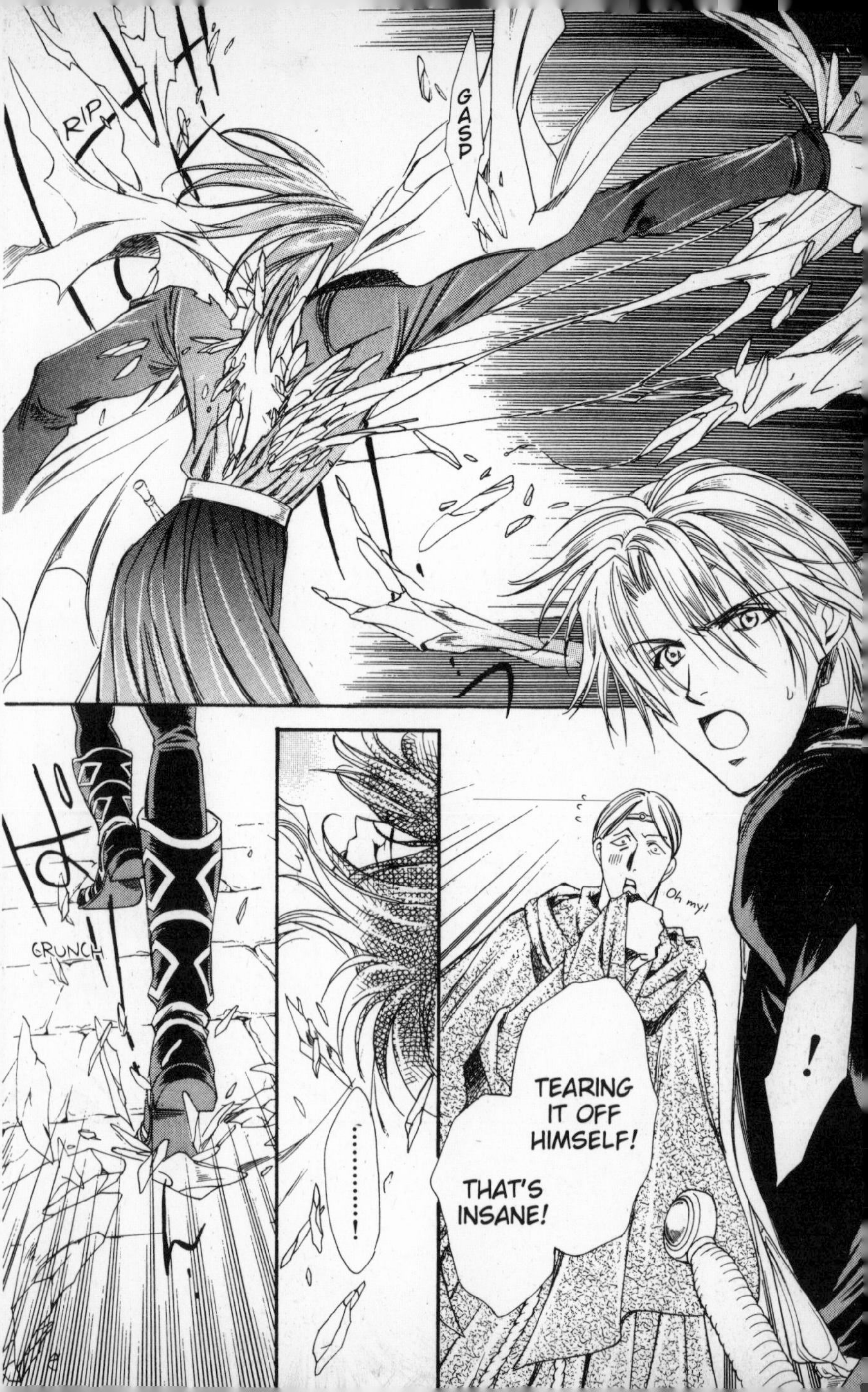
GASP
RIP
!
Oh my!
TEARING IT OFF HIMSELF!
THAT'S INSANE!
......!
GRUNCH

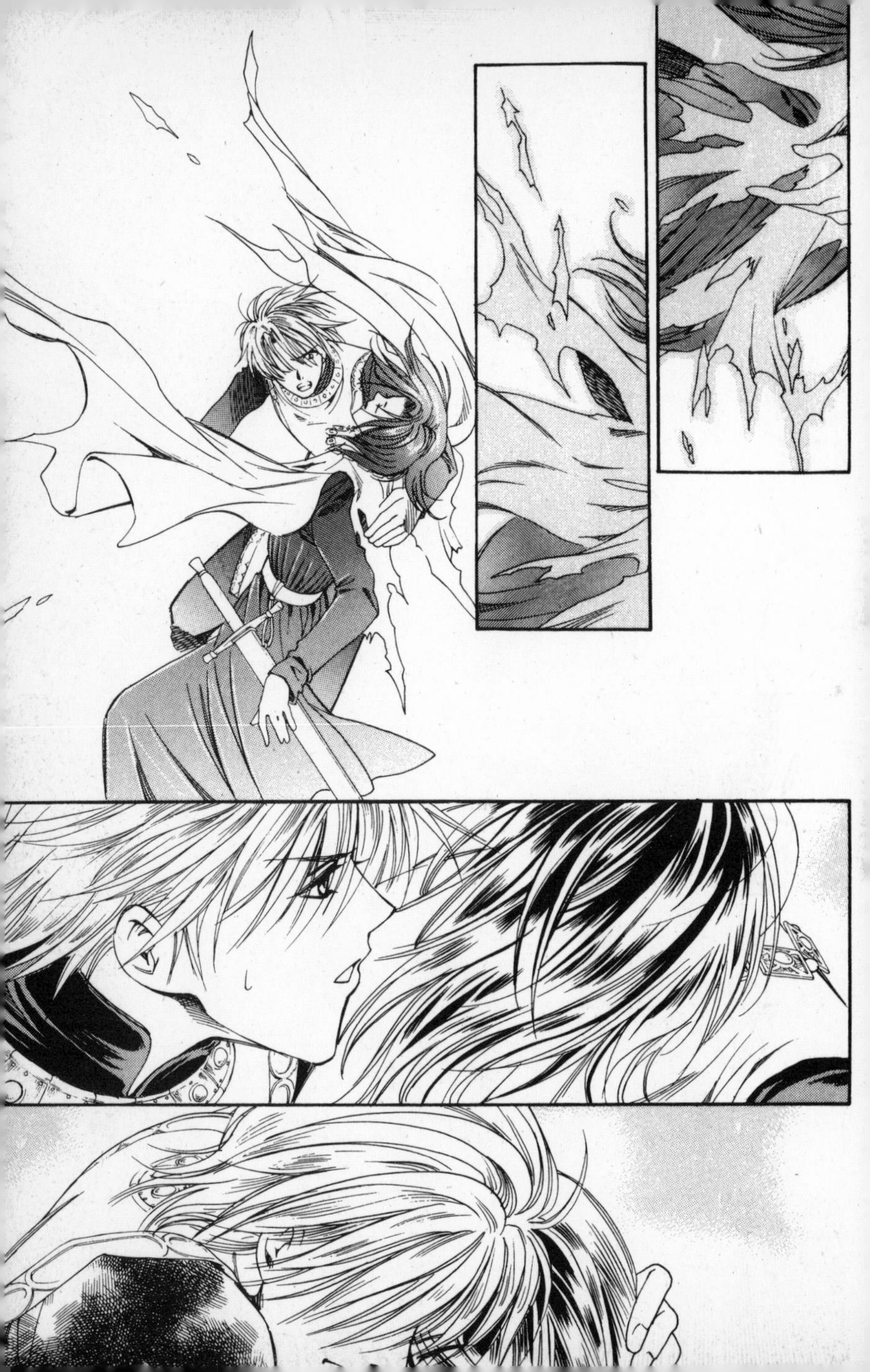

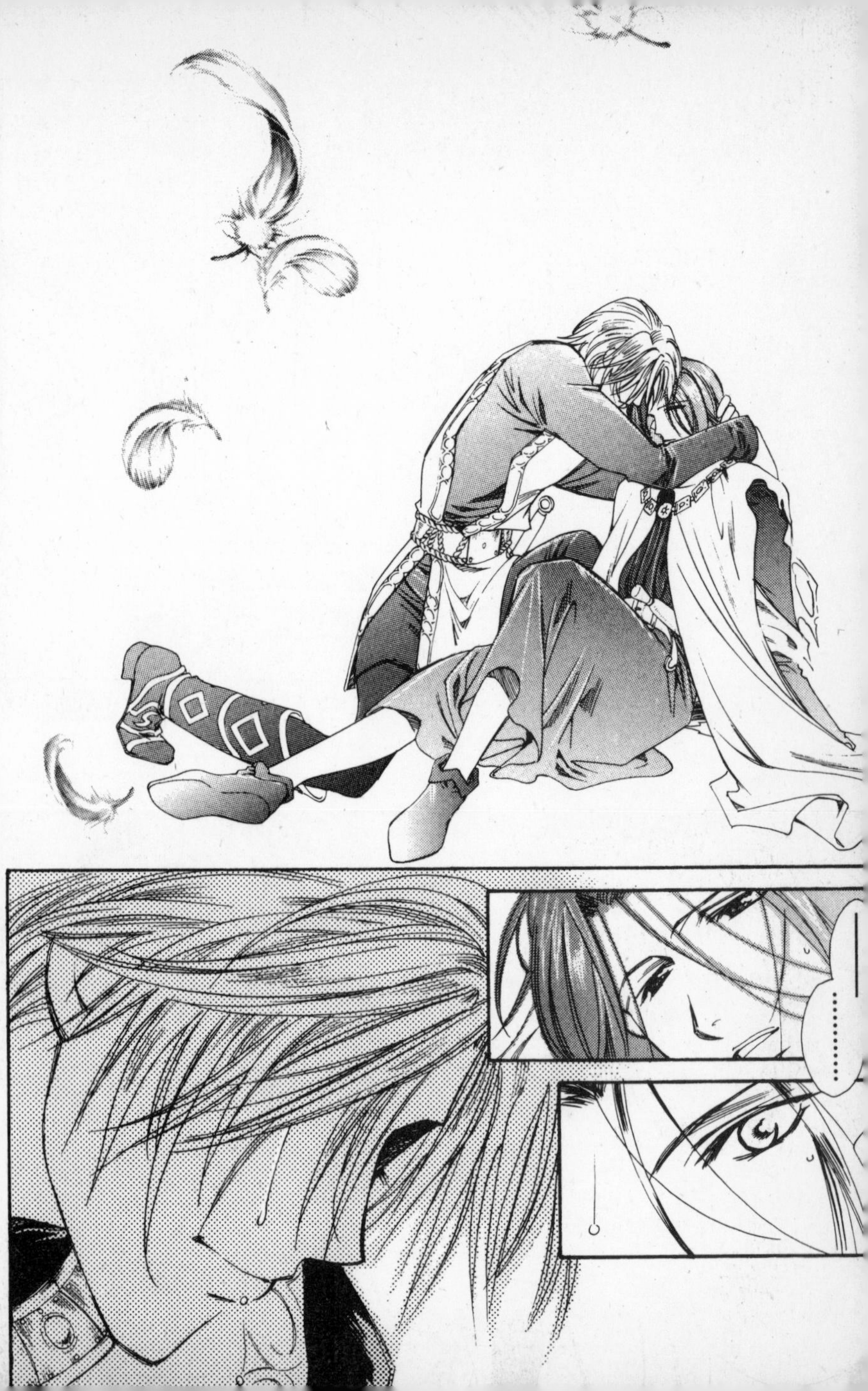
......

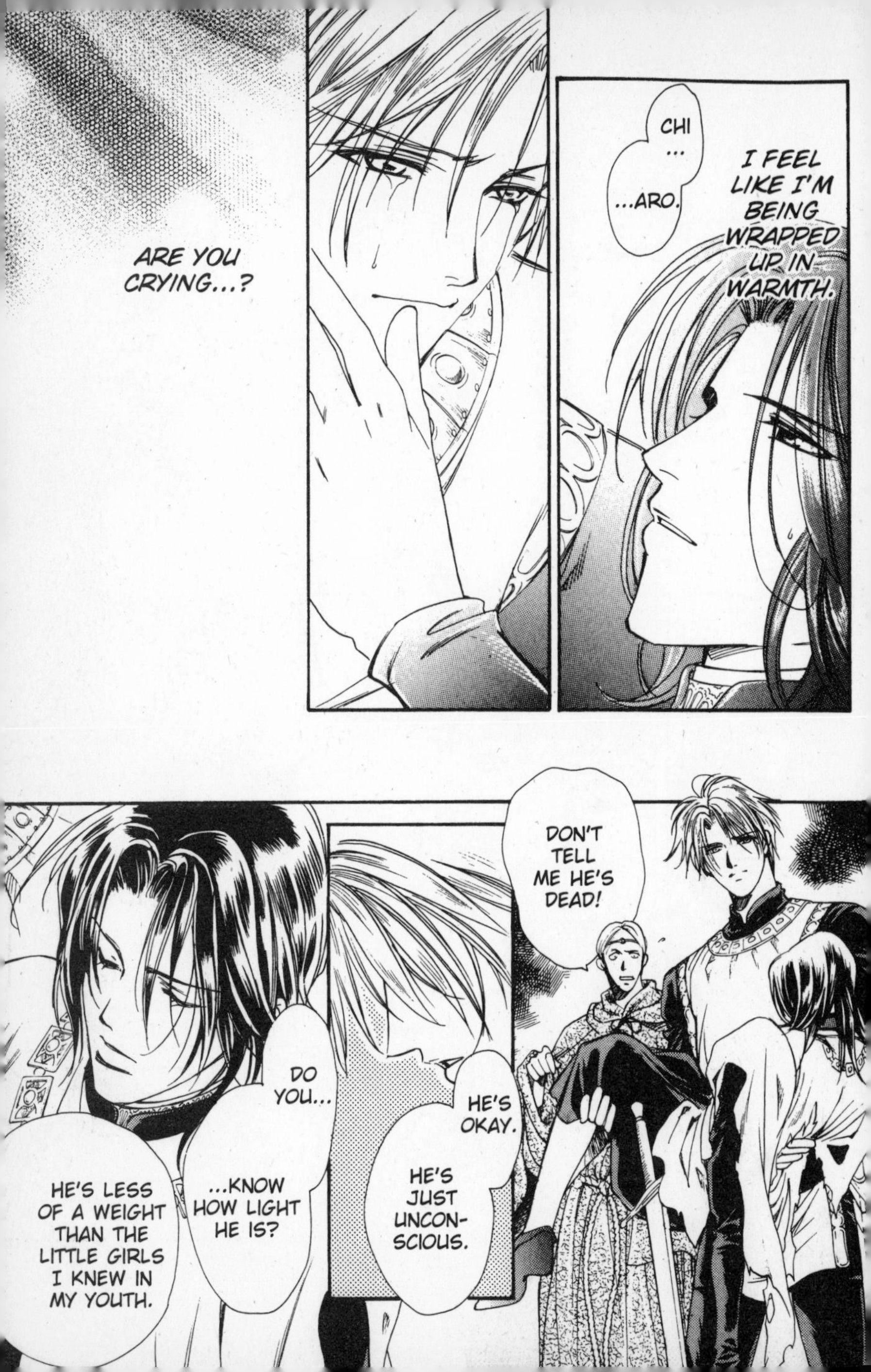
I FEEL LIKE I'M BEING WRAPPED UP IN WARMTH.
CHI ...
...ARO.
ARE YOU CRYING...?
DON'T TELL ME HE'S DEAD!
HE'S OKAY.
HE'S JUST UNCONSCIOUS.
DO YOU...
...KNOW HOW LIGHT HE IS?
HE'S LESS OF A WEIGHT THAN THE LITTLE GIRLS I KNEW IN MY YOUTH.

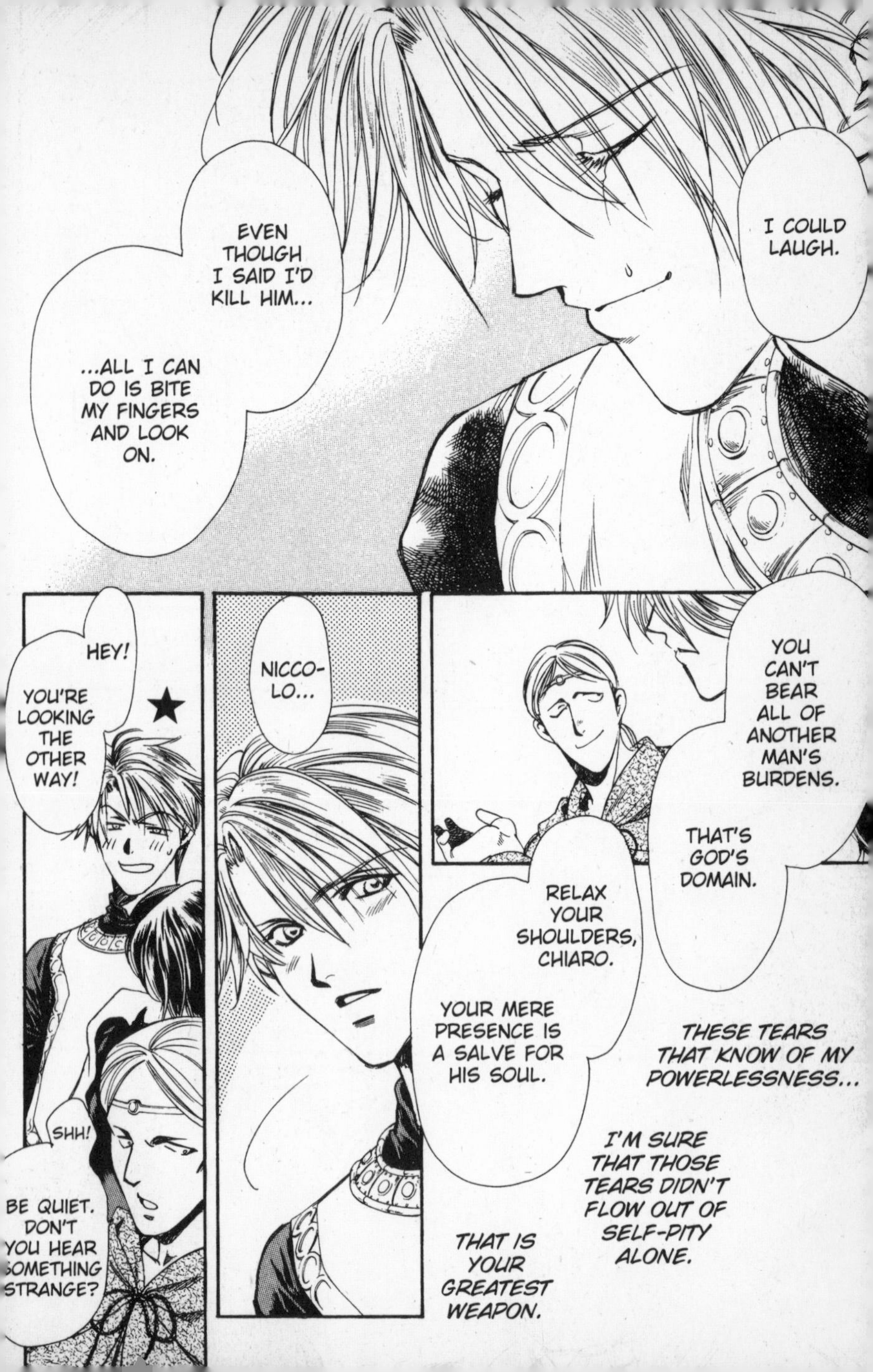
I COULD LAUGH.
EVEN THOUGH I SAID I'D KILL HIM...
...ALL I CAN DO IS BITE MY FINGERS AND LOOK ON.
YOU CAN'T BEAR ALL OF ANOTHER MAN'S BURDENS.
THAT'S GOD'S DOMAIN.
RELAX YOUR SHOULDERS, CHIARO.
YOUR MERE PRESENCE IS A SALVE FOR HIS SOUL.
THESE TEARS THAT KNOW OF MY POWERLESSNESS...
I'M SURE THAT THOSE TEARS DIDN'T FLOW OUT OF SELF-PITY ALONE.
THAT IS YOUR GREATEST WEAPON.
NICCO-LO...
HEY!
YOU'RE LOOKING THE OTHER WAY!
SHH!
BE QUIET. DON'T YOU HEAR SOMETHING STRANGE?

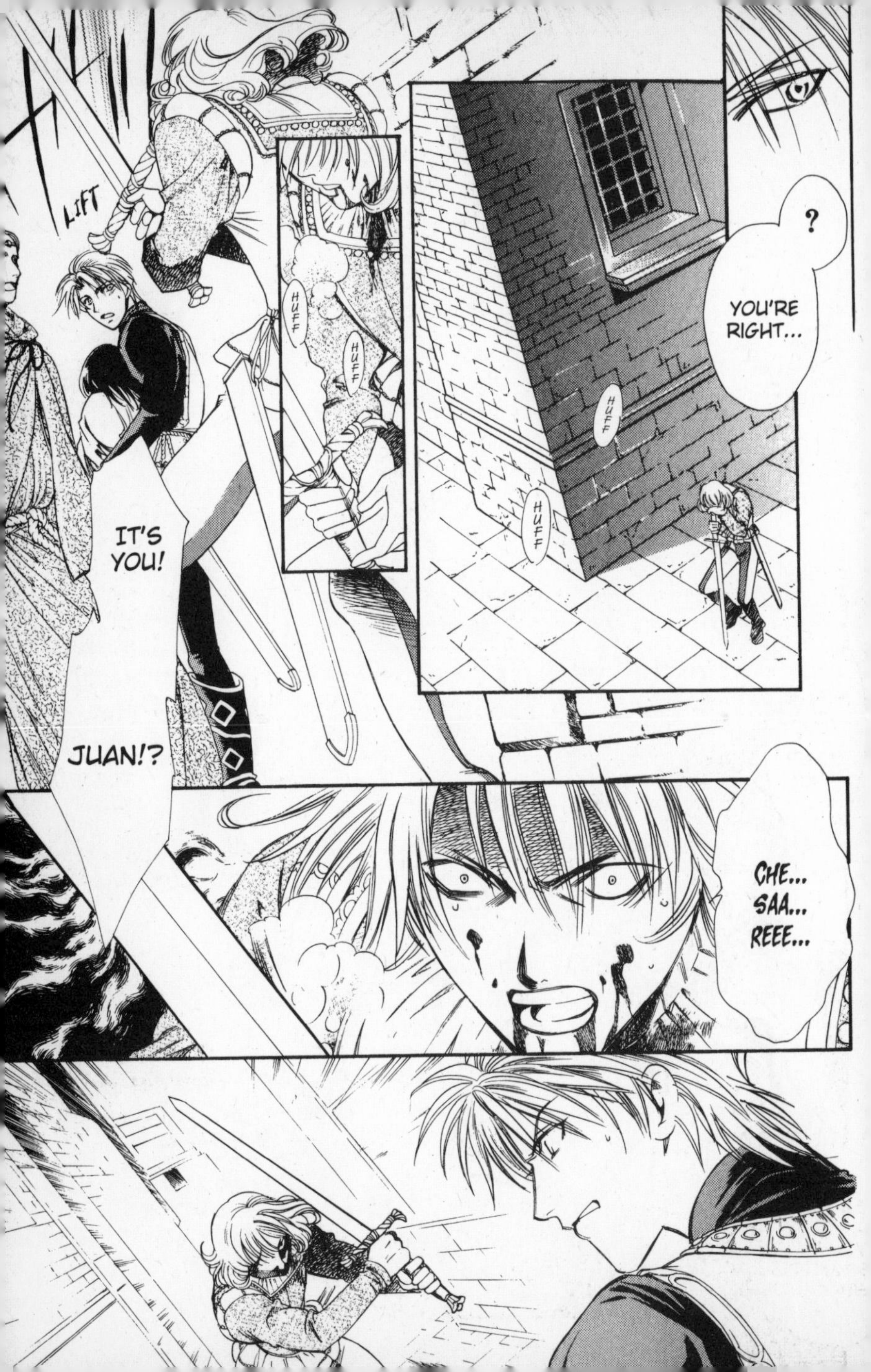
?
YOU'RE RIGHT...
HUFF
HUFF
HUFF
HUFF
LIFT
IT'S YOU!
JUAN!?
CHE... SAA... REEE...

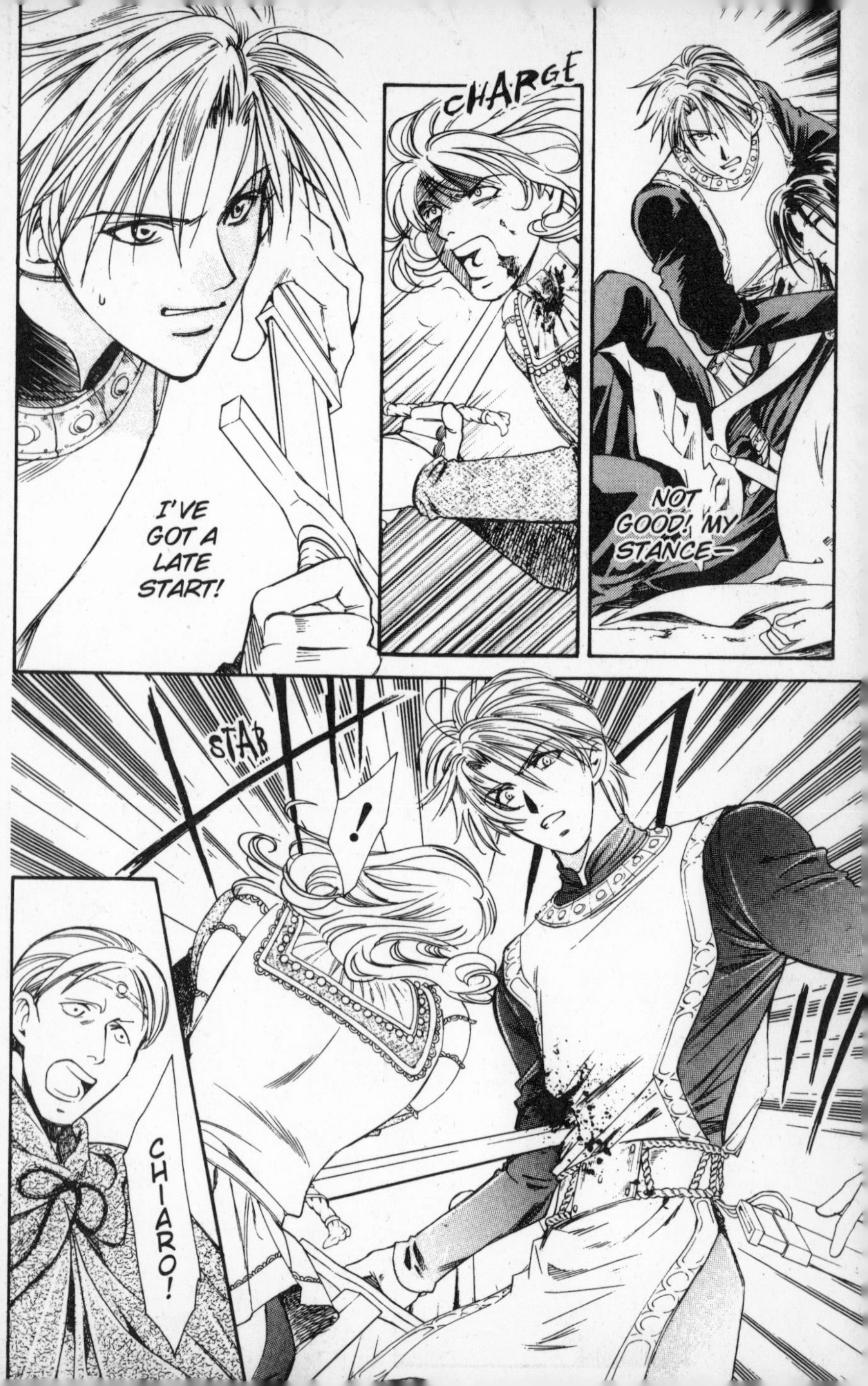
NOT GOOD! MY STANCE—
CHARGE
I'VE GOT A LATE START!
STAB
!
CHIARO!

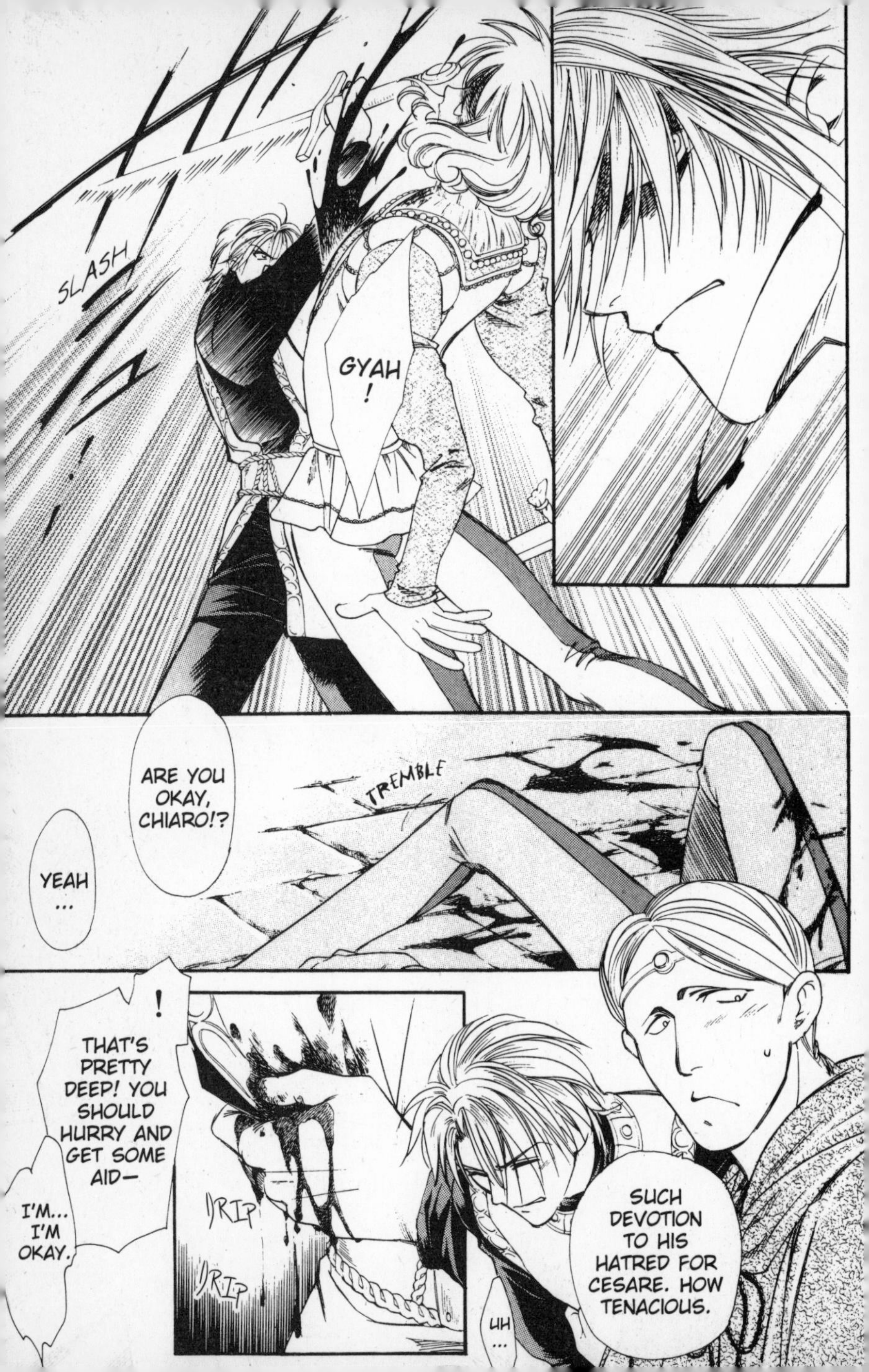
SLASH
GYAH!
TREMBLE
ARE YOU OKAY, CHIARO!?
YEAH...
SUCH DEVOTION TO HIS HATRED FOR CESARE. HOW TENACIOUS.
UH...
!
THAT'S PRETTY DEEP! YOU SHOULD HURRY AND GET SOME AID—
DRIP
I'M... I'M OKAY.
DRIP

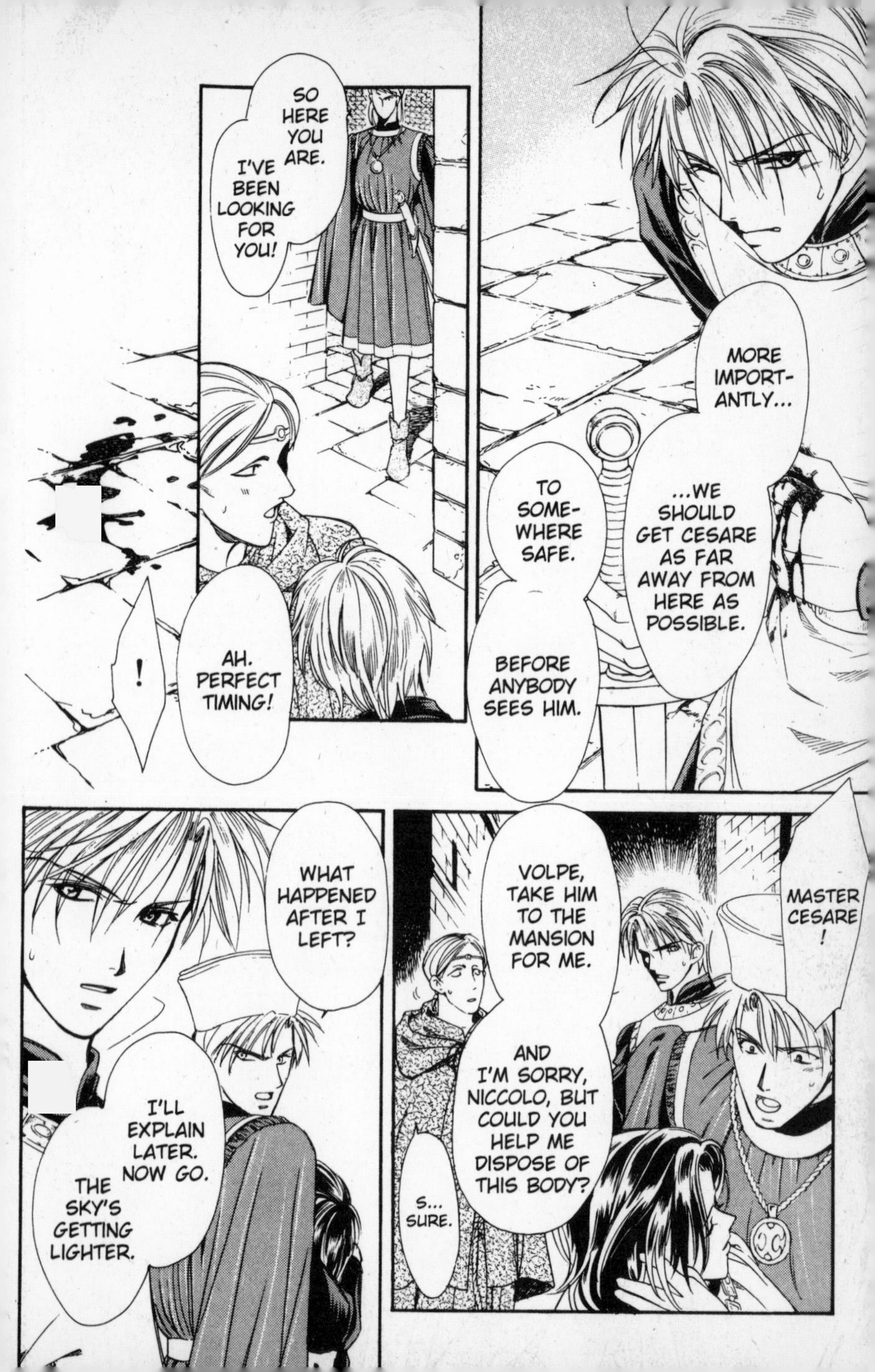

MORE IMPORTANTLY...
...WE SHOULD GET CESARE AS FAR AWAY FROM HERE AS POSSIBLE.
TO SOMEWHERE SAFE.
BEFORE ANYBODY SEES HIM.
SO HERE YOU ARE.
I'VE BEEN LOOKING FOR YOU!
AH. PERFECT TIMING!
!
MASTER CESARE!
VOLPE, TAKE HIM TO THE MANSION FOR ME.
AND I'M SORRY, NICCOLO, BUT COULD YOU HELP ME DISPOSE OF THIS BODY?
S... SURE.
WHAT HAPPENED AFTER I LEFT?
I'LL EXPLAIN LATER. NOW GO.
THE SKY'S GETTING LIGHTER.

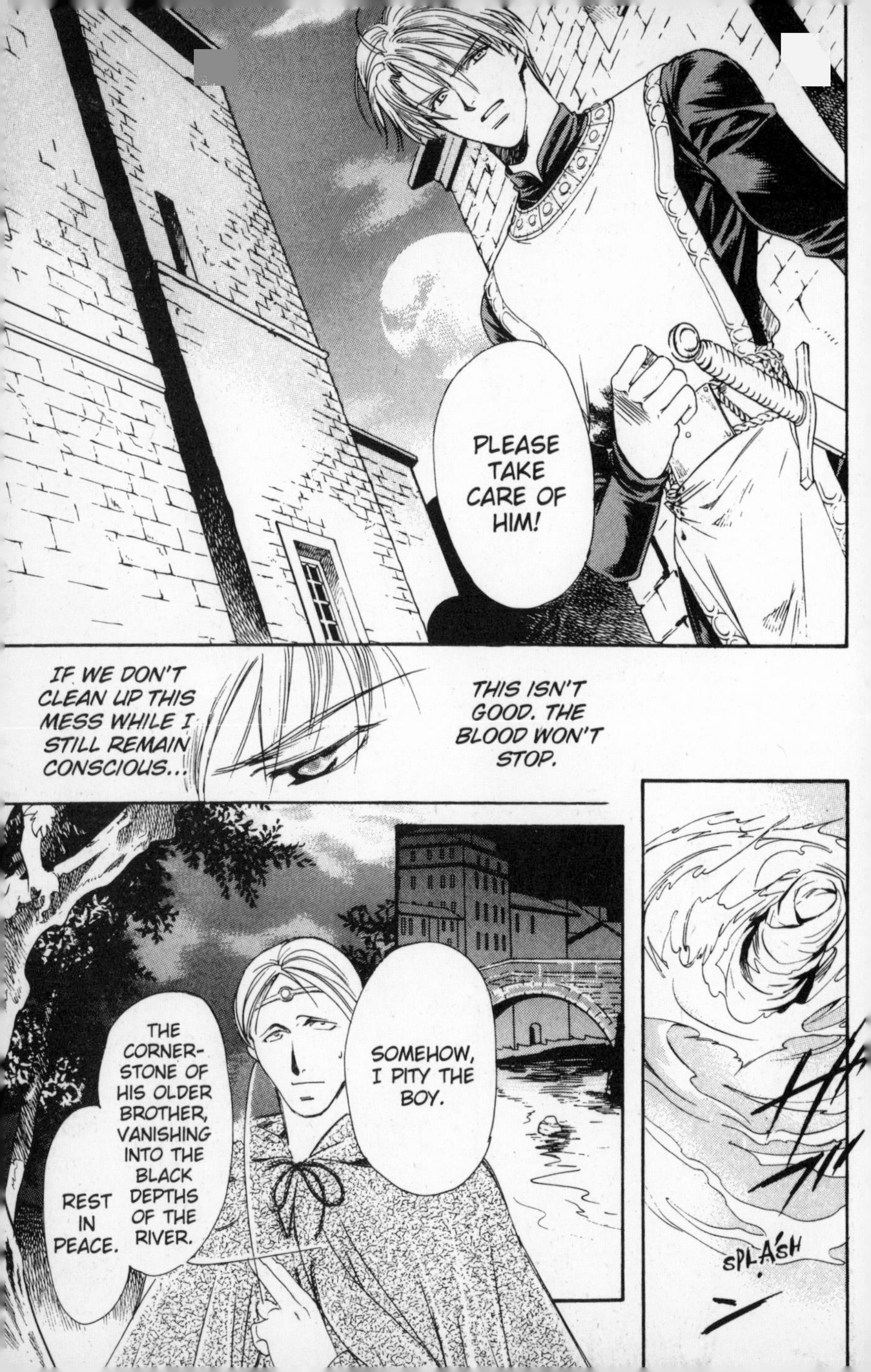
PLEASE TAKE CARE OF HIM!
THIS ISN'T GOOD. THE BLOOD WON'T STOP.
IF WE DON'T CLEAN UP THIS MESS WHILE I STILL REMAIN CONSCIOUS...
SPLASH
SOMEHOW, I PITY THE BOY.
THE CORNER-STONE OF HIS OLDER BROTHER, VANISHING INTO THE BLACK DEPTHS OF THE RIVER.
REST IN PEACE.

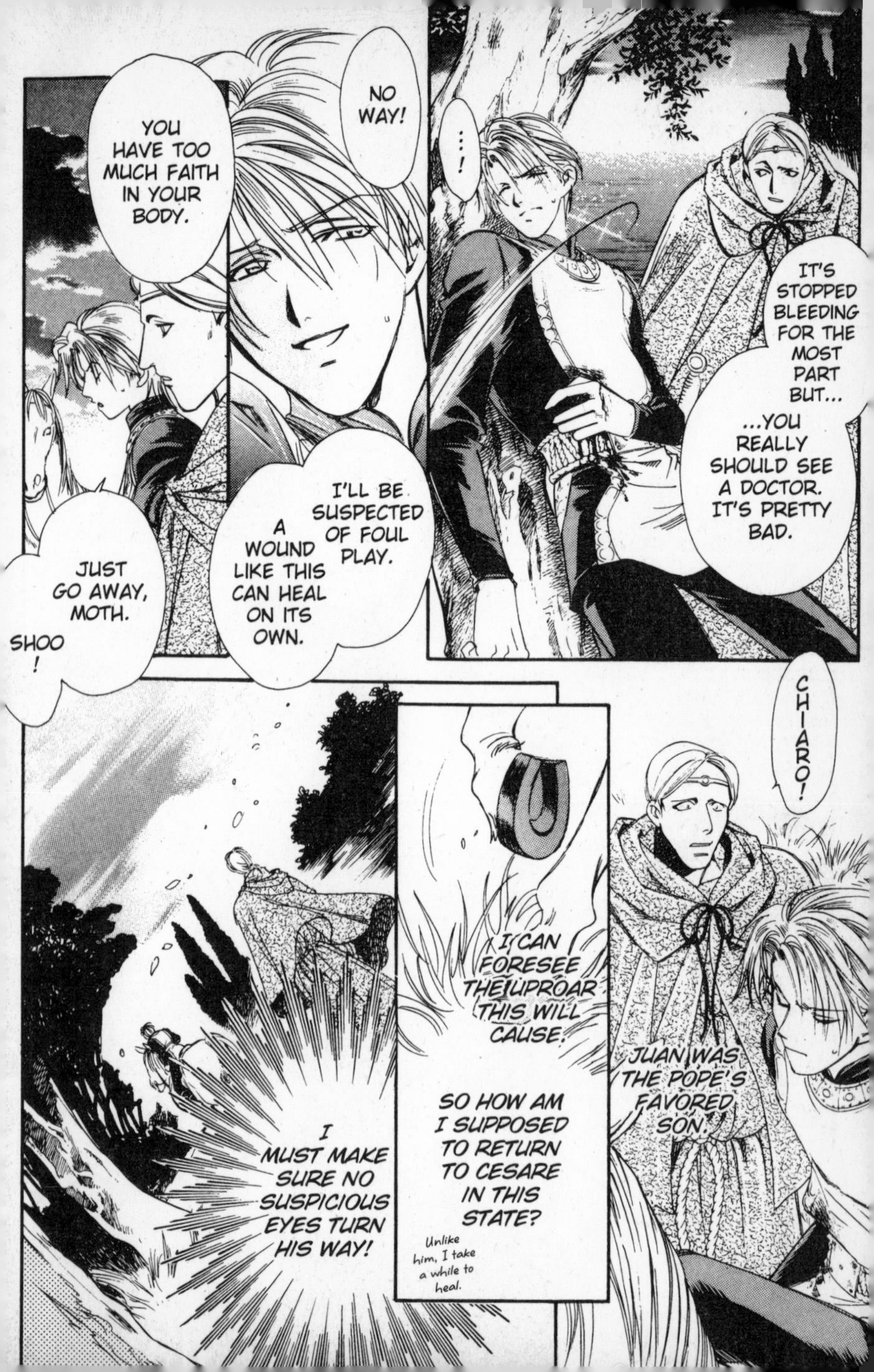
...!
IT'S STOPPED BLEEDING FOR THE MOST PART BUT...
...YOU REALLY SHOULD SEE A DOCTOR. IT'S PRETTY BAD.
NO WAY!
I'LL BE SUSPECTED OF FOUL PLAY.
A WOUND LIKE THIS CAN HEAL ON ITS OWN.
YOU HAVE TOO MUCH FAITH IN YOUR BODY.
JUST GO AWAY, MOTH.
SHOO!
CHIARO!
JUAN WAS THE POPE'S FAVORED SON.
I CAN FORESEE THE UPROAR THIS WILL CAUSE.
SO HOW AM I SUPPOSED TO RETURN TO CESARE IN THIS STATE?
Unlike him, I take a while to heal.
I MUST MAKE SURE NO SUSPICIOUS EYES TURN HIS WAY!

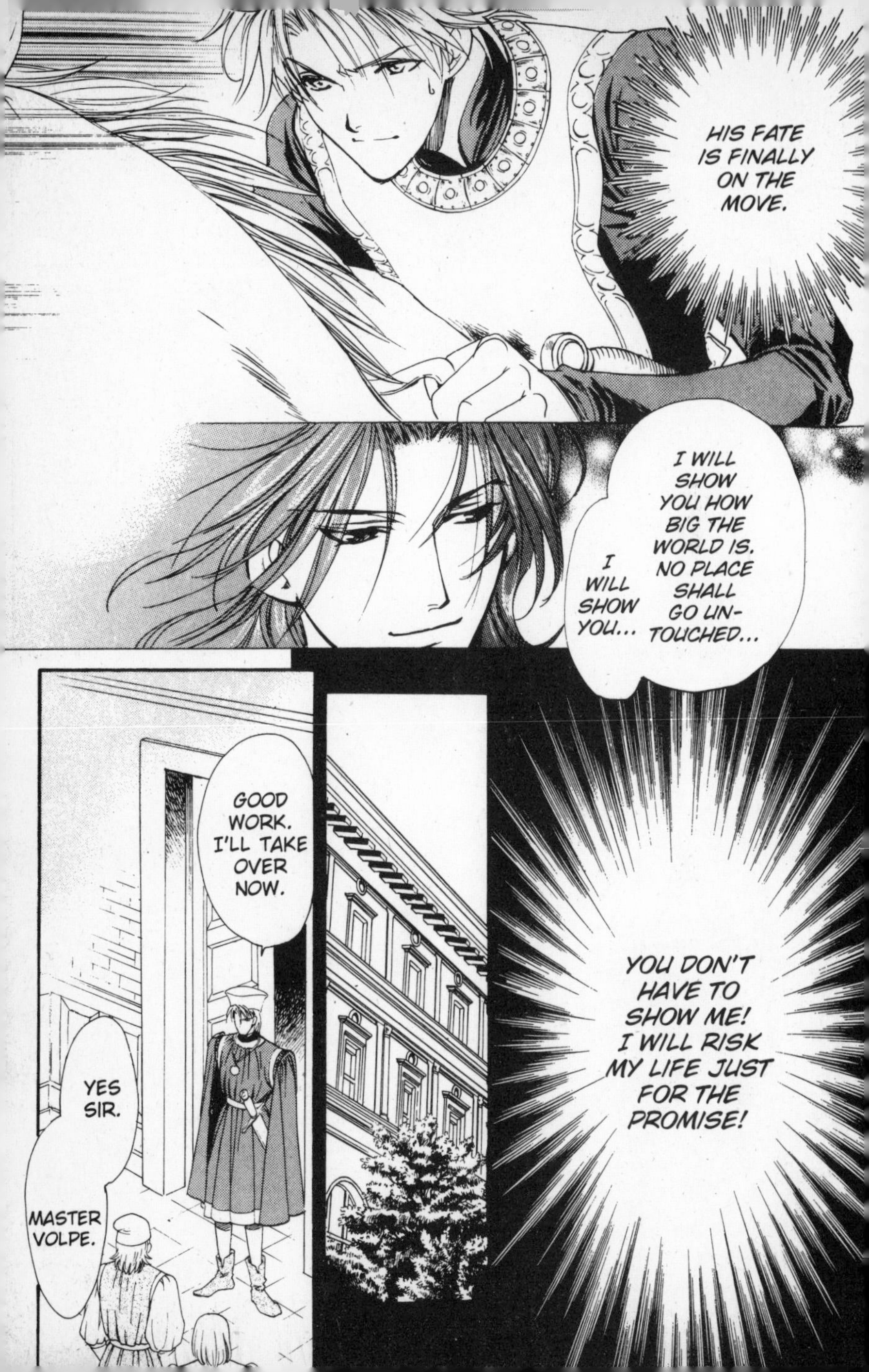
HIS FATE IS FINALLY ON THE MOVE.
I WILL SHOW YOU HOW BIG THE WORLD IS. NO PLACE SHALL GO UN-TOUCHED...
I WILL SHOW YOU...
YOU DON'T HAVE TO SHOW ME! I WILL RISK MY LIFE JUST FOR THE PROMISE!
GOOD WORK. I'LL TAKE OVER NOW.
YES SIR.
MASTER VOLPE.

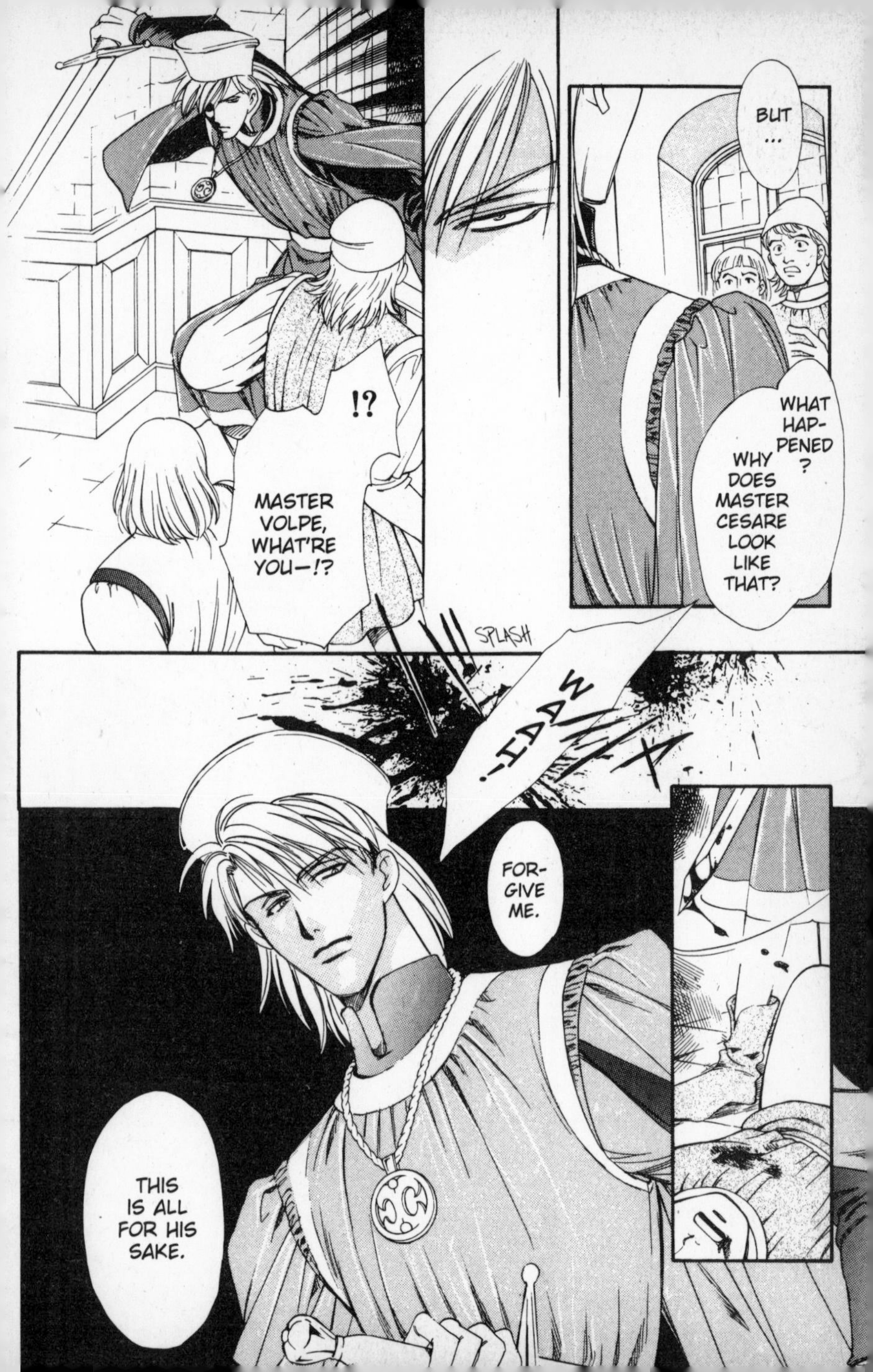
BUT ...
WHAT HAPPENED? WHY DOES MASTER CESARE LOOK LIKE THAT?
!?
MASTER VOLPE, WHAT'RE YOU—!?
SPLASH
WAAAH!
FORGIVE ME.
THIS IS ALL FOR HIS SAKE.

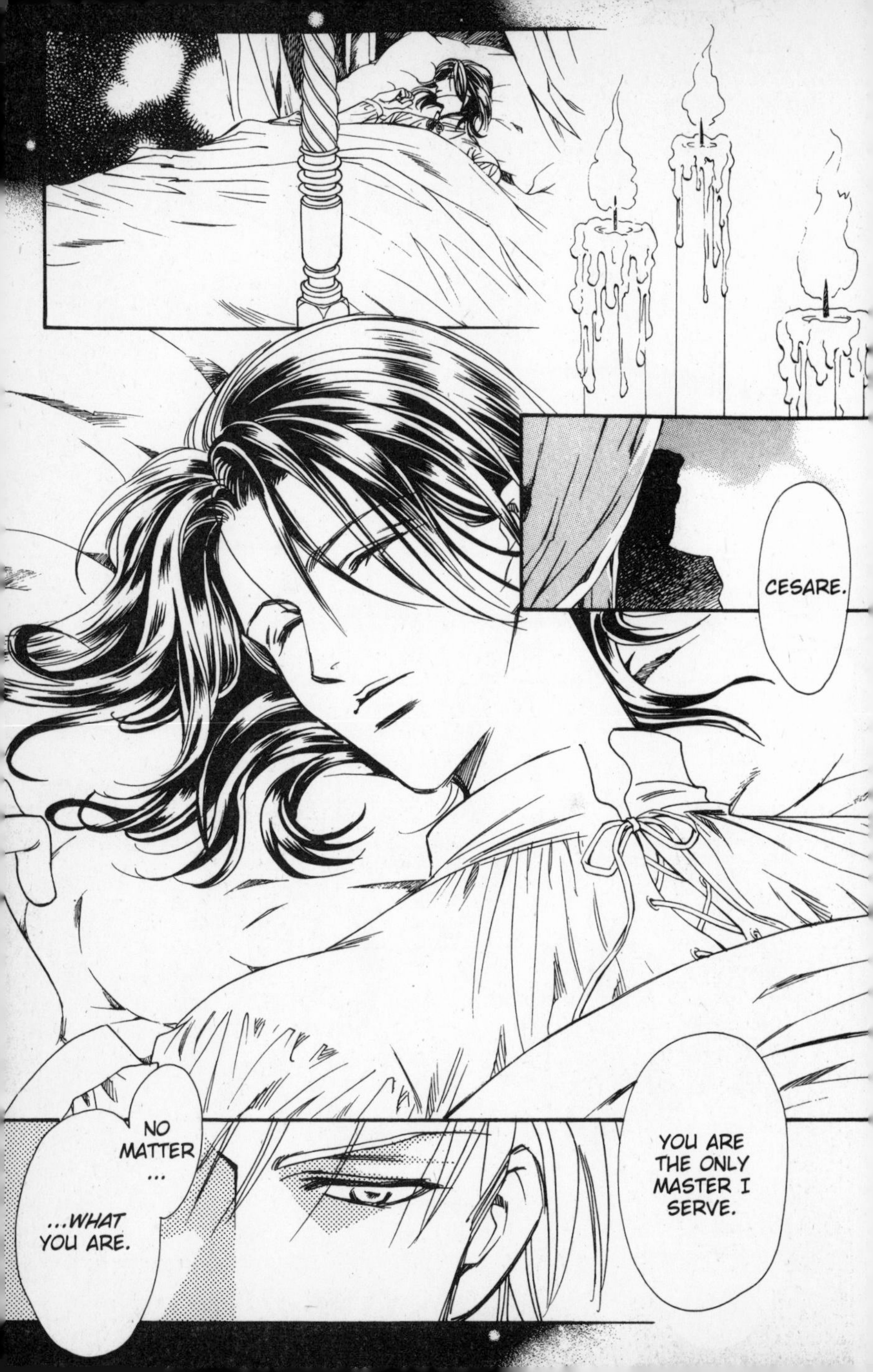
CESARE.
YOU ARE THE ONLY MASTER I SERVE.
NO MATTER ...
...WHAT YOU ARE.

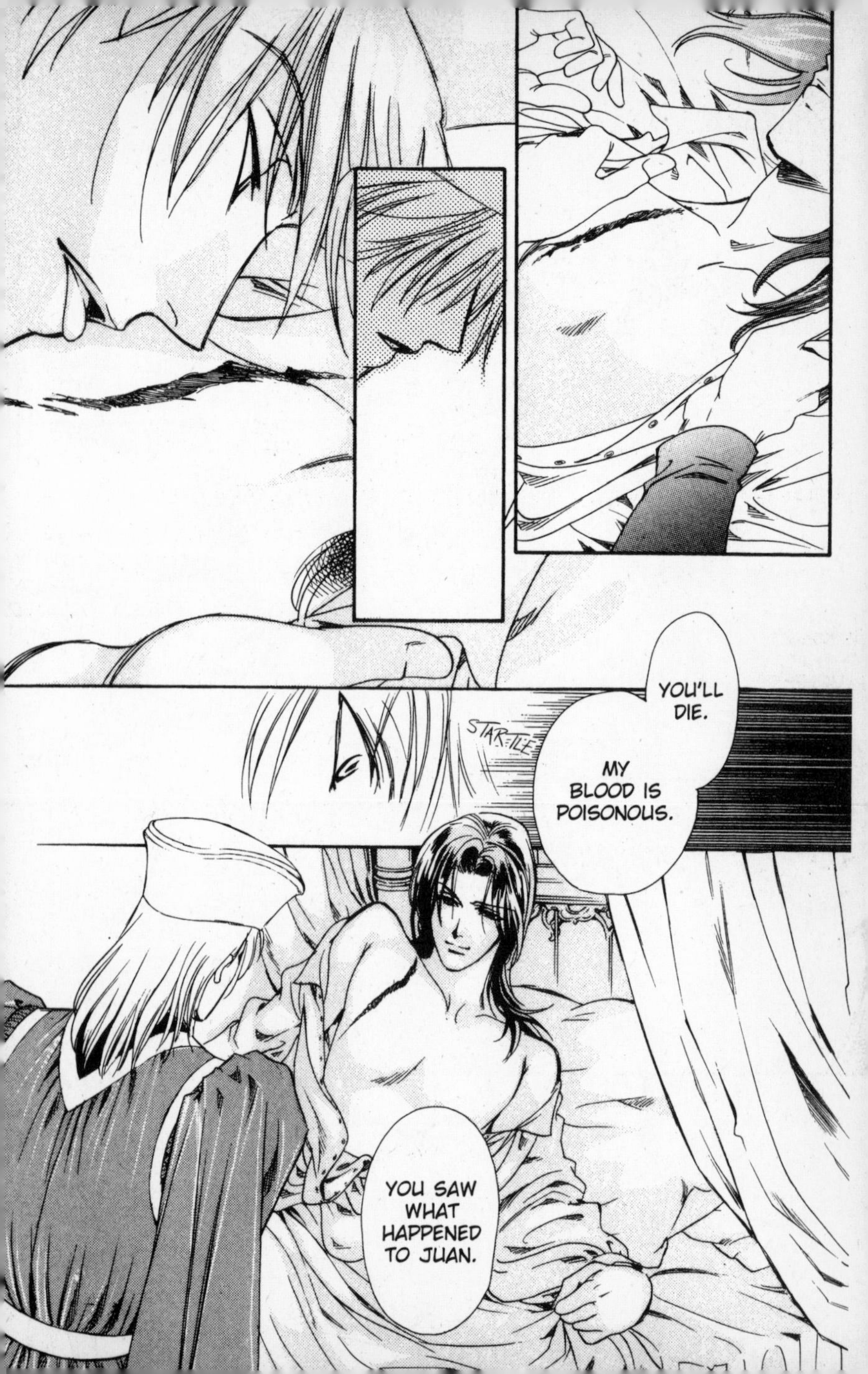
YOU'LL DIE.
STARTLE
MY BLOOD IS POISONOUS.
YOU SAW WHAT HAPPENED TO JUAN.

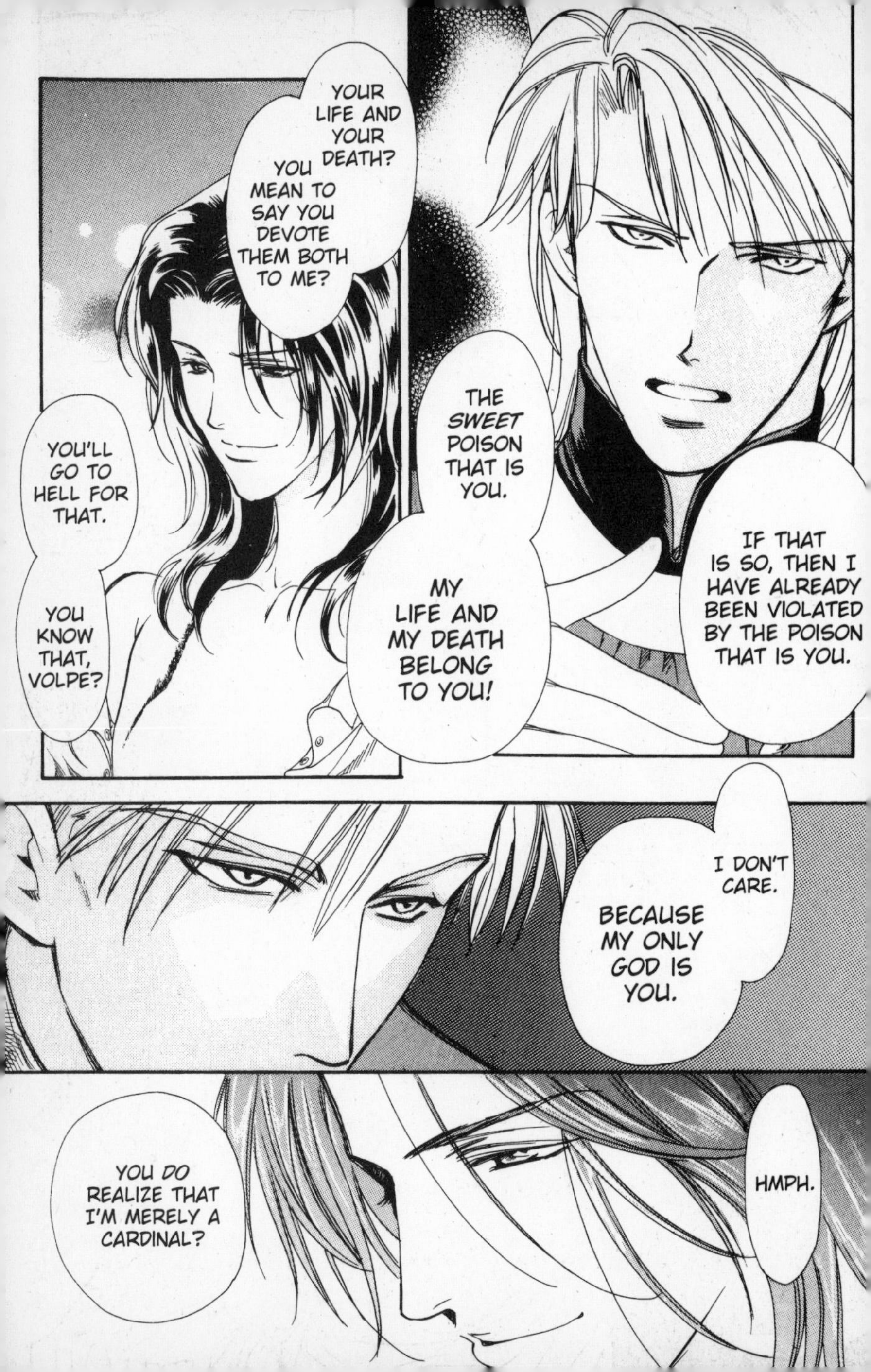
IF THAT IS SO, THEN I HAVE ALREADY BEEN VIOLATED BY THE POISON THAT IS YOU.
THE *SWEET* POISON THAT IS YOU.
MY LIFE AND MY DEATH BELONG TO YOU!
YOUR LIFE AND YOUR DEATH? YOU MEAN TO SAY YOU DEVOTE THEM BOTH TO ME?
YOU'LL GO TO HELL FOR THAT.
YOU KNOW THAT, VOLPE?
I DON'T CARE.
BECAUSE MY ONLY GOD IS YOU.
HMPH.
YOU *DO* REALIZE THAT I'M MERELY A CARDINAL?

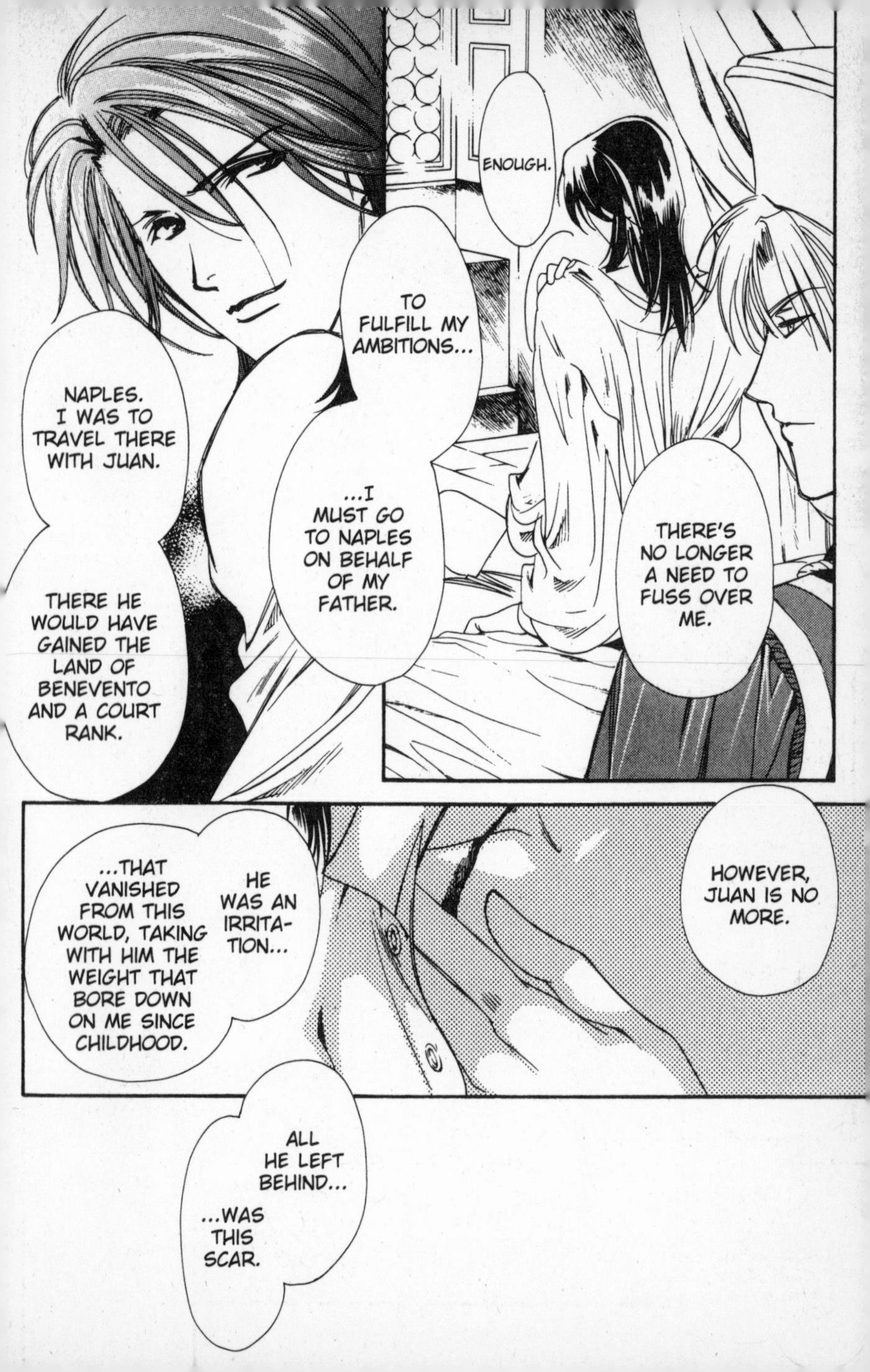
ENOUGH.
THERE'S NO LONGER A NEED TO FUSS OVER ME.
TO FULFILL MY AMBITIONS...
...I MUST GO TO NAPLES ON BEHALF OF MY FATHER.
NAPLES. I WAS TO TRAVEL THERE WITH JUAN.
THERE HE WOULD HAVE GAINED THE LAND OF BENEVENTO AND A COURT RANK.
HOWEVER, JUAN IS NO MORE.
HE WAS AN IRRITA-TION...
...THAT VANISHED FROM THIS WORLD, TAKING WITH HIM THE WEIGHT THAT BORE DOWN ON ME SINCE CHILDHOOD.
ALL HE LEFT BEHIND...
...WAS THIS SCAR.

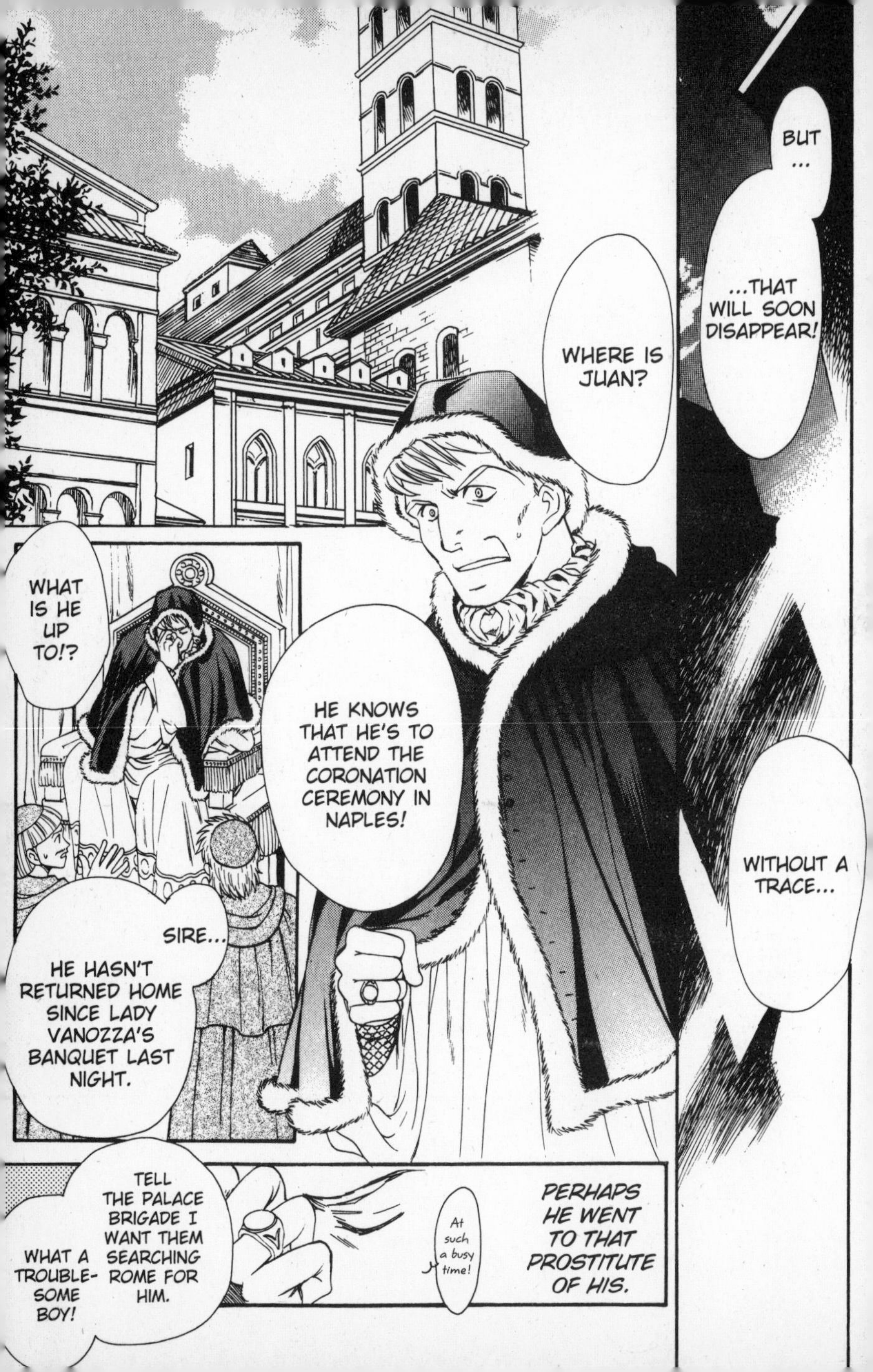
BUT...
...THAT WILL SOON DISAPPEAR!
WITHOUT A TRACE...
WHERE IS JUAN?
WHAT IS HE UP TO!?
HE KNOWS THAT HE'S TO ATTEND THE CORONATION CEREMONY IN NAPLES!
SIRE...
HE HASN'T RETURNED HOME SINCE LADY VANOZZA'S BANQUET LAST NIGHT.
PERHAPS HE WENT TO THAT PROSTITUTE OF HIS.
At such a busy time!
TELL THE PALACE BRIGADE I WANT THEM SEARCHING ROME FOR HIM.
WHAT A TROUBLE-SOME BOY!

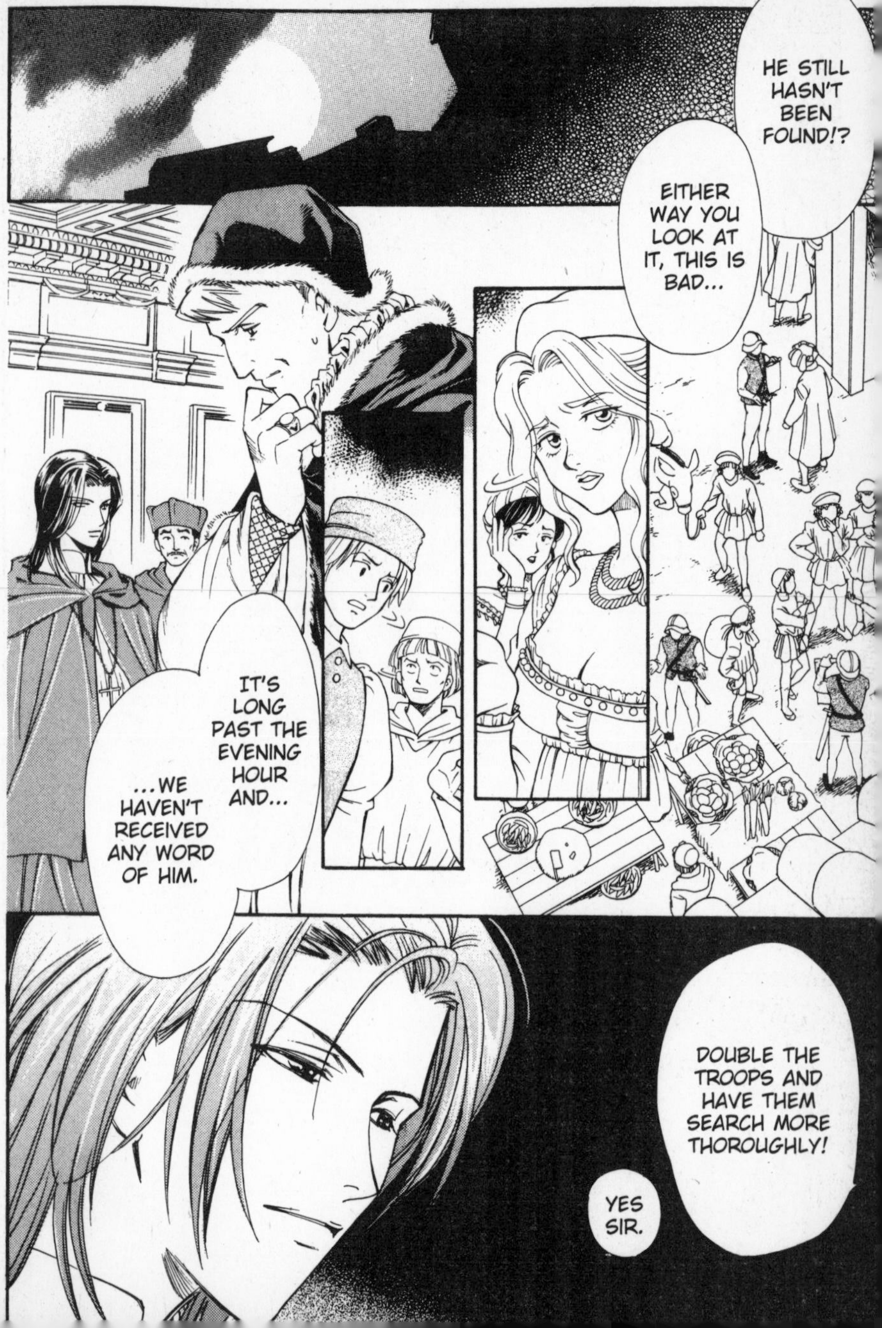
HE STILL HASN'T BEEN FOUND!?
EITHER WAY YOU LOOK AT IT, THIS IS BAD...
IT'S LONG PAST THE EVENING HOUR AND...
...WE HAVEN'T RECEIVED ANY WORD OF HIM.
DOUBLE THE TROOPS AND HAVE THEM SEARCH MORE THOROUGHLY!
YES SIR.

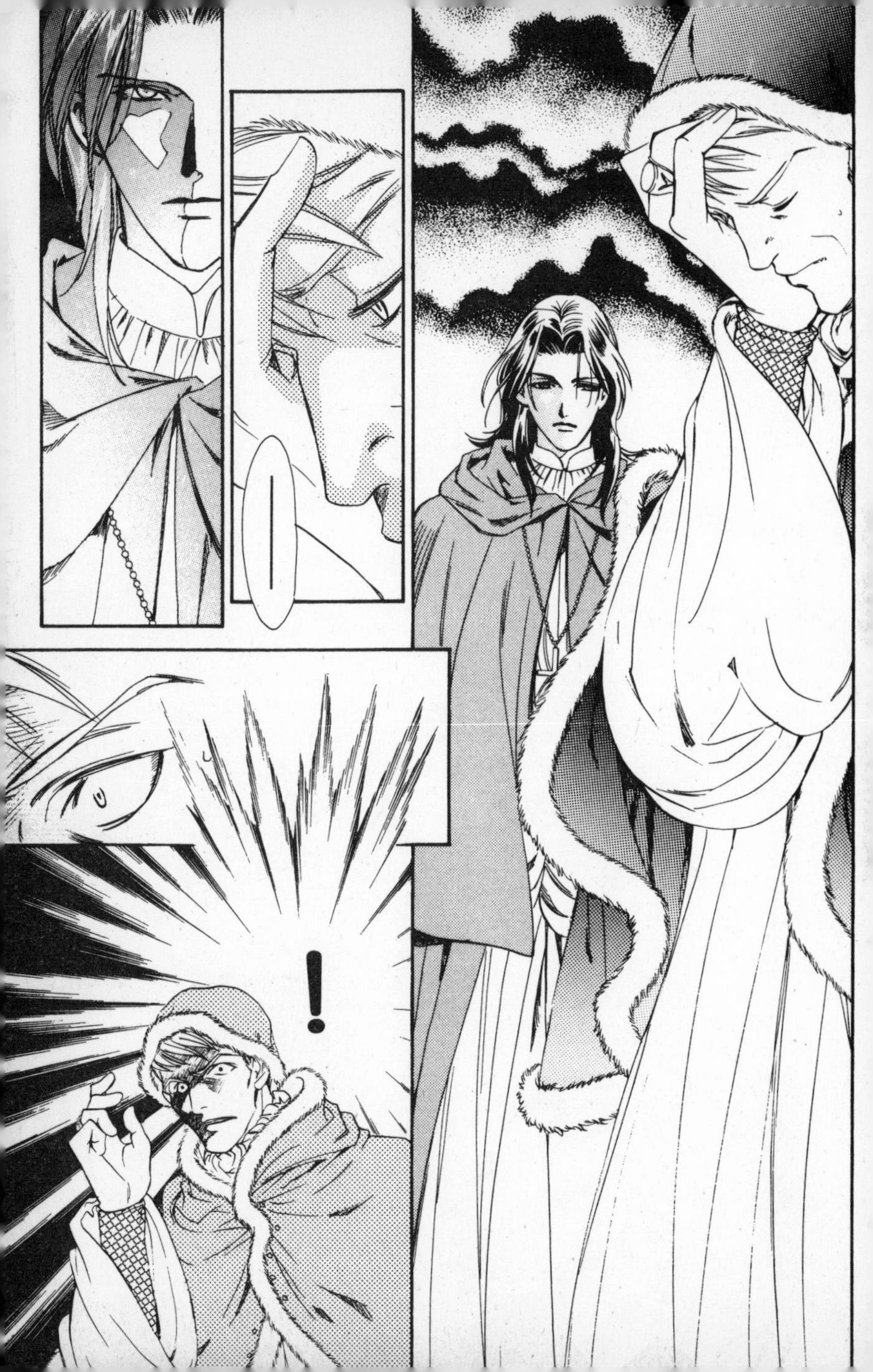
!

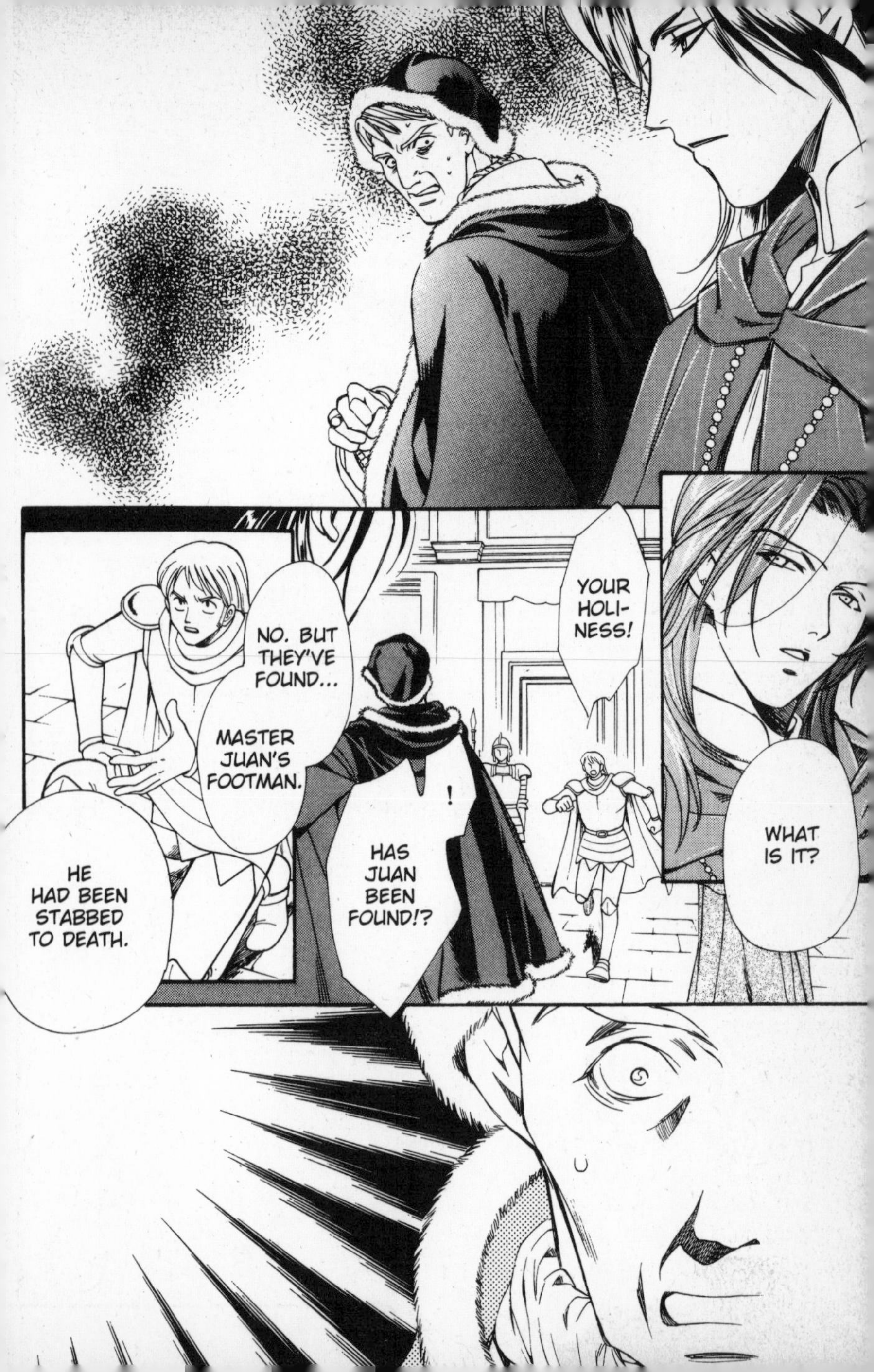
YOUR HOLINESS!
WHAT IS IT?
!
HAS JUAN BEEN FOUND!?
NO. BUT THEY'VE FOUND...
MASTER JUAN'S FOOTMAN.
HE HAD BEEN STABBED TO DEATH.

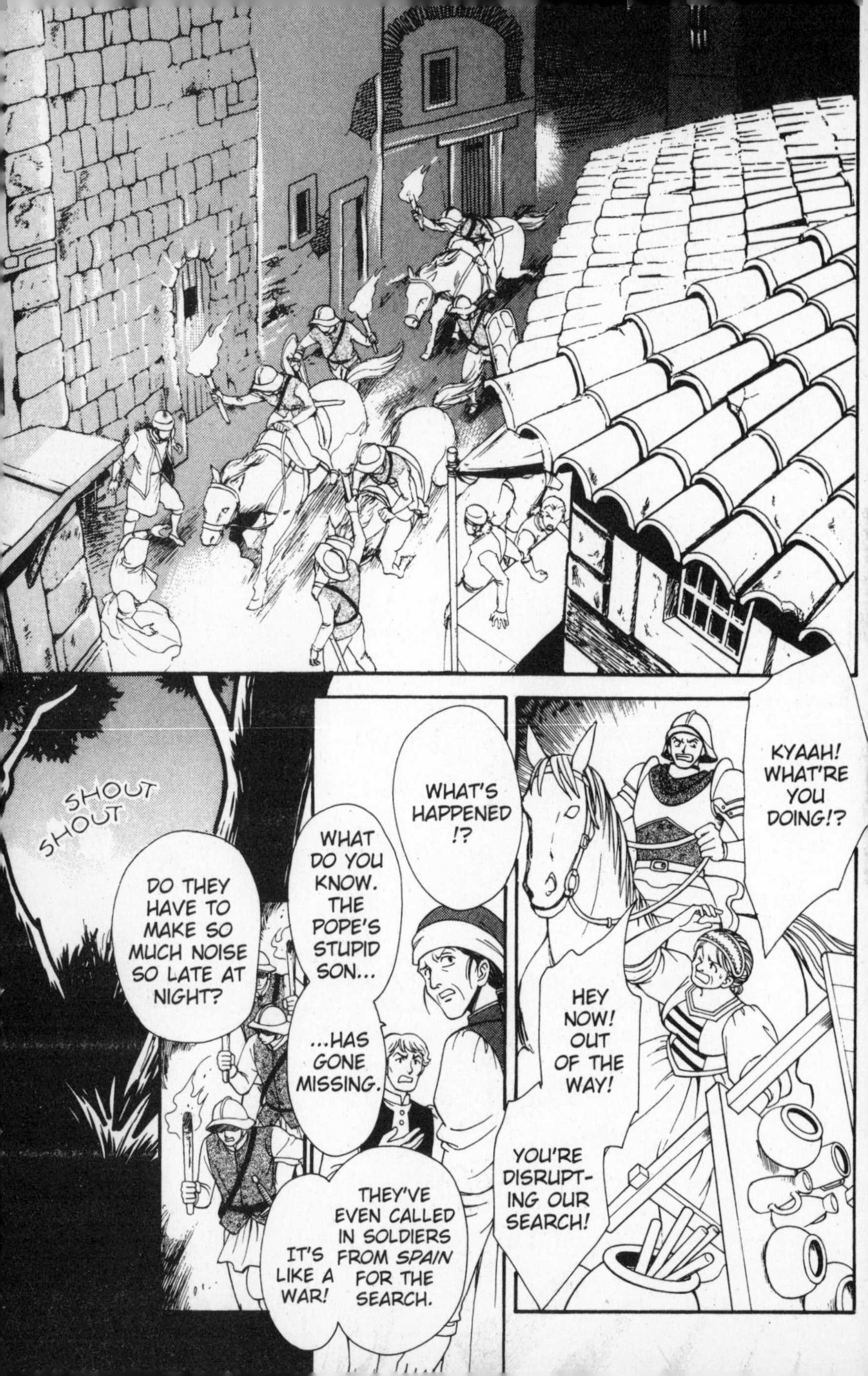
KYAAH! WHAT'RE YOU DOING!?
HEY NOW! OUT OF THE WAY!
YOU'RE DISRUPT-ING OUR SEARCH!
WHAT'S HAPPENED!?
WHAT DO YOU KNOW. THE POPE'S STUPID SON...
...HAS GONE MISSING.
THEY'VE EVEN CALLED IN SOLDIERS FROM *SPAIN* FOR THE SEARCH.
IT'S LIKE A WAR!
SHOUT SHOUT
DO THEY HAVE TO MAKE SO MUCH NOISE SO LATE AT NIGHT?

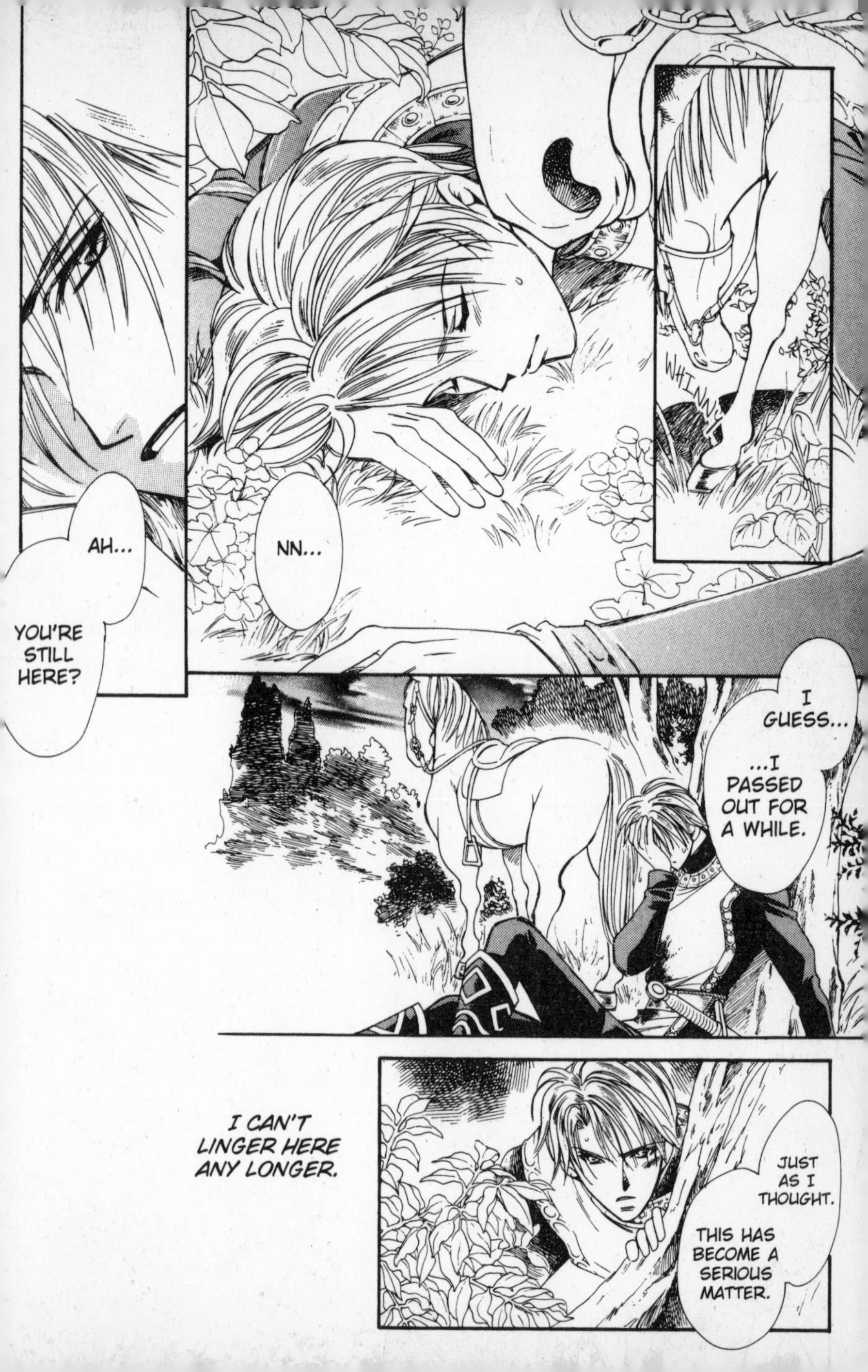
WHINNY
NN...
AH...
YOU'RE STILL HERE?
I GUESS...
...I PASSED OUT FOR A WHILE.
JUST AS I THOUGHT.
THIS HAS BECOME A SERIOUS MATTER.
I CAN'T LINGER HERE ANY LONGER.

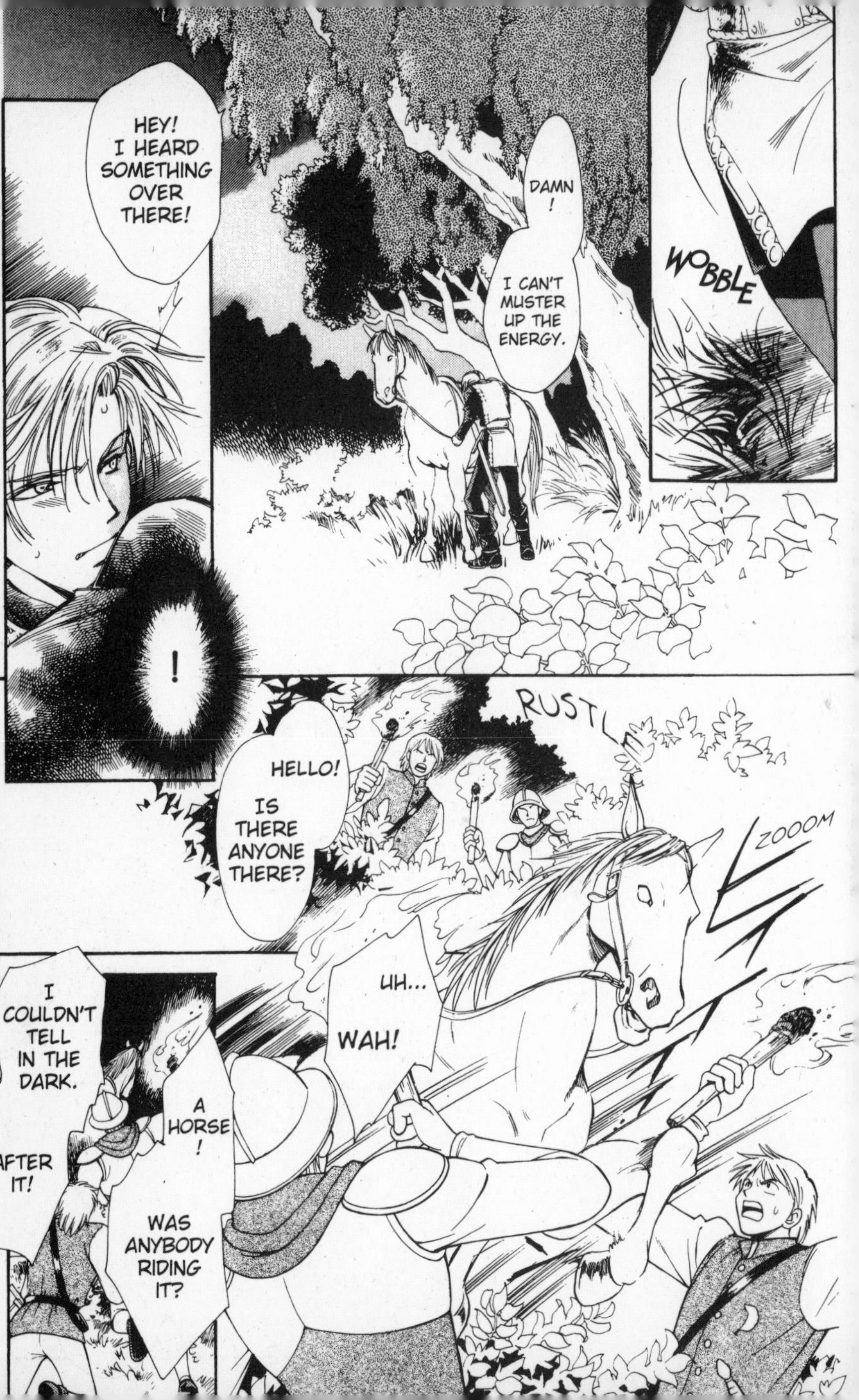
WOBBLE
DAMN!
I CAN'T MUSTER UP THE ENERGY.
HEY! I HEARD SOMETHING OVER THERE!
!
RUSTLE
HELLO!
IS THERE ANYONE THERE?
ZOOOM
UH...
WAH!
A HORSE!
WAS ANYBODY RIDING IT?
I COULDN'T TELL IN THE DARK.
AFTER IT!

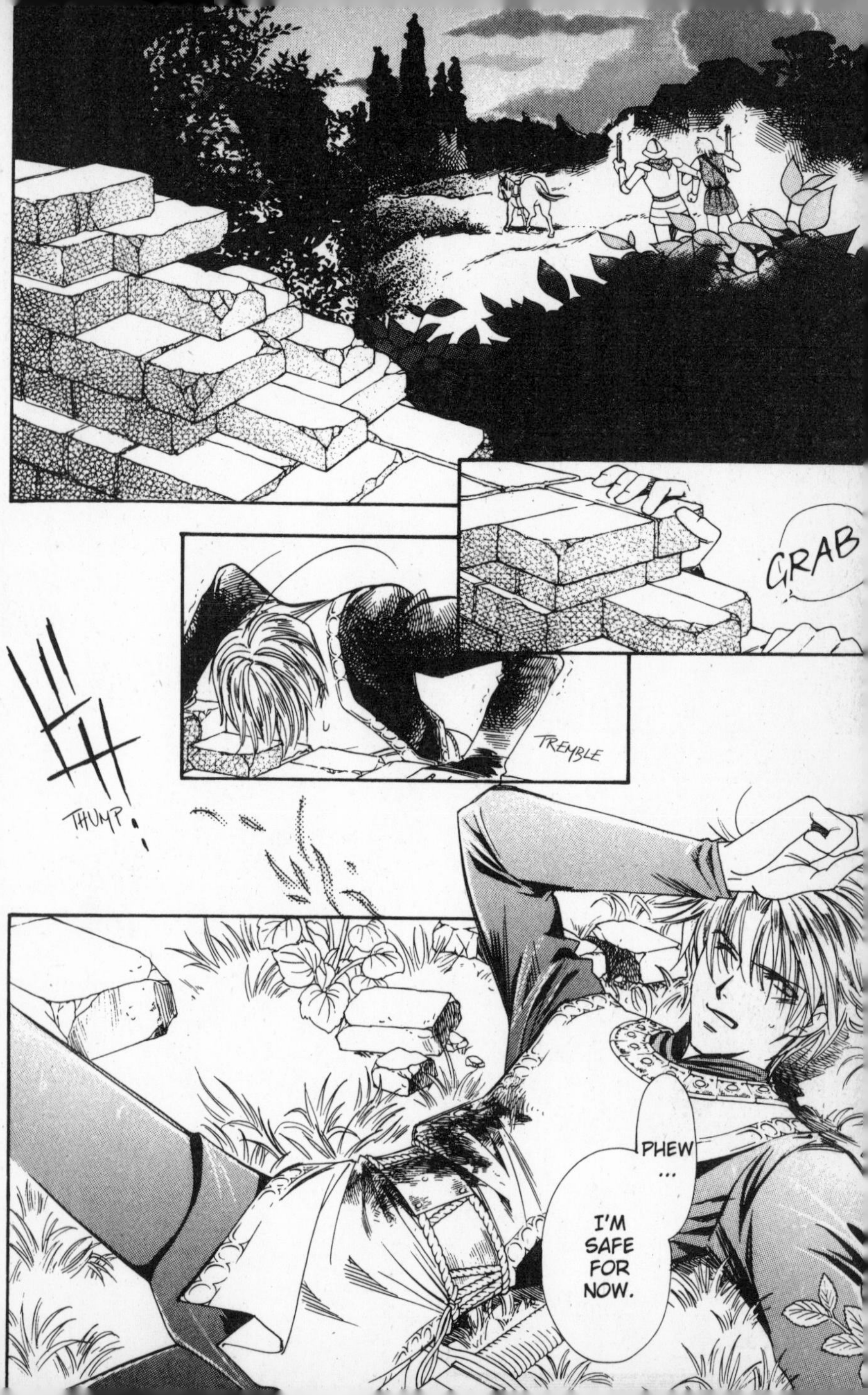
GRAB
TREMBLE
THUMP!
PHEW ...
I'M SAFE FOR NOW.

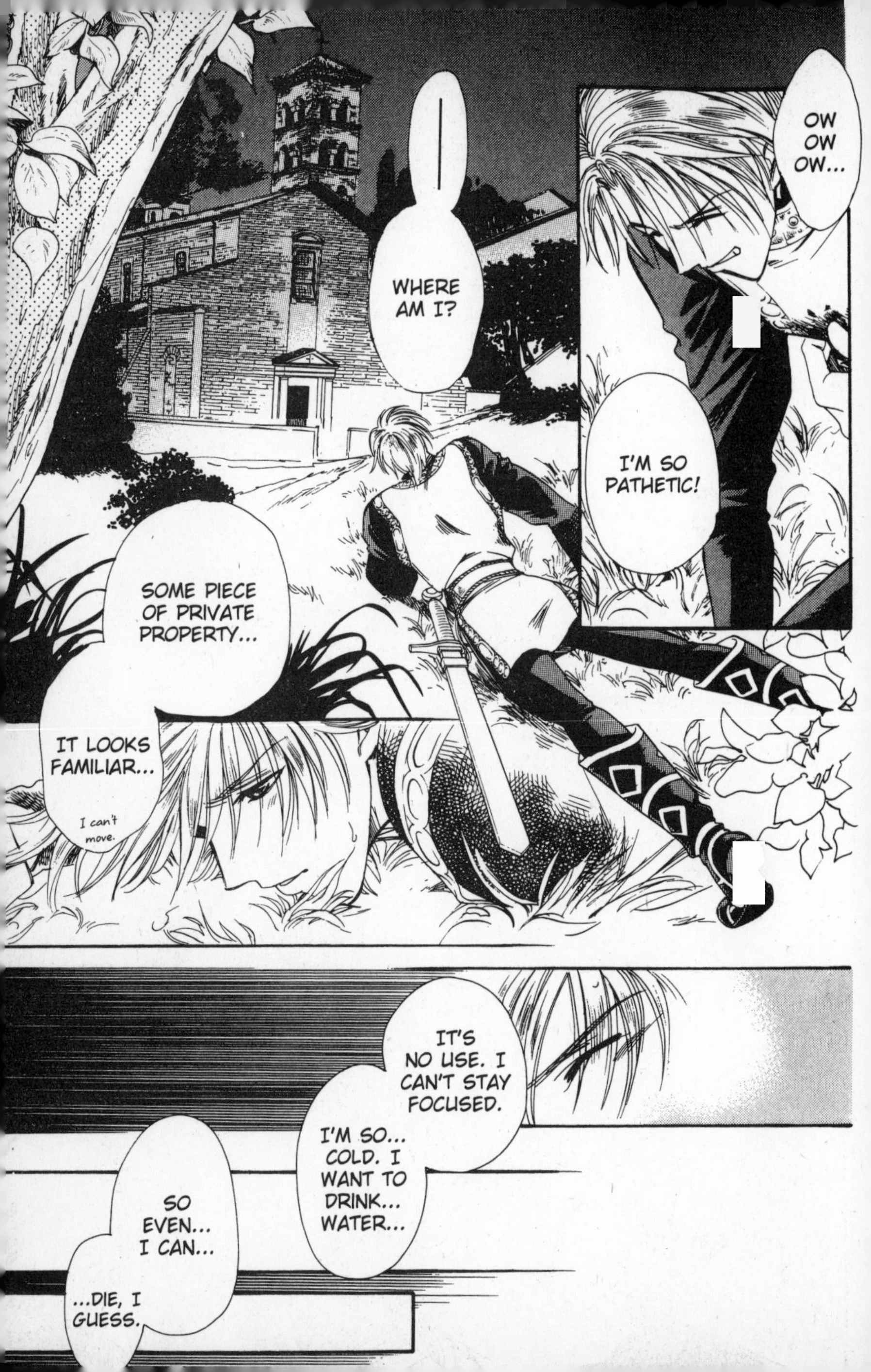
OW OW OW...
I'M SO PATHETIC!
!
WHERE AM I?
SOME PIECE OF PRIVATE PROPERTY...
IT LOOKS FAMILIAR...
I can't move.
IT'S NO USE. I CAN'T STAY FOCUSED.
I'M SO... COLD. I WANT TO DRINK... WATER...
SO EVEN... I CAN...
...DIE, I GUESS.

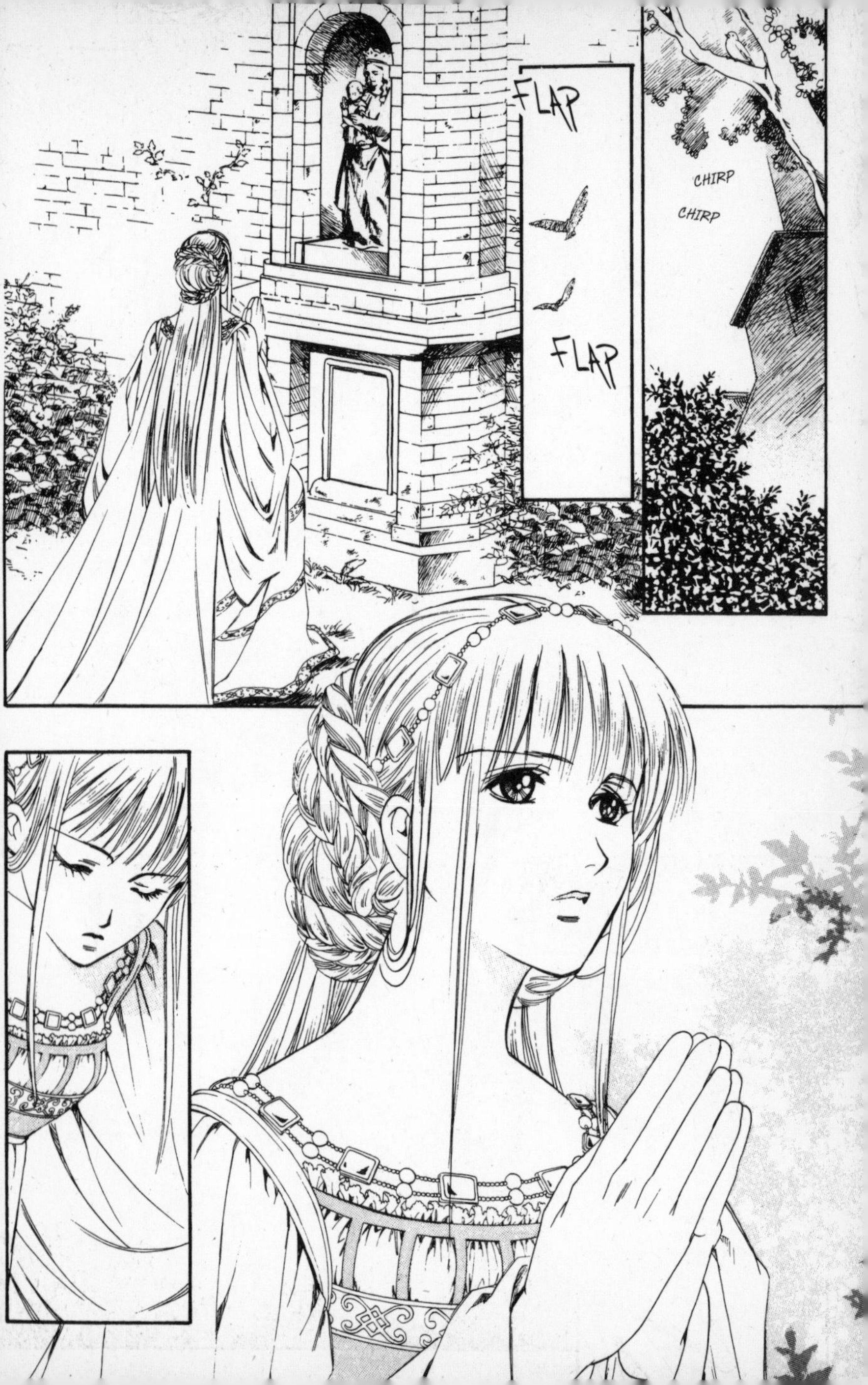
CHIRP
CHIRP
FLAP
FLAP

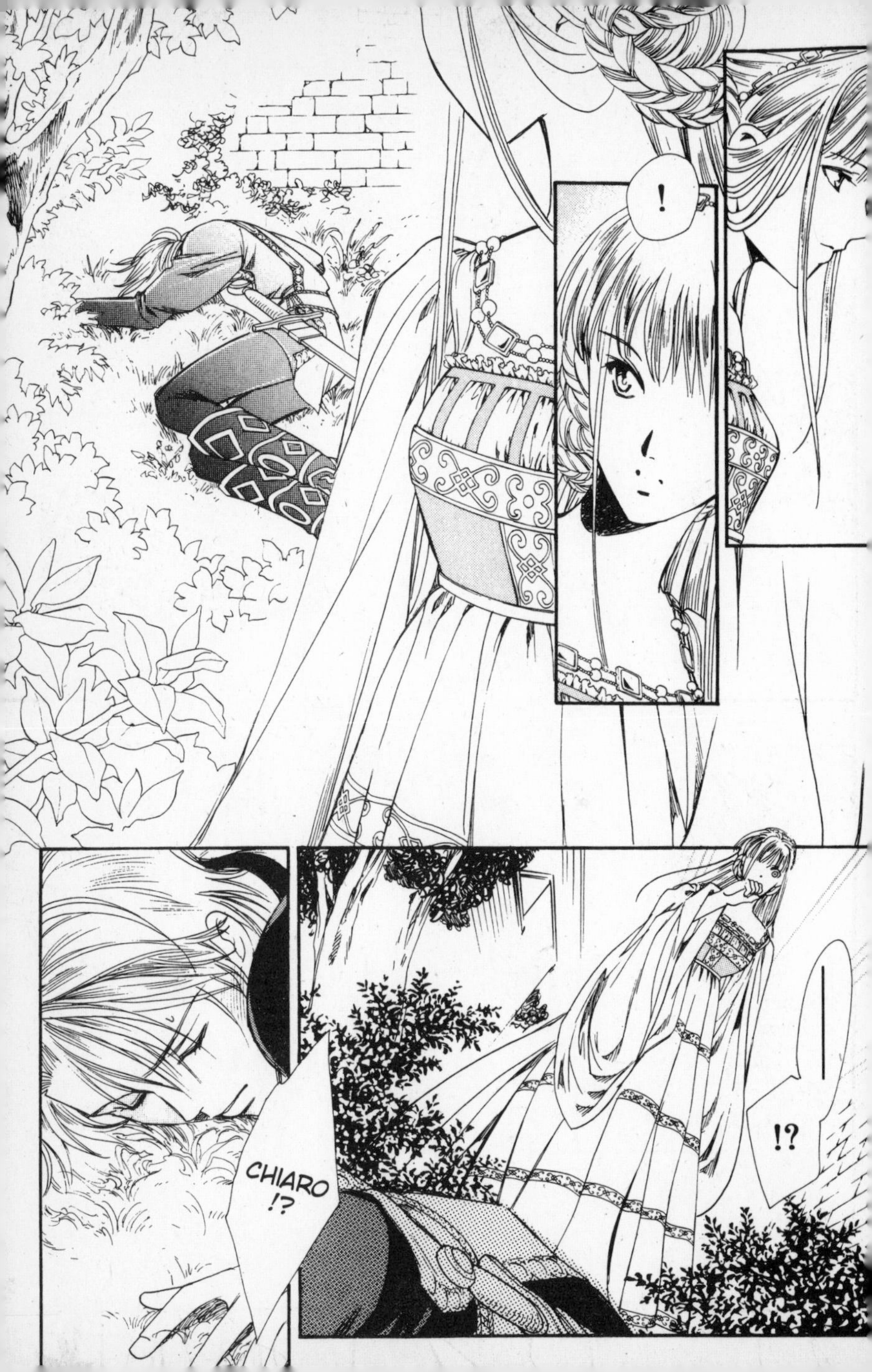
!
!?
CHIARO !?

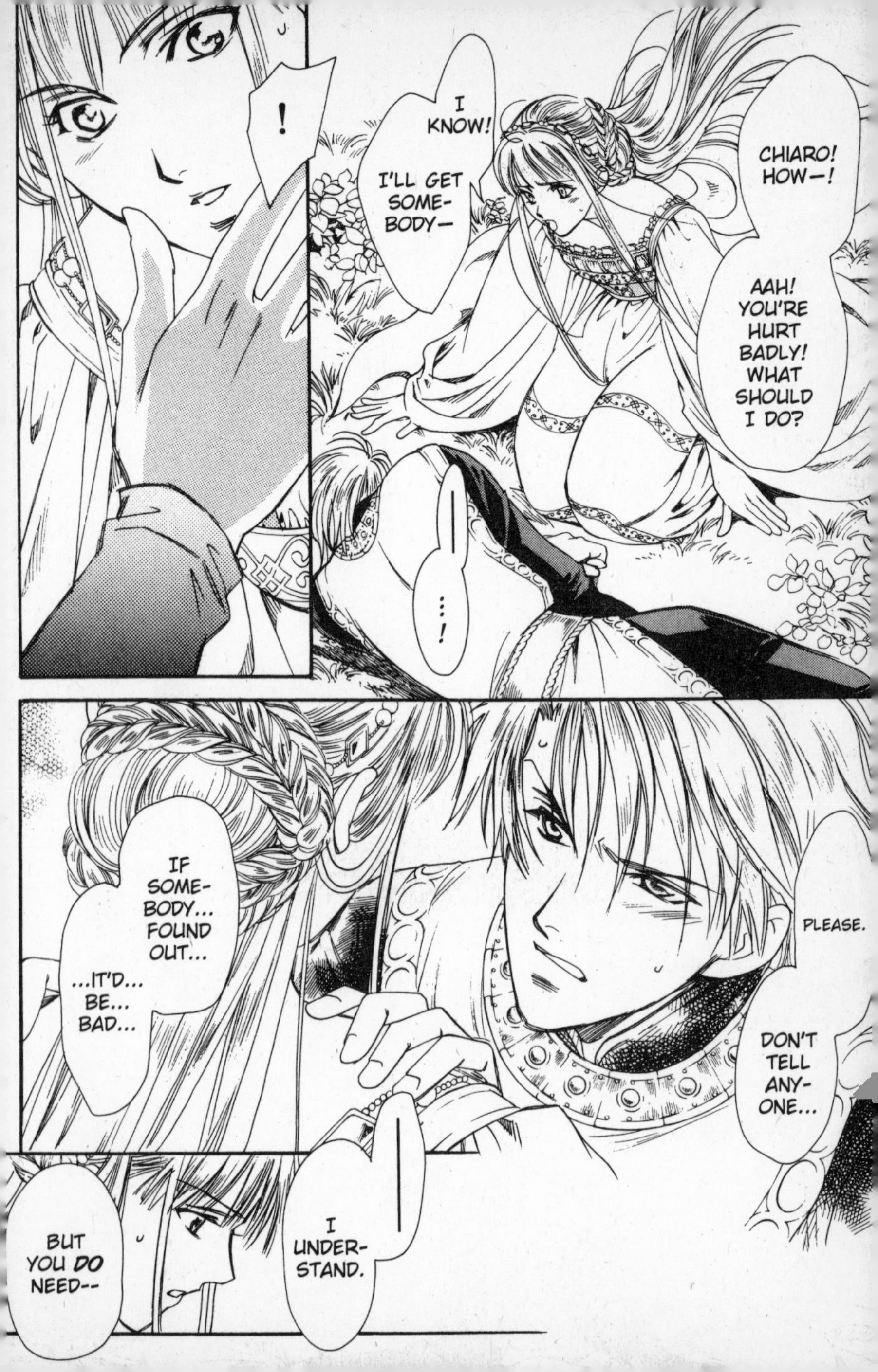
CHIARO! HOW—!
AAH! YOU'RE HURT BADLY! WHAT SHOULD I DO?
I KNOW! I'LL GET SOME-BODY—
—...!
!
PLEASE.
DON'T TELL ANY-ONE...
IF SOME-BODY... FOUND OUT...
...IT'D... BE... BAD...
—
I UNDER-STAND.
BUT YOU ***DO*** NEED--

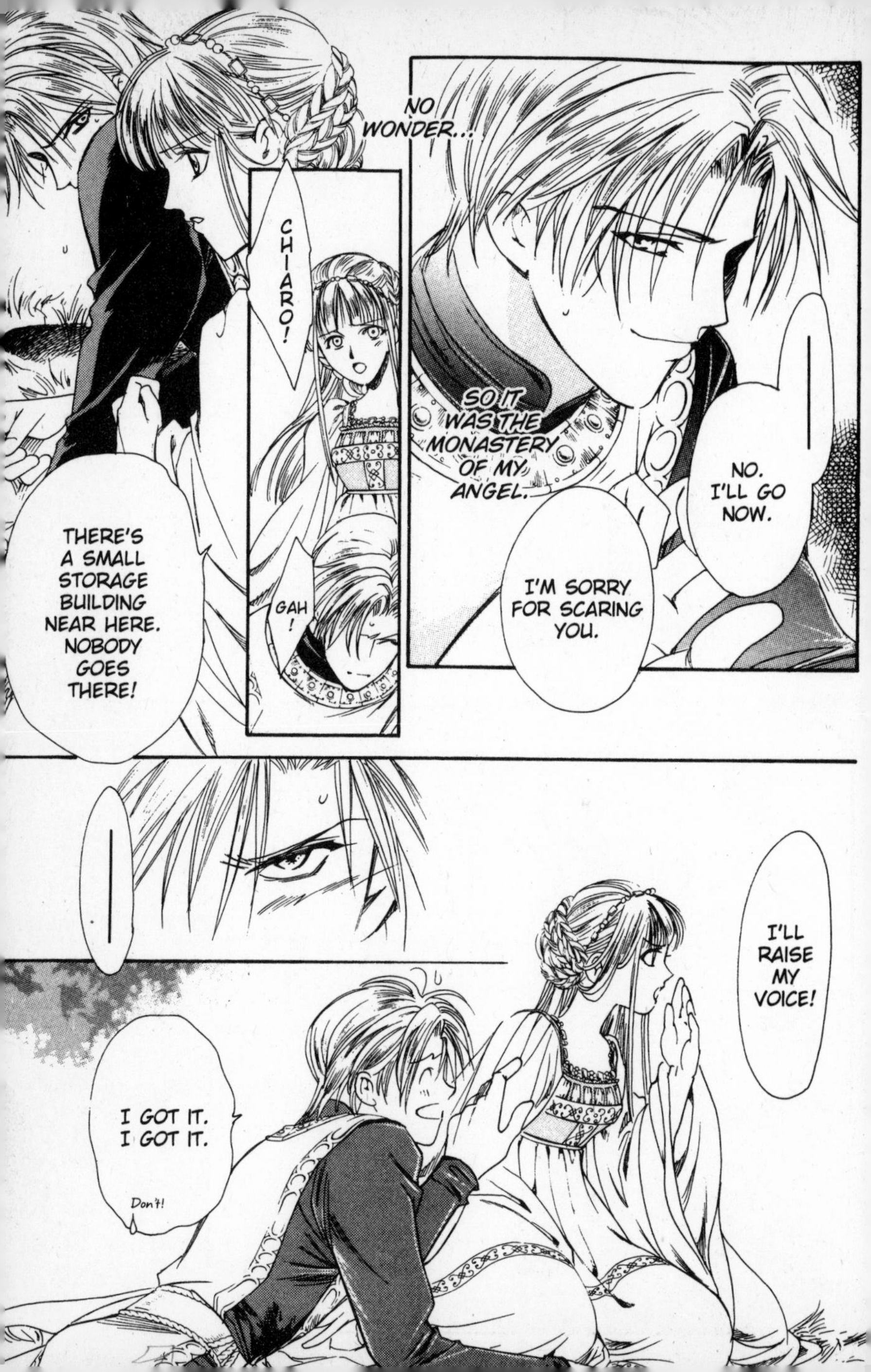
NO WONDER...
SO IT WAS THE MONASTERY OF MY ANGEL.
—
NO. I'LL GO NOW.
I'M SORRY FOR SCARING YOU.
CHIARO!
GAH!
THERE'S A SMALL STORAGE BUILDING NEAR HERE. NOBODY GOES THERE!
—
I'LL RAISE MY VOICE!
I GOT IT. I GOT IT.
Don't!

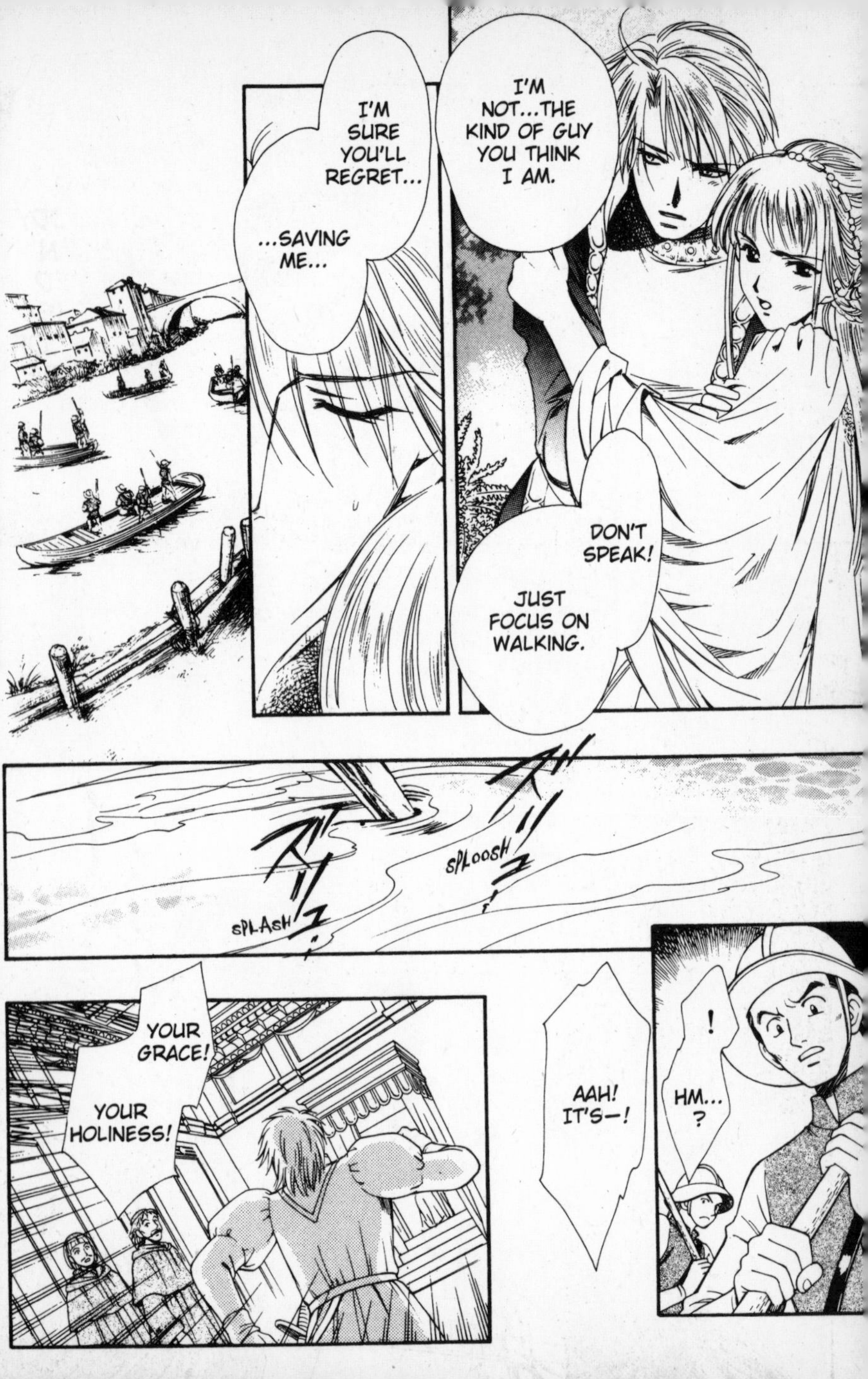
I'M NOT...THE KIND OF GUY YOU THINK I AM.
DON'T SPEAK!
JUST FOCUS ON WALKING.
I'M SURE YOU'LL REGRET...
...SAVING ME...
SPLOOSH
SPLASH
!
HM...?
AAH! IT'S—!
YOUR GRACE!
YOUR HOLINESS!

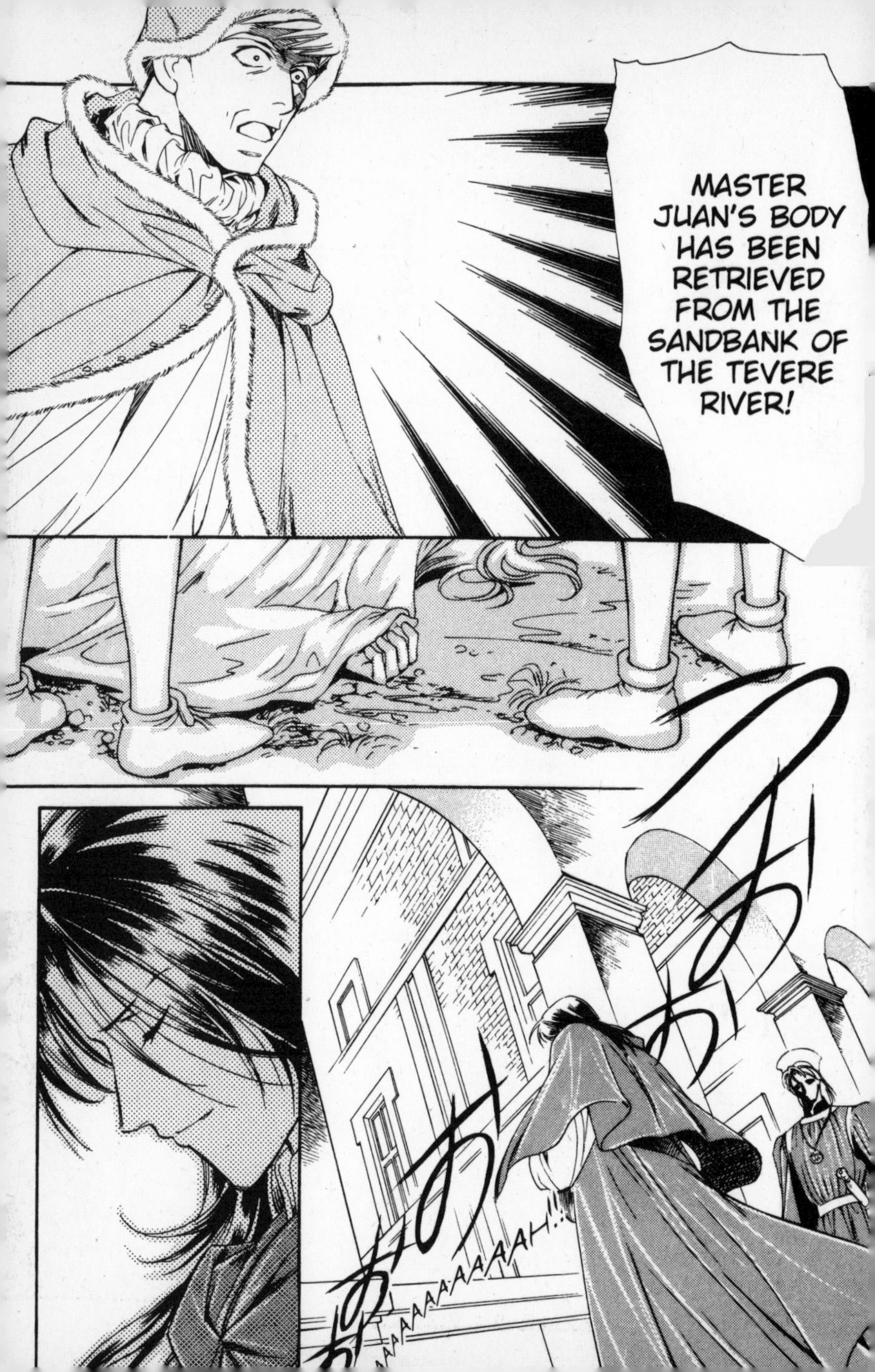
MASTER JUAN'S BODY HAS BEEN RETRIEVED FROM THE SANDBANK OF THE TEVERE RIVER!
AAAAAAAAAAAAAH!!

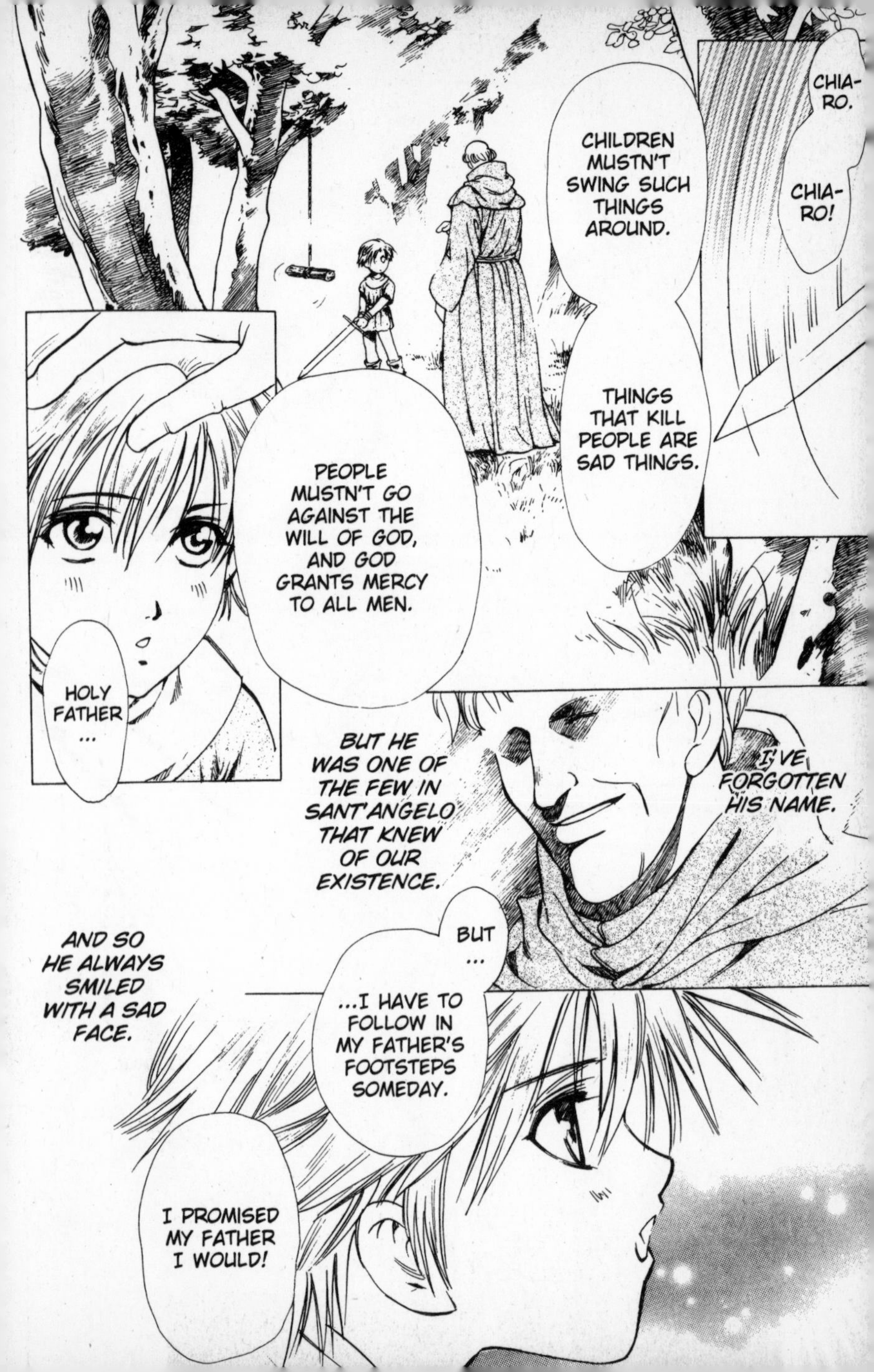
CHIA-RO.
CHIA-RO!
CHILDREN MUSTN'T SWING SUCH THINGS AROUND.
THINGS THAT KILL PEOPLE ARE SAD THINGS.
PEOPLE MUSTN'T GO AGAINST THE WILL OF GOD, AND GOD GRANTS MERCY TO ALL MEN.
HOLY FATHER ...
I'VE FORGOTTEN HIS NAME.
BUT HE WAS ONE OF THE FEW IN SANT'ANGELO THAT KNEW OF OUR EXISTENCE.
AND SO HE ALWAYS SMILED WITH A SAD FACE.
BUT ...
...I HAVE TO FOLLOW IN MY FATHER'S FOOTSTEPS SOMEDAY.
I PROMISED MY FATHER I WOULD!

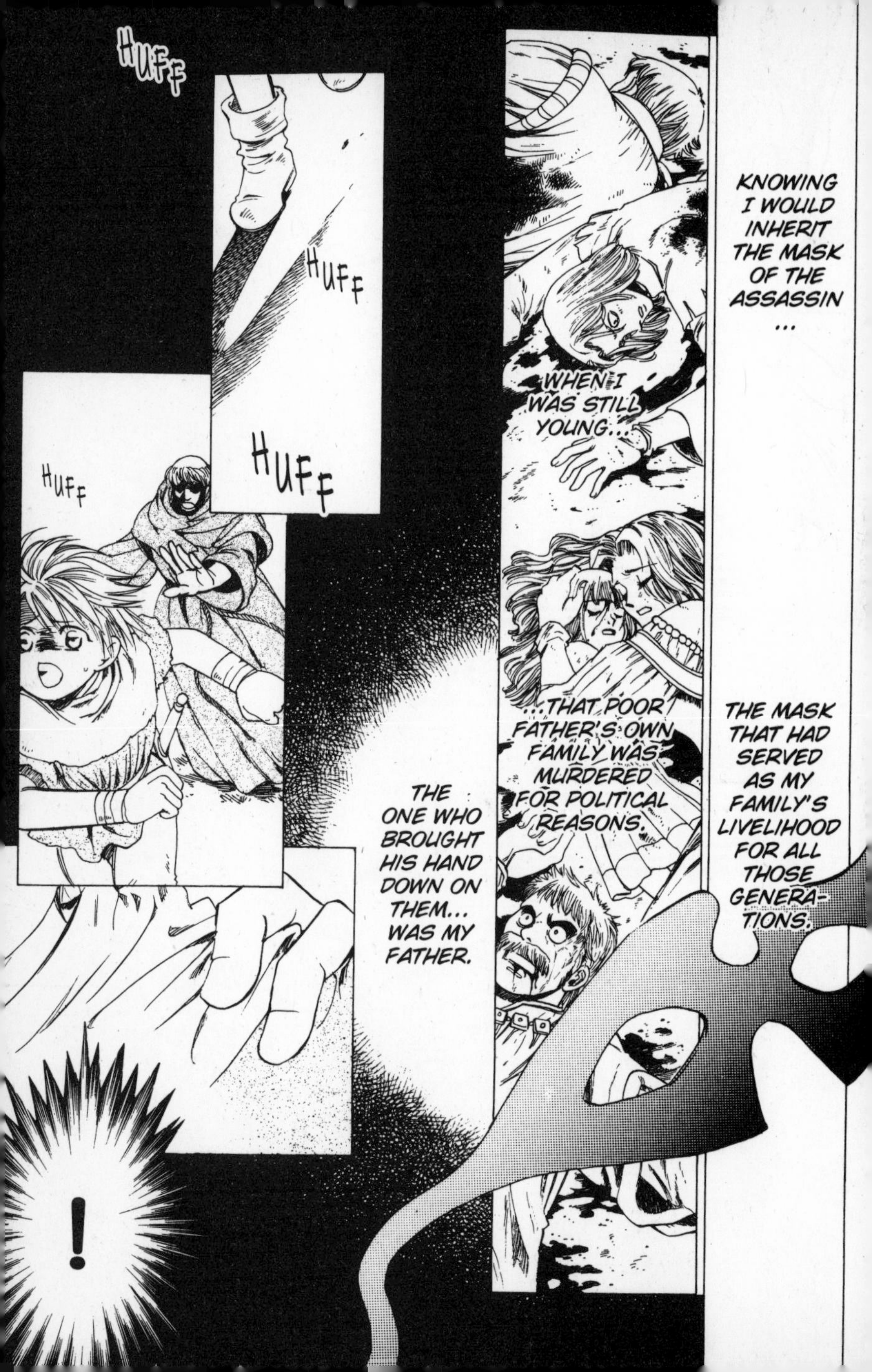
KNOWING I WOULD INHERIT THE MASK OF THE ASSASSIN ...
THE MASK THAT HAD SERVED AS MY FAMILY'S LIVELIHOOD FOR ALL THOSE GENERA-TIONS.
WHEN I WAS STILL YOUNG...
...THAT POOR FATHER'S OWN FAMILY WAS MURDERED FOR POLITICAL REASONS.
THE ONE WHO BROUGHT HIS HAND DOWN ON THEM... WAS MY FATHER.
HUFF
HUFF
HUFF
HUFF
!

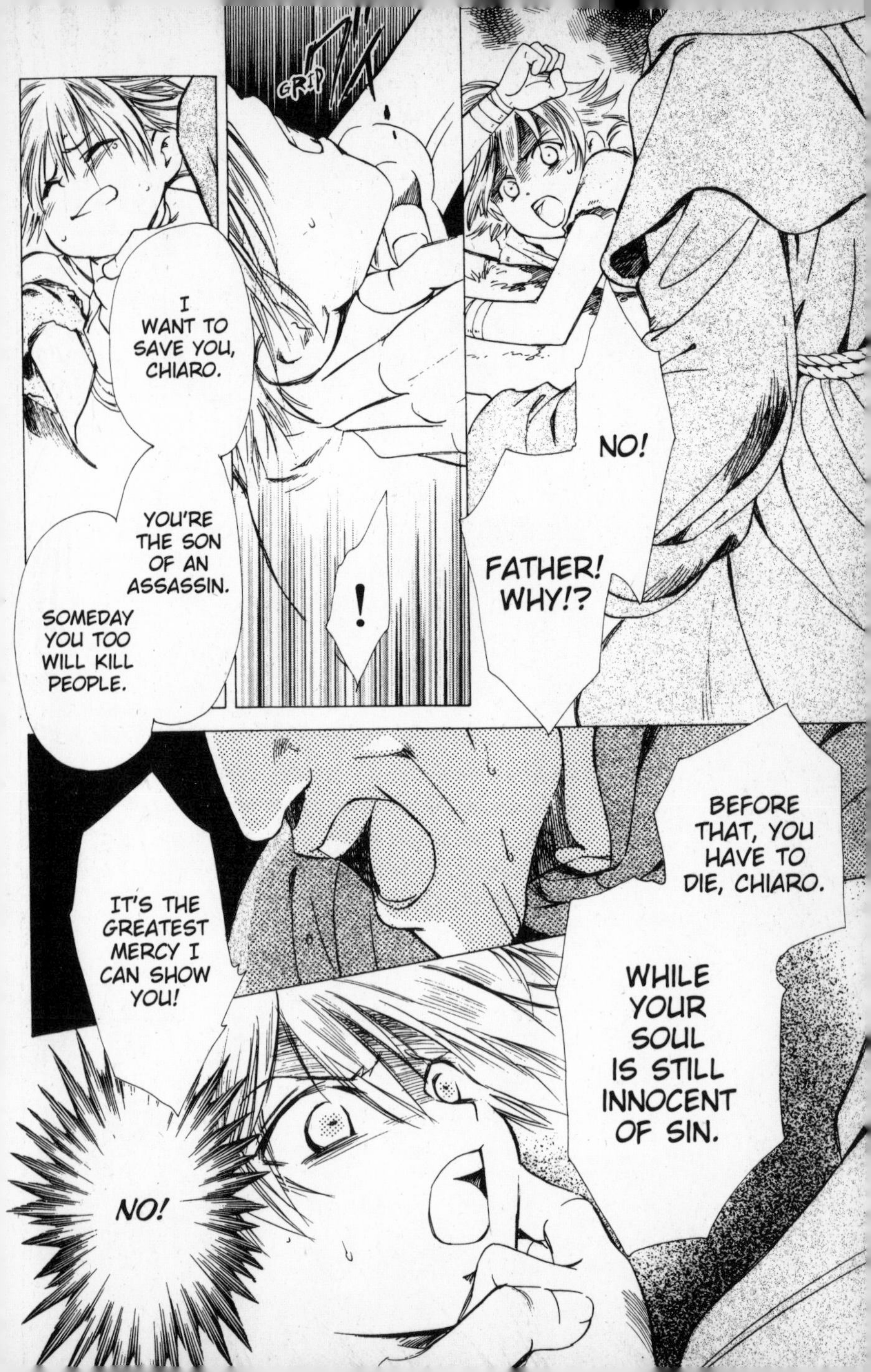
NO!
FATHER! WHY!?
GRIP
!
I WANT TO SAVE YOU, CHIARO.
YOU'RE THE SON OF AN ASSASSIN.
SOMEDAY YOU TOO WILL KILL PEOPLE.
BEFORE THAT, YOU HAVE TO DIE, CHIARO.
WHILE YOUR SOUL IS STILL INNOCENT OF SIN.
IT'S THE GREATEST MERCY I CAN SHOW YOU!
NO!

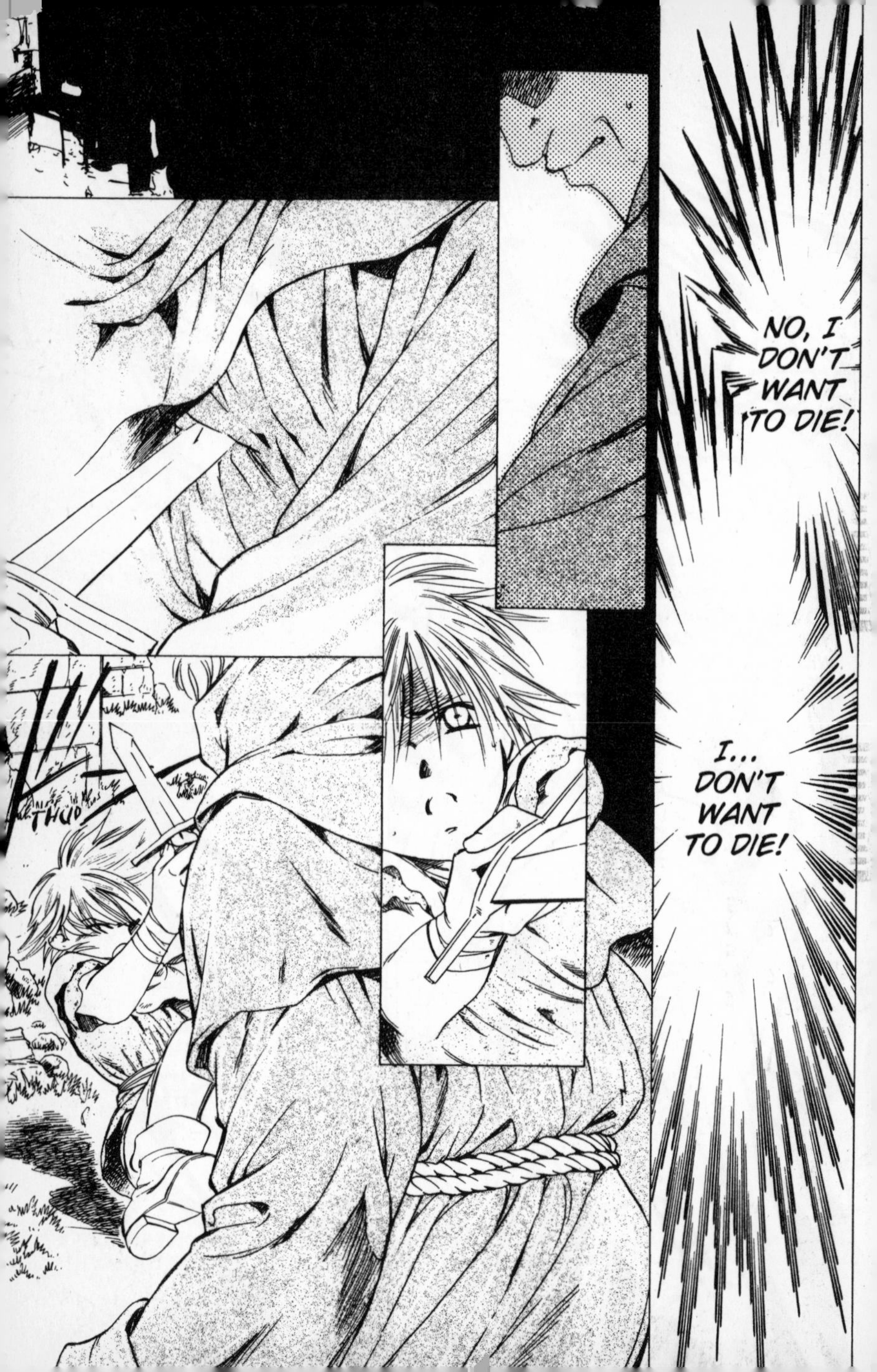
NO, I DON'T WANT TO DIE!
I... DON'T WANT TO DIE!
THUD

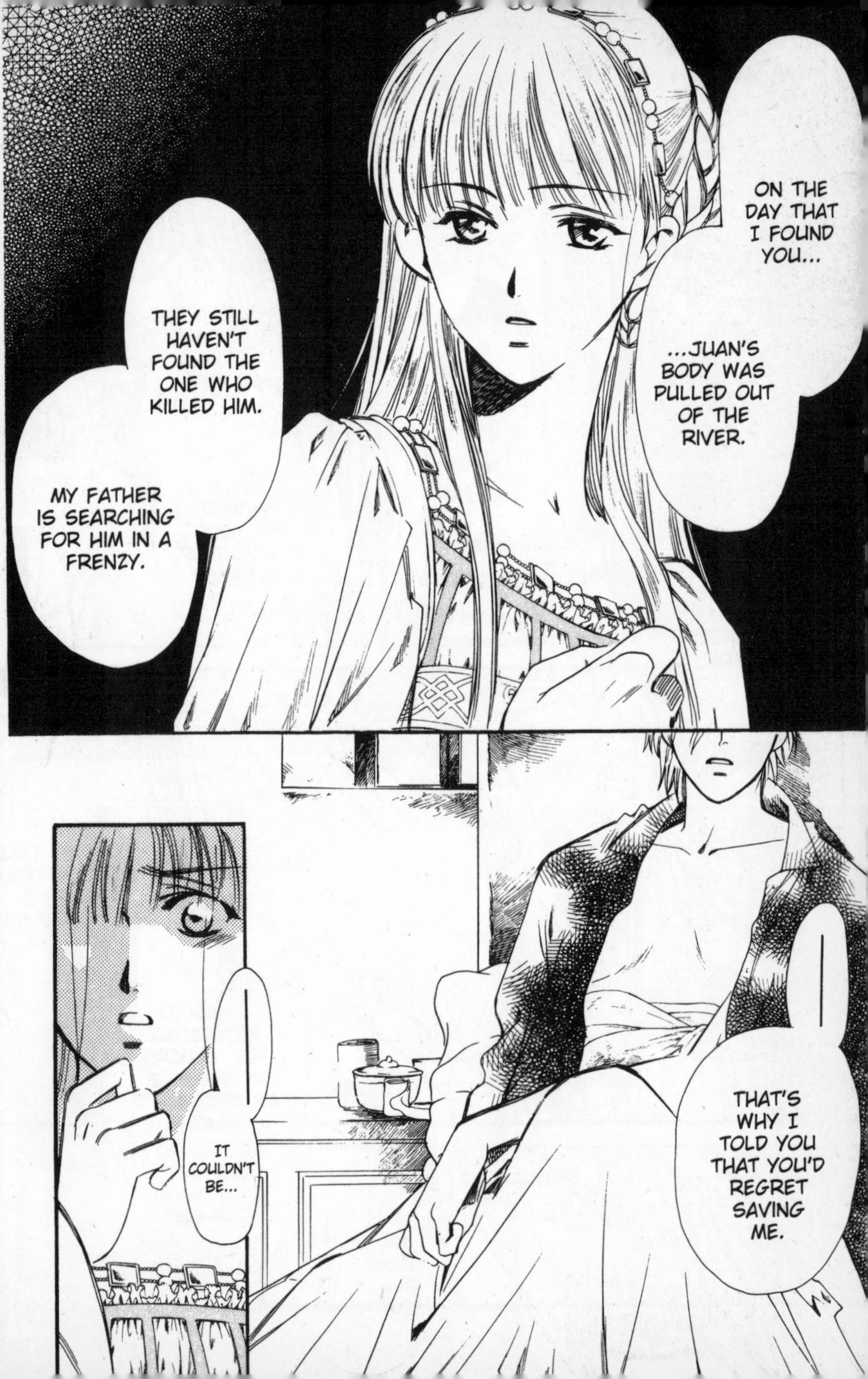
ON THE DAY THAT I FOUND YOU...
...JUAN'S BODY WAS PULLED OUT OF THE RIVER.
THEY STILL HAVEN'T FOUND THE ONE WHO KILLED HIM.
MY FATHER IS SEARCHING FOR HIM IN A FRENZY.
THAT'S WHY I TOLD YOU THAT YOU'D REGRET SAVING ME.
IT COULDN'T BE...

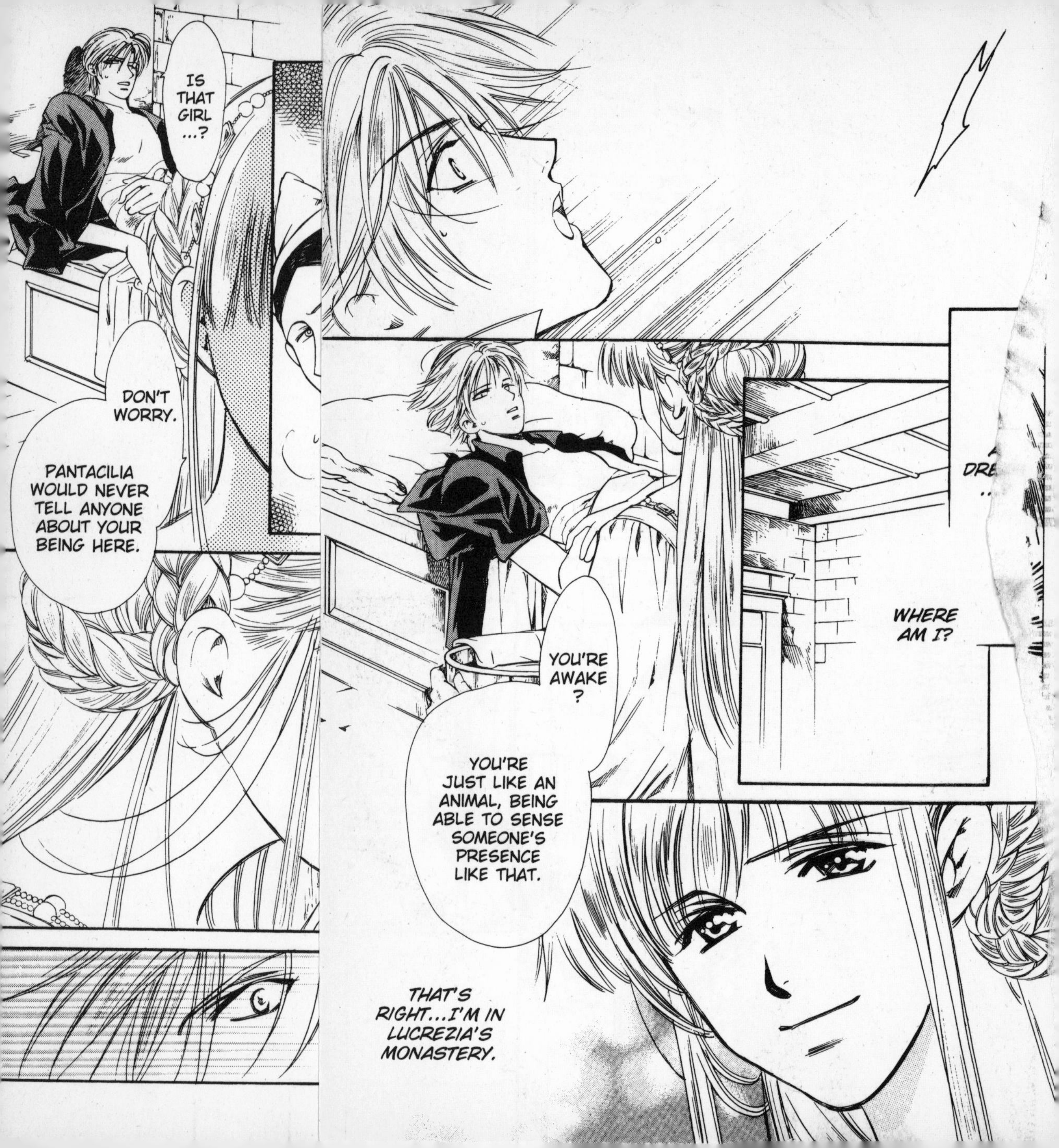
A DRE...
WHERE AM I?
YOU'RE AWAKE?
YOU'RE JUST LIKE AN ANIMAL, BEING ABLE TO SENSE SOMEONE'S PRESENCE LIKE THAT.
THAT'S RIGHT...I'M IN LUCREZIA'S MONASTERY.
IS THAT GIRL...?
DON'T WORRY.
PANTACILIA WOULD NEVER TELL ANYONE ABOUT YOUR BEING HERE.

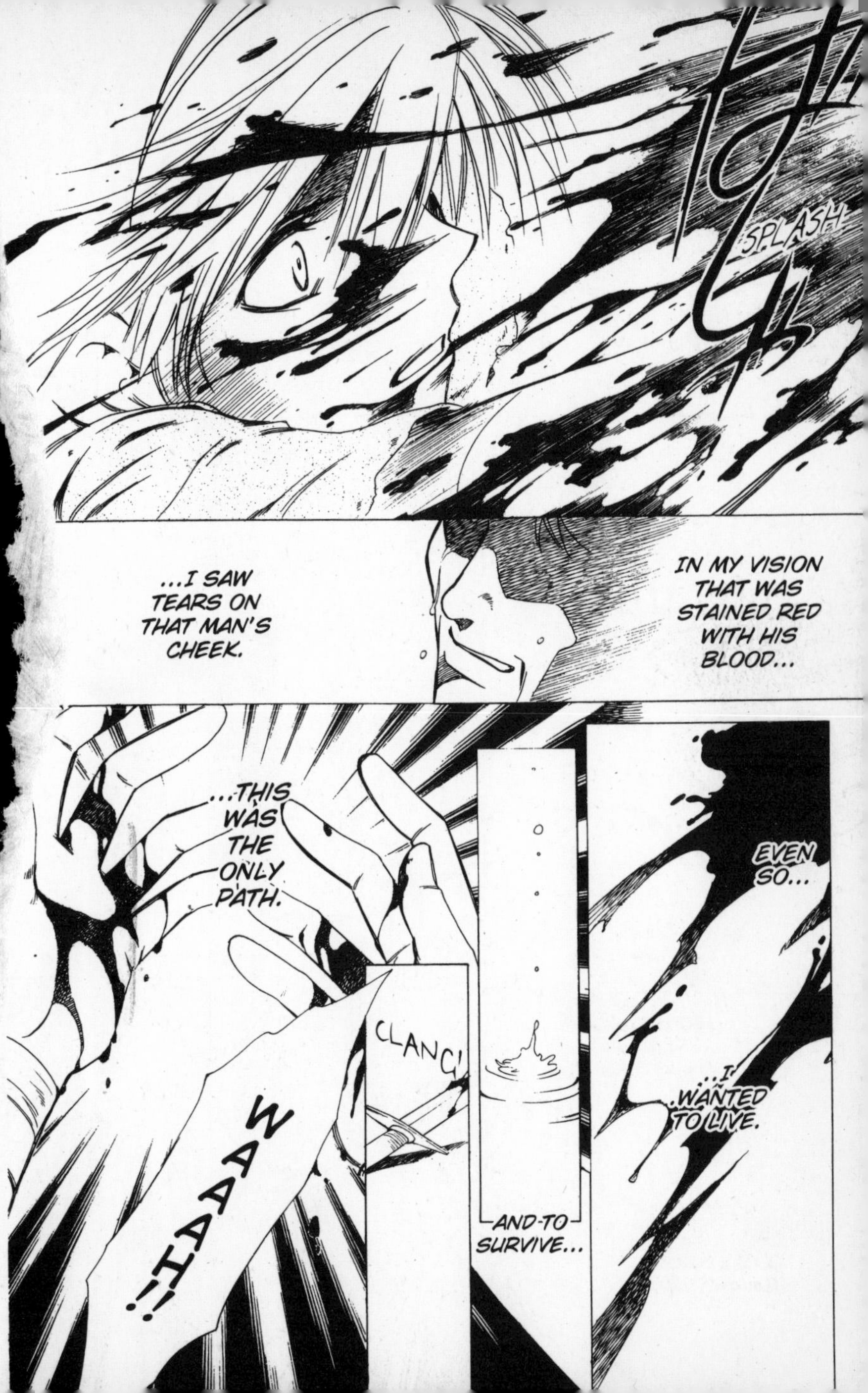
SPLASH
IN MY VISION THAT WAS STAINED RED WITH HIS BLOOD...
...I SAW TEARS ON THAT MAN'S CHEEK.
EVEN SO...
...I WANTED TO LIVE.
AND TO SURVIVE...
CLANG!
...THIS WAS THE ONLY PATH.
WAAAAH!!

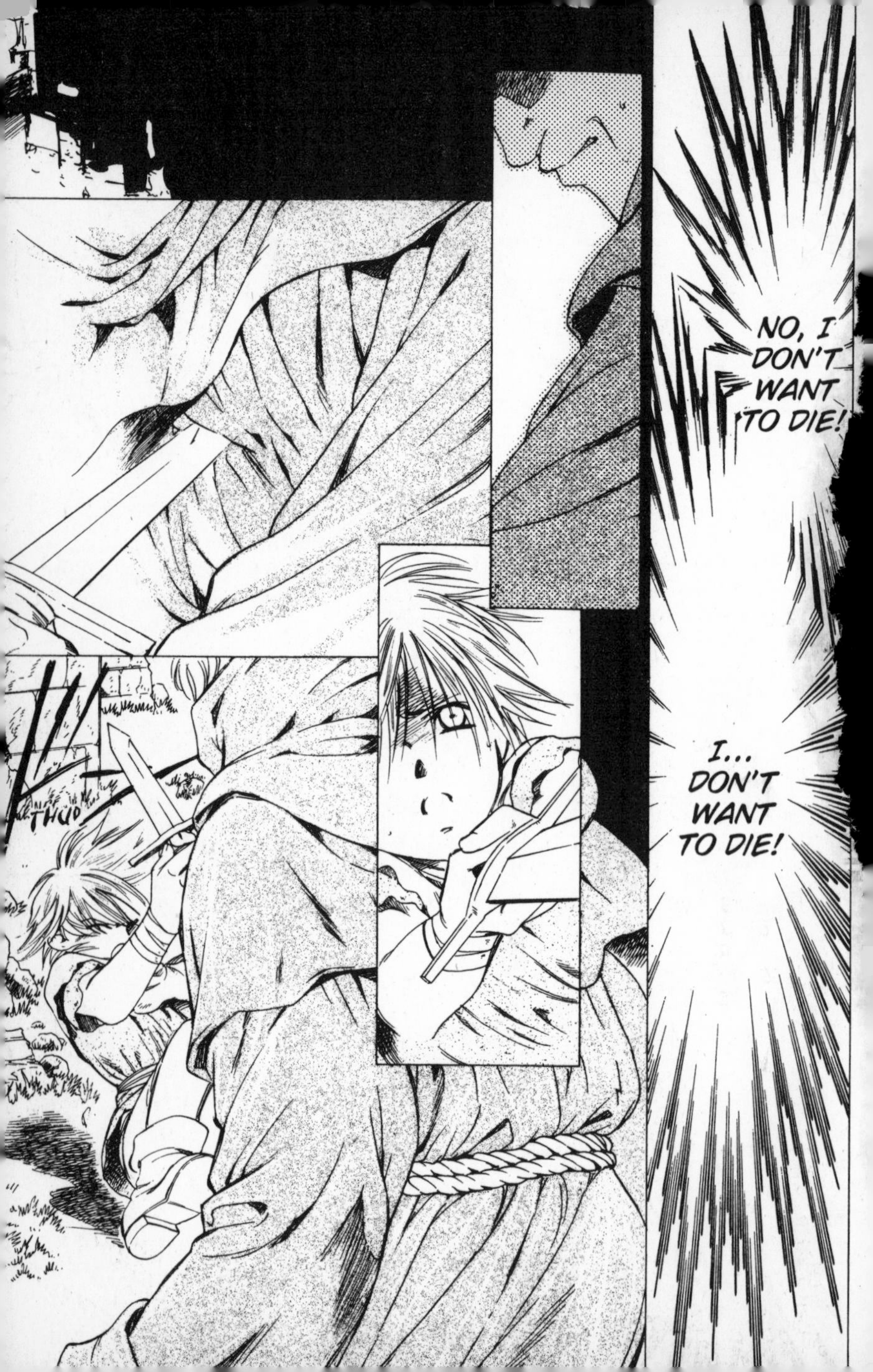
NO, I DON'T WANT TO DIE!
I... DON'T WANT TO DIE!
THUD

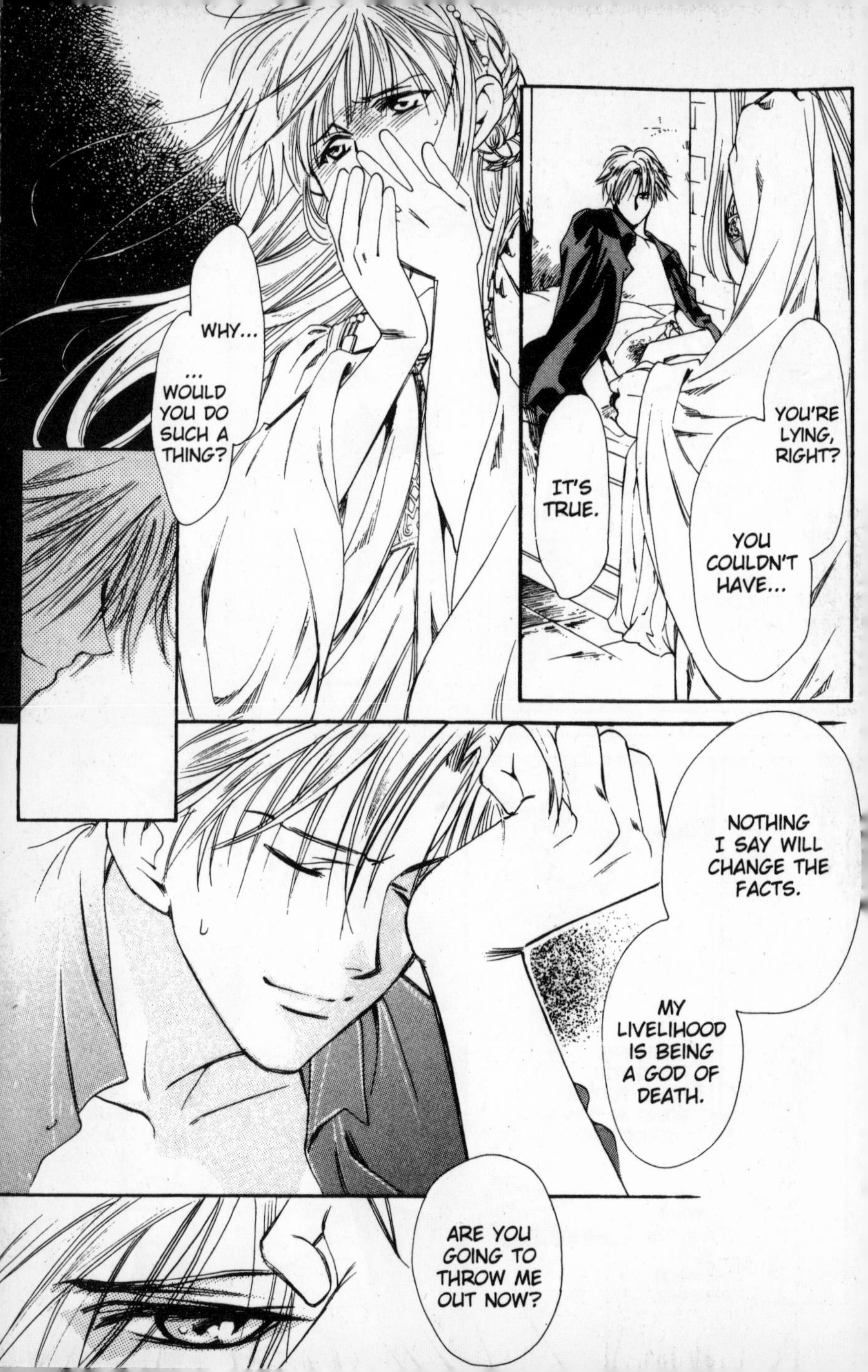
YOU'RE LYING, RIGHT?
YOU COULDN'T HAVE...
IT'S TRUE.
WHY...
... WOULD YOU DO SUCH A THING?
NOTHING I SAY WILL CHANGE THE FACTS.
MY LIVELIHOOD IS BEING A GOD OF DEATH.
ARE YOU GOING TO THROW ME OUT NOW?

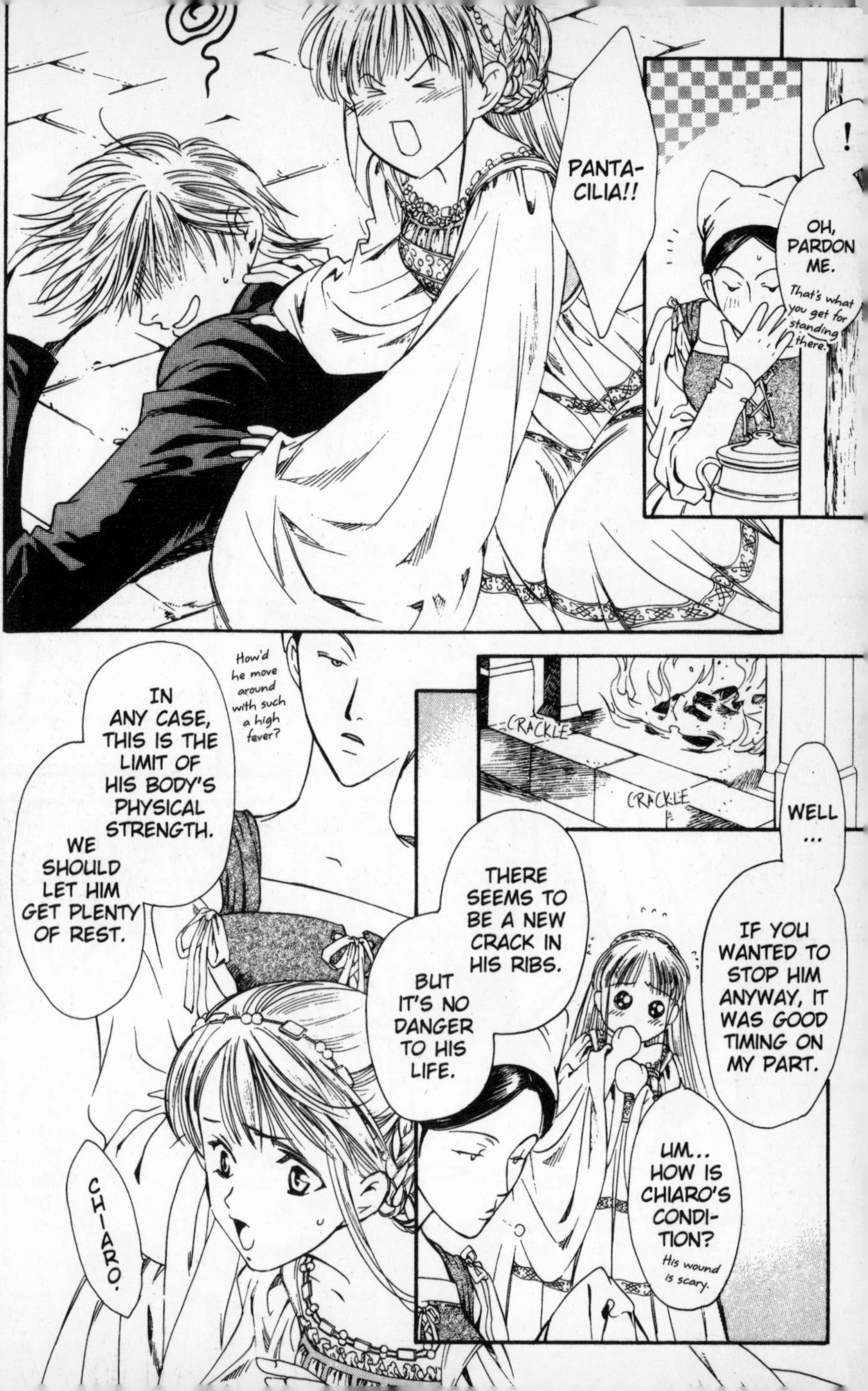
!
OH, PARDON ME.
That's what you get for standing there.
PANTA-CILIA!!
CRACKLE
CRACKLE
WELL...
IF YOU WANTED TO STOP HIM ANYWAY, IT WAS GOOD TIMING ON MY PART.
THERE SEEMS TO BE A NEW CRACK IN HIS RIBS.
BUT IT'S NO DANGER TO HIS LIFE.
UM.. HOW IS CHIARO'S CONDITION?
His wound is scary.
IN ANY CASE, THIS IS THE LIMIT OF HIS BODY'S PHYSICAL STRENGTH.
WE SHOULD LET HIM GET PLENTY OF REST.
How'd he move around with such a high fever?
CHIARO.

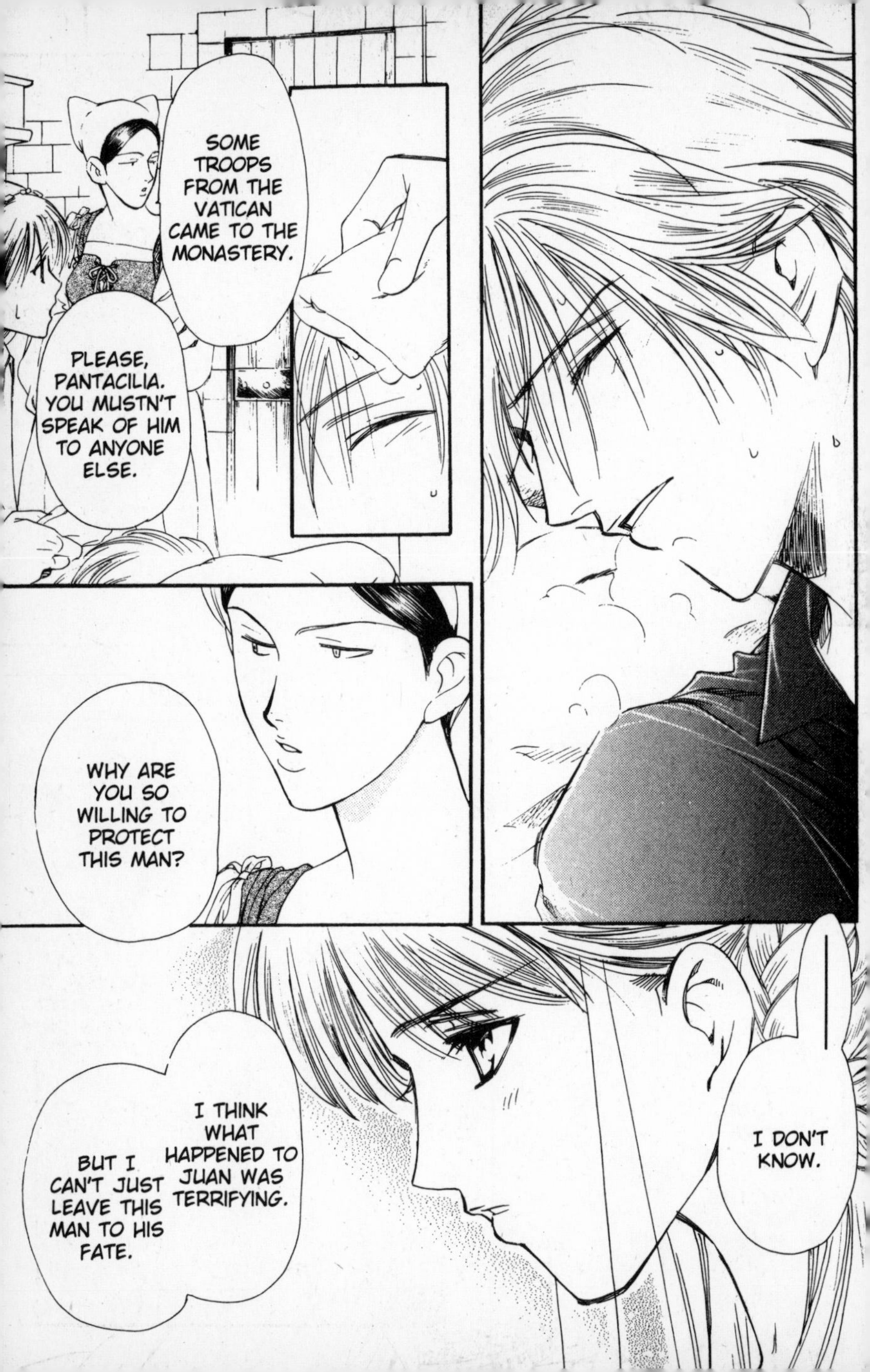
SOME TROOPS FROM THE VATICAN CAME TO THE MONASTERY.
PLEASE, PANTACILIA. YOU MUSTN'T SPEAK OF HIM TO ANYONE ELSE.
WHY ARE YOU SO WILLING TO PROTECT THIS MAN?
I DON'T KNOW.
I THINK WHAT HAPPENED TO JUAN WAS TERRIFYING.
BUT I CAN'T JUST LEAVE THIS MAN TO HIS FATE.

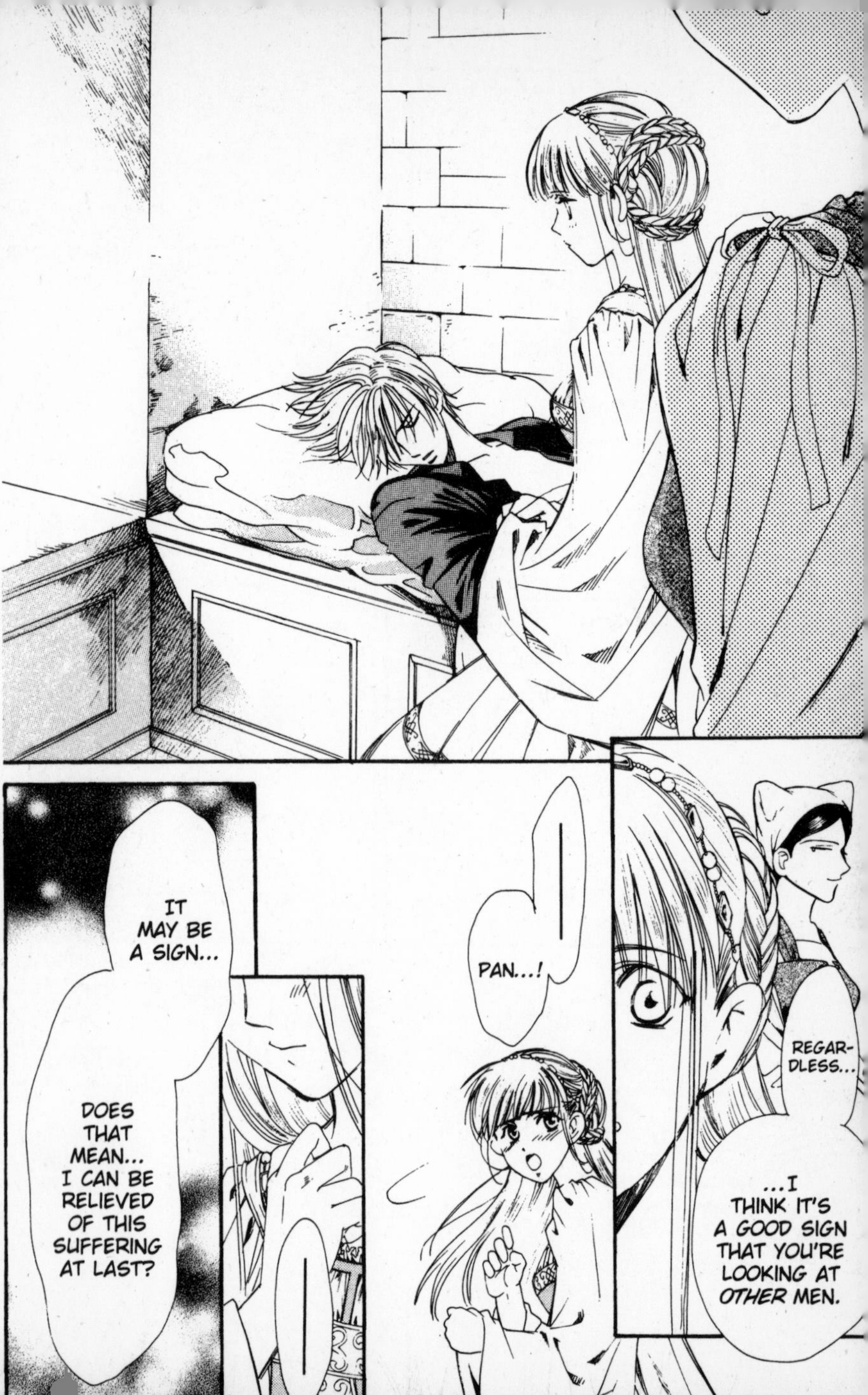
REGARDLESS...
...I THINK IT'S A GOOD SIGN THAT YOU'RE LOOKING AT *OTHER* MEN.
PAN...!
IT MAY BE A SIGN...
DOES THAT MEAN... I CAN BE RELIEVED OF THIS SUFFERING AT LAST?

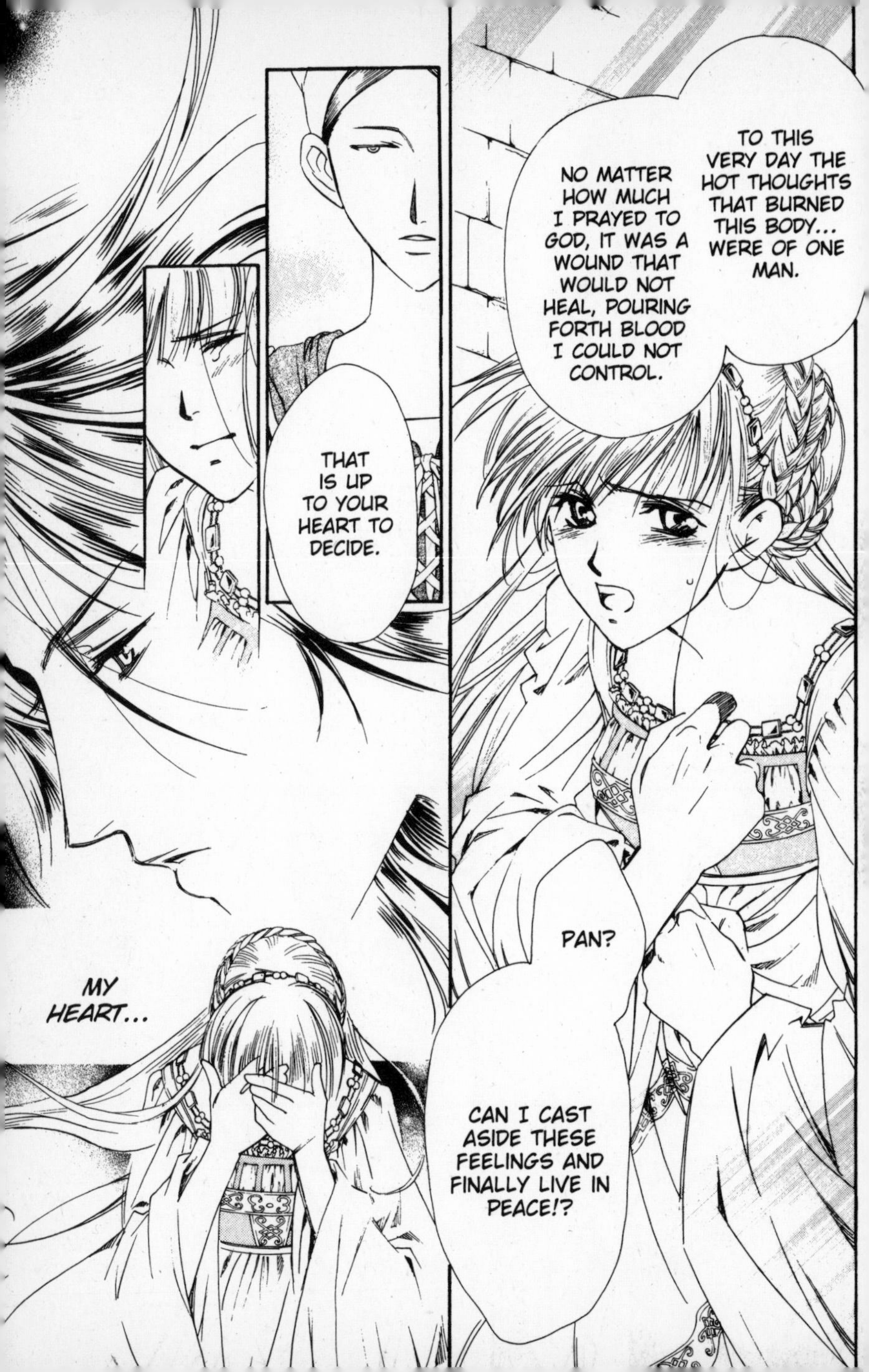
TO THIS VERY DAY THE HOT THOUGHTS THAT BURNED THIS BODY... WERE OF ONE MAN.
NO MATTER HOW MUCH I PRAYED TO GOD, IT WAS A WOUND THAT WOULD NOT HEAL, POURING FORTH BLOOD I COULD NOT CONTROL.
PAN?
CAN I CAST ASIDE THESE FEELINGS AND FINALLY LIVE IN PEACE!?
THAT IS UP TO YOUR HEART TO DECIDE.
MY HEART...

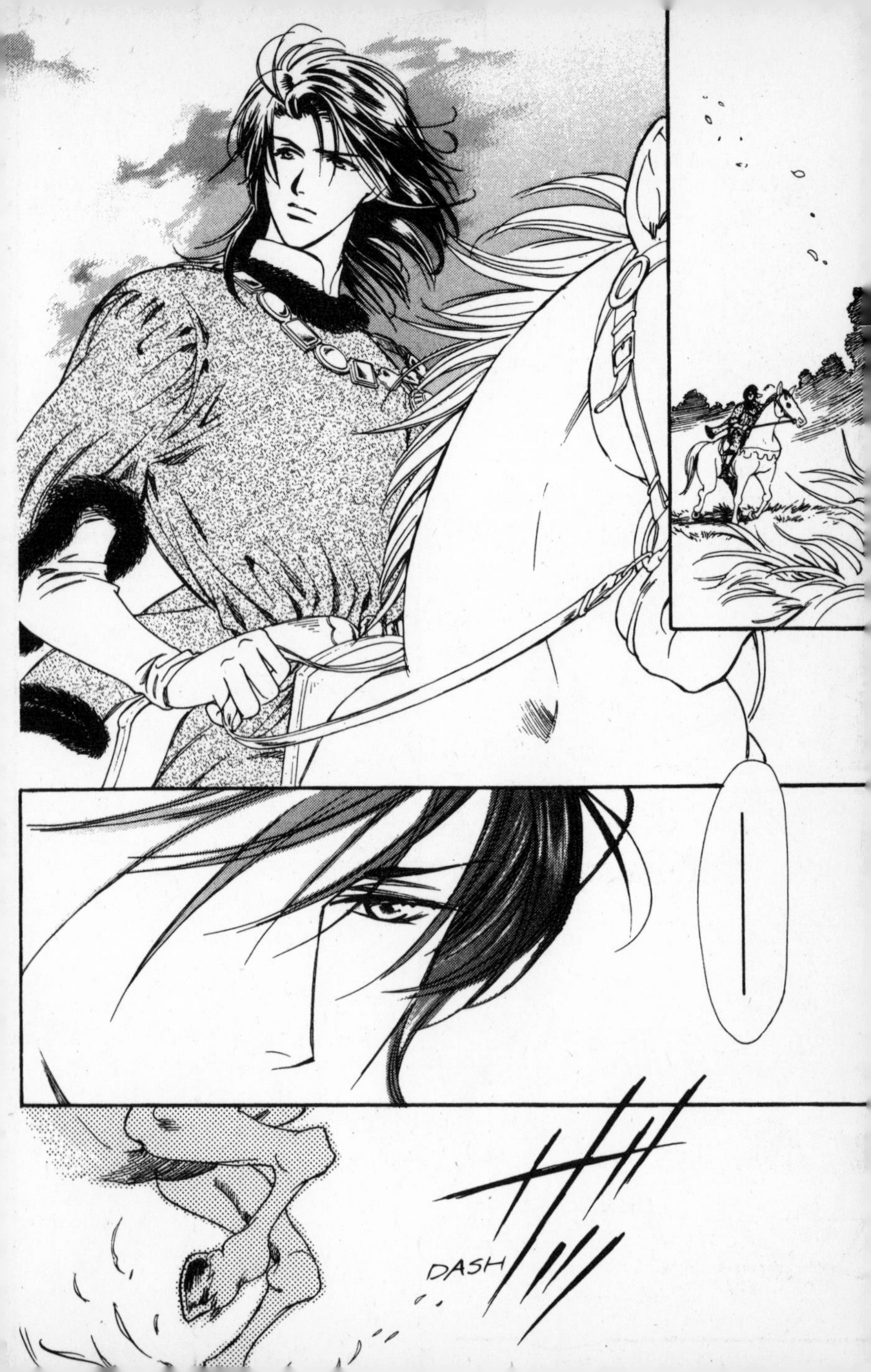
DASH

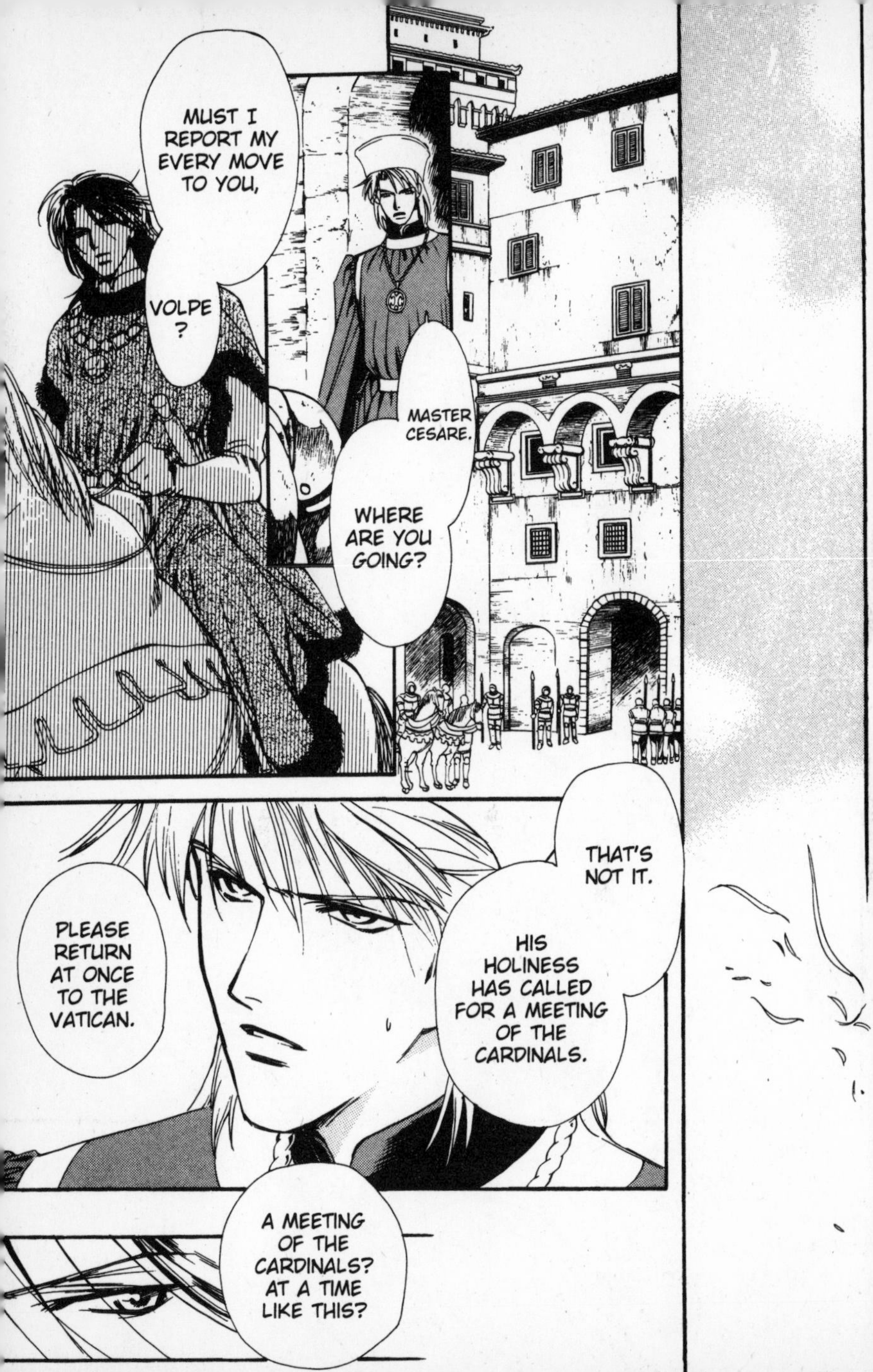
MASTER CESARE.
WHERE ARE YOU GOING?
MUST I REPORT MY EVERY MOVE TO YOU,
VOLPE?
THAT'S NOT IT.
HIS HOLINESS HAS CALLED FOR A MEETING OF THE CARDINALS.
PLEASE RETURN AT ONCE TO THE VATICAN.
A MEETING OF THE CARDINALS? AT A TIME LIKE THIS?

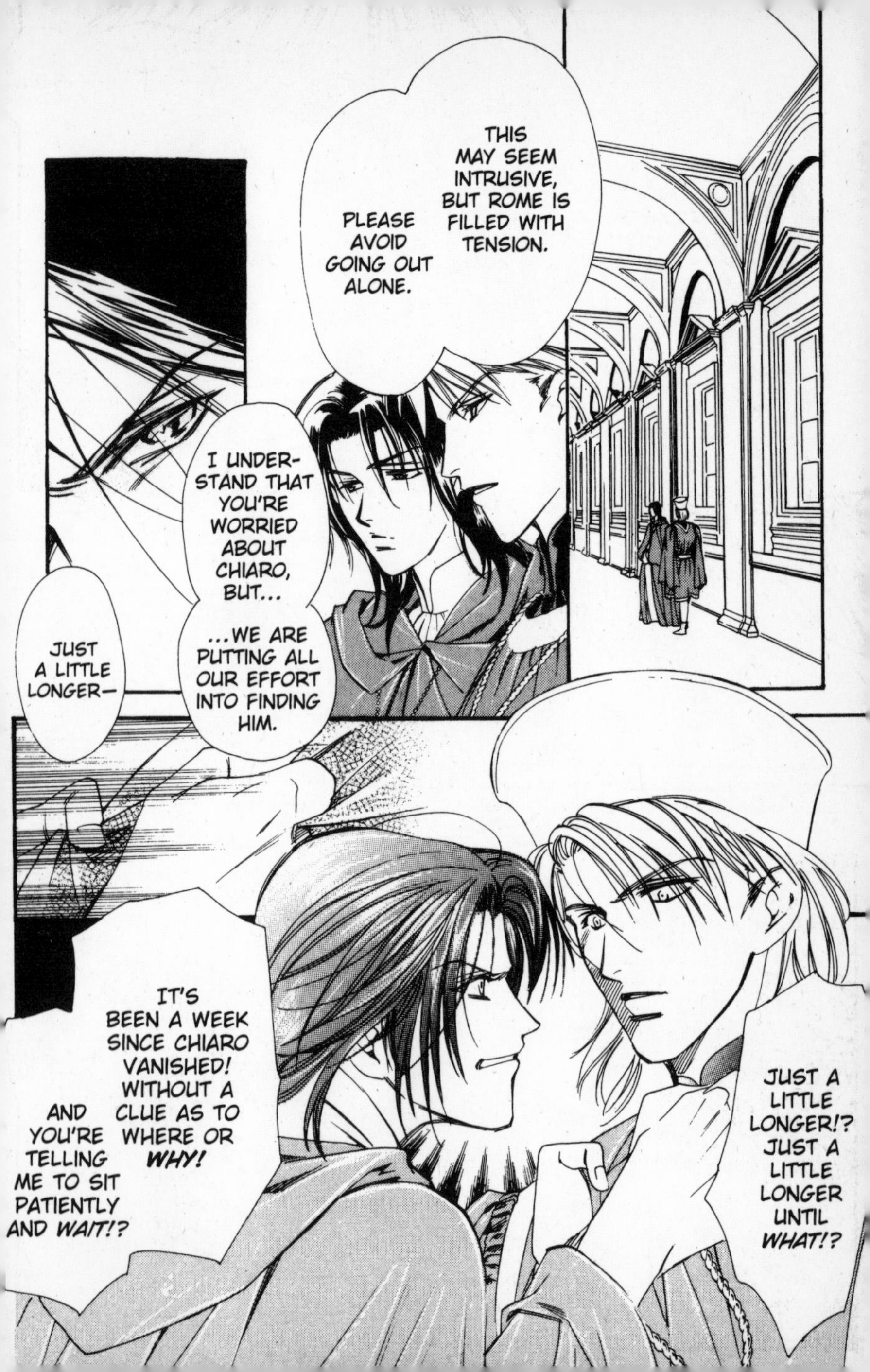
THIS MAY SEEM INTRUSIVE, BUT ROME IS FILLED WITH TENSION.
PLEASE AVOID GOING OUT ALONE.
I UNDER-STAND THAT YOU'RE WORRIED ABOUT CHIARO, BUT...
...WE ARE PUTTING ALL OUR EFFORT INTO FINDING HIM.
JUST A LITTLE LONGER—
JUST A LITTLE LONGER!? JUST A LITTLE LONGER UNTIL *WHAT!?*
IT'S BEEN A WEEK SINCE CHIARO VANISHED! WITHOUT A CLUE AS TO WHERE OR *WHY!*
AND YOU'RE TELLING ME TO SIT PATIENTLY AND *WAIT!?*

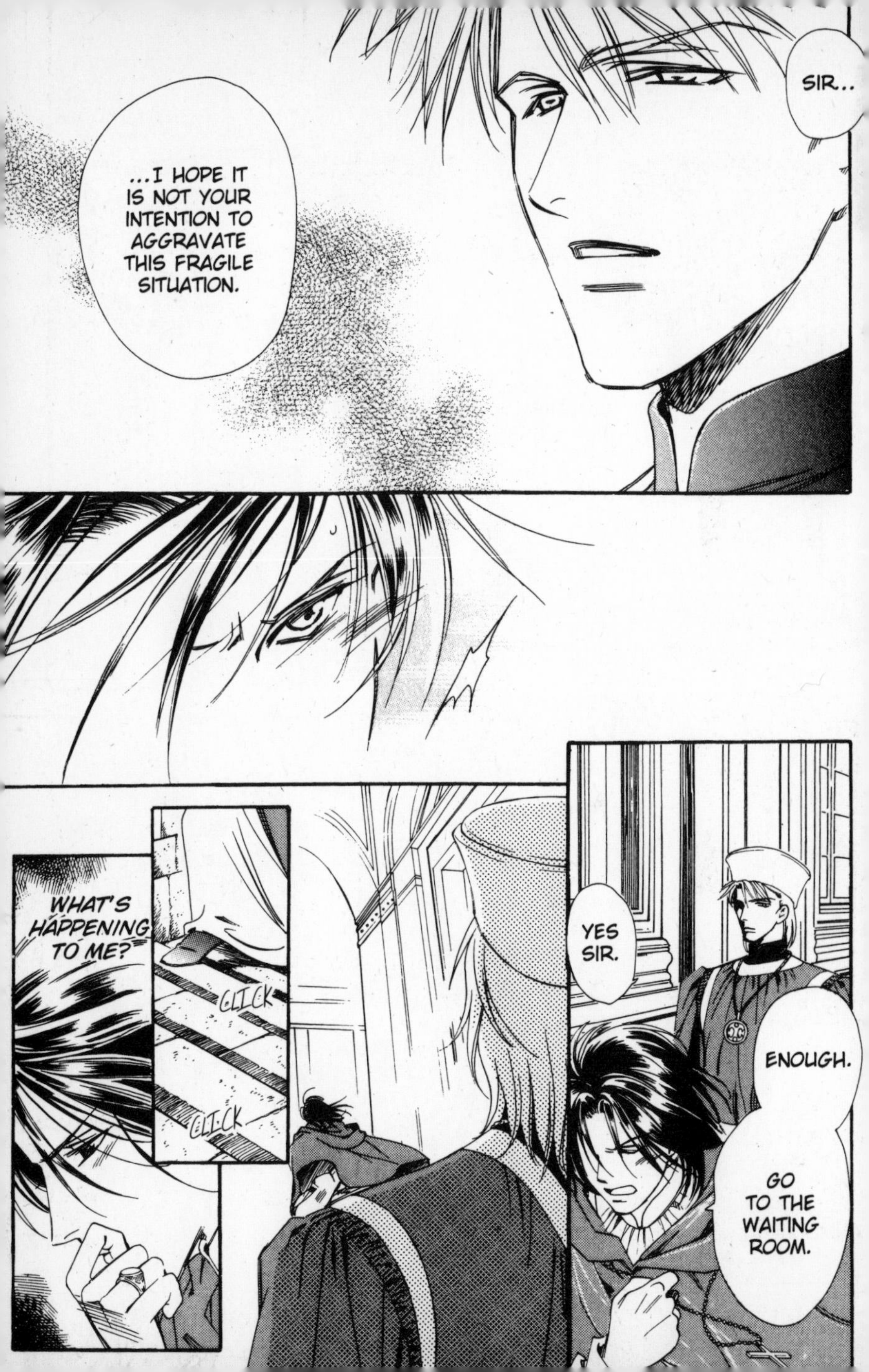
SIR...
...I HOPE IT IS NOT YOUR INTENTION TO AGGRAVATE THIS FRAGILE SITUATION.
ENOUGH.
GO TO THE WAITING ROOM.
YES SIR.
CLICK
CLICK
WHAT'S HAPPENING TO ME?

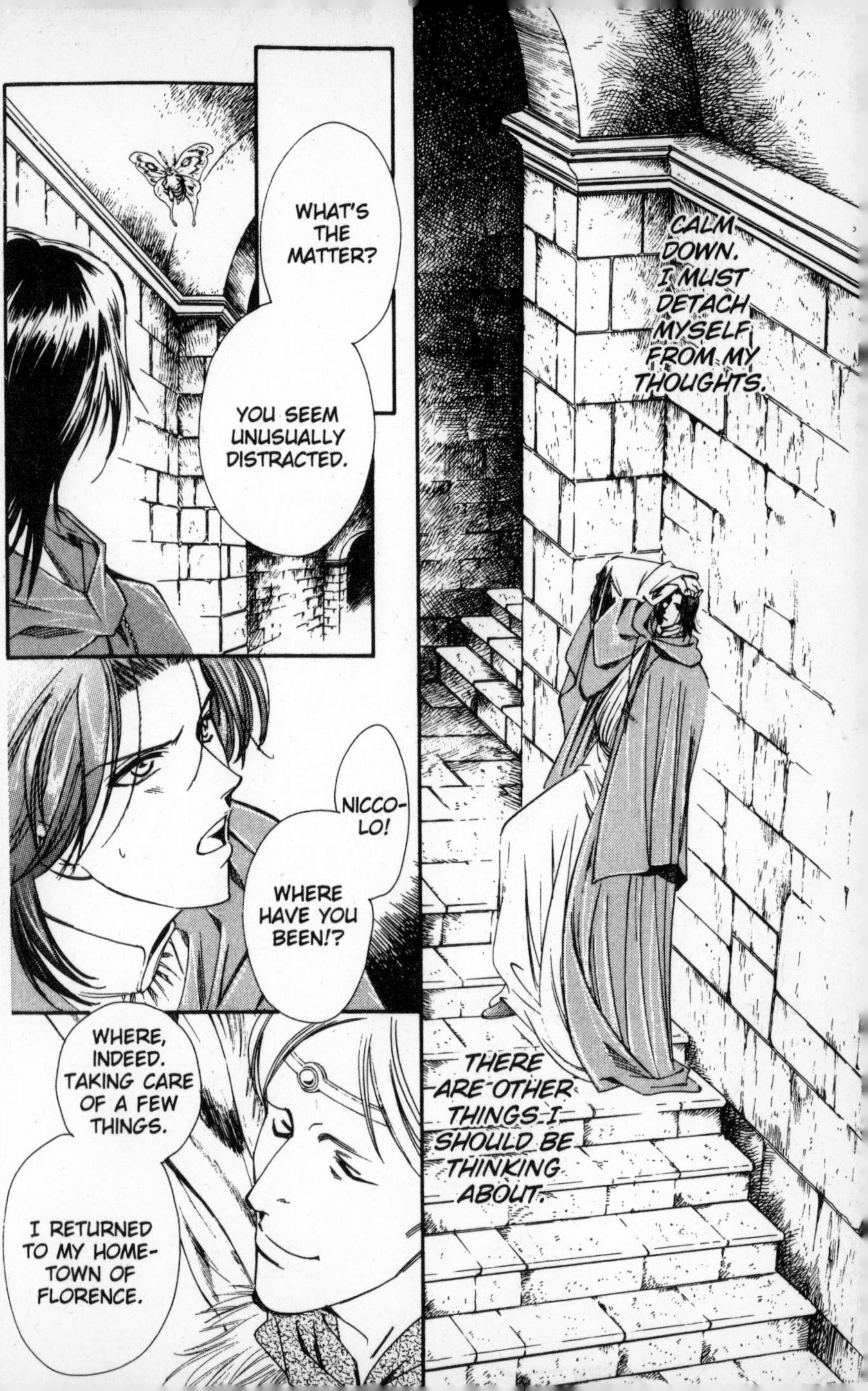
CALM DOWN. I MUST DETACH MYSELF FROM MY THOUGHTS.
THERE ARE OTHER THINGS I SHOULD BE THINKING ABOUT.
WHAT'S THE MATTER?
YOU SEEM UNUSUALLY DISTRACTED.
NICCO-LO!
WHERE HAVE YOU BEEN!?
WHERE, INDEED. TAKING CARE OF A FEW THINGS.
I RETURNED TO MY HOME-TOWN OF FLORENCE.

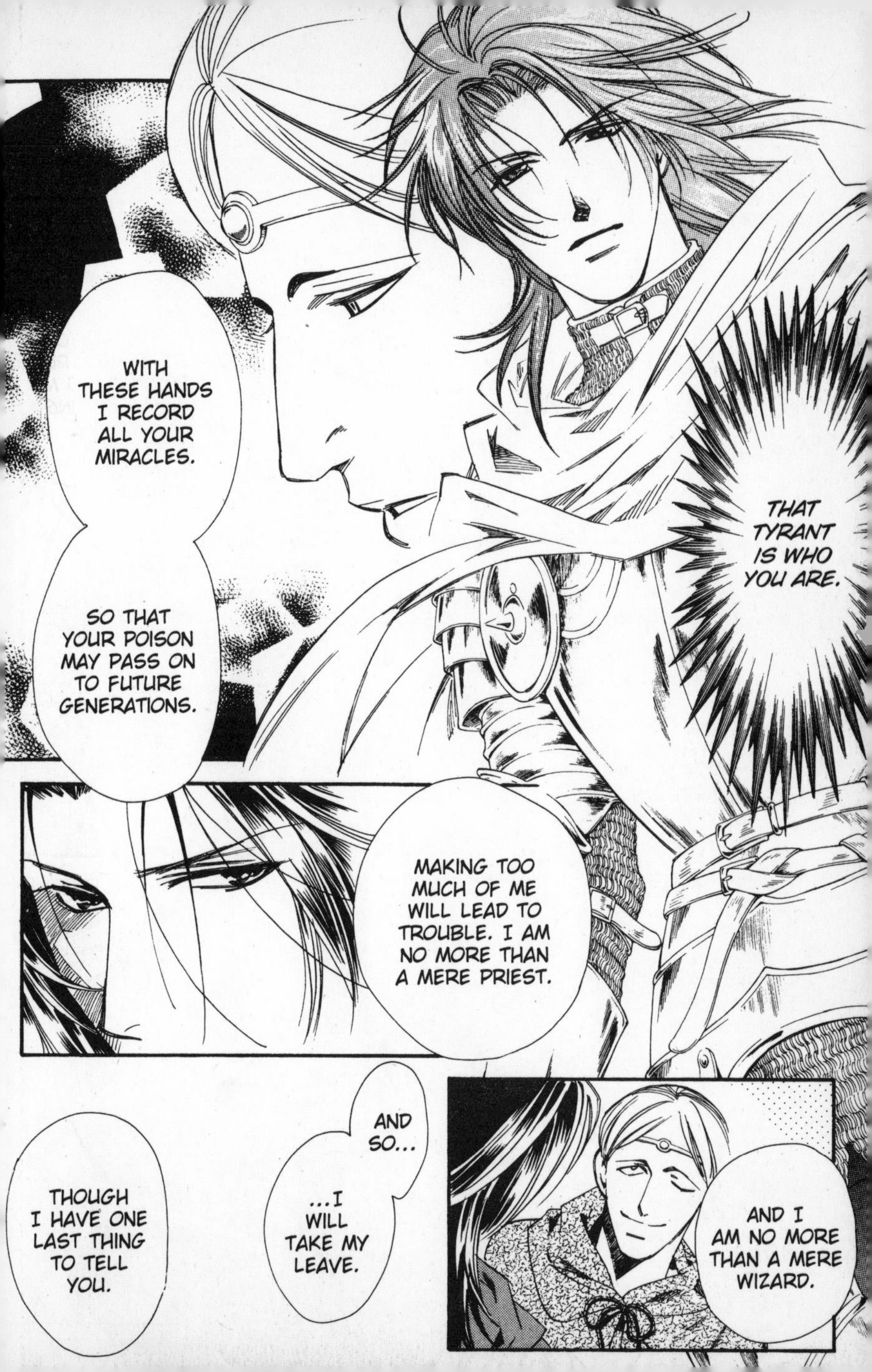
THAT TYRANT IS WHO YOU ARE.
WITH THESE HANDS I RECORD ALL YOUR MIRACLES.
SO THAT YOUR POISON MAY PASS ON TO FUTURE GENERATIONS.
MAKING TOO MUCH OF ME WILL LEAD TO TROUBLE. I AM NO MORE THAN A MERE PRIEST.
AND I AM NO MORE THAN A MERE WIZARD.
AND SO...
...I WILL TAKE MY LEAVE.
THOUGH I HAVE ONE LAST THING TO TELL YOU.

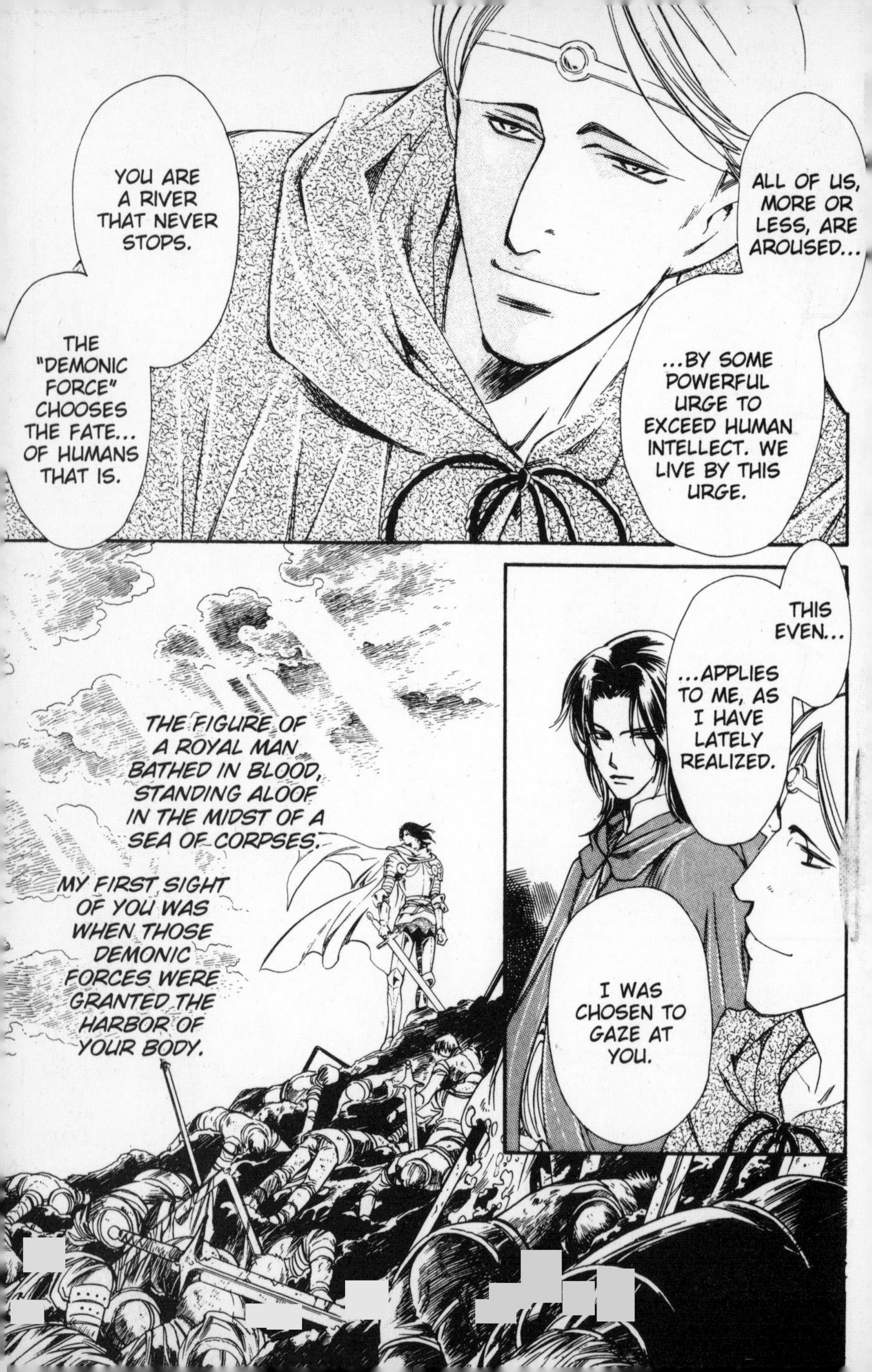
ALL OF US, MORE OR LESS, ARE AROUSED...
...BY SOME POWERFUL URGE TO EXCEED HUMAN INTELLECT. WE LIVE BY THIS URGE.
YOU ARE A RIVER THAT NEVER STOPS.
THE "DEMONIC FORCE" CHOOSES THE FATE... OF HUMANS THAT IS.
THIS EVEN...
...APPLIES TO ME, AS I HAVE LATELY REALIZED.
I WAS CHOSEN TO GAZE AT YOU.
THE FIGURE OF A ROYAL MAN BATHED IN BLOOD, STANDING ALOOF IN THE MIDST OF A SEA OF CORPSES.
MY FIRST SIGHT OF YOU WAS WHEN THOSE DEMONIC FORCES WERE GRANTED THE HARBOR OF YOUR BODY.

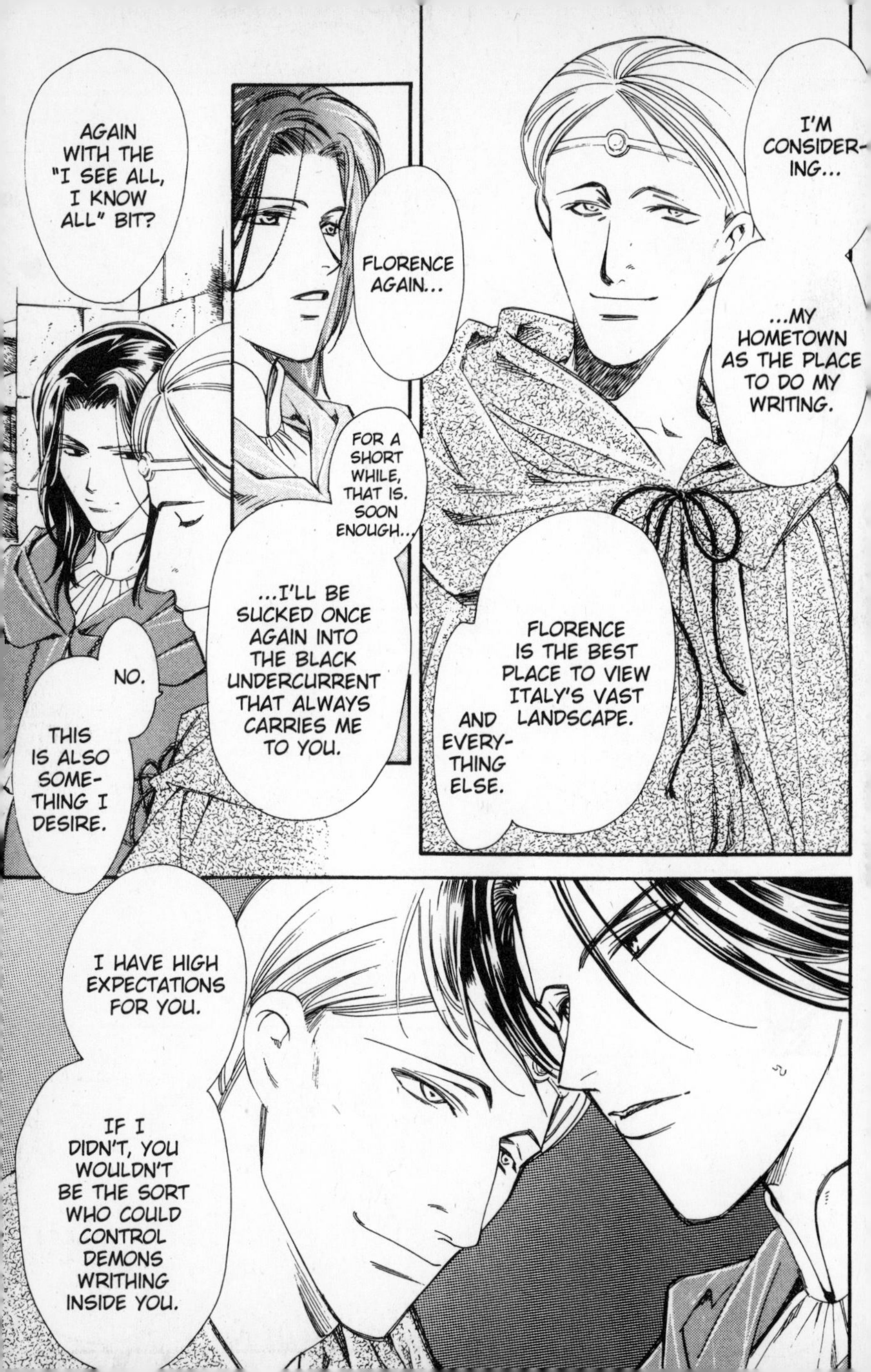
I'M CONSIDERING...
...MY HOMETOWN AS THE PLACE TO DO MY WRITING.
FLORENCE IS THE BEST PLACE TO VIEW ITALY'S VAST LANDSCAPE.
AND EVERYTHING ELSE.
FLORENCE AGAIN...
FOR A SHORT WHILE, THAT IS. SOON ENOUGH...
...I'LL BE SUCKED ONCE AGAIN INTO THE BLACK UNDERCURRENT THAT ALWAYS CARRIES ME TO YOU.
AGAIN WITH THE "I SEE ALL, I KNOW ALL" BIT?
NO.
THIS IS ALSO SOMETHING I DESIRE.
I HAVE HIGH EXPECTATIONS FOR YOU.
IF I DIDN'T, YOU WOULDN'T BE THE SORT WHO COULD CONTROL DEMONS WRITHING INSIDE YOU.

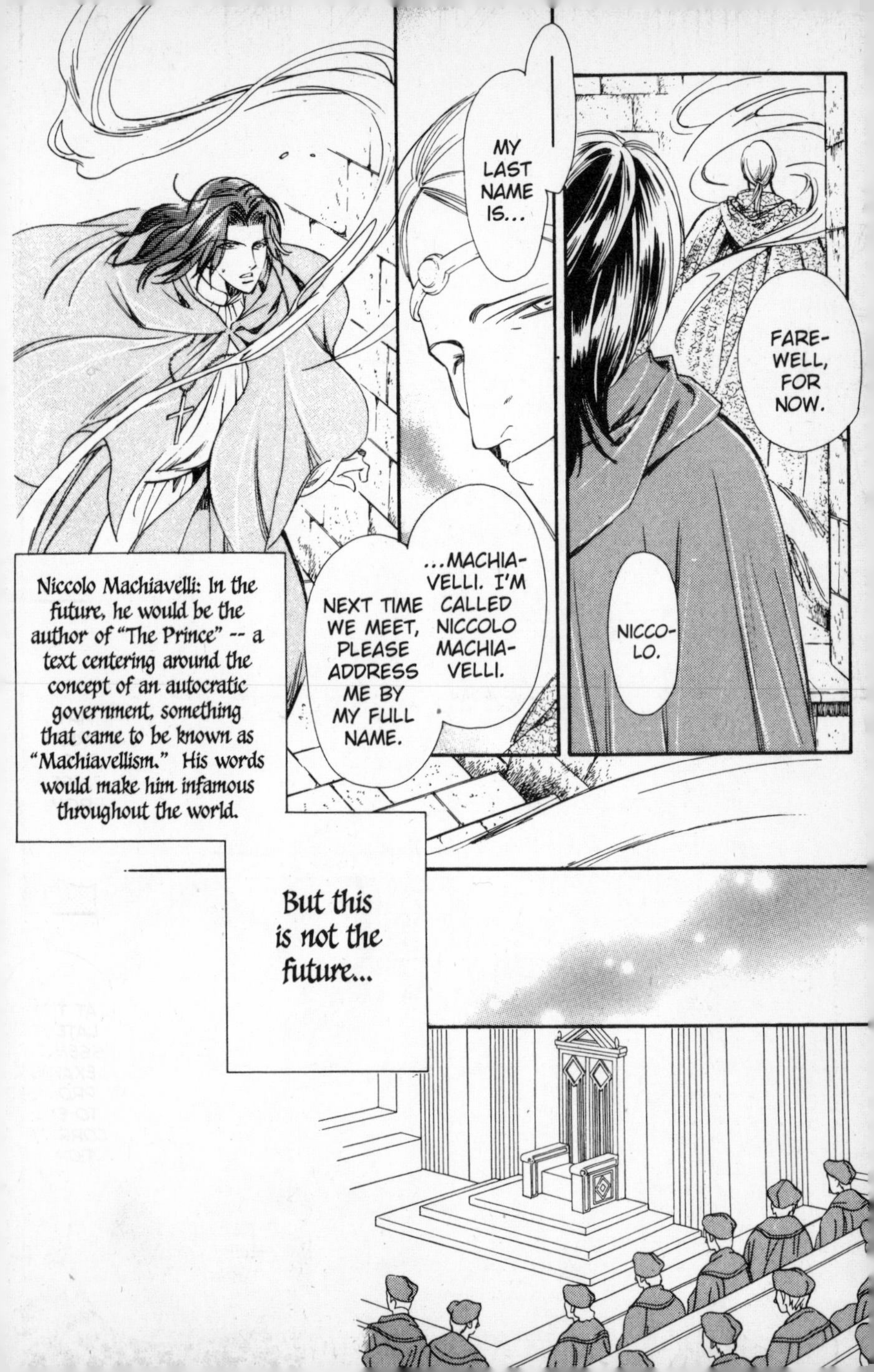
FARE-WELL, FOR NOW.
NICCO-LO.
MY LAST NAME IS...
...MACHIA-VELLI. I'M CALLED NICCOLO MACHIA-VELLI.
NEXT TIME WE MEET, PLEASE ADDRESS ME BY MY FULL NAME.
Niccolo Machiavelli: In the future, he would be the author of "The Prince" -- a text centering around the concept of an autocratic government, something that came to be known as "Machiavellism." His words would make him infamous throughout the world.
But this is not the future...

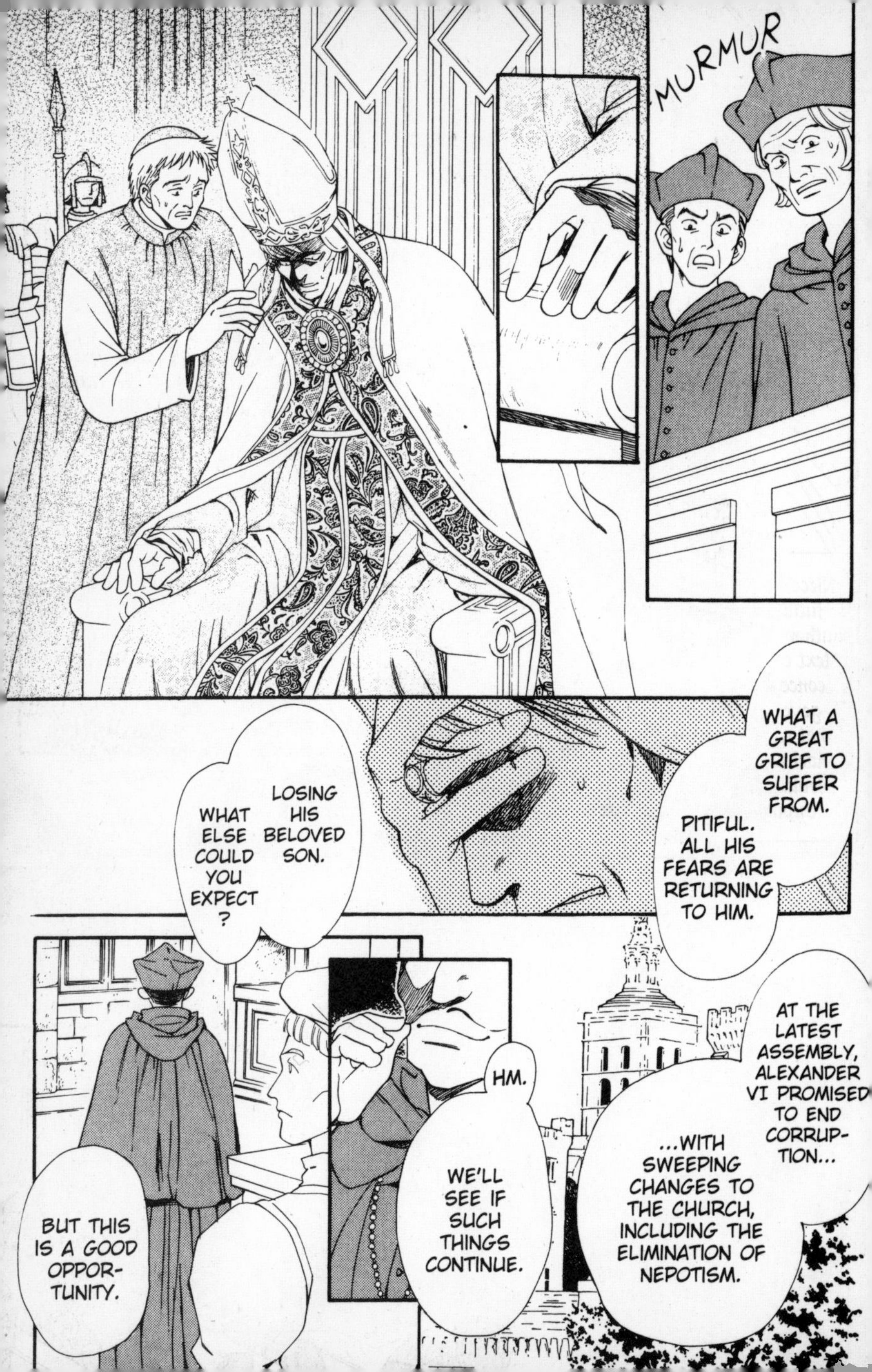
MURMUR
WHAT A GREAT GRIEF TO SUFFER FROM.
PITIFUL. ALL HIS FEARS ARE RETURNING TO HIM.
LOSING HIS BELOVED SON.
WHAT ELSE COULD YOU EXPECT?
AT THE LATEST ASSEMBLY, ALEXANDER VI PROMISED TO END CORRUP-TION...
...WITH SWEEPING CHANGES TO THE CHURCH, INCLUDING THE ELIMINATION OF NEPOTISM.
HM.
WE'LL SEE IF SUCH THINGS CONTINUE.
BUT THIS IS A GOOD OPPOR-TUNITY.

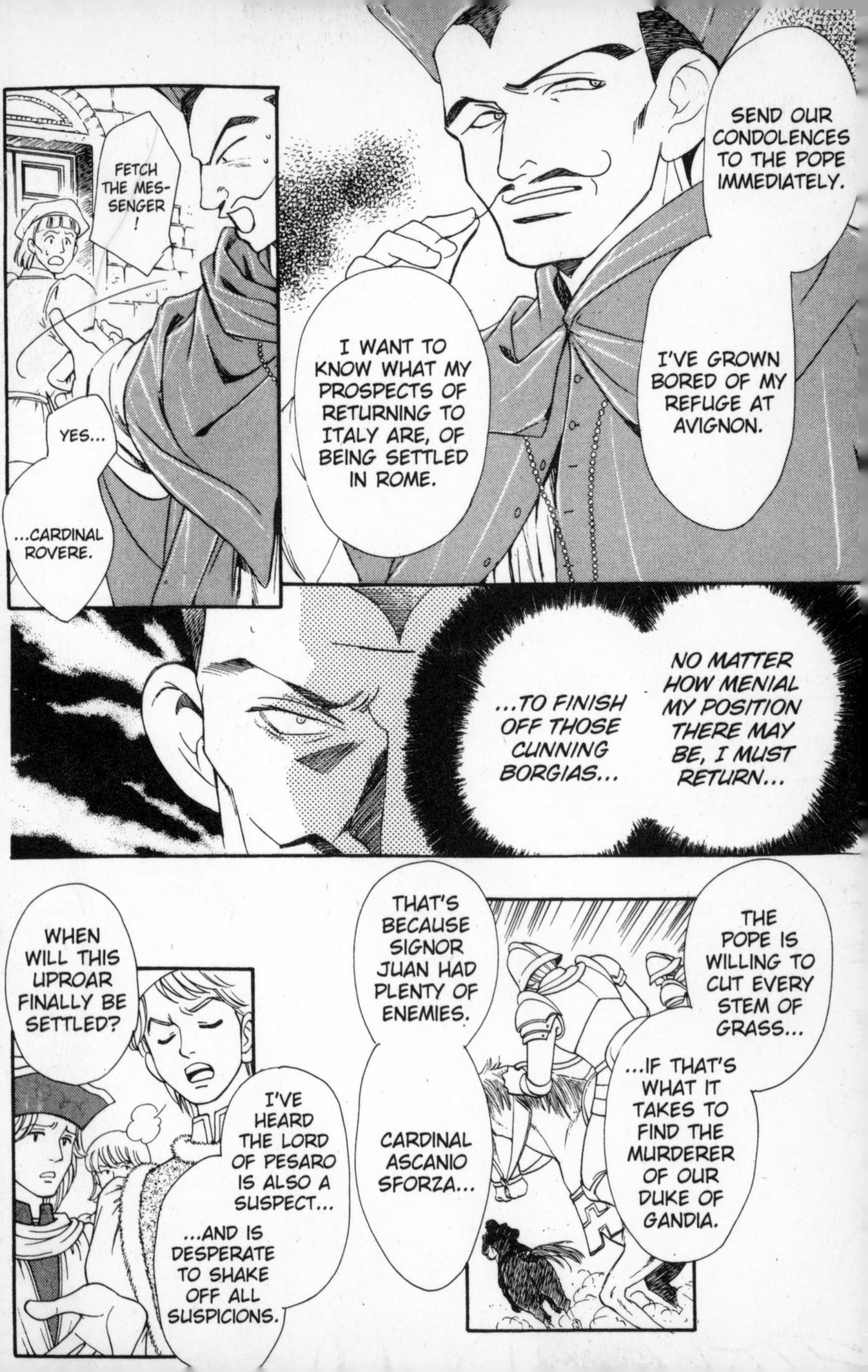
SEND OUR CONDOLENCES TO THE POPE IMMEDIATELY.
I'VE GROWN BORED OF MY REFUGE AT AVIGNON.
I WANT TO KNOW WHAT MY PROSPECTS OF RETURNING TO ITALY ARE, OF BEING SETTLED IN ROME.
FETCH THE MES-SENGER!
YES...
...CARDINAL ROVERE.
NO MATTER HOW MENIAL MY POSITION THERE MAY BE, I MUST RETURN...
...TO FINISH OFF THOSE CUNNING BORGIAS...
THE POPE IS WILLING TO CUT EVERY STEM OF GRASS...
...IF THAT'S WHAT IT TAKES TO FIND THE MURDERER OF OUR DUKE OF GANDIA.
WHEN WILL THIS UPROAR FINALLY BE SETTLED?
THAT'S BECAUSE SIGNOR JUAN HAD PLENTY OF ENEMIES.
CARDINAL ASCANIO SFORZA...
I'VE HEARD THE LORD OF PESARO IS ALSO A SUSPECT...
...AND IS DESPERATE TO SHAKE OFF ALL SUSPICIONS.

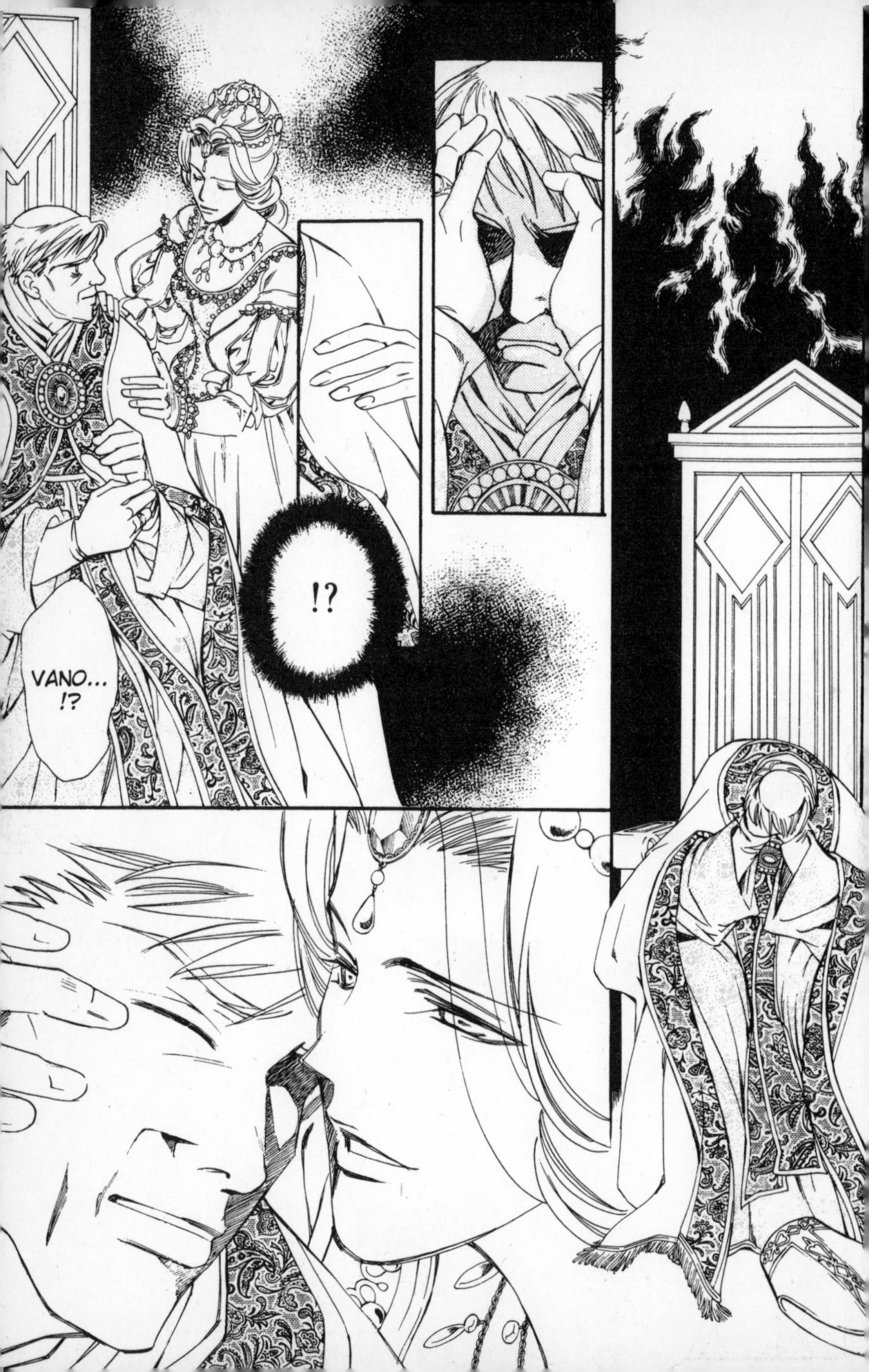
!?
VANO... !?

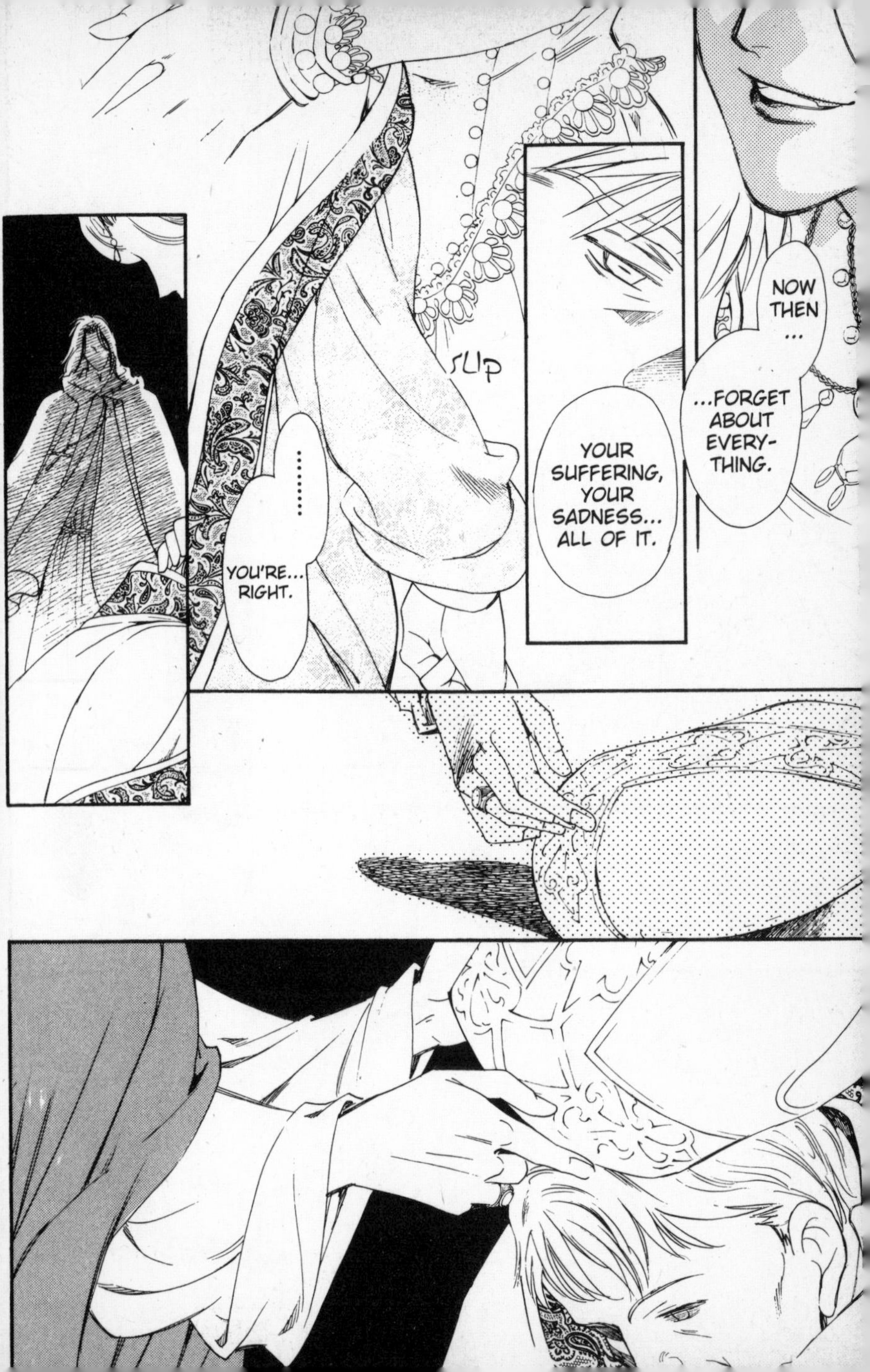
NOW THEN ...
...FORGET ABOUT EVERY-THING.
YOUR SUFFERING, YOUR SADNESS... ALL OF IT.
SLIP
......
YOU'RE... RIGHT.

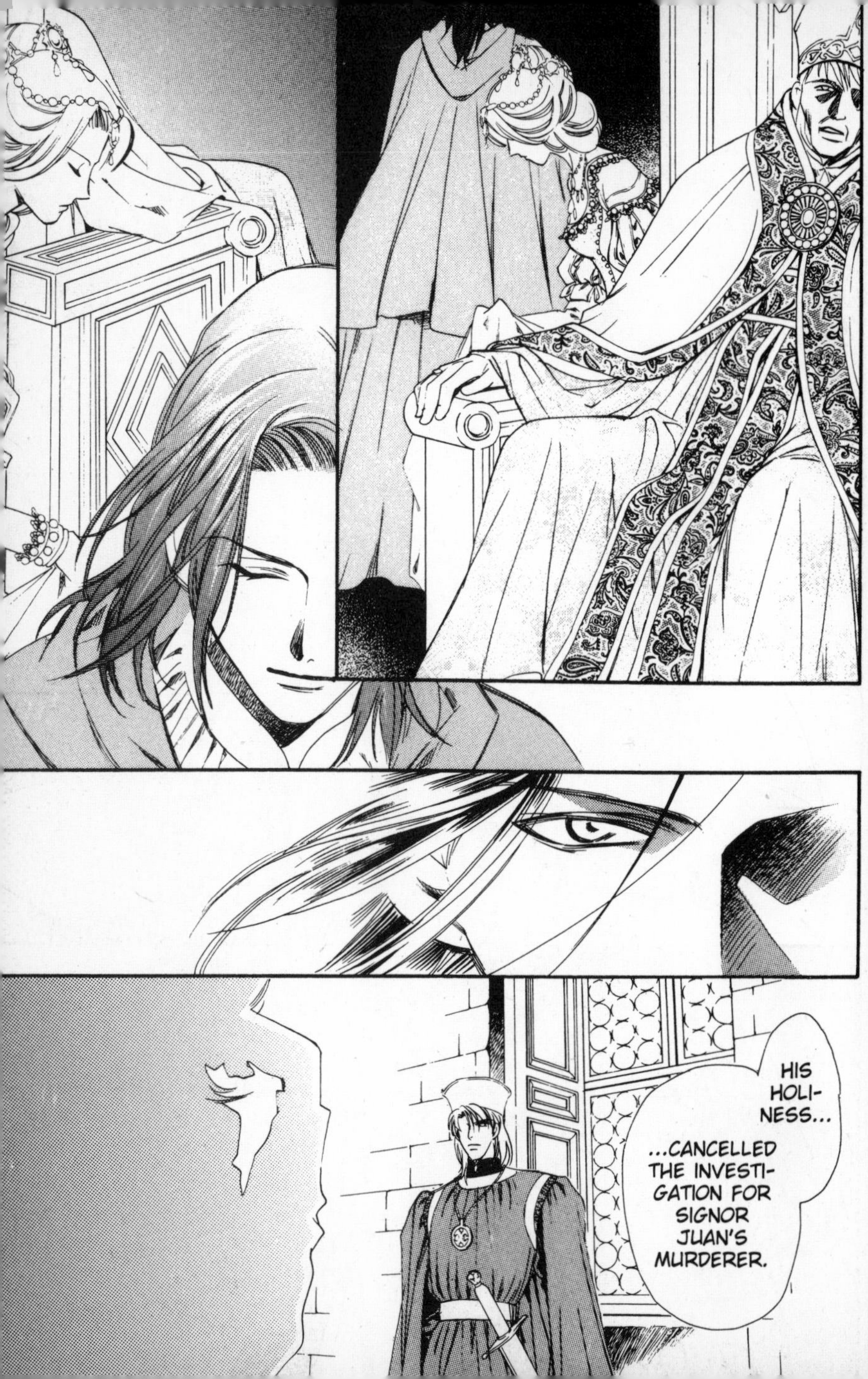
HIS HOLI- NESS...
...CANCELLED THE INVESTI- GATION FOR SIGNOR JUAN'S MURDERER.

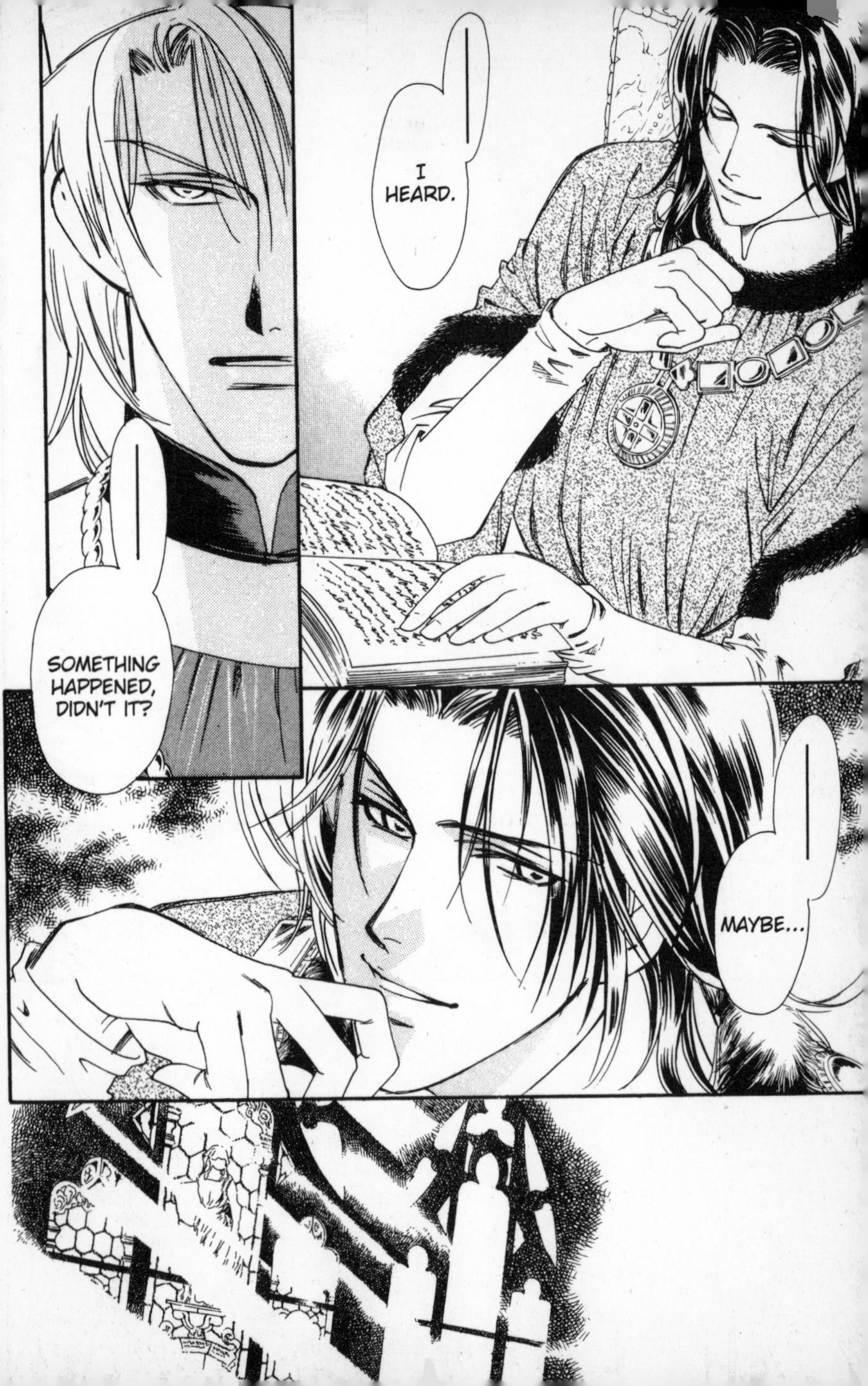
I HEARD.
SOMETHING HAPPENED, DIDN'T IT?
MAYBE...

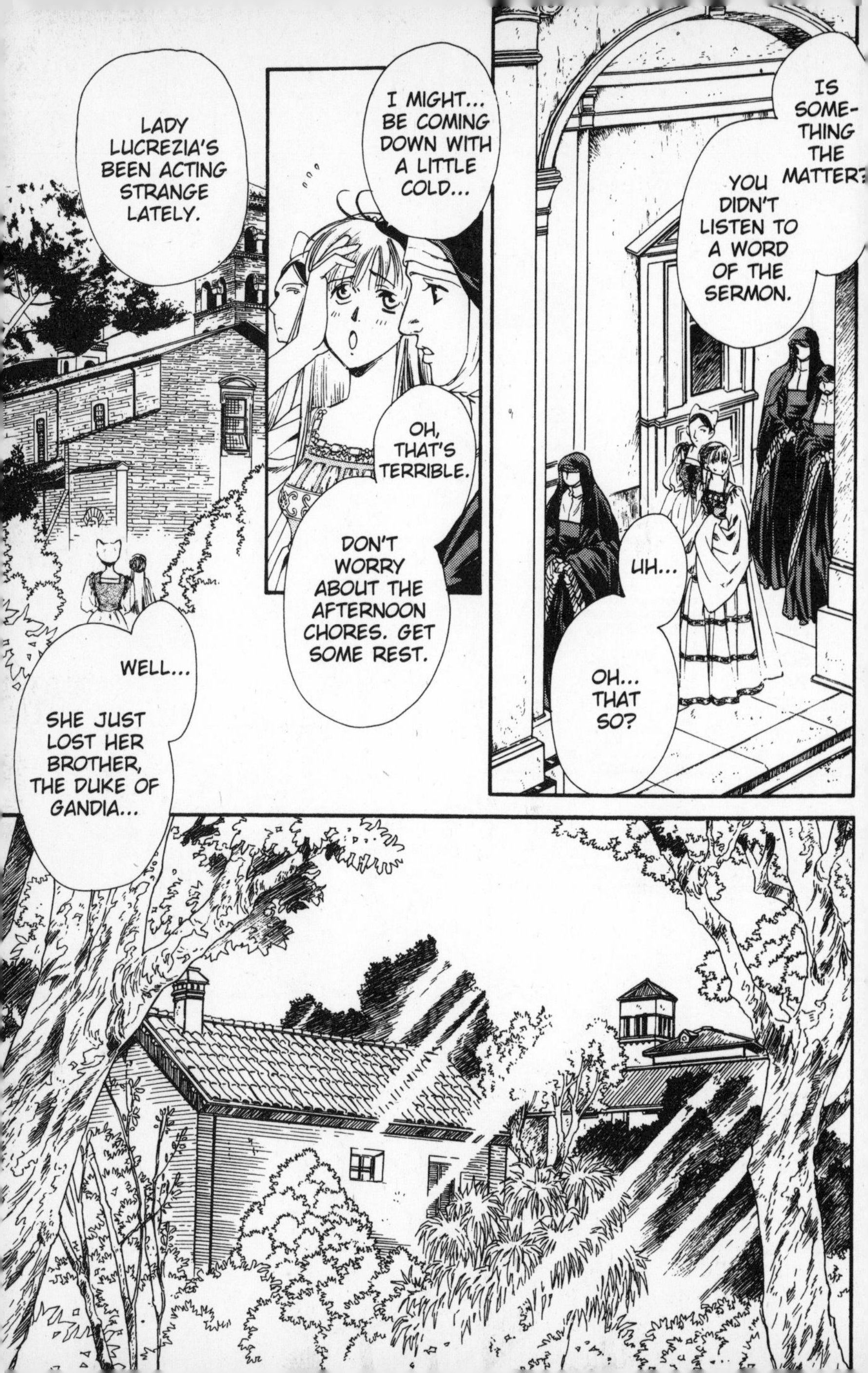
IS SOMETHING THE MATTER?
YOU DIDN'T LISTEN TO A WORD OF THE SERMON.
UH...
OH... THAT SO?
I MIGHT... BE COMING DOWN WITH A LITTLE COLD...
OH, THAT'S TERRIBLE.
DON'T WORRY ABOUT THE AFTERNOON CHORES. GET SOME REST.
LADY LUCREZIA'S BEEN ACTING STRANGE LATELY.
WELL...
SHE JUST LOST HER BROTHER, THE DUKE OF GANDIA...

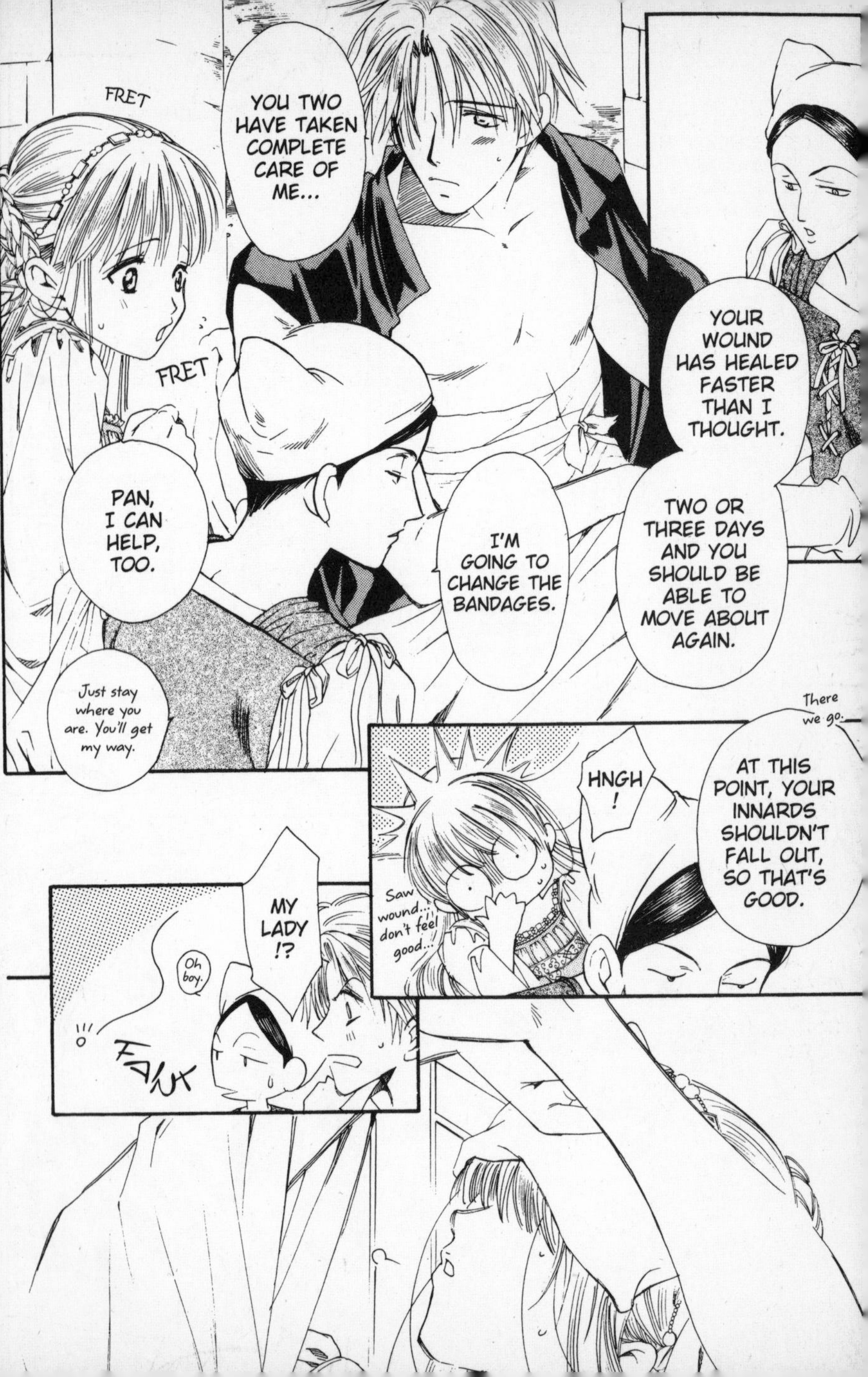
YOUR WOUND HAS HEALED FASTER THAN I THOUGHT.
TWO OR THREE DAYS AND YOU SHOULD BE ABLE TO MOVE ABOUT AGAIN.
YOU TWO HAVE TAKEN COMPLETE CARE OF ME...
FRET
FRET
I'M GOING TO CHANGE THE BANDAGES.
PAN, I CAN HELP, TOO.
Just stay where you are. You'll get my way.
There we go.
AT THIS POINT, YOUR INNARDS SHOULDN'T FALL OUT, SO THAT'S GOOD.
HNGH!
Saw wound... don't feel good...
MY LADY!?
Oh boy.
FAINT

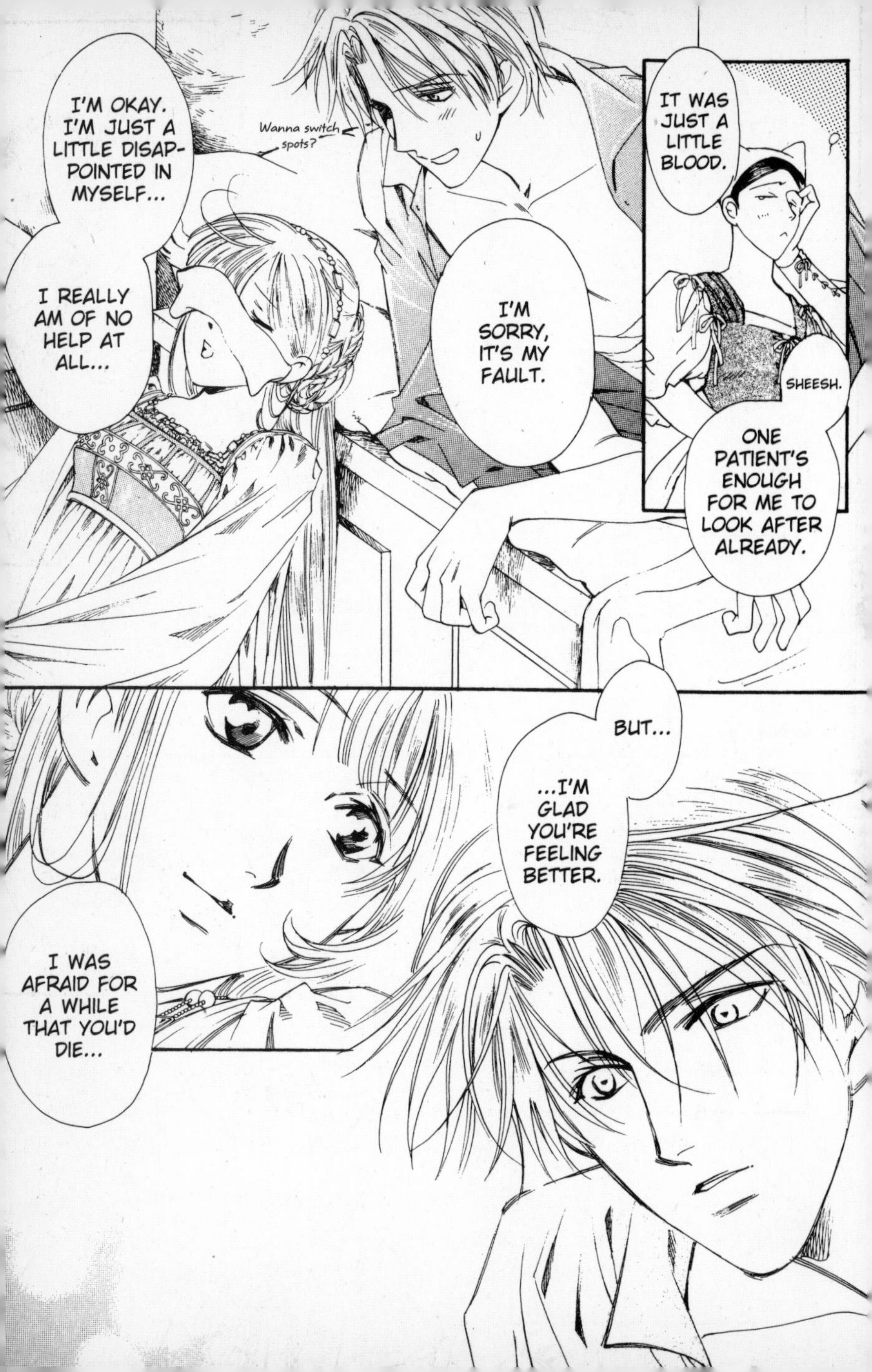
IT WAS JUST A LITTLE BLOOD.
SHEESH.
ONE PATIENT'S ENOUGH FOR ME TO LOOK AFTER ALREADY.
I'M SORRY, IT'S MY FAULT.
Wanna switch spots?
I'M OKAY. I'M JUST A LITTLE DISAPPOINTED IN MYSELF...
I REALLY AM OF NO HELP AT ALL...
BUT...
...I'M GLAD YOU'RE FEELING BETTER.
I WAS AFRAID FOR A WHILE THAT YOU'D DIE...

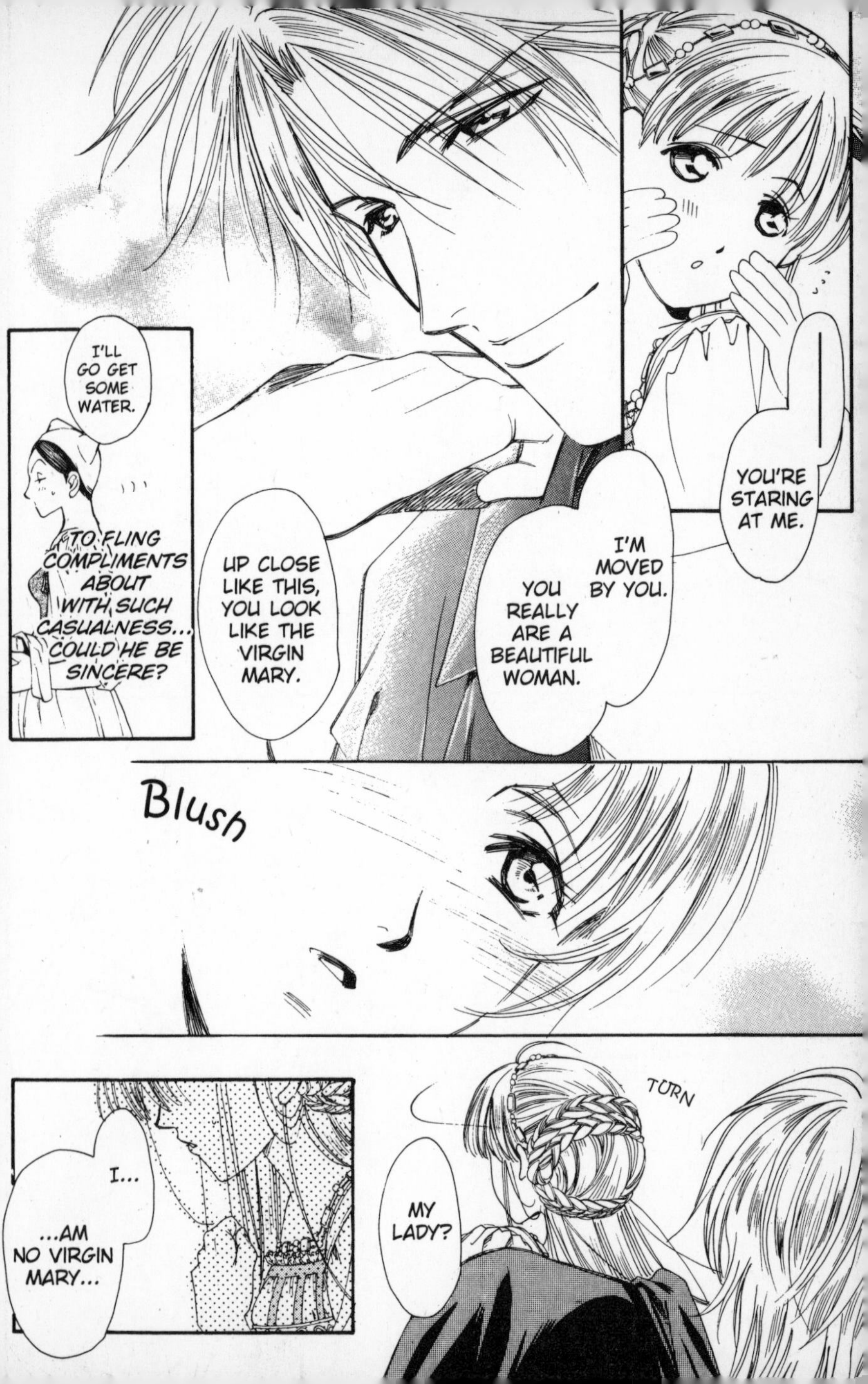
YOU'RE STARING AT ME.
I'M MOVED BY YOU.
YOU REALLY ARE A BEAUTIFUL WOMAN.
UP CLOSE LIKE THIS, YOU LOOK LIKE THE VIRGIN MARY.
I'LL GO GET SOME WATER.
TO FLING COMPLIMENTS ABOUT WITH SUCH CASUALNESS... COULD HE BE SINCERE?
Blush
TURN
MY LADY?
I...
...AM NO VIRGIN MARY...

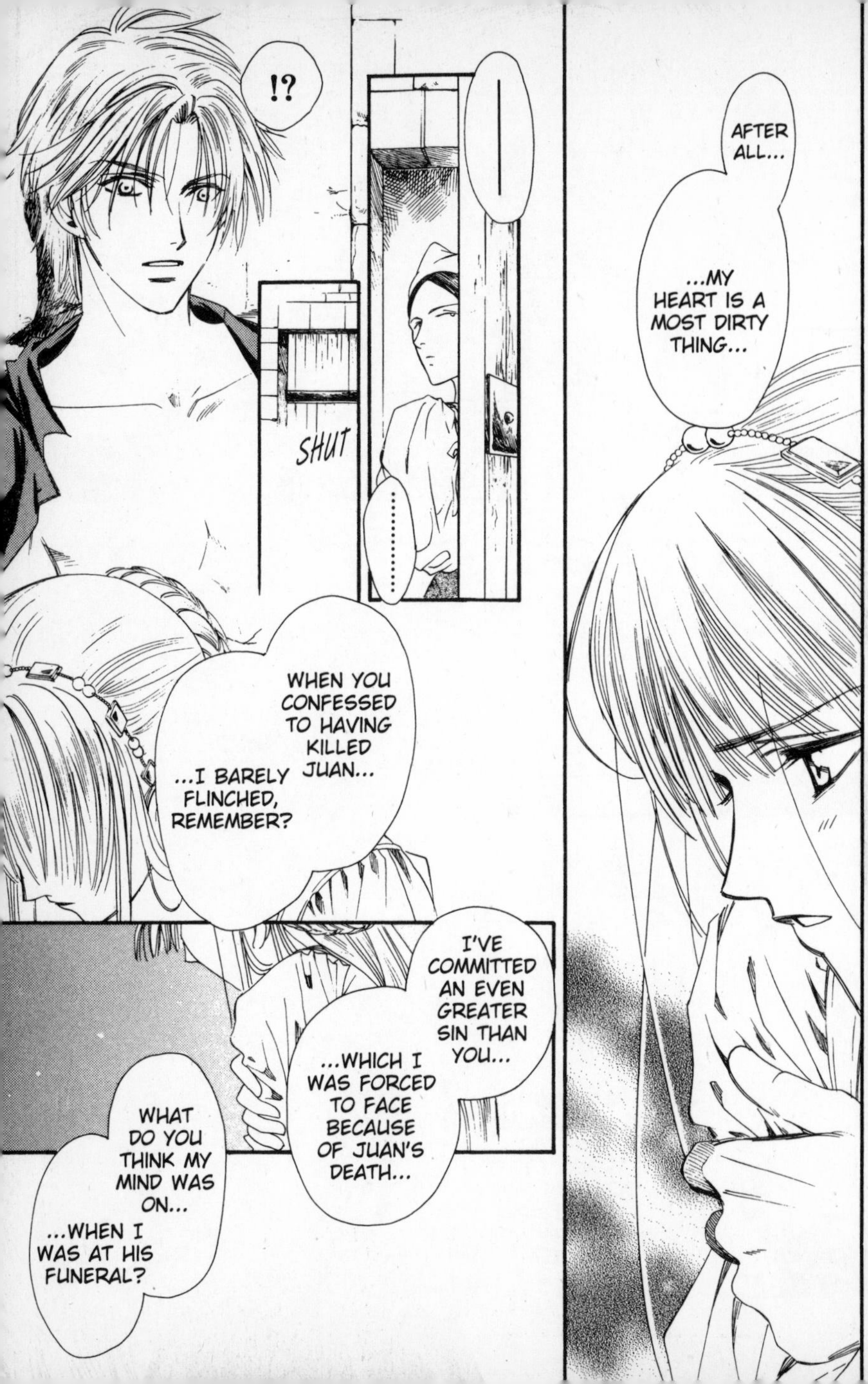
AFTER ALL...
...MY HEART IS A MOST DIRTY THING...
......
SHUT
!?
WHEN YOU CONFESSED TO HAVING KILLED JUAN...
...I BARELY FLINCHED, REMEMBER?
I'VE COMMITTED AN EVEN GREATER SIN THAN YOU...
...WHICH I WAS FORCED TO FACE BECAUSE OF JUAN'S DEATH...
WHAT DO YOU THINK MY MIND WAS ON...
...WHEN I WAS AT HIS FUNERAL?

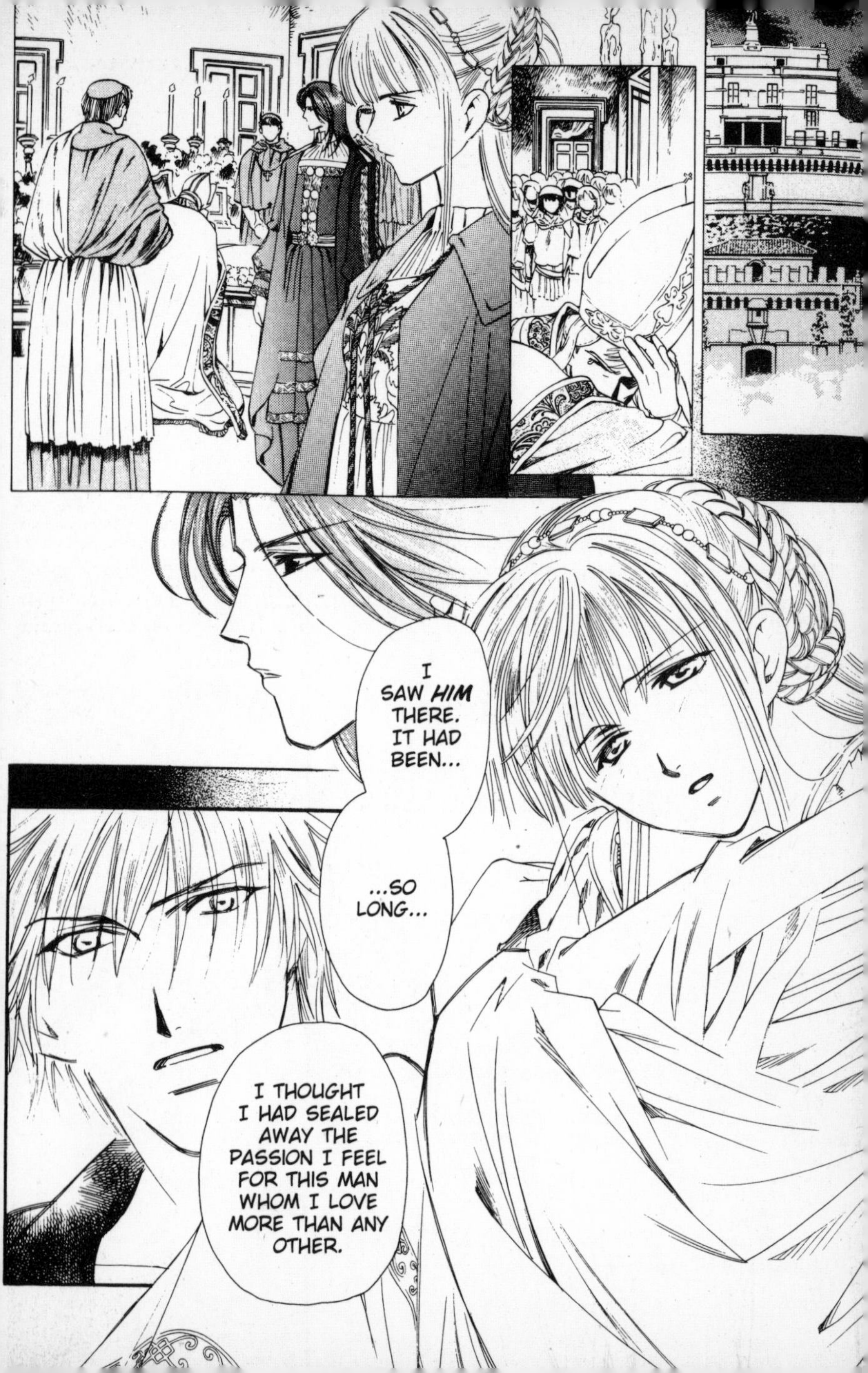
I SAW *HIM* THERE. IT HAD BEEN...
...SO LONG...
I THOUGHT I HAD SEALED AWAY THE PASSION I FEEL FOR THIS MAN WHOM I LOVE MORE THAN ANY OTHER.

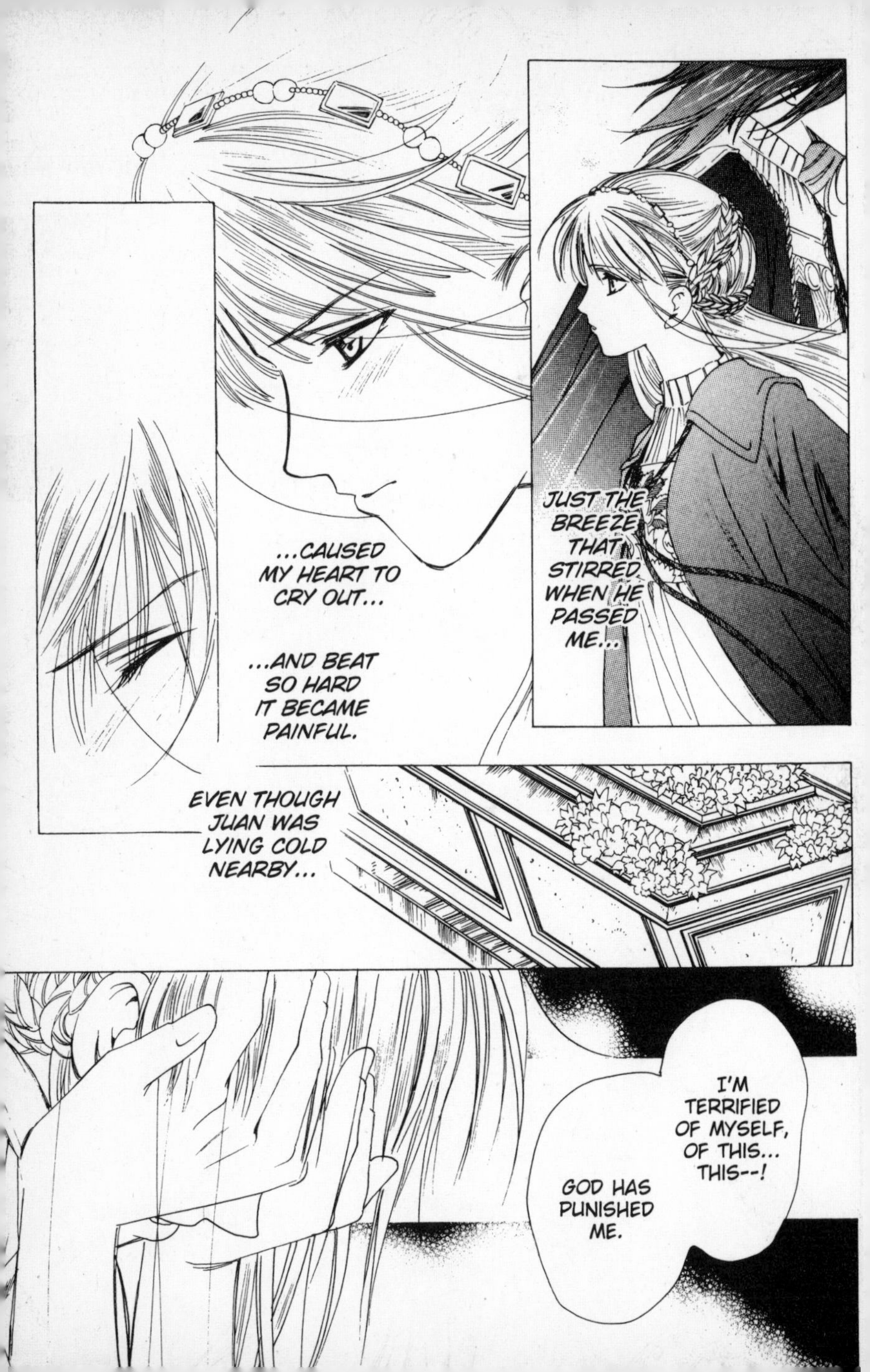
JUST THE BREEZE THAT STIRRED WHEN HE PASSED ME...
...CAUSED MY HEART TO CRY OUT...
...AND BEAT SO HARD IT BECAME PAINFUL.
EVEN THOUGH JUAN WAS LYING COLD NEARBY...
I'M TERRIFIED OF MYSELF, OF THIS... THIS--!
GOD HAS PUNISHED ME.

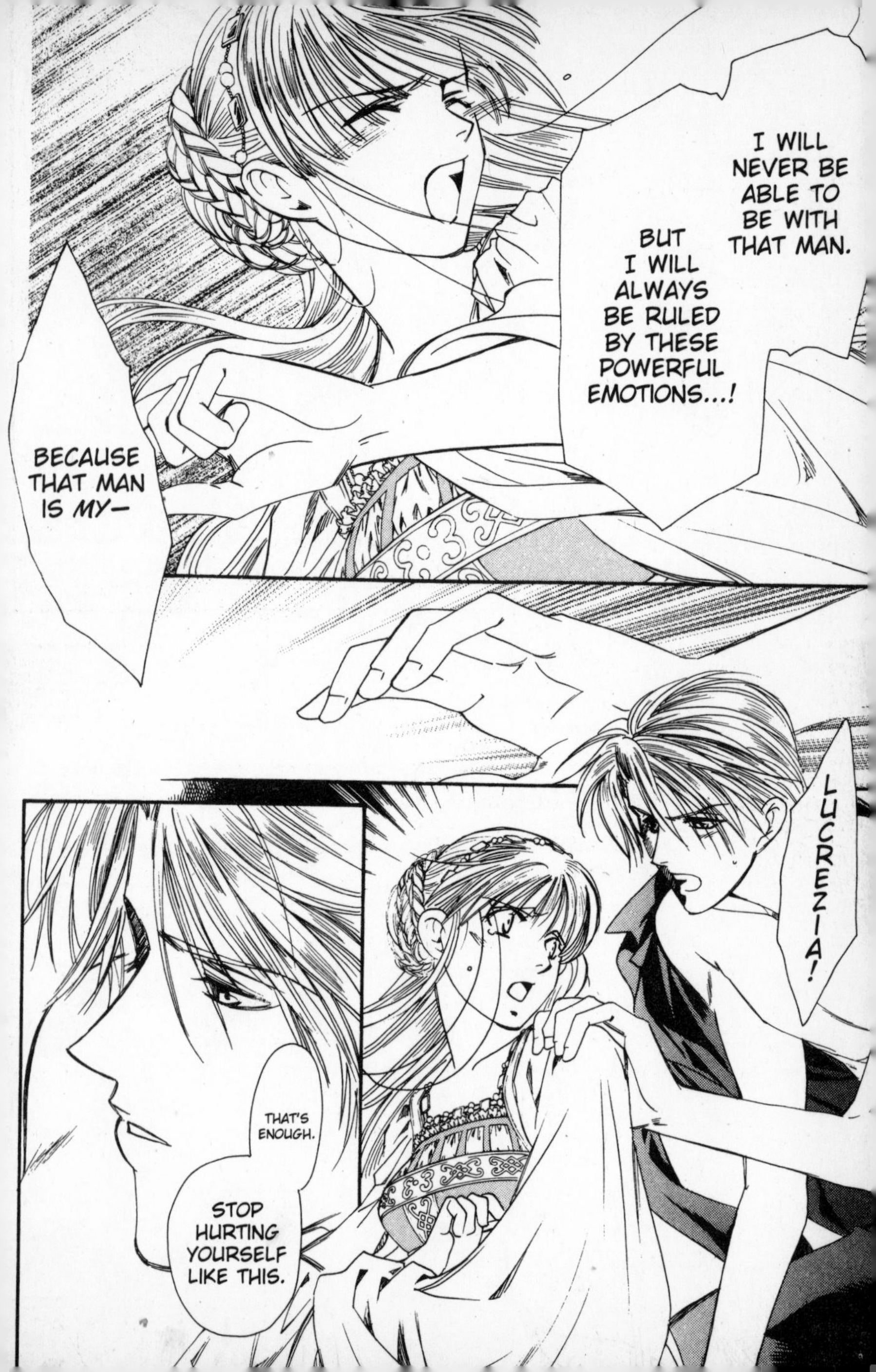
I WILL NEVER BE ABLE TO BE WITH THAT MAN.
BUT I WILL ALWAYS BE RULED BY THESE POWERFUL EMOTIONS...!
BECAUSE THAT MAN IS *MY*—
LUCREZIA!
THAT'S ENOUGH.
STOP HURTING YOURSELF LIKE THIS.

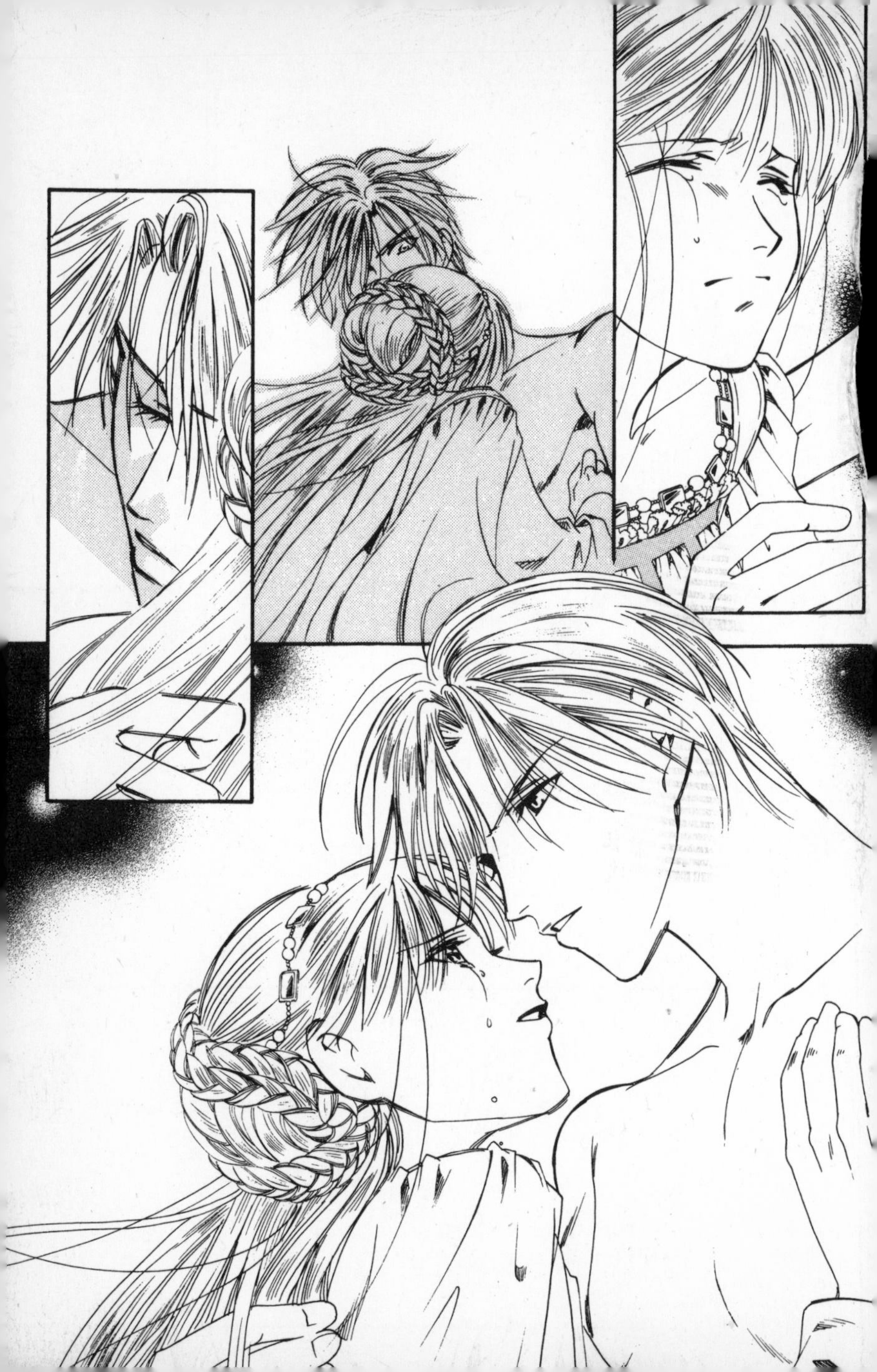

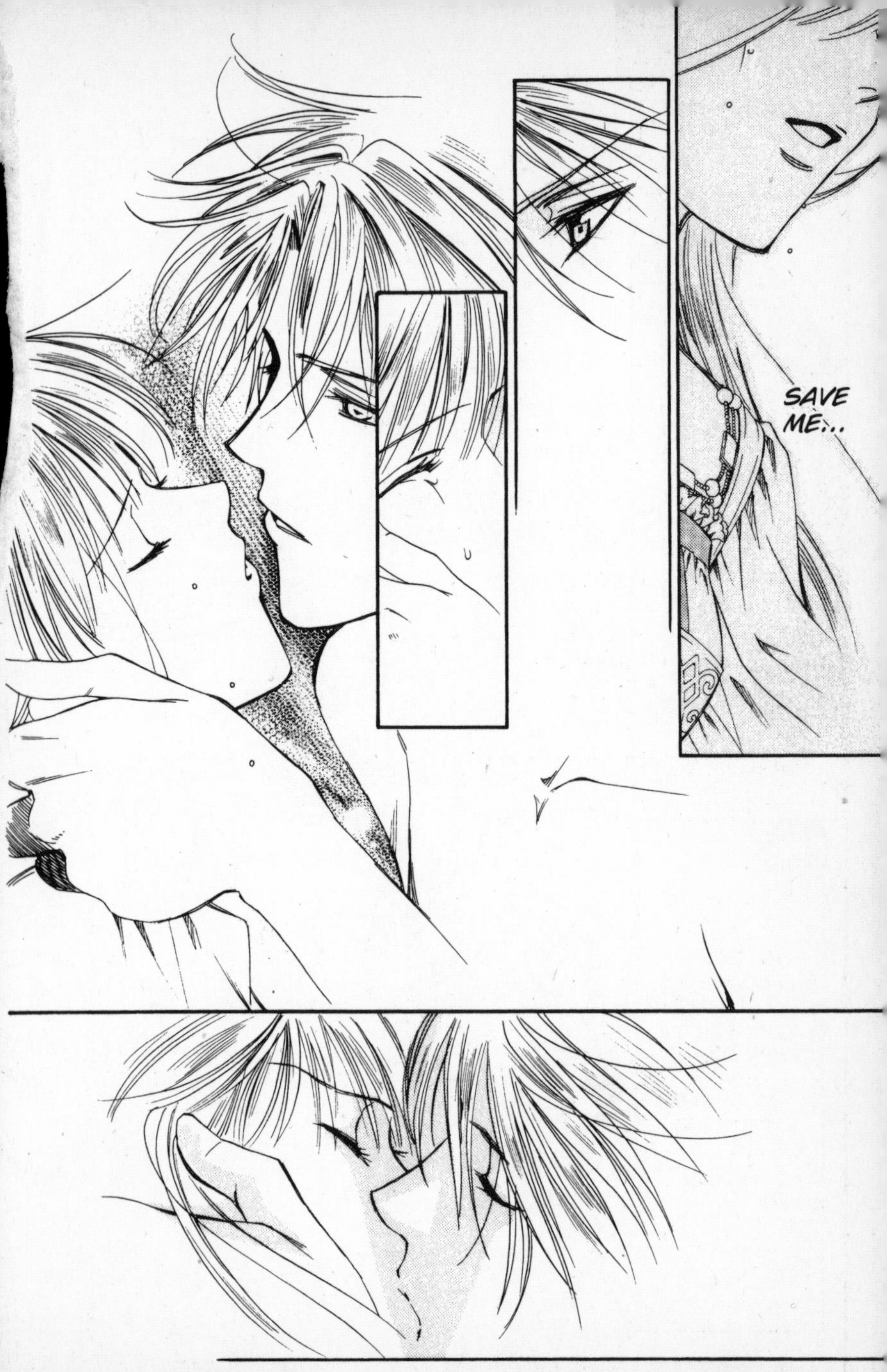
SAVE ME...

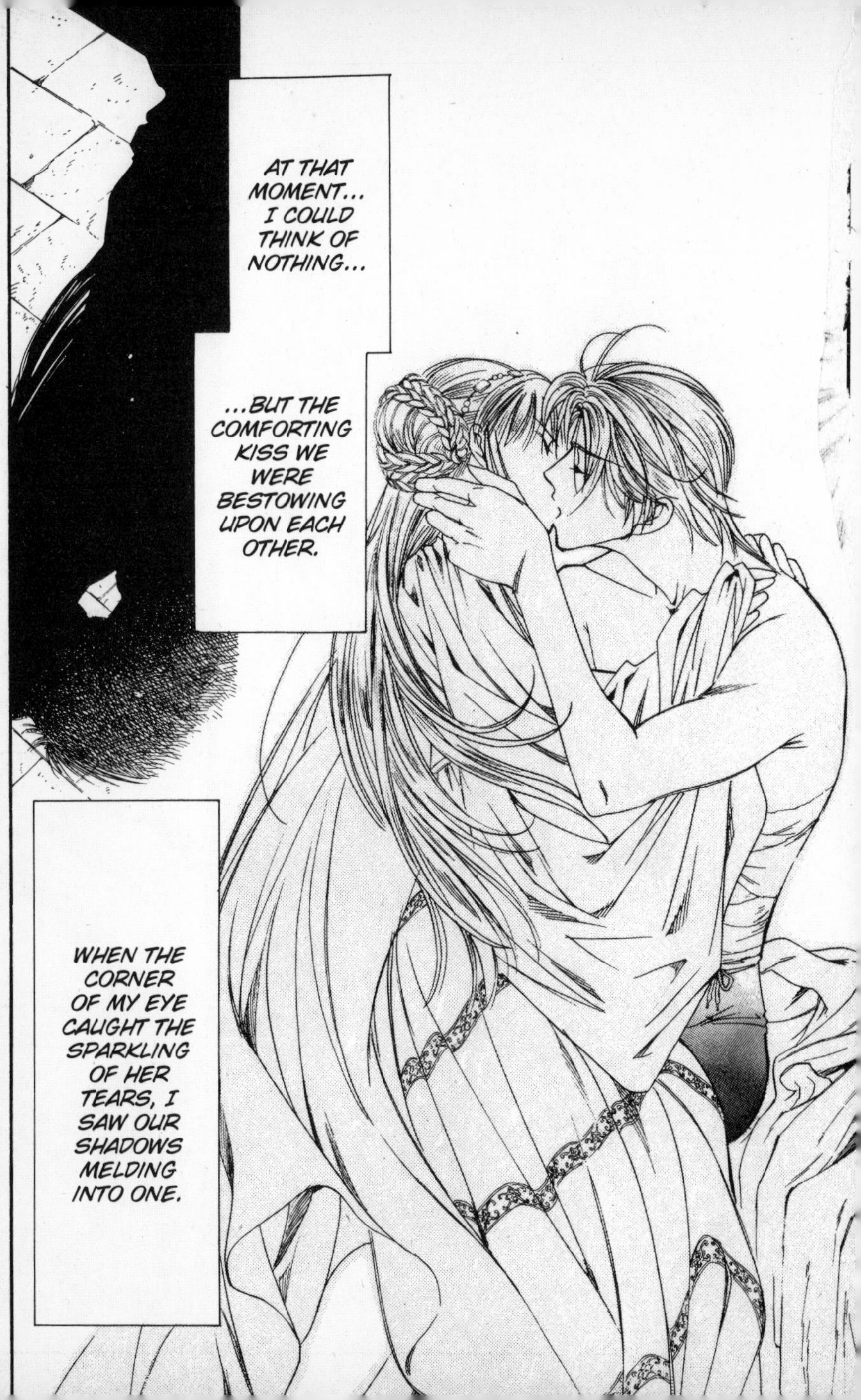
AT THAT MOMENT... I COULD THINK OF NOTHING...
...BUT THE COMFORTING KISS WE WERE BESTOWING UPON EACH OTHER.
WHEN THE CORNER OF MY EYE CAUGHT THE SPARKLING OF HER TEARS, I SAW OUR SHADOWS MELDING INTO ONE.

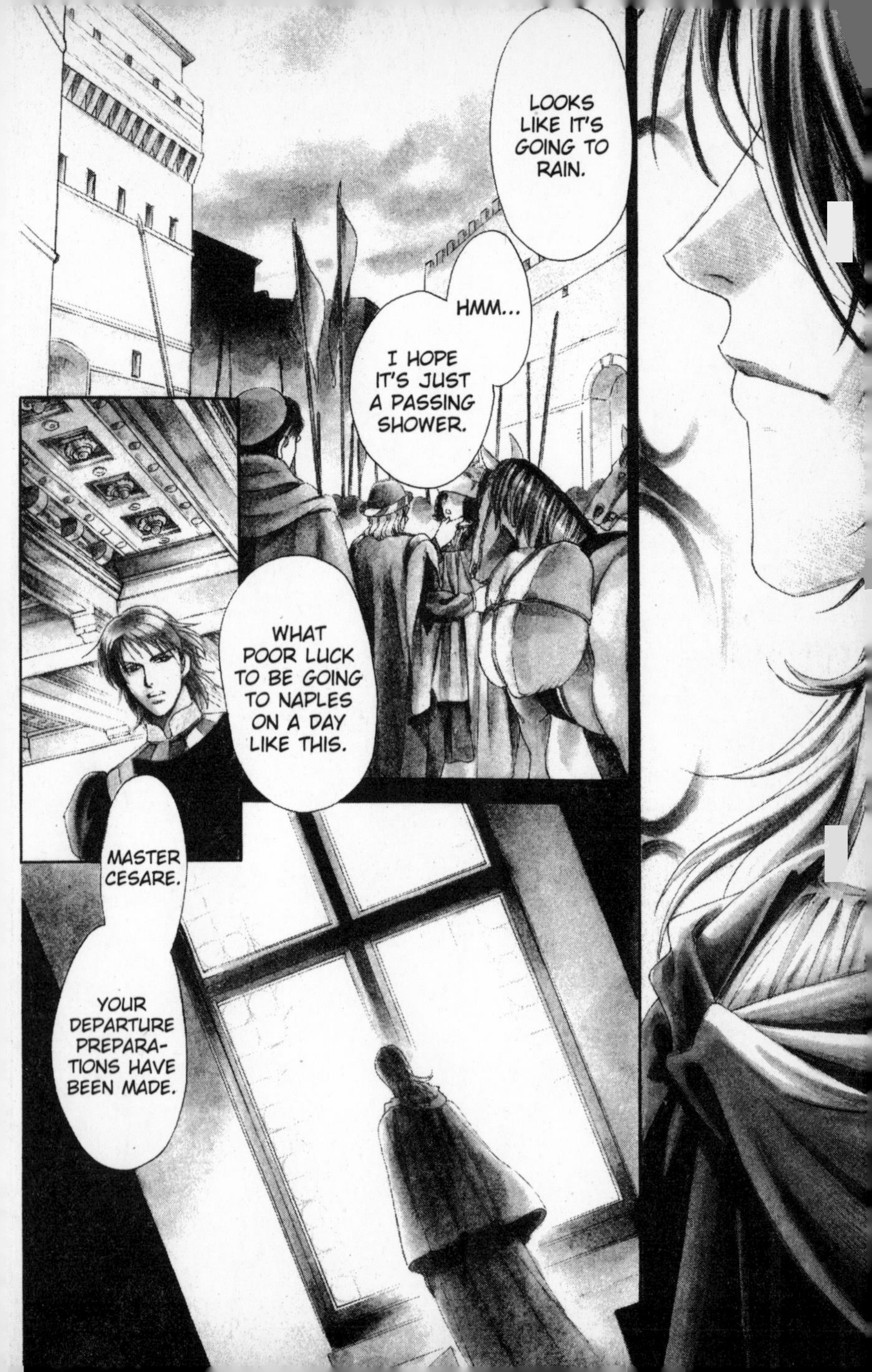
LOOKS LIKE IT'S GOING TO RAIN.
HMM...
I HOPE IT'S JUST A PASSING SHOWER.
WHAT POOR LUCK TO BE GOING TO NAPLES ON A DAY LIKE THIS.
MASTER CESARE.
YOUR DEPARTURE PREPARA-TIONS HAVE BEEN MADE.

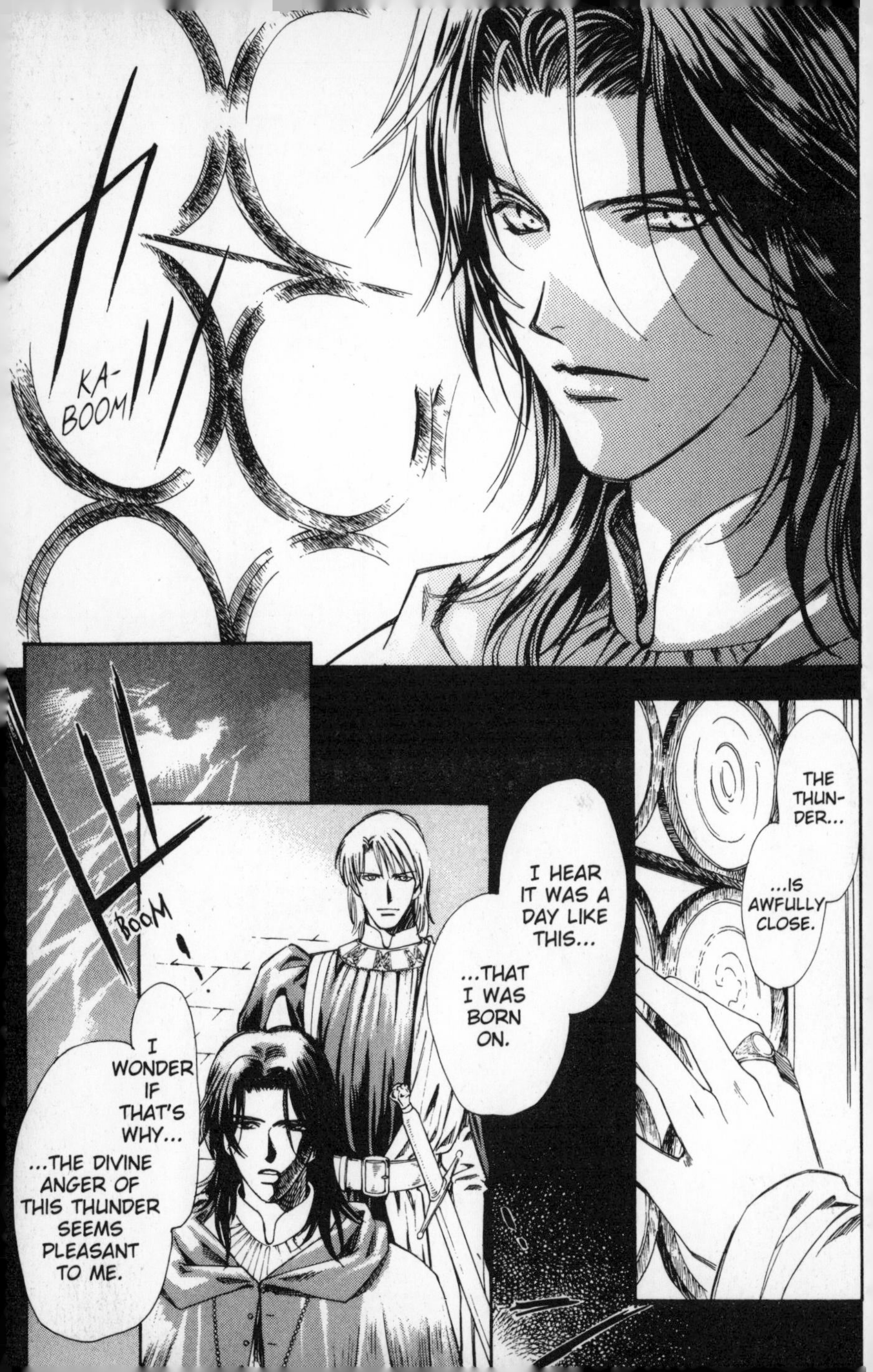
KA-BOOM
THE THUNDER...
...IS AWFULLY CLOSE.
BOOM
I HEAR IT WAS A DAY LIKE THIS...
...THAT I WAS BORN ON.
I WONDER IF THAT'S WHY...
...THE DIVINE ANGER OF THIS THUNDER SEEMS PLEASANT TO ME.

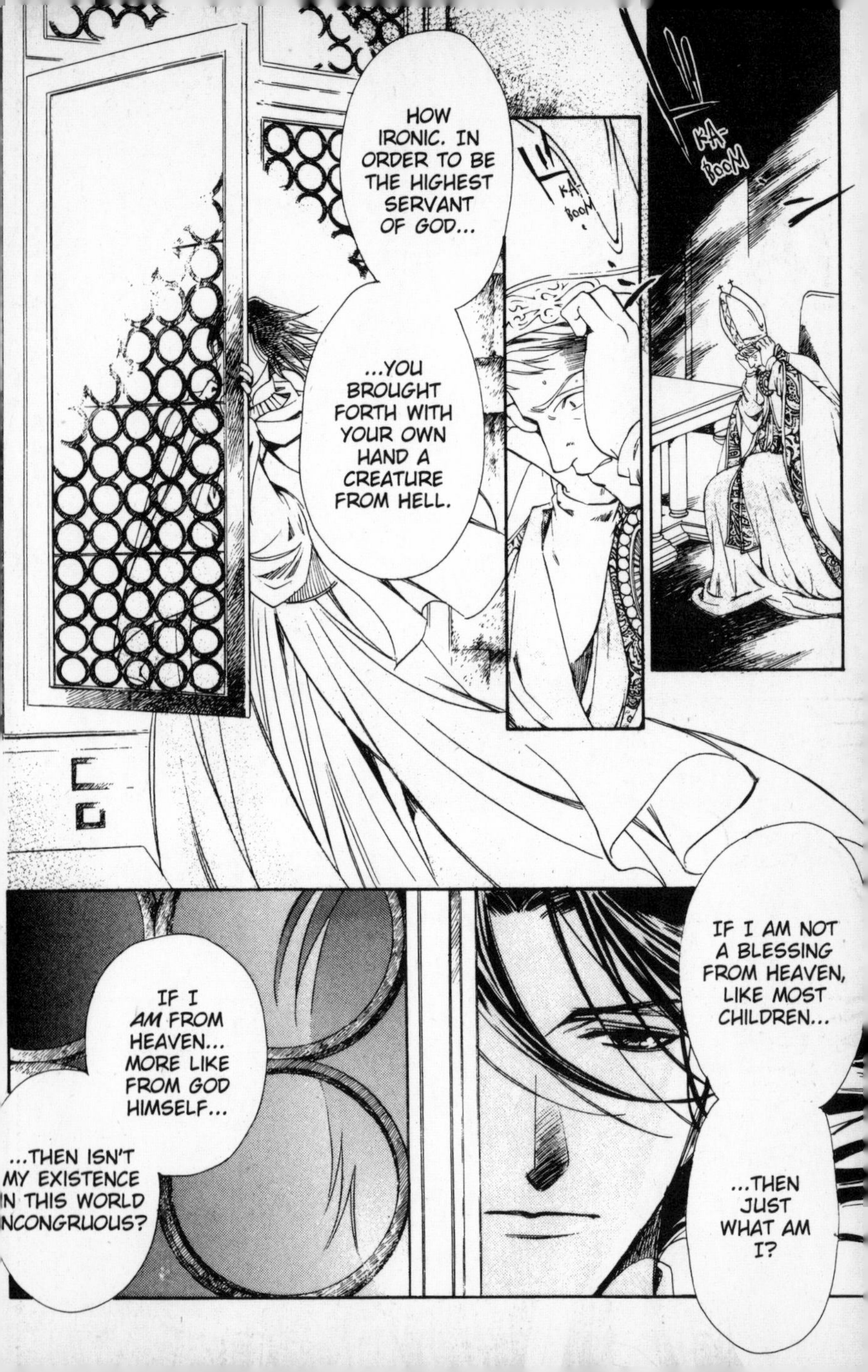
KA-BOOM
KA-BOOM
HOW IRONIC. IN ORDER TO BE THE HIGHEST SERVANT OF GOD...
...YOU BROUGHT FORTH WITH YOUR OWN HAND A CREATURE FROM HELL.
IF I AM NOT A BLESSING FROM HEAVEN, LIKE MOST CHILDREN...
...THEN JUST WHAT AM I?
IF I AM FROM HEAVEN... MORE LIKE FROM GOD HIMSELF...
...THEN ISN'T MY EXISTENCE N THIS WORLD NCONGRUOUS?

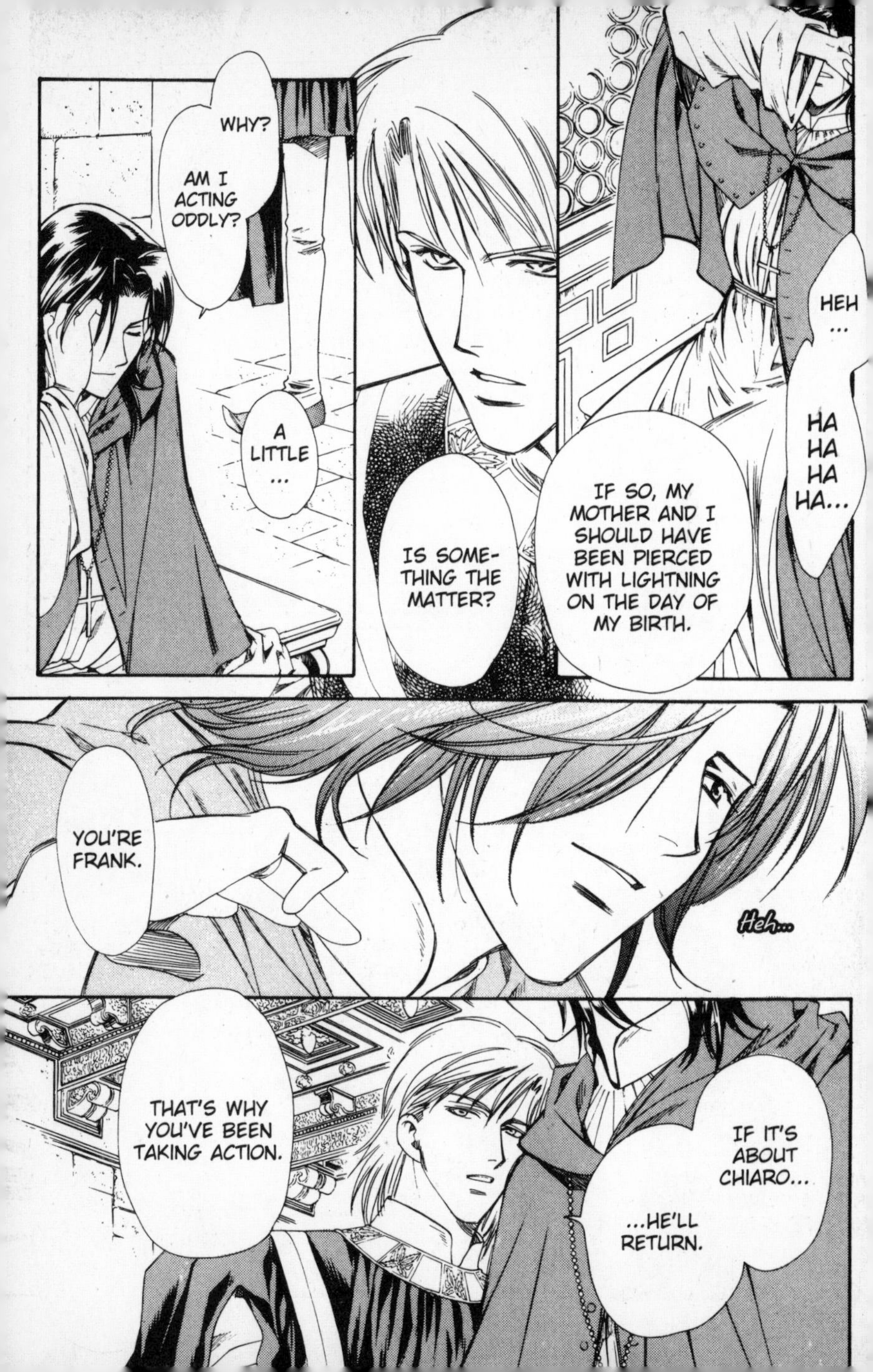
HEH ...
HA HA HA HA...
IF SO, MY MOTHER AND I SHOULD HAVE BEEN PIERCED WITH LIGHTNING ON THE DAY OF MY BIRTH.
IS SOME-THING THE MATTER?
WHY?
AM I ACTING ODDLY?
A LITTLE ...
Heh...
YOU'RE FRANK.
IF IT'S ABOUT CHIARO...
...HE'LL RETURN.
THAT'S WHY YOU'VE BEEN TAKING ACTION.

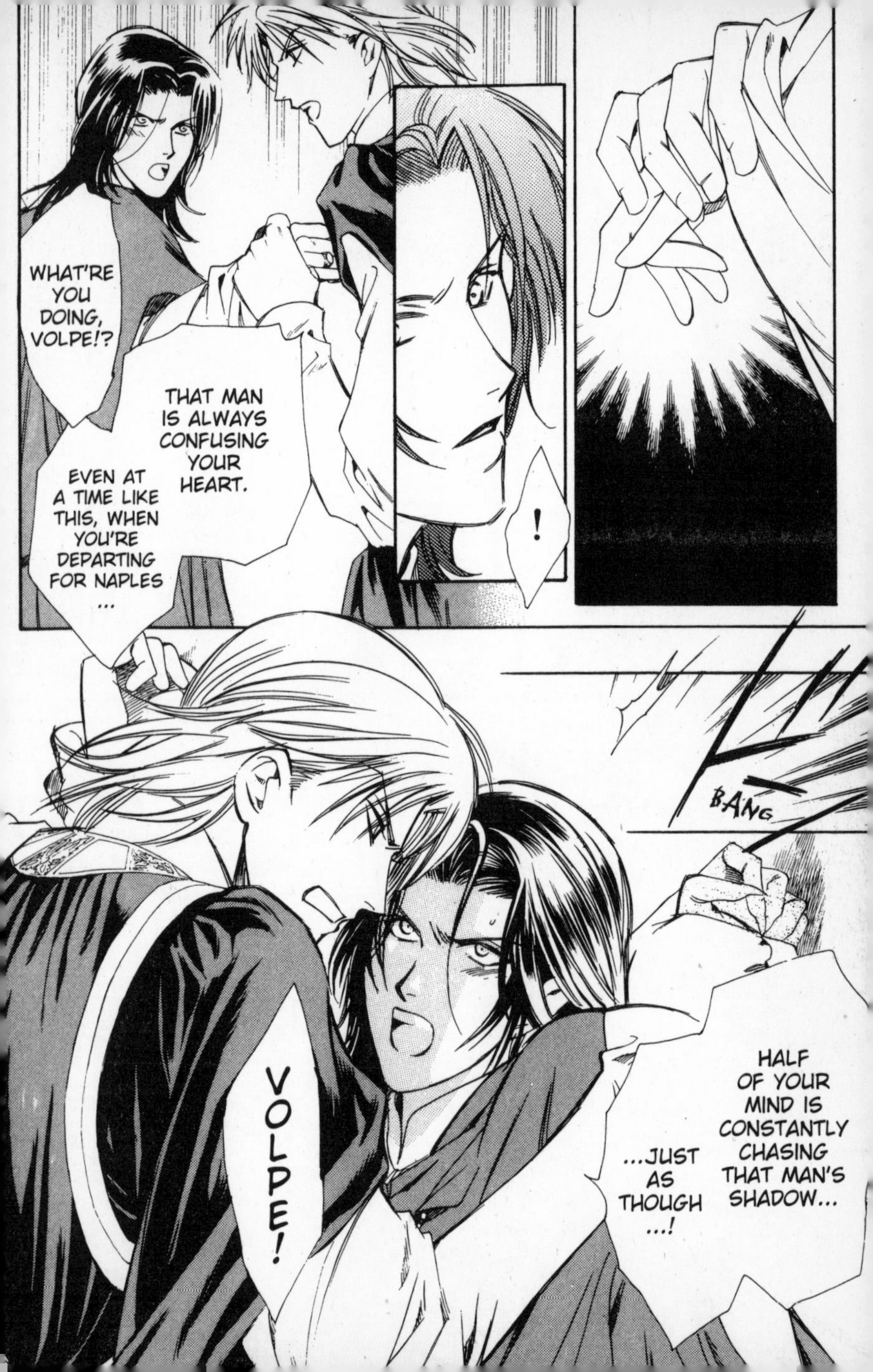
!
WHAT'RE YOU DOING, VOLPE!?
THAT MAN IS ALWAYS CONFUSING YOUR HEART.
EVEN AT A TIME LIKE THIS, WHEN YOU'RE DEPARTING FOR NAPLES ...
BANG
HALF OF YOUR MIND IS CONSTANTLY CHASING THAT MAN'S SHADOW...
...JUST AS THOUGH ...!
VOLPE!

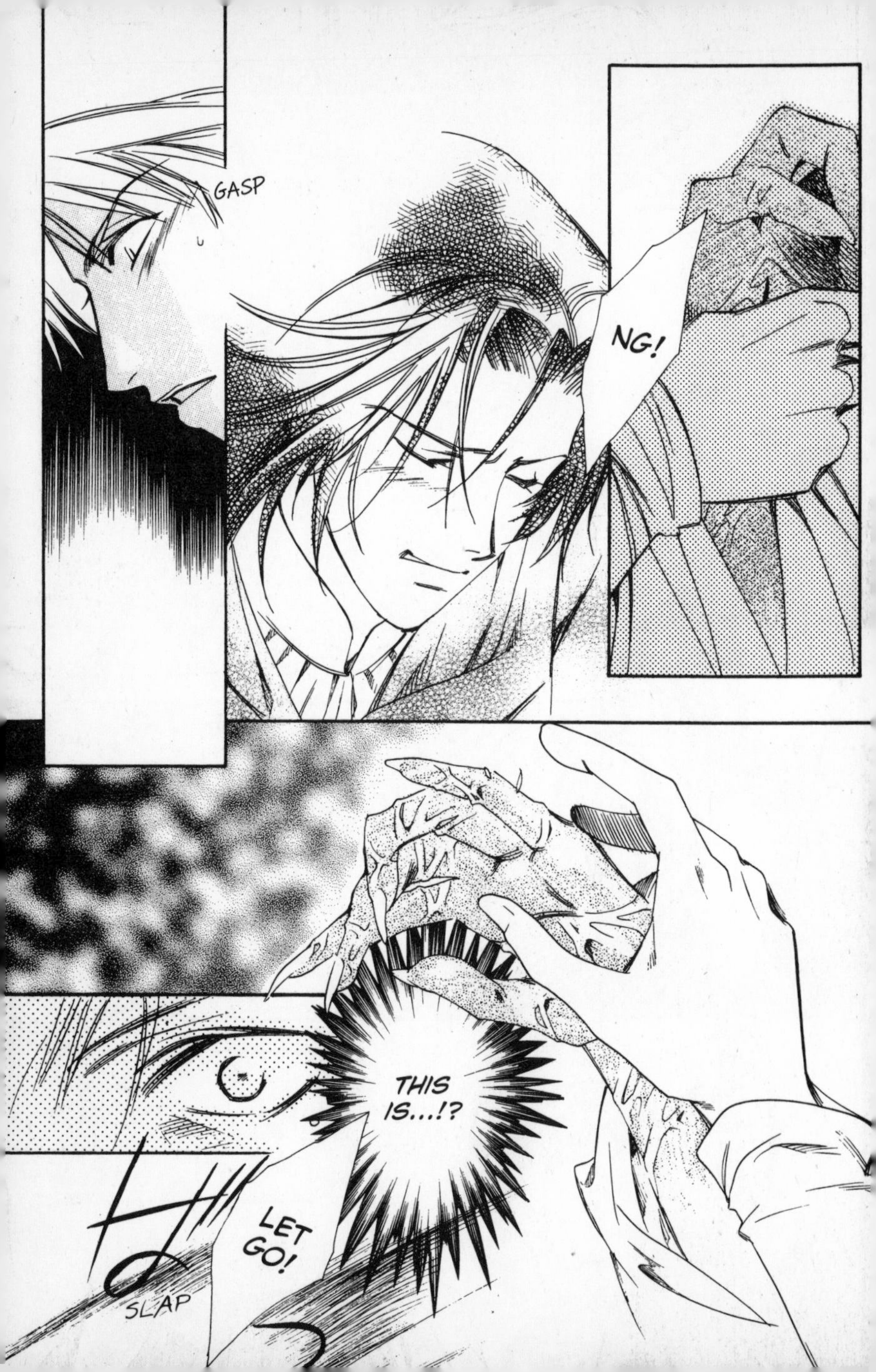
NG!
GASP
THIS IS...!?
LET GO!
SLAP

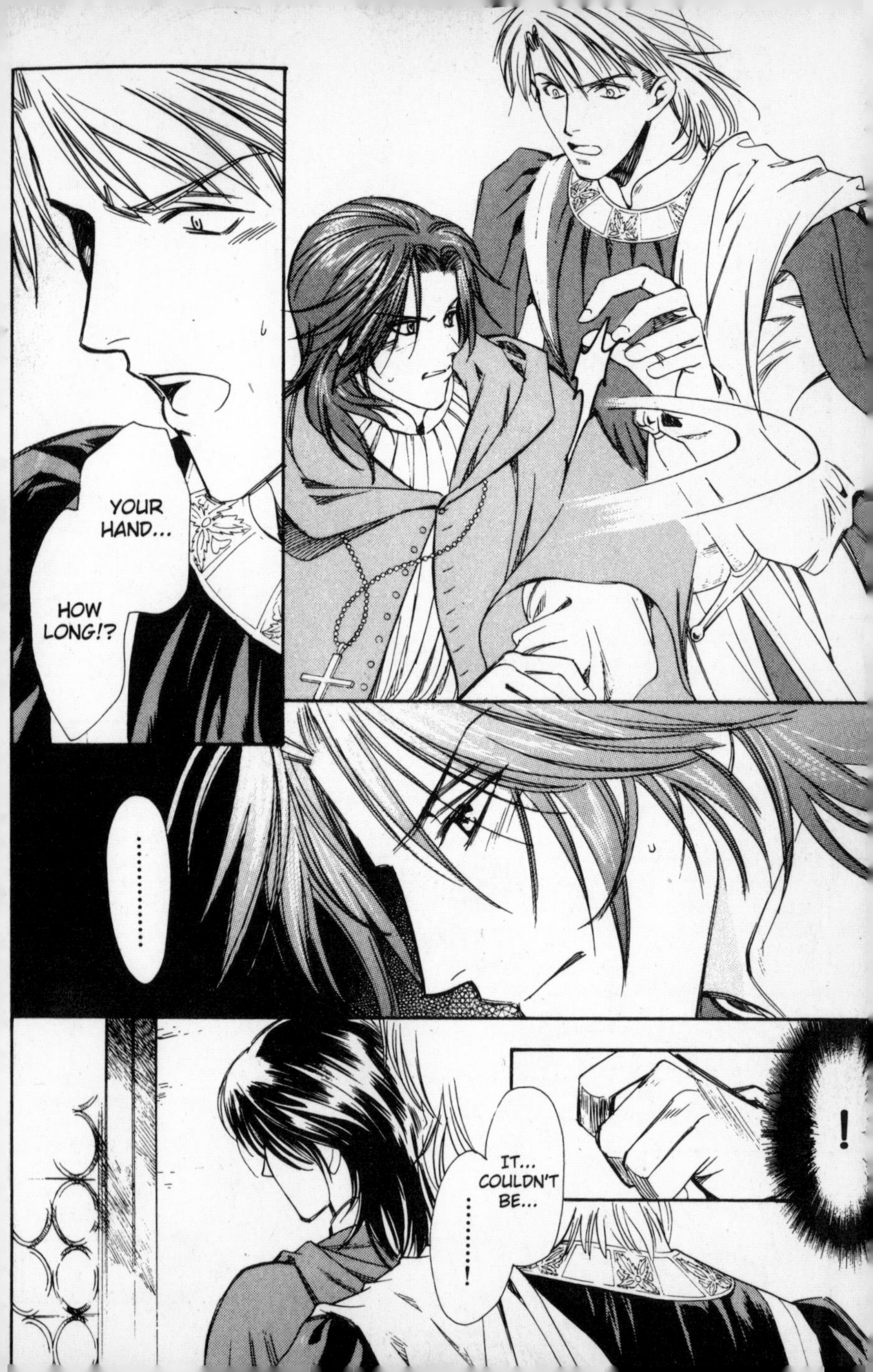
YOUR HAND...
HOW LONG!?
......
!
IT... COULDN'T BE...
......!

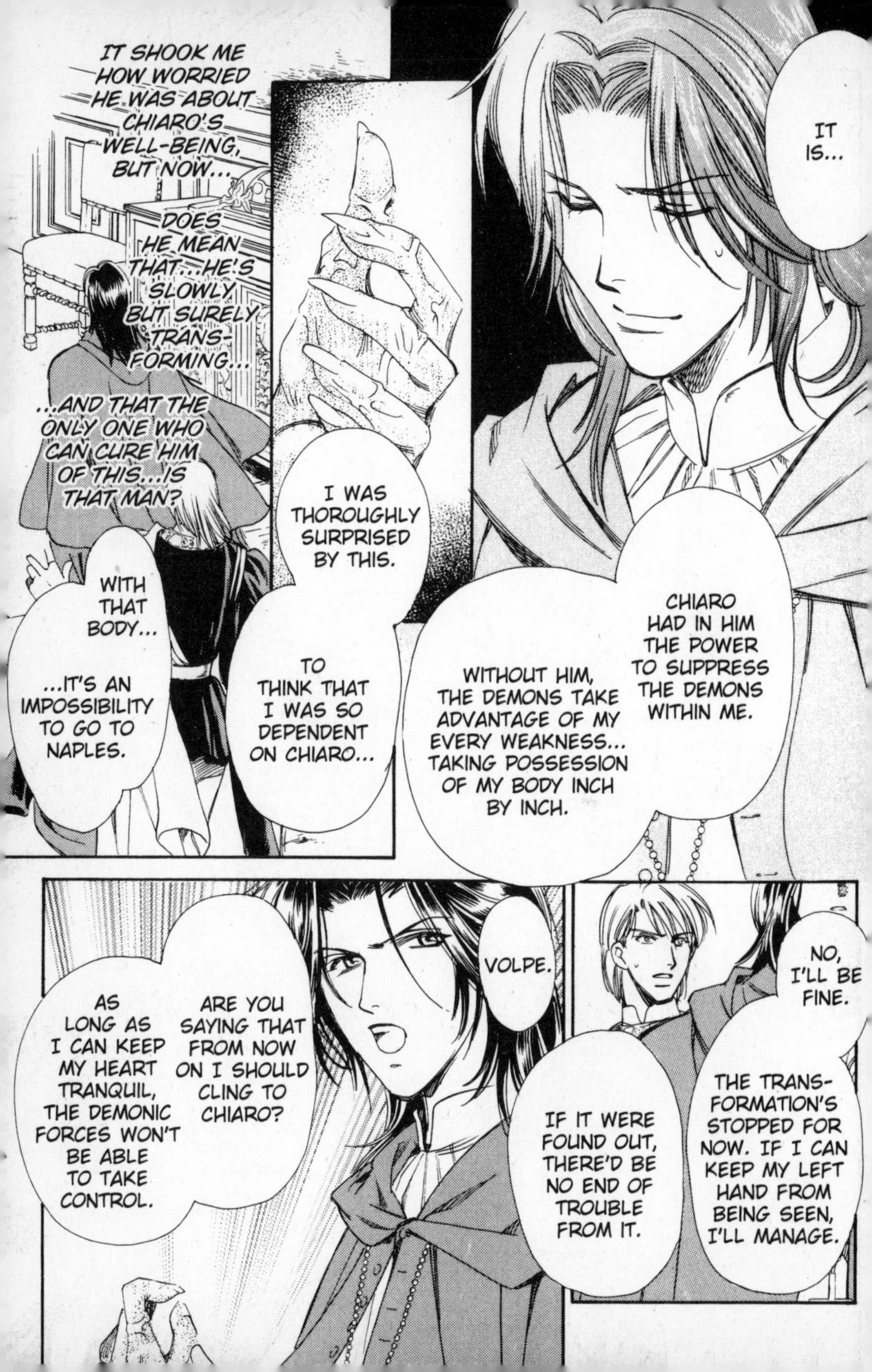
IT IS...
CHIARO HAD IN HIM THE POWER TO SUPPRESS THE DEMONS WITHIN ME.
WITHOUT HIM, THE DEMONS TAKE ADVANTAGE OF MY EVERY WEAKNESS... TAKING POSSESSION OF MY BODY INCH BY INCH.
I WAS THOROUGHLY SURPRISED BY THIS.
TO THINK THAT I WAS SO DEPENDENT ON CHIARO...
IT SHOOK ME HOW WORRIED HE WAS ABOUT CHIARO'S WELL-BEING, BUT NOW...
DOES HE MEAN THAT...HE'S SLOWLY BUT SURELY TRANS-FORMING...
...AND THAT THE ONLY ONE WHO CAN CURE HIM OF THIS...IS THAT MAN?
WITH THAT BODY...
...IT'S AN IMPOSSIBILITY TO GO TO NAPLES.
NO, I'LL BE FINE.
THE TRANS-FORMATION'S STOPPED FOR NOW. IF I CAN KEEP MY LEFT HAND FROM BEING SEEN, I'LL MANAGE.
IF IT WERE FOUND OUT, THERE'D BE NO END OF TROUBLE FROM IT.
VOLPE.
ARE YOU SAYING THAT FROM NOW ON I SHOULD CLING TO CHIARO?
AS LONG AS I CAN KEEP MY HEART TRANQUIL, THE DEMONIC FORCES WON'T BE ABLE TO TAKE CONTROL.

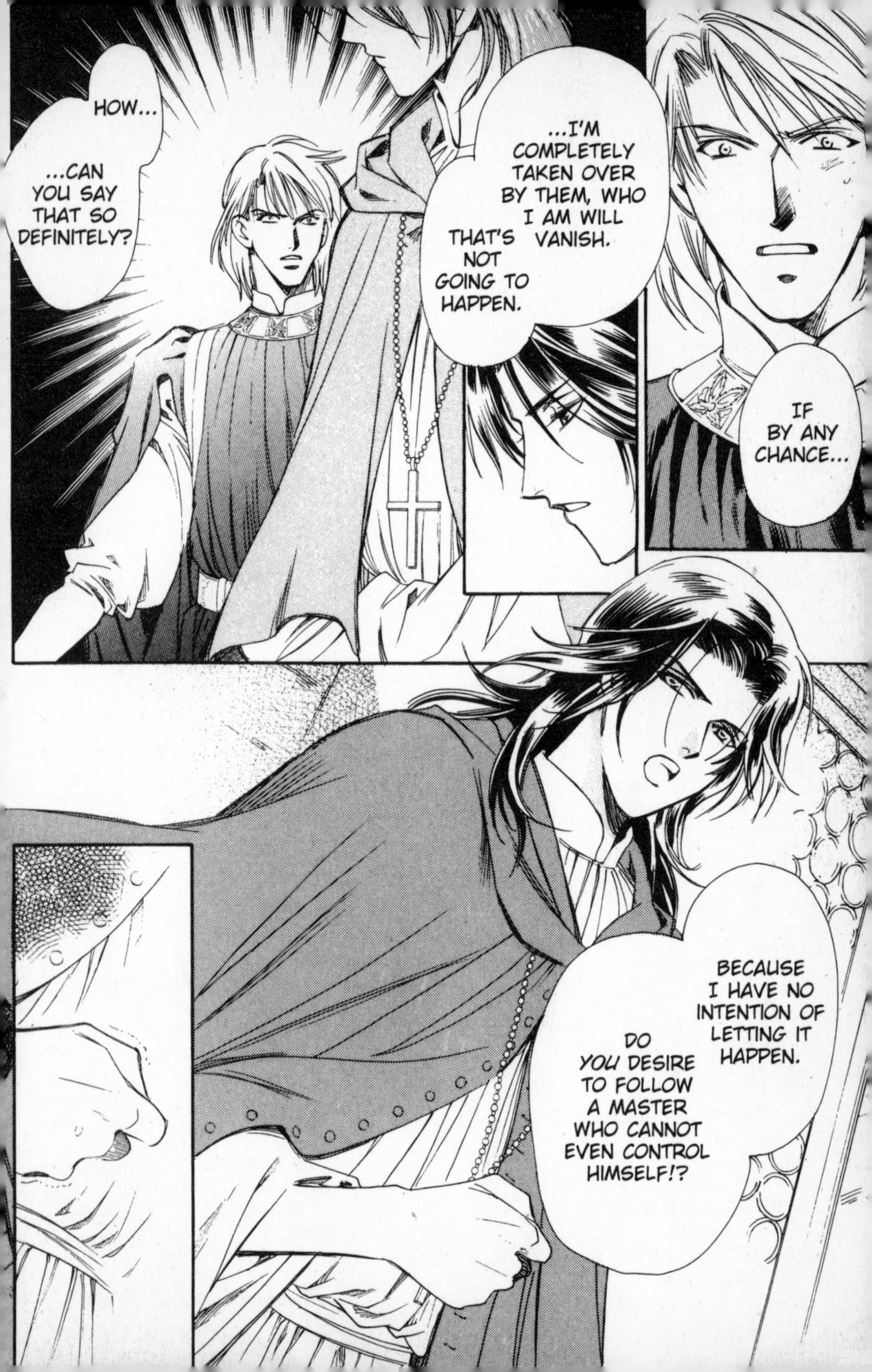
IF BY ANY CHANCE...
...I'M COMPLETELY TAKEN OVER BY THEM, WHO I AM WILL VANISH.
THAT'S NOT GOING TO HAPPEN.
HOW...
...CAN YOU SAY THAT SO DEFINITELY?
BECAUSE I HAVE NO INTENTION OF LETTING IT HAPPEN.
DO *YOU* DESIRE TO FOLLOW A MASTER WHO CANNOT EVEN CONTROL HIMSELF!?

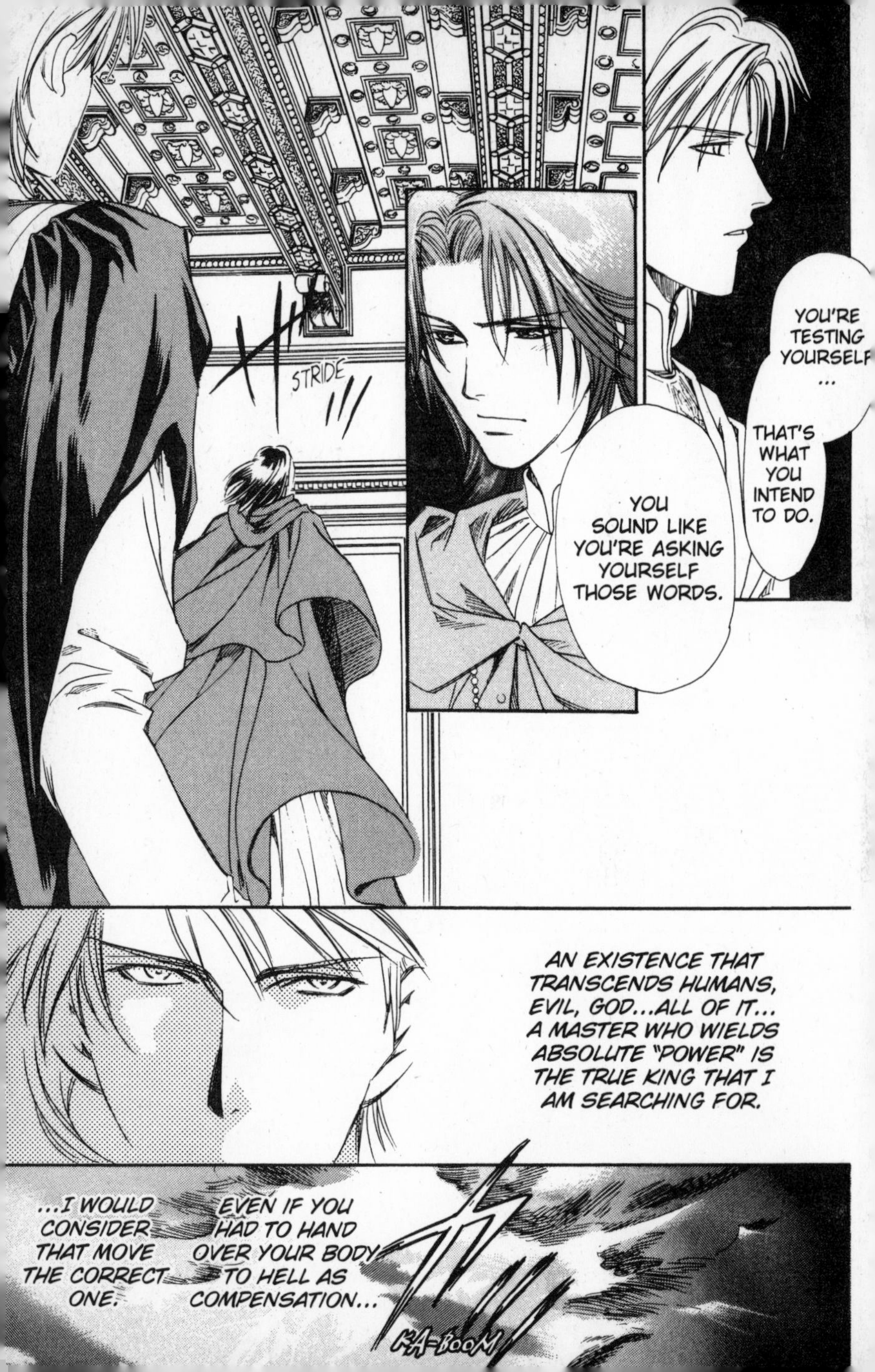
YOU'RE TESTING YOURSELF ...
THAT'S WHAT YOU INTEND TO DO.
YOU SOUND LIKE YOU'RE ASKING YOURSELF THOSE WORDS.
STRIDE
AN EXISTENCE THAT TRANSCENDS HUMANS, EVIL, GOD...ALL OF IT... A MASTER WHO WIELDS ABSOLUTE "POWER" IS THE TRUE KING THAT I AM SEARCHING FOR.
EVEN IF YOU HAD TO HAND OVER YOUR BODY TO HELL AS COMPENSATION...
...I WOULD CONSIDER THAT MOVE THE CORRECT ONE.
KA-BOOM

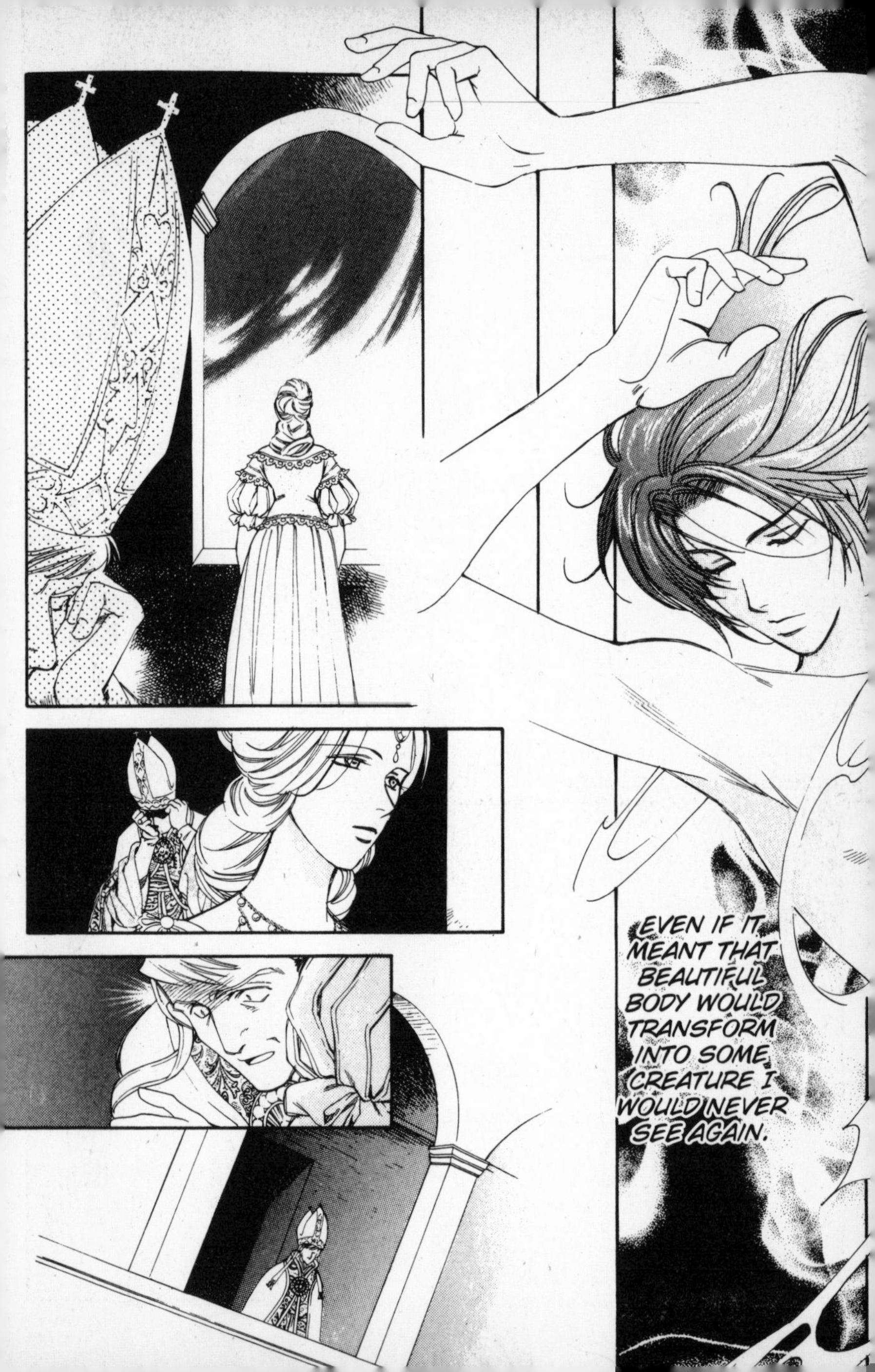
EVEN IF IT MEANT THAT BEAUTIFUL BODY WOULD TRANSFORM INTO SOME CREATURE I WOULD NEVER SEE AGAIN.

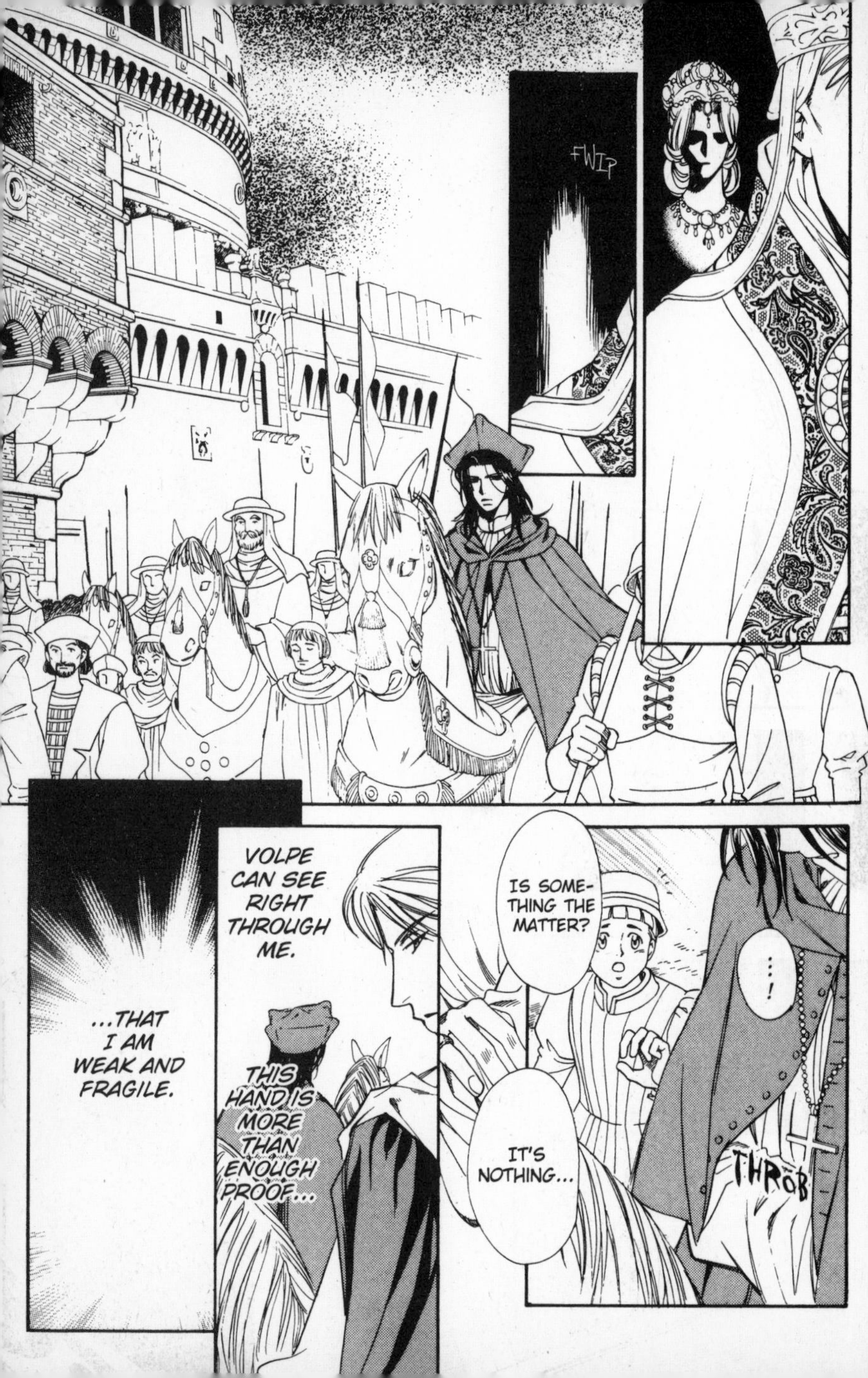
FWIP
IS SOMETHING THE MATTER?
...!
IT'S NOTHING...
THROB
VOLPE CAN SEE RIGHT THROUGH ME.
THIS HAND IS MORE THAN ENOUGH PROOF...
...THAT I AM WEAK AND FRAGILE.

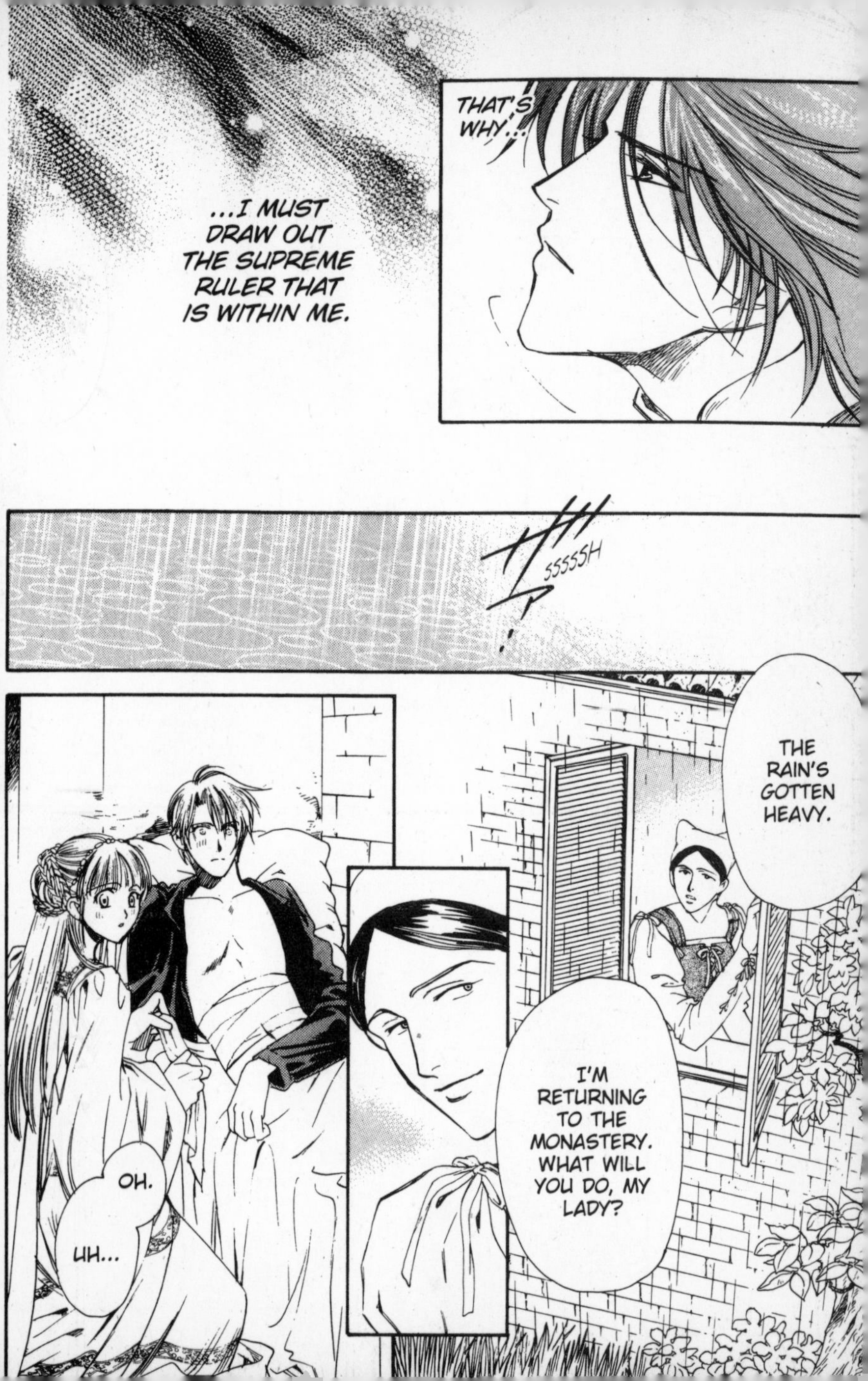
THAT'S WHY...
...I MUST DRAW OUT THE SUPREME RULER THAT IS WITHIN ME.
SSSSSH
THE RAIN'S GOTTEN HEAVY.
I'M RETURNING TO THE MONASTERY. WHAT WILL YOU DO, MY LADY?
OH.
UH...

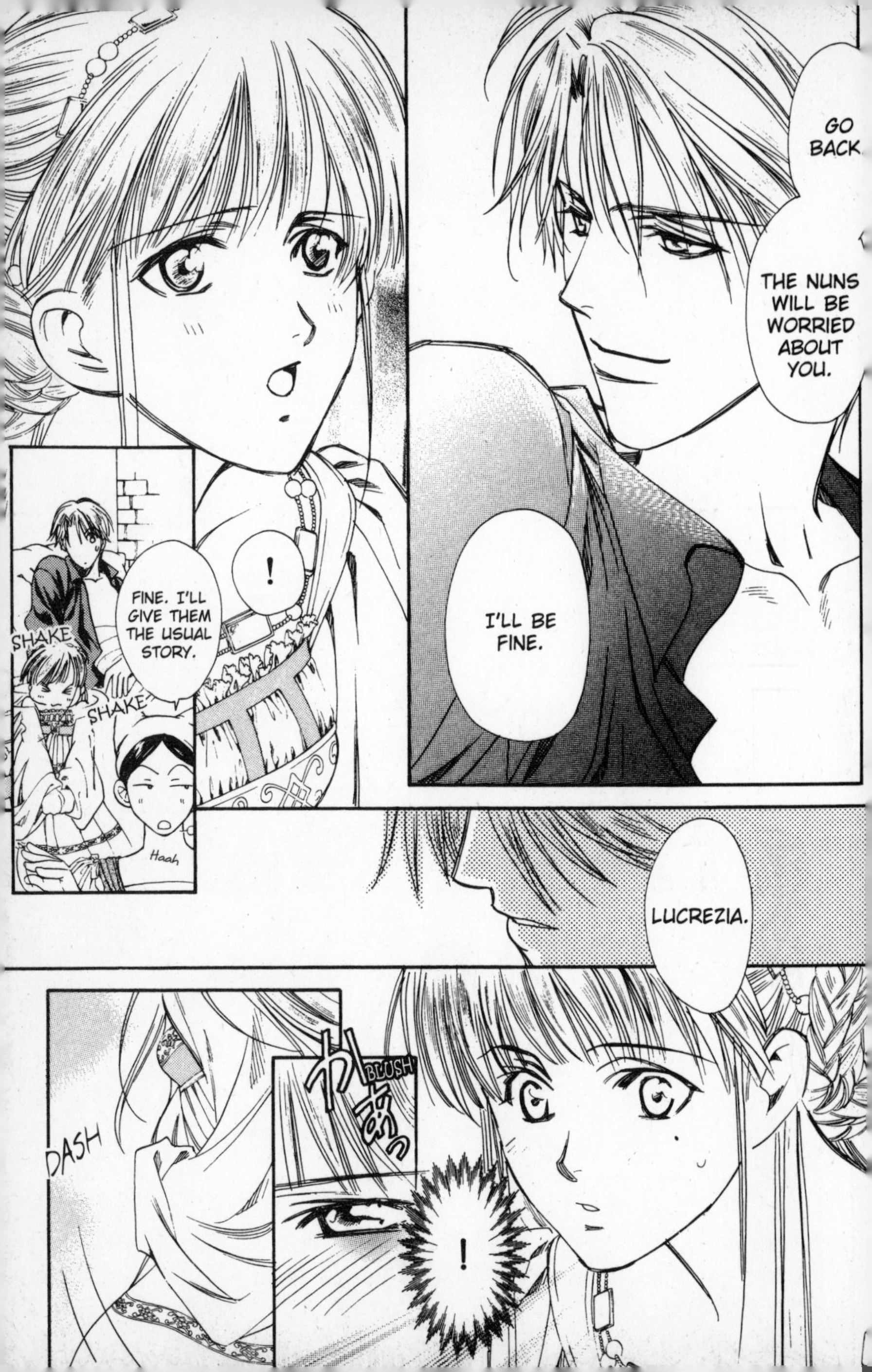
GO BACK
THE NUNS WILL BE WORRIED ABOUT YOU.
I'LL BE FINE.
!
FINE. I'LL GIVE THEM THE USUAL STORY.
SHAKE
SHAKE
Haah
LUCREZIA.
!
BLUSH
DASH

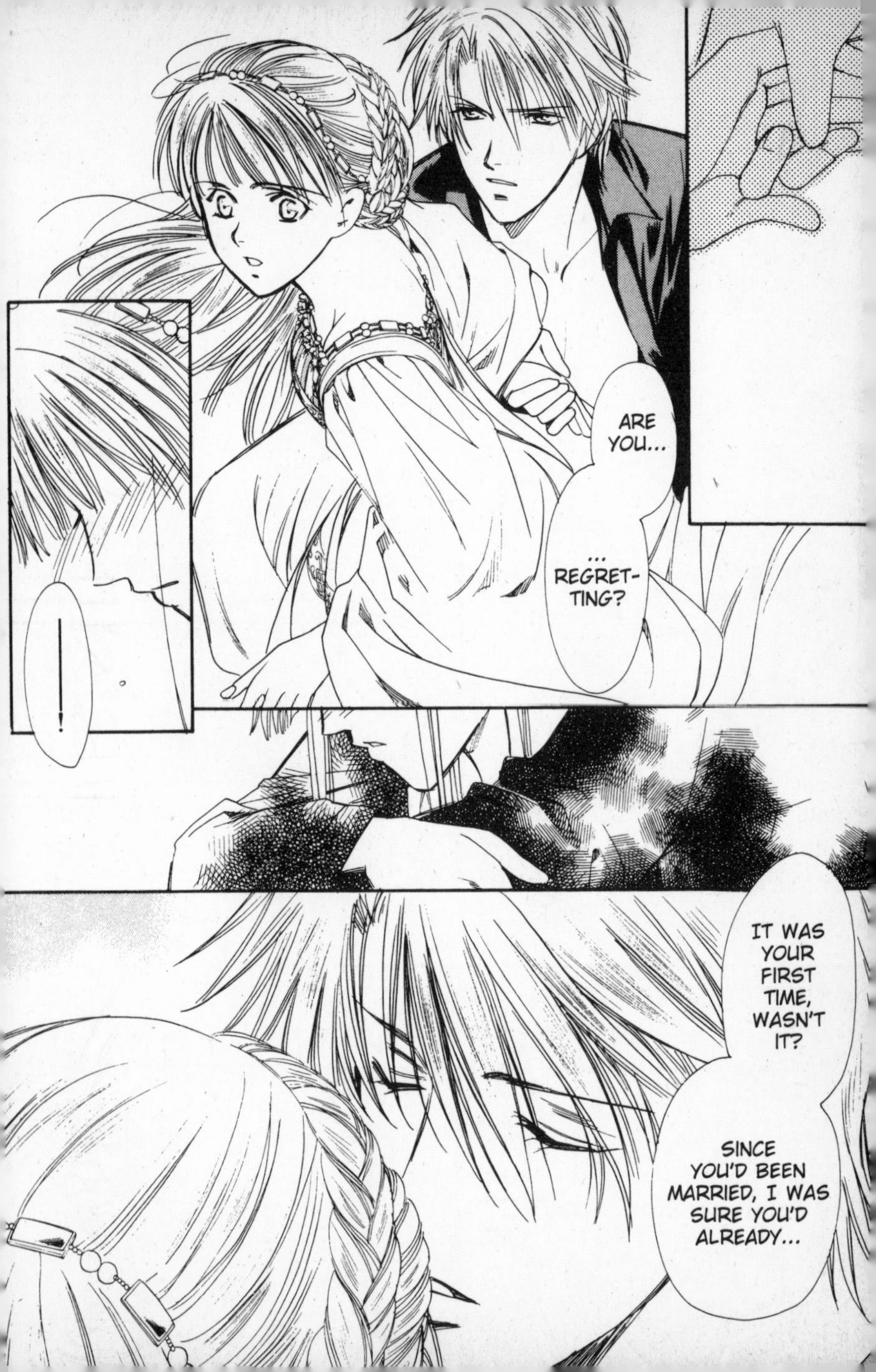
ARE YOU...
... REGRET-TING?
!
IT WAS YOUR FIRST TIME, WASN'T IT?
SINCE YOU'D BEEN MARRIED, I WAS SURE YOU'D ALREADY...

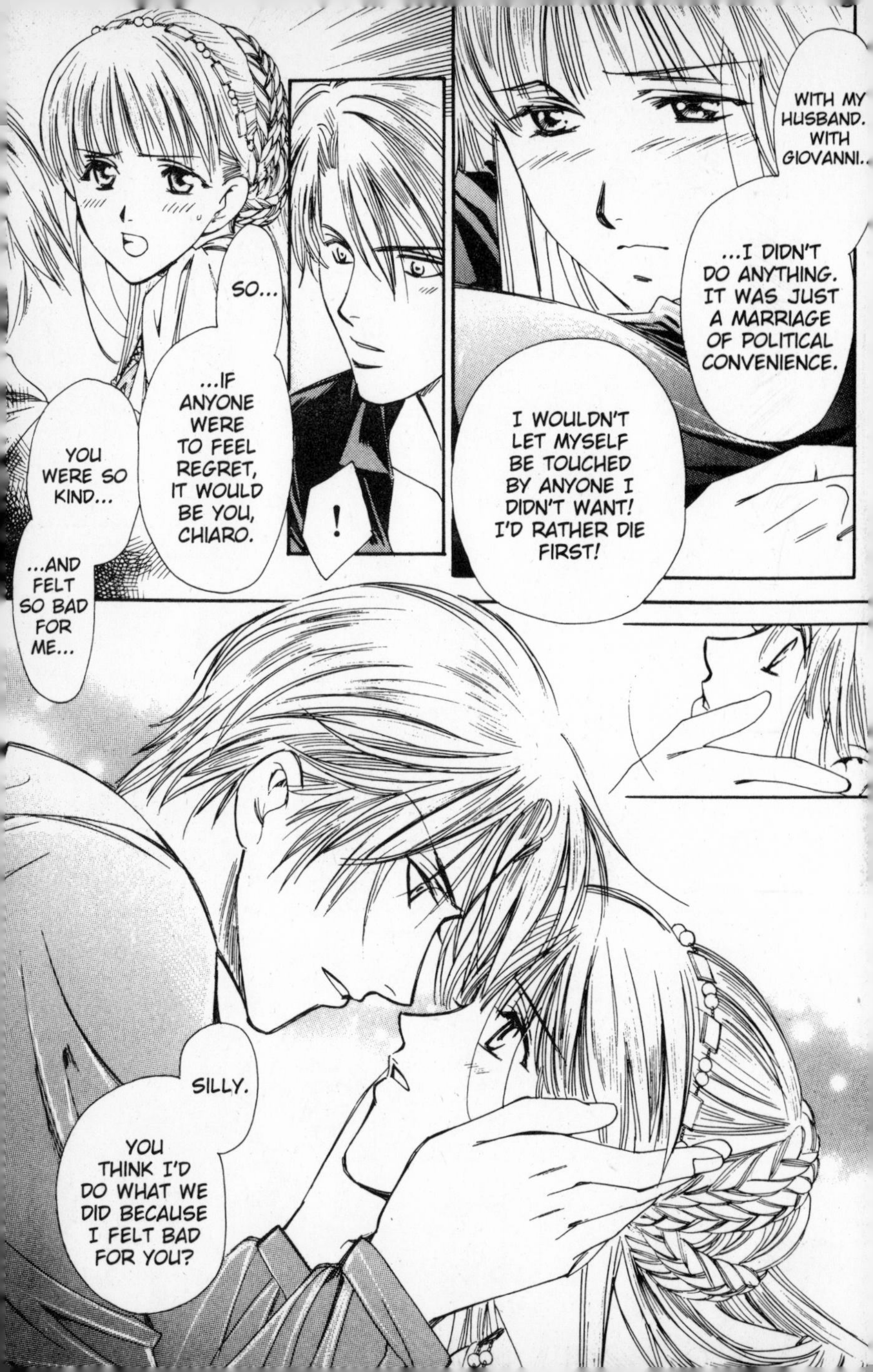
WITH MY HUSBAND. WITH GIOVANNI..
...I DIDN'T DO ANYTHING. IT WAS JUST A MARRIAGE OF POLITICAL CONVENIENCE.
I WOULDN'T LET MYSELF BE TOUCHED BY ANYONE I DIDN'T WANT! I'D RATHER DIE FIRST!
!
SO...
...IF ANYONE WERE TO FEEL REGRET, IT WOULD BE YOU, CHIARO.
YOU WERE SO KIND...
...AND FELT SO BAD FOR ME...
SILLY.
YOU THINK I'D DO WHAT WE DID BECAUSE I FELT BAD FOR YOU?

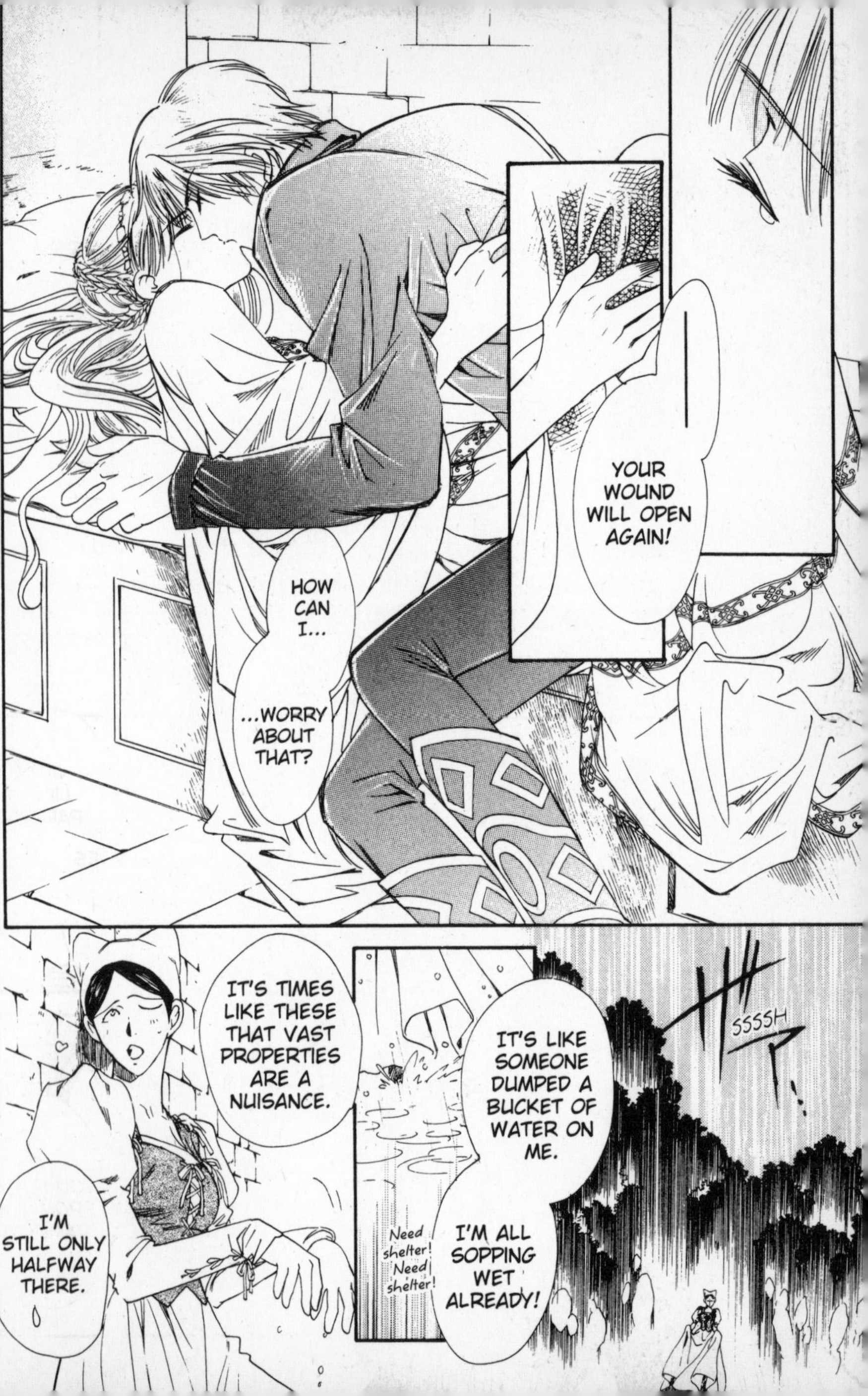
YOUR WOUND WILL OPEN AGAIN!
HOW CAN I...
...WORRY ABOUT THAT?
SSSSH
IT'S LIKE SOMEONE DUMPED A BUCKET OF WATER ON ME.
I'M ALL SOPPING WET ALREADY!
Need shelter! Need shelter!
IT'S TIMES LIKE THESE THAT VAST PROPERTIES ARE A NUISANCE.
I'M STILL ONLY HALFWAY THERE.

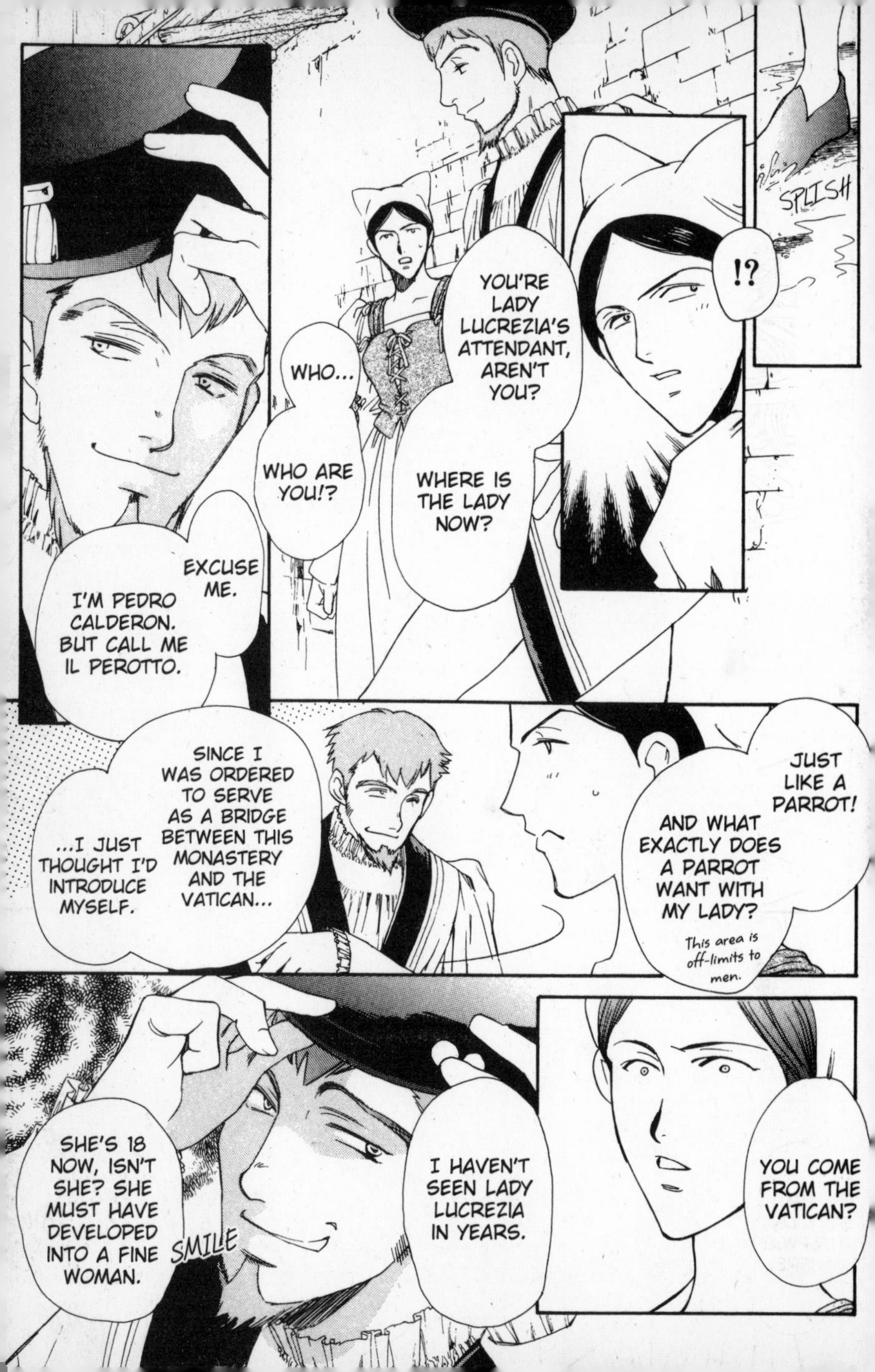
SPLISH
!?
YOU'RE LADY LUCREZIA'S ATTENDANT, AREN'T YOU?
WHERE IS THE LADY NOW?
WHO...
WHO ARE YOU!?
EXCUSE ME.
I'M PEDRO CALDERON. BUT CALL ME IL PEROTTO.
JUST LIKE A PARROT!
AND WHAT EXACTLY DOES A PARROT WANT WITH MY LADY?
This area is off-limits to men.
SINCE I WAS ORDERED TO SERVE AS A BRIDGE BETWEEN THIS MONASTERY AND THE VATICAN...
...I JUST THOUGHT I'D INTRODUCE MYSELF.
YOU COME FROM THE VATICAN?
I HAVEN'T SEEN LADY LUCREZIA IN YEARS.
SHE'S 18 NOW, ISN'T SHE? SHE MUST HAVE DEVELOPED INTO A FINE WOMAN.
SMILE

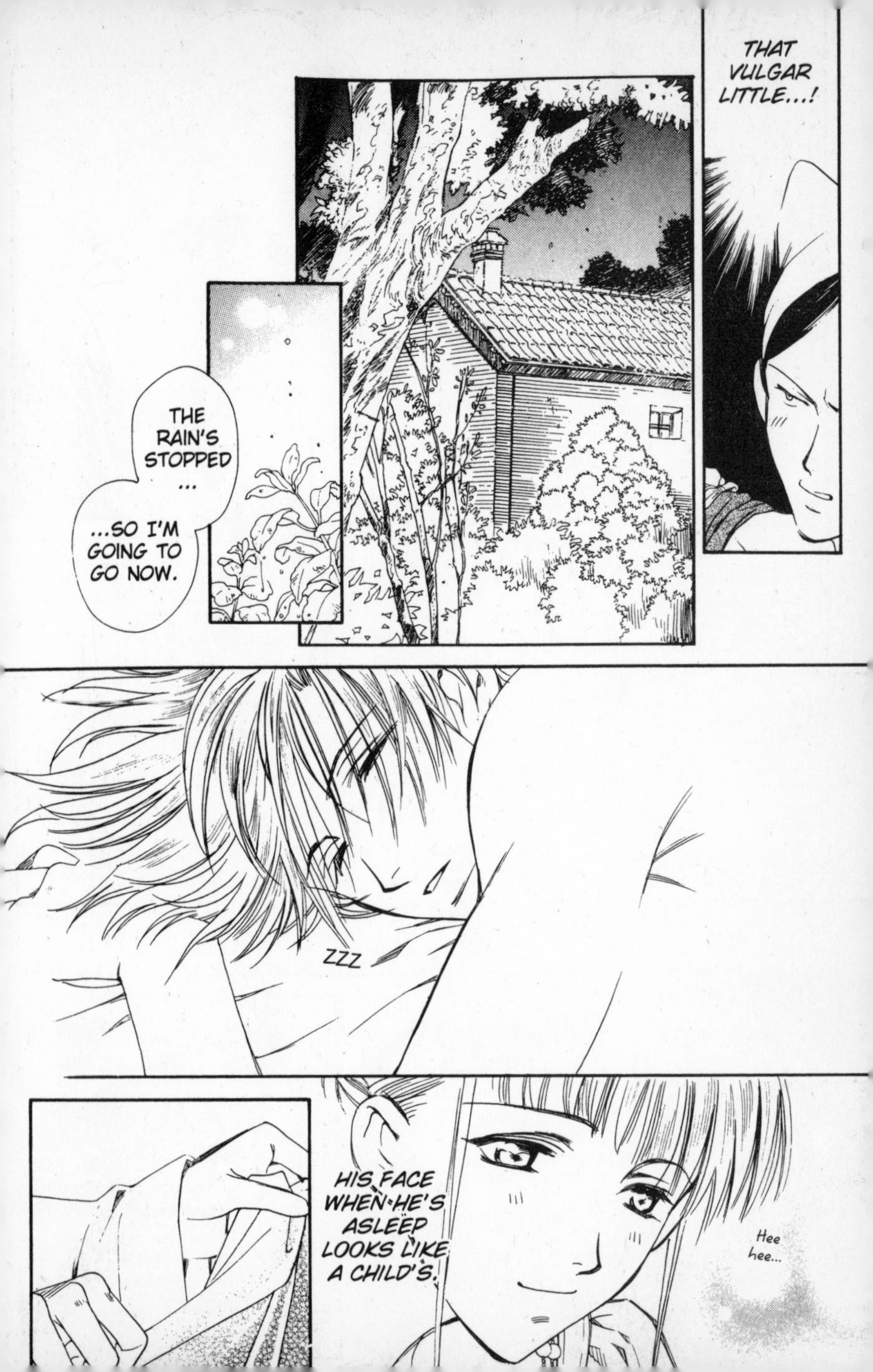
THAT VULGAR LITTLE...!
THE RAIN'S STOPPED ...
...SO I'M GOING TO GO NOW.
ZZZ
Hee hee...
HIS FACE WHEN HE'S ASLEEP LOOKS LIKE A CHILD'S.

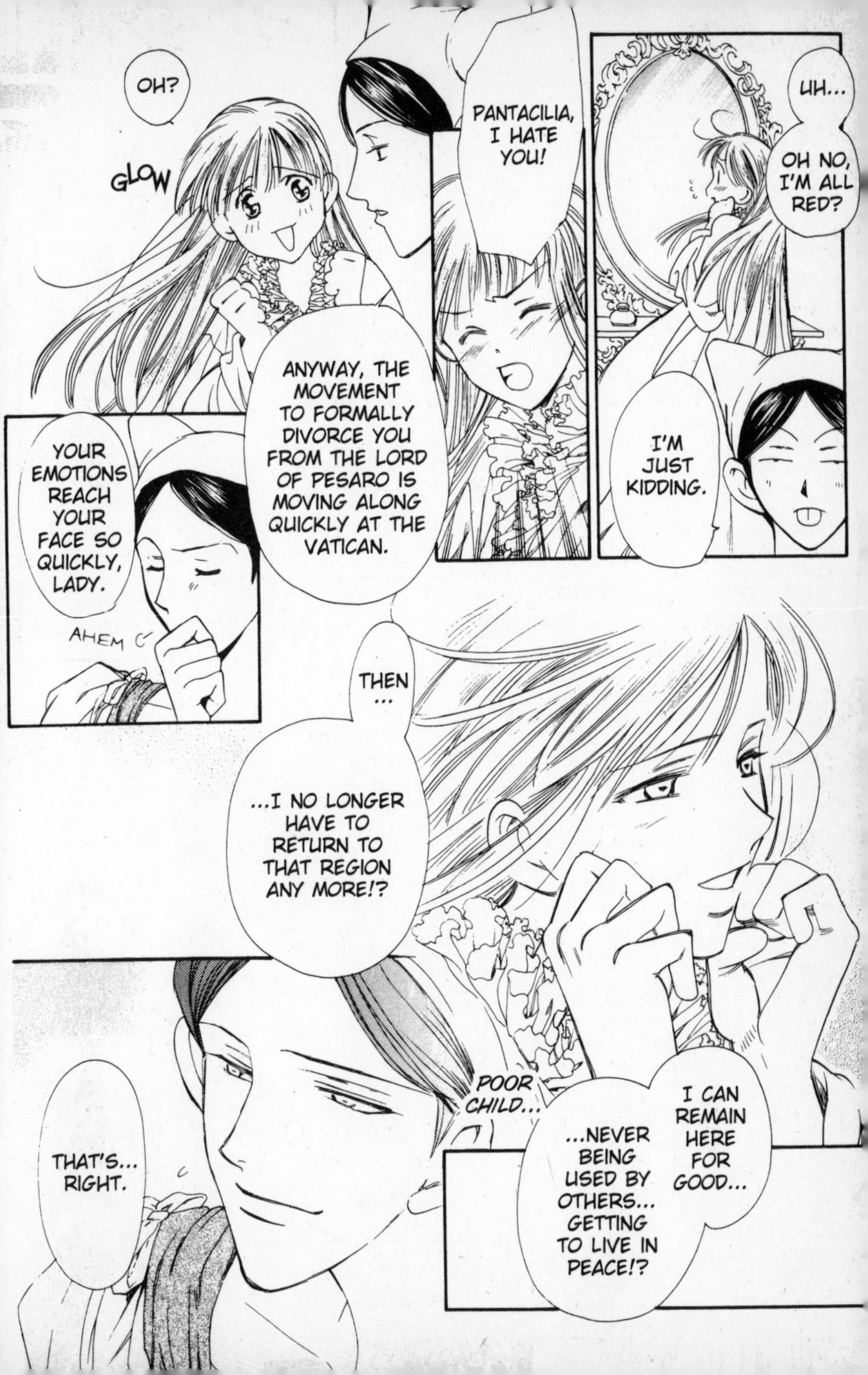
UH...
OH NO, I'M ALL RED?
I'M JUST KIDDING.
PANTACILIA, I HATE YOU!
OH?
GLOW
ANYWAY, THE MOVEMENT TO FORMALLY DIVORCE YOU FROM THE LORD OF PESARO IS MOVING ALONG QUICKLY AT THE VATICAN.
YOUR EMOTIONS REACH YOUR FACE SO QUICKLY, LADY.
AHEM
THEN...
...I NO LONGER HAVE TO RETURN TO THAT REGION ANY MORE!?
I CAN REMAIN HERE FOR GOOD...
...NEVER BEING USED BY OTHERS... GETTING TO LIVE IN PEACE!?
POOR CHILD...
THAT'S... RIGHT.

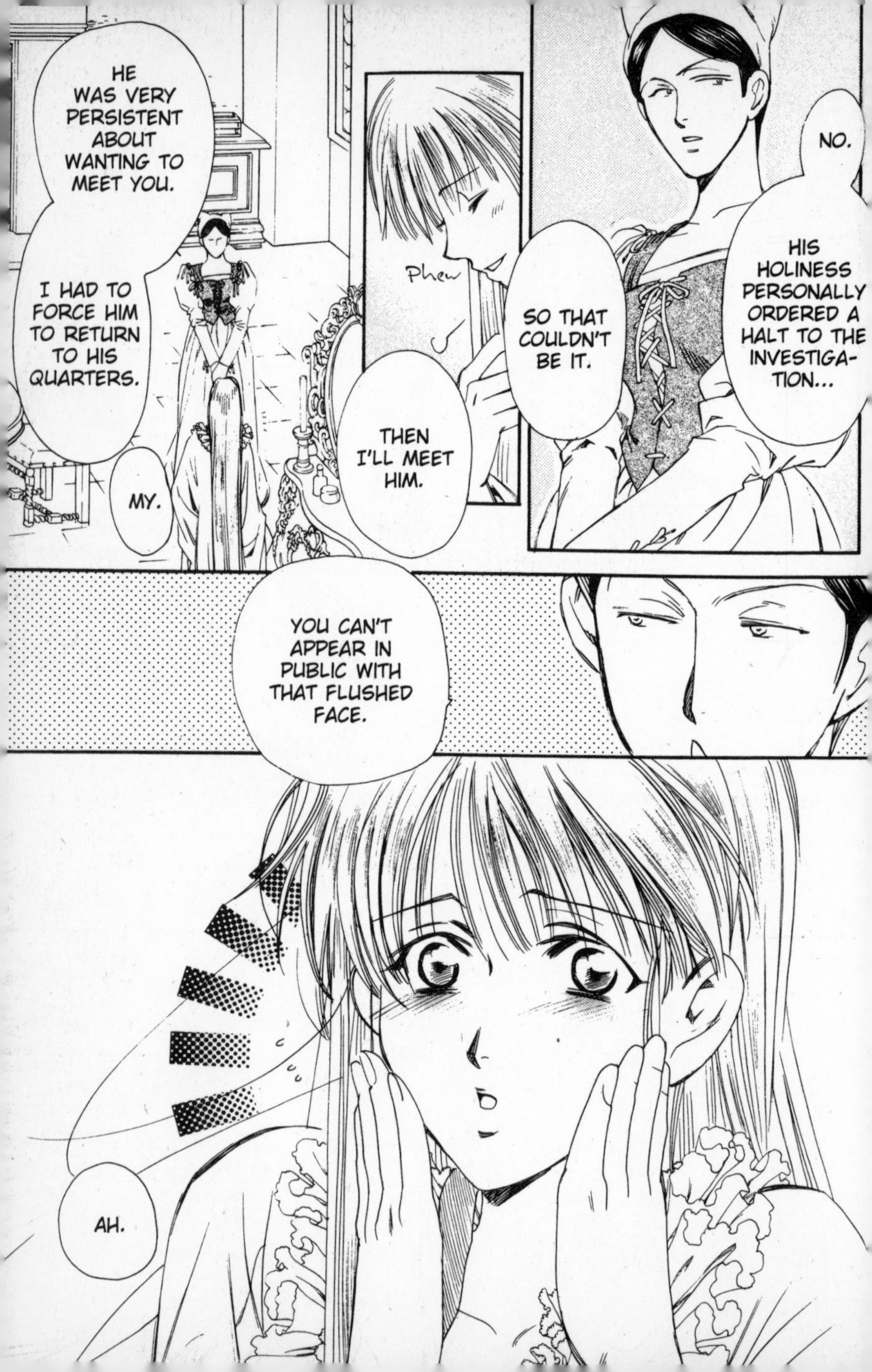

NO.
HIS HOLINESS PERSONALLY ORDERED A HALT TO THE INVESTIGATION...
SO THAT COULDN'T BE IT.
Phew
THEN I'LL MEET HIM.
HE WAS VERY PERSISTENT ABOUT WANTING TO MEET YOU.
I HAD TO FORCE HIM TO RETURN TO HIS QUARTERS.
MY.
YOU CAN'T APPEAR IN PUBLIC WITH THAT FLUSHED FACE.
AH.

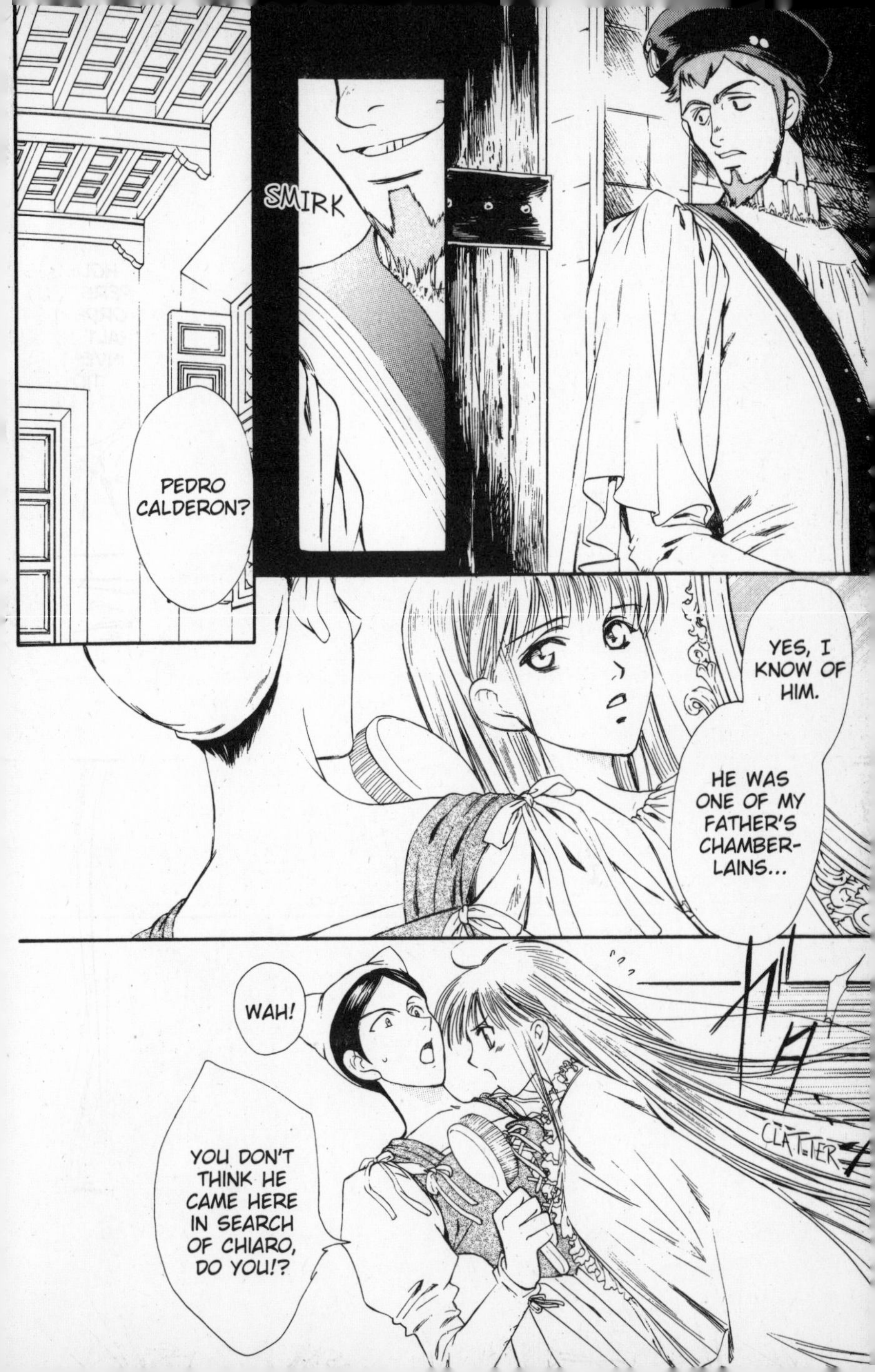
SMIRK
PEDRO CALDERON?
YES, I KNOW OF HIM.
HE WAS ONE OF MY FATHER'S CHAMBER-LAINS...
CLATTER
WAH!
YOU DON'T THINK HE CAME HERE IN SEARCH OF CHIARO, DO YOU!?

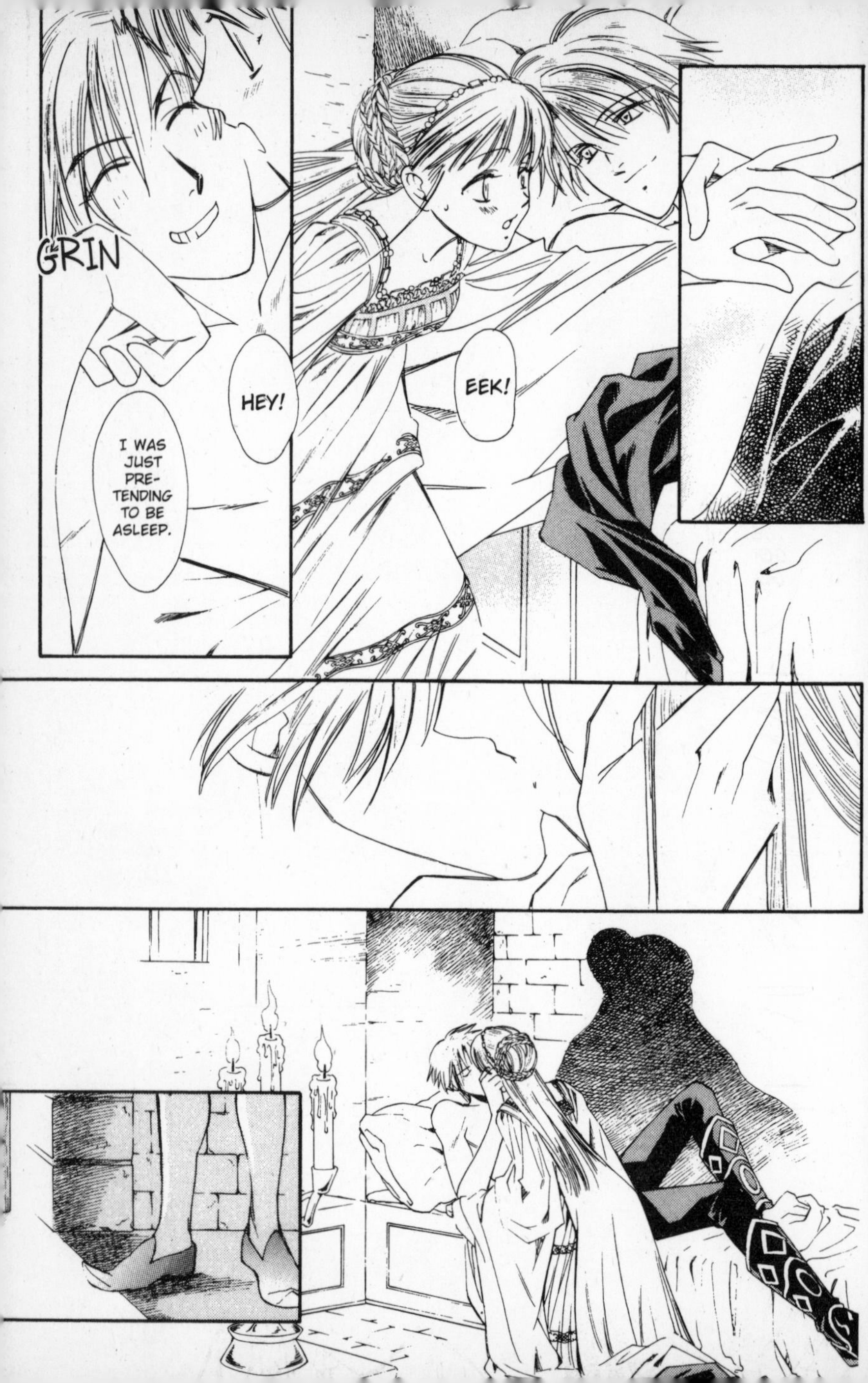
EEK!
HEY!
GRIN
I WAS JUST PRE-TENDING TO BE ASLEEP.

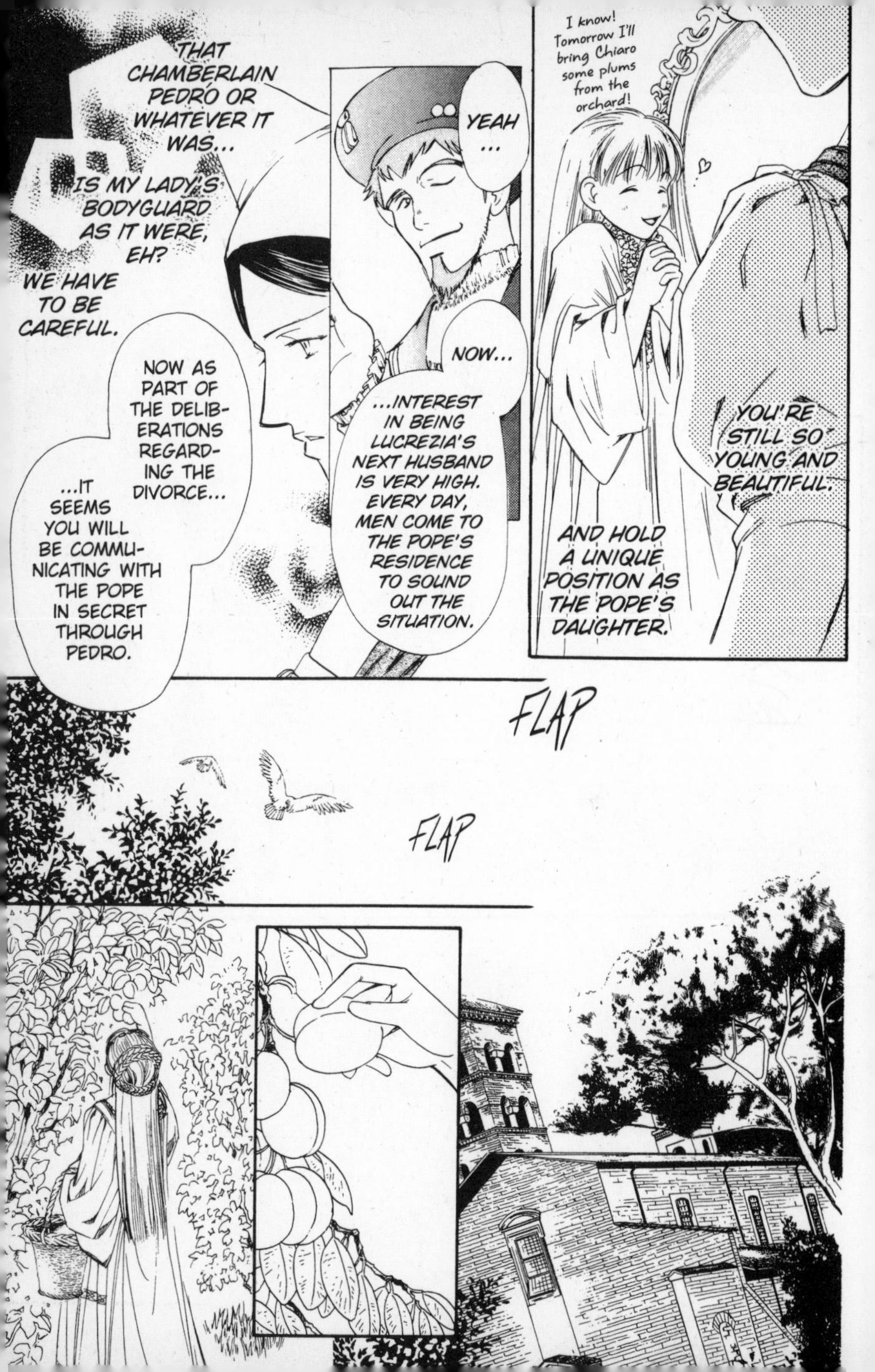
I know! Tomorrow I'll bring Chiaro some plums from the orchard!
YOU'RE STILL SO YOUNG AND BEAUTIFUL.
AND HOLD A UNIQUE POSITION AS THE POPE'S DAUGHTER.
YEAH ...
NOW...
...INTEREST IN BEING LUCREZIA'S NEXT HUSBAND IS VERY HIGH. EVERY DAY, MEN COME TO THE POPE'S RESIDENCE TO SOUND OUT THE SITUATION.
THAT CHAMBERLAIN PEDRO OR WHATEVER IT WAS...
IS MY LADY'S BODYGUARD AS IT WERE, EH?
WE HAVE TO BE CAREFUL.
NOW AS PART OF THE DELIB-ERATIONS REGARD-ING THE DIVORCE...
...IT SEEMS YOU WILL BE COMMU-NICATING WITH THE POPE IN SECRET THROUGH PEDRO.
FLAP
FLAP

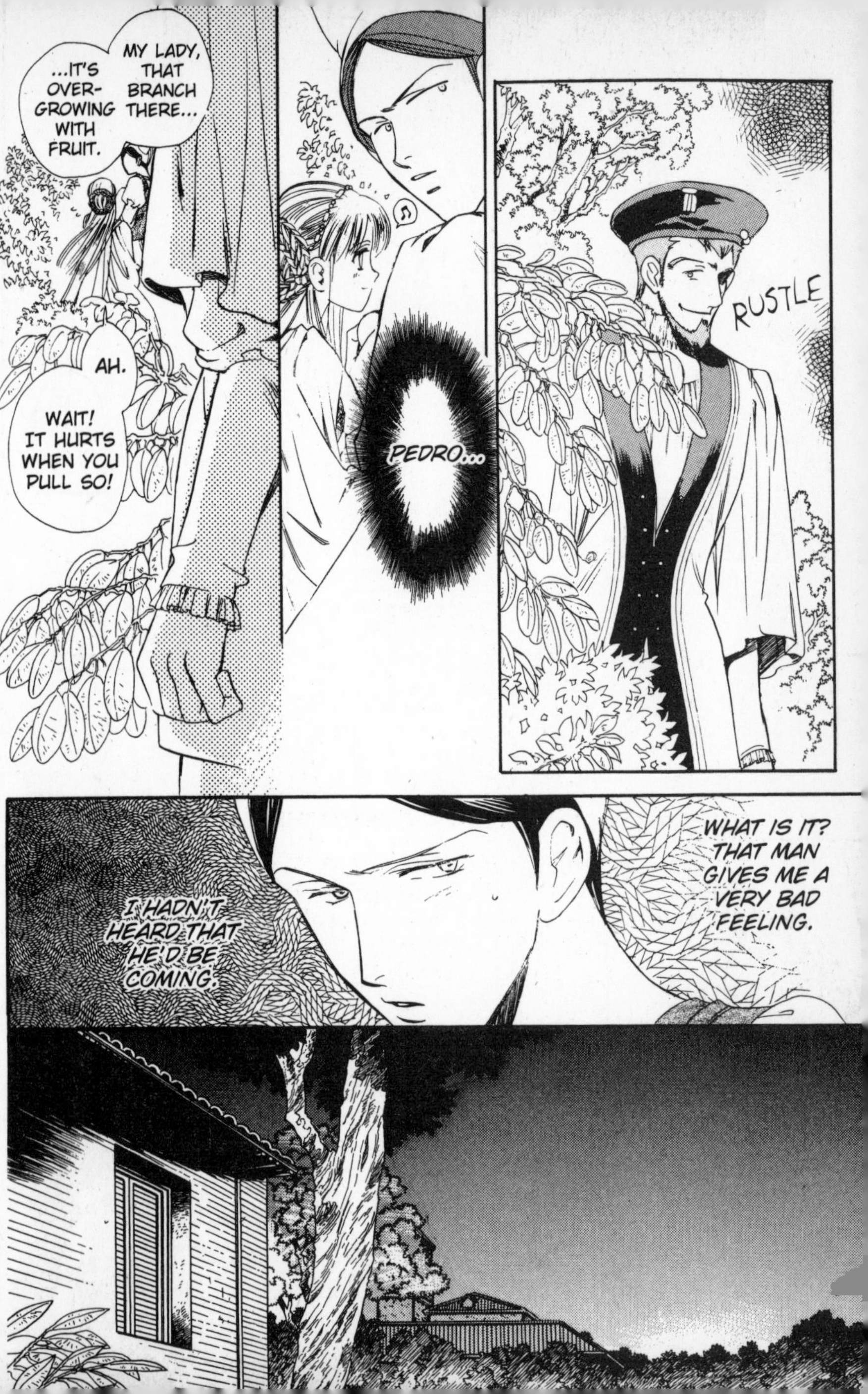
RUSTLE
PEDRO...
MY LADY, THAT BRANCH THERE...
...IT'S OVER-GROWING WITH FRUIT.
AH.
WAIT! IT HURTS WHEN YOU PULL SO!
WHAT IS IT? THAT MAN GIVES ME A VERY BAD FEELING.
I HADN'T HEARD THAT HE'D BE COMING.

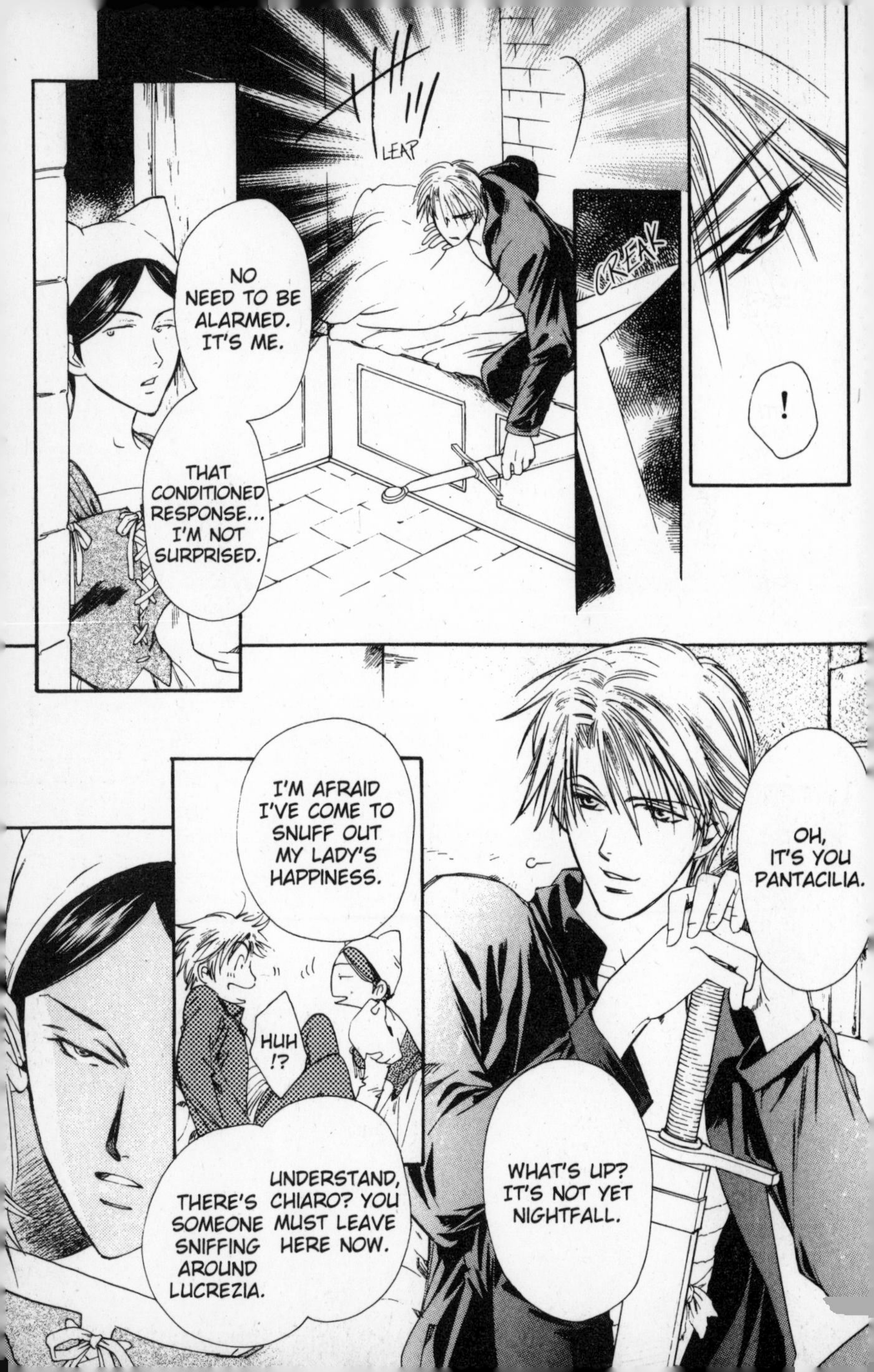
!
LEAP
CREAK
NO NEED TO BE ALARMED. IT'S ME.
THAT CONDITIONED RESPONSE... I'M NOT SURPRISED.
OH, IT'S YOU PANTACILIA.
WHAT'S UP? IT'S NOT YET NIGHTFALL.
I'M AFRAID I'VE COME TO SNUFF OUT MY LADY'S HAPPINESS.
HUH !?
THERE'S SOMEONE SNIFFING AROUND LUCREZIA.
UNDERSTAND, CHIARO? YOU MUST LEAVE HERE NOW.

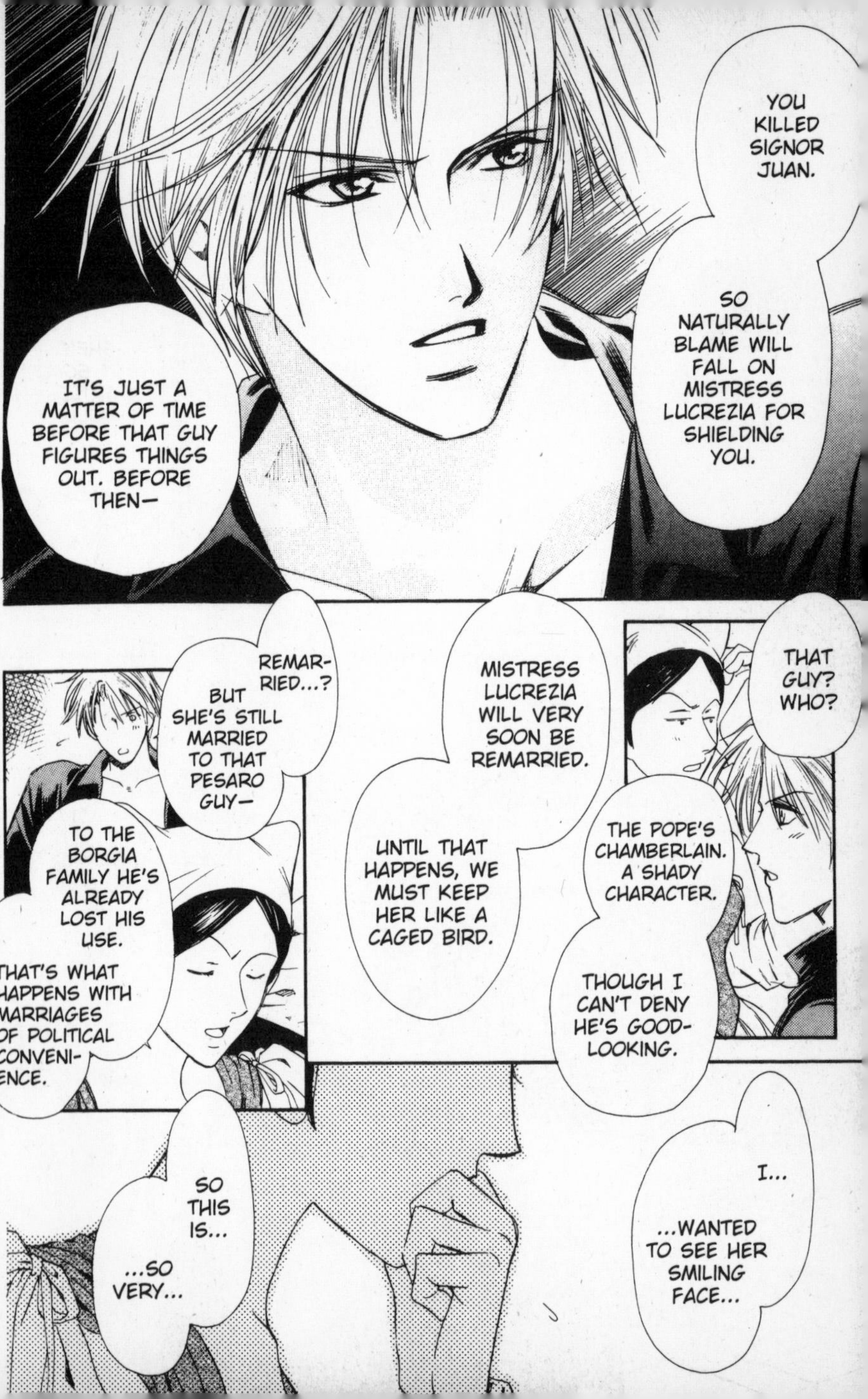
YOU KILLED SIGNOR JUAN.
SO NATURALLY BLAME WILL FALL ON MISTRESS LUCREZIA FOR SHIELDING YOU.
IT'S JUST A MATTER OF TIME BEFORE THAT GUY FIGURES THINGS OUT. BEFORE THEN—
THAT GUY? WHO?
THE POPE'S CHAMBERLAIN. A SHADY CHARACTER.
THOUGH I CAN'T DENY HE'S GOOD-LOOKING.
MISTRESS LUCREZIA WILL VERY SOON BE REMARRIED.
UNTIL THAT HAPPENS, WE MUST KEEP HER LIKE A CAGED BIRD.
REMARRIED...? BUT SHE'S STILL MARRIED TO THAT PESARO GUY—
TO THE BORGIA FAMILY HE'S ALREADY LOST HIS USE.
THAT'S WHAT HAPPENS WITH MARRIAGES OF POLITICAL CONVENIENCE.
I...
...WANTED TO SEE HER SMILING FACE...
SO THIS IS...
...SO VERY...

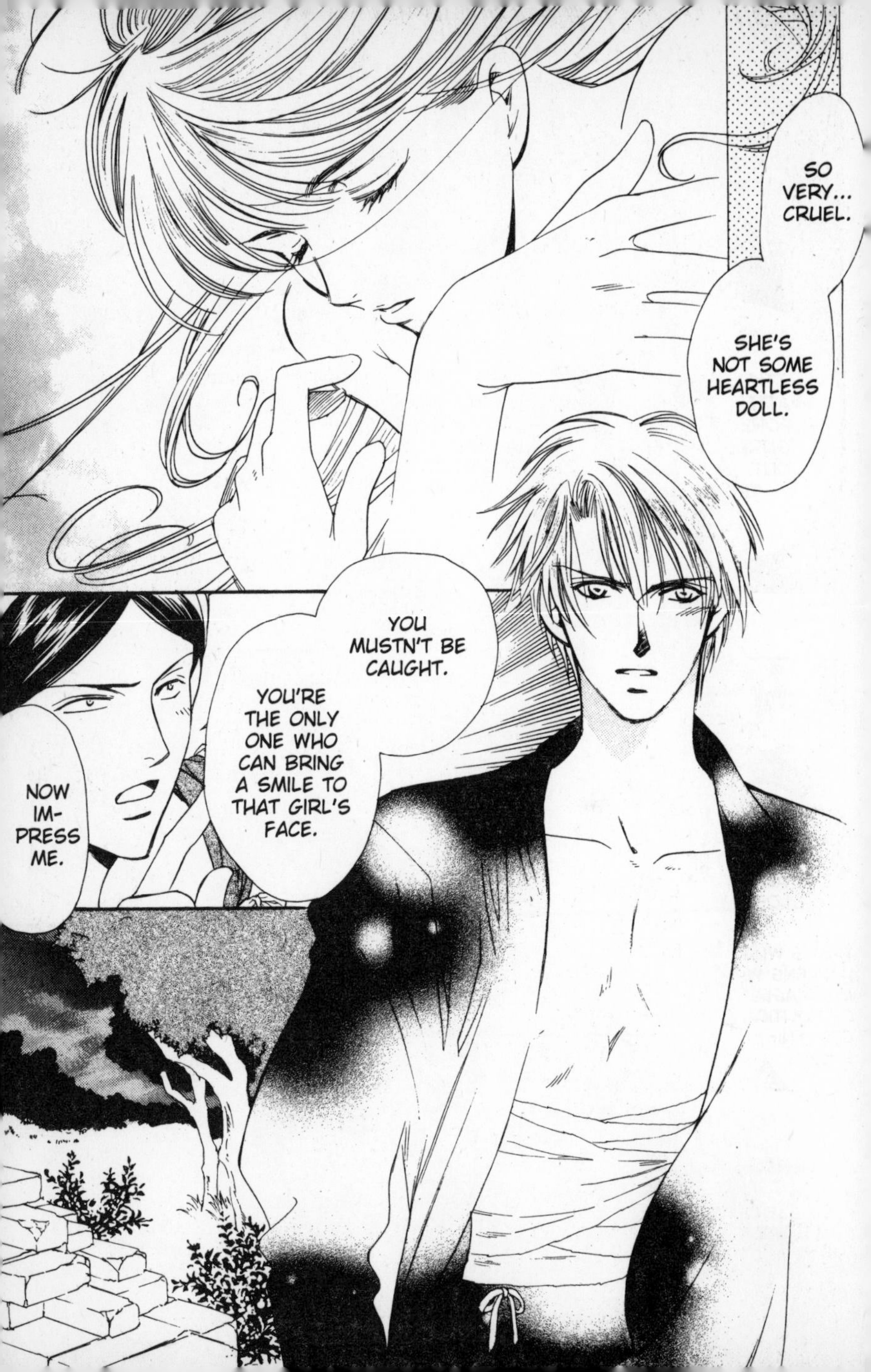
SO VERY... CRUEL.
SHE'S NOT SOME HEARTLESS DOLL.
YOU MUSTN'T BE CAUGHT.
YOU'RE THE ONLY ONE WHO CAN BRING A SMILE TO THAT GIRL'S FACE.
NOW IM-PRESS ME.

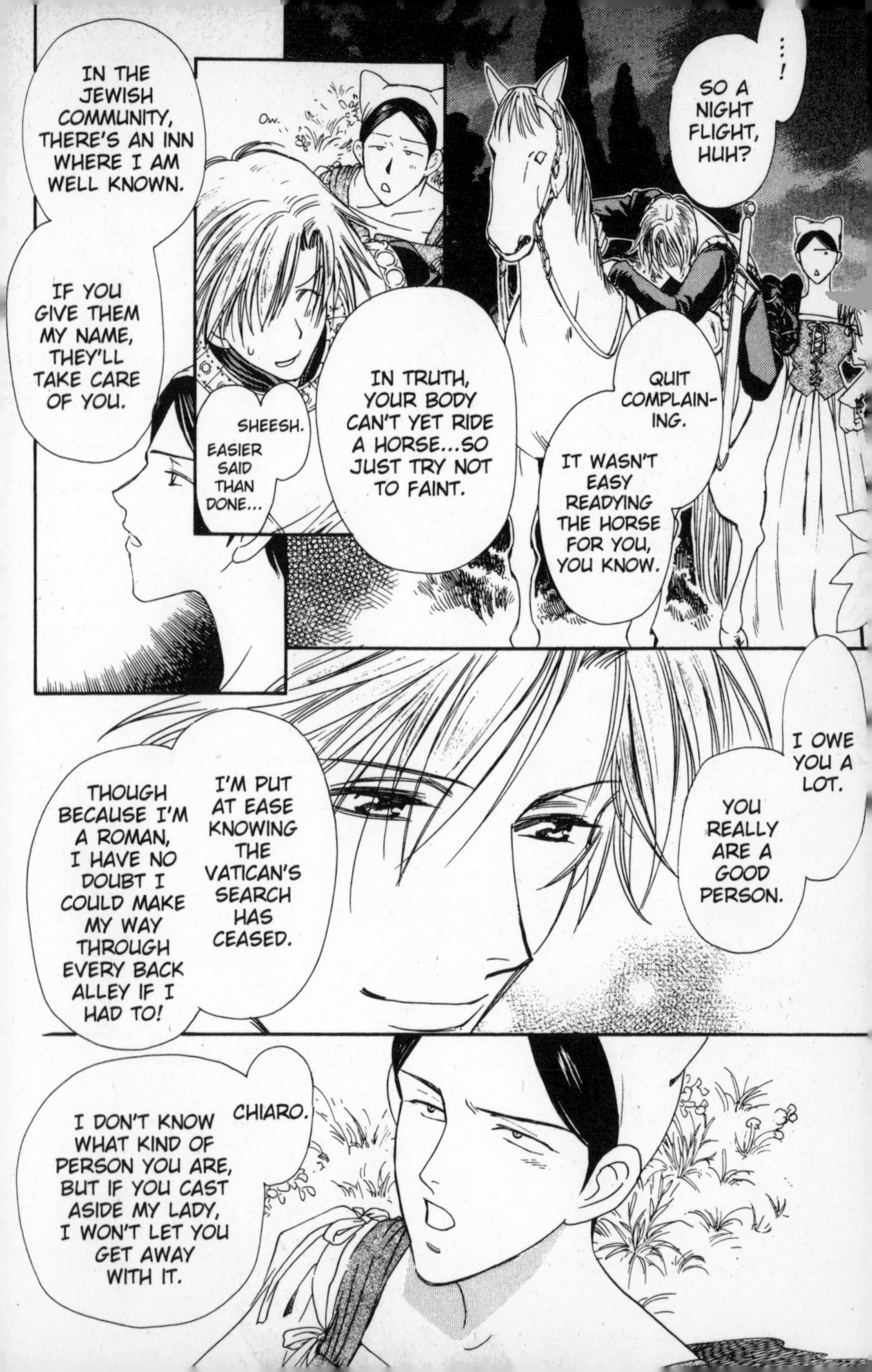
...!
SO A NIGHT FLIGHT, HUH?
QUIT COMPLAINING.
IT WASN'T EASY READYING THE HORSE FOR YOU, YOU KNOW.
IN TRUTH, YOUR BODY CAN'T YET RIDE A HORSE...SO JUST TRY NOT TO FAINT.
Ow.
SHEESH.
EASIER SAID THAN DONE...
IN THE JEWISH COMMUNITY, THERE'S AN INN WHERE I AM WELL KNOWN.
IF YOU GIVE THEM MY NAME, THEY'LL TAKE CARE OF YOU.
I OWE YOU A LOT.
YOU REALLY ARE A GOOD PERSON.
I'M PUT AT EASE KNOWING THE VATICAN'S SEARCH HAS CEASED.
THOUGH BECAUSE I'M A ROMAN, I HAVE NO DOUBT I COULD MAKE MY WAY THROUGH EVERY BACK ALLEY IF I HAD TO!
CHIARO.
I DON'T KNOW WHAT KIND OF PERSON YOU ARE, BUT IF YOU CAST ASIDE MY LADY, I WON'T LET YOU GET AWAY WITH IT.

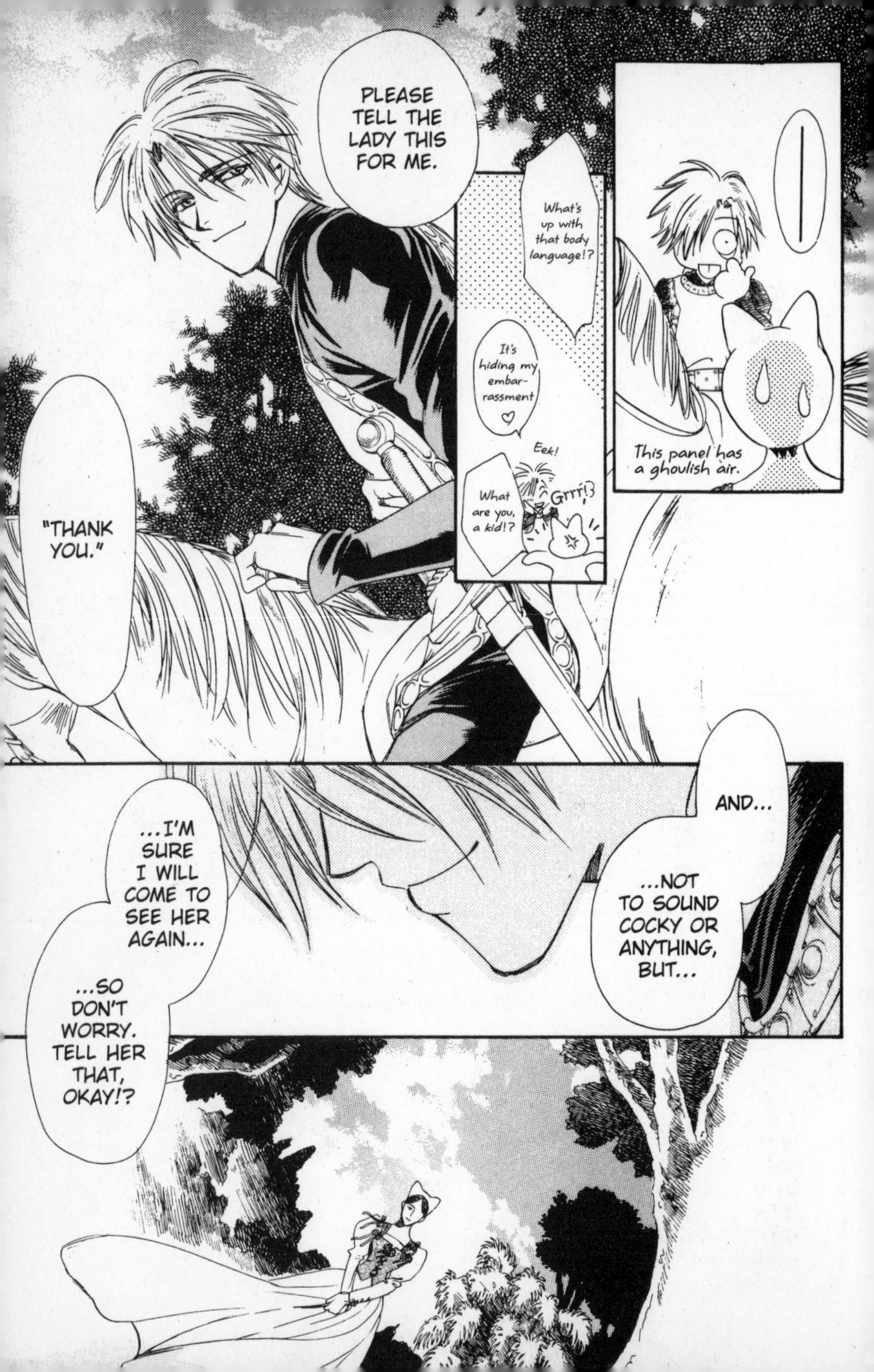
PLEASE TELL THE LADY THIS FOR ME.
"THANK YOU."
!
This panel has a ghoulish air.
What's up with that body language!?
It's hiding my embarrassment ♡
Eek!
Grrr!
What are you, a kid!?
AND...
...NOT TO SOUND COCKY OR ANYTHING, BUT...
...I'M SURE I WILL COME TO SEE HER AGAIN...
...SO DON'T WORRY. TELL HER THAT, OKAY!?

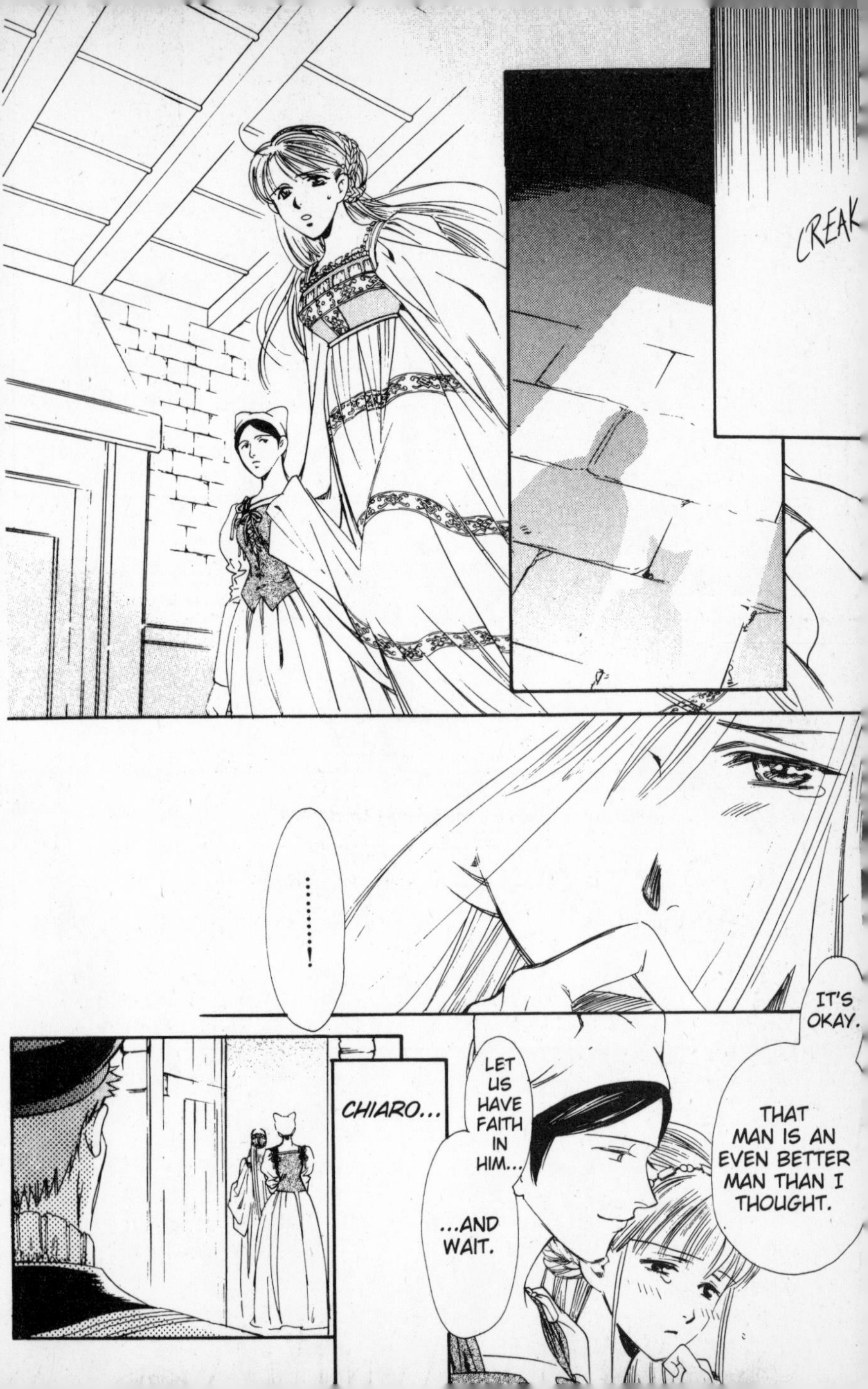
CREAK
......!
IT'S OKAY.
THAT MAN IS AN EVEN BETTER MAN THAN I THOUGHT.
LET US HAVE FAITH IN HIM...
...AND WAIT.
CHIARO...

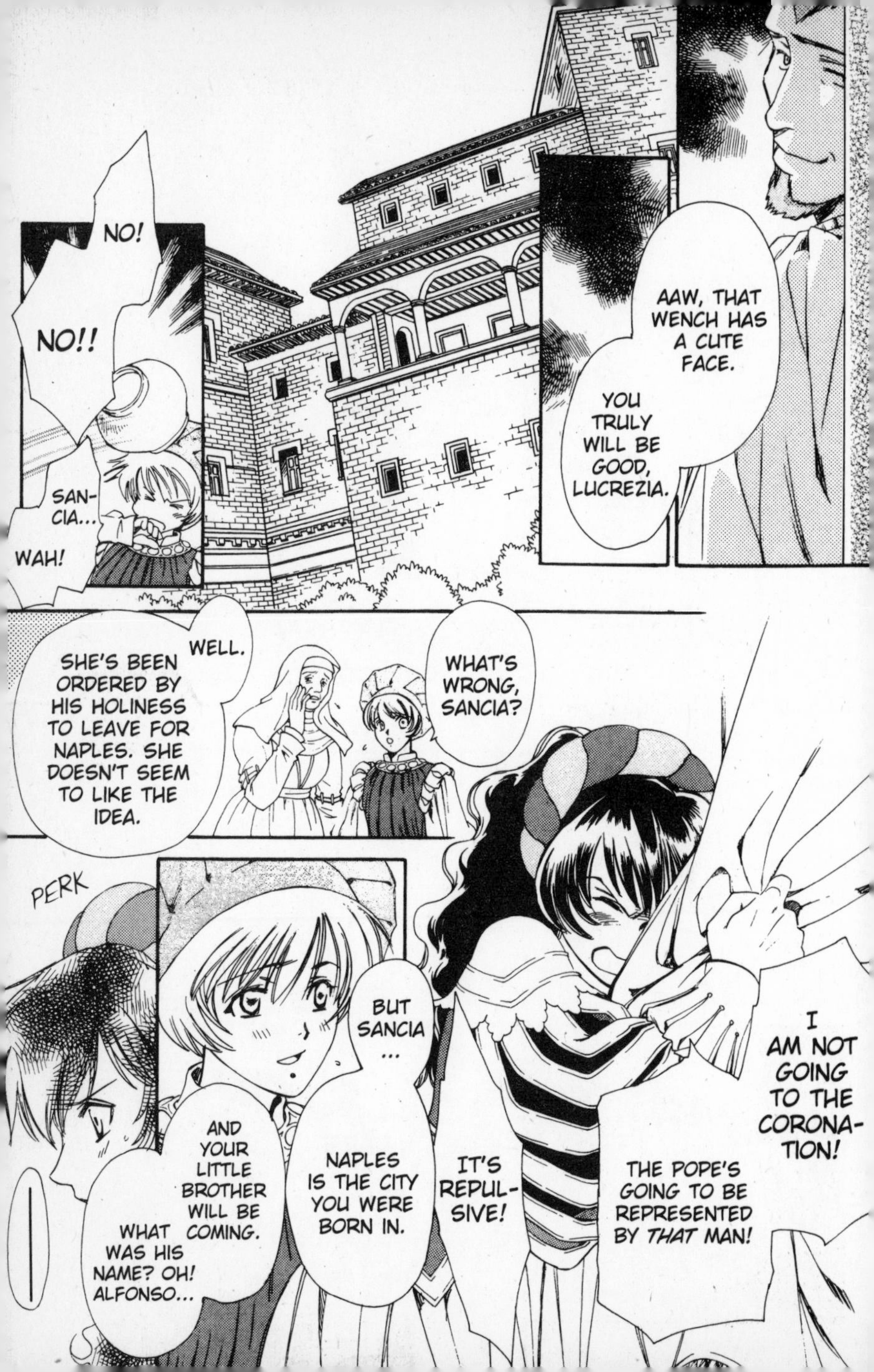
AAW, THAT WENCH HAS A CUTE FACE.
YOU TRULY WILL BE GOOD, LUCREZIA.
NO!
NO!!
SAN-CIA...
WAH!
WHAT'S WRONG, SANCIA?
WELL.
SHE'S BEEN ORDERED BY HIS HOLINESS TO LEAVE FOR NAPLES. SHE DOESN'T SEEM TO LIKE THE IDEA.
I AM NOT GOING TO THE CORONA-TION!
THE POPE'S GOING TO BE REPRESENTED BY *THAT* MAN!
IT'S REPUL-SIVE!
BUT SANCIA ...
NAPLES IS THE CITY YOU WERE BORN IN.
AND YOUR LITTLE BROTHER WILL BE COMING.
WHAT WAS HIS NAME? OH! ALFONSO...
PERK
!

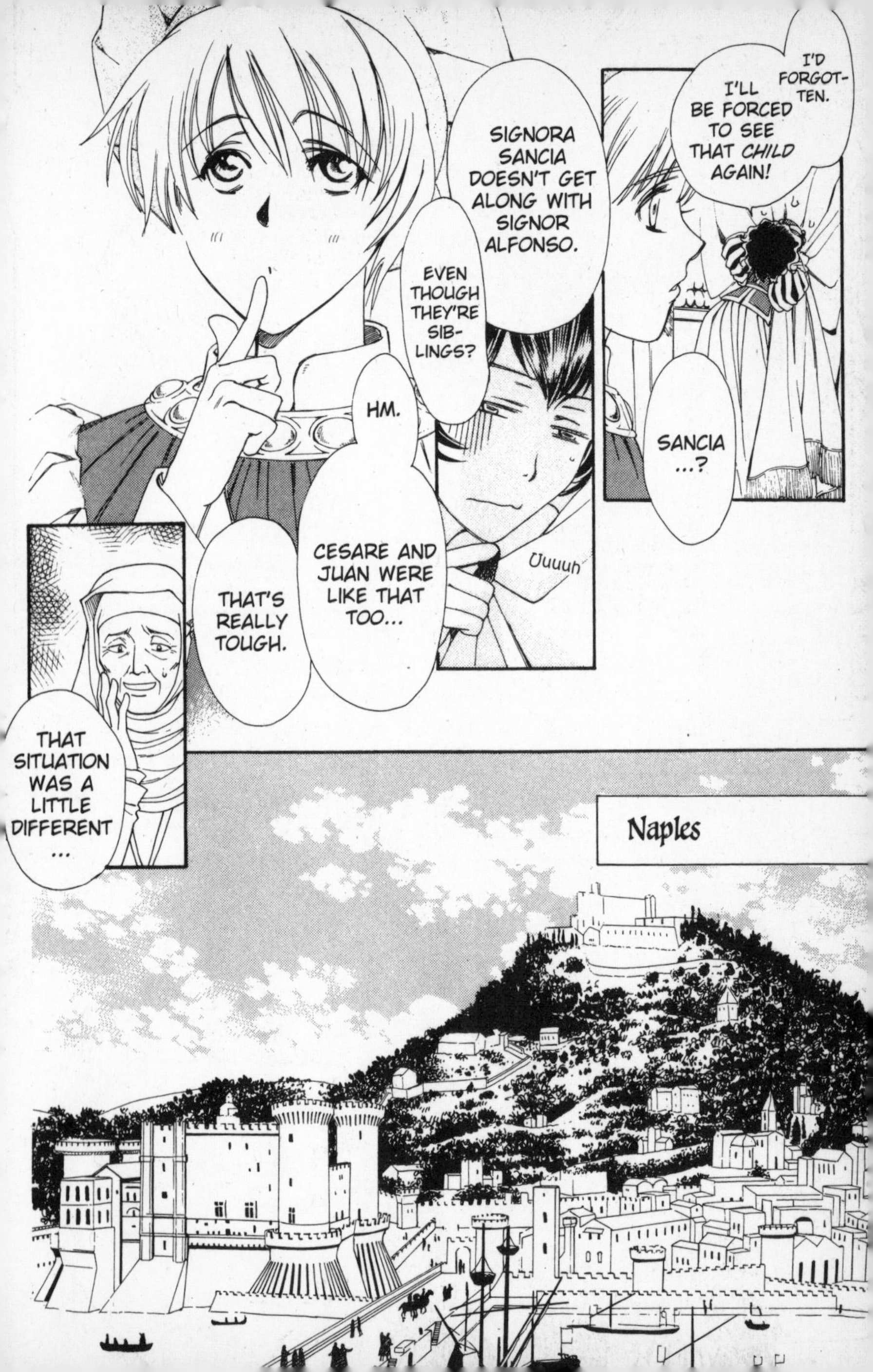
I'D FORGOT-TEN.
I'LL BE FORCED TO SEE THAT *CHILD* AGAIN!
SANCIA ...?
SIGNORA SANCIA DOESN'T GET ALONG WITH SIGNOR ALFONSO.
EVEN THOUGH THEY'RE SIB-LINGS?
HM.
CESARE AND JUAN WERE LIKE THAT TOO...
Uuuuh
THAT'S REALLY TOUGH.
THAT SITUATION WAS A LITTLE DIFFERENT ...
Naples

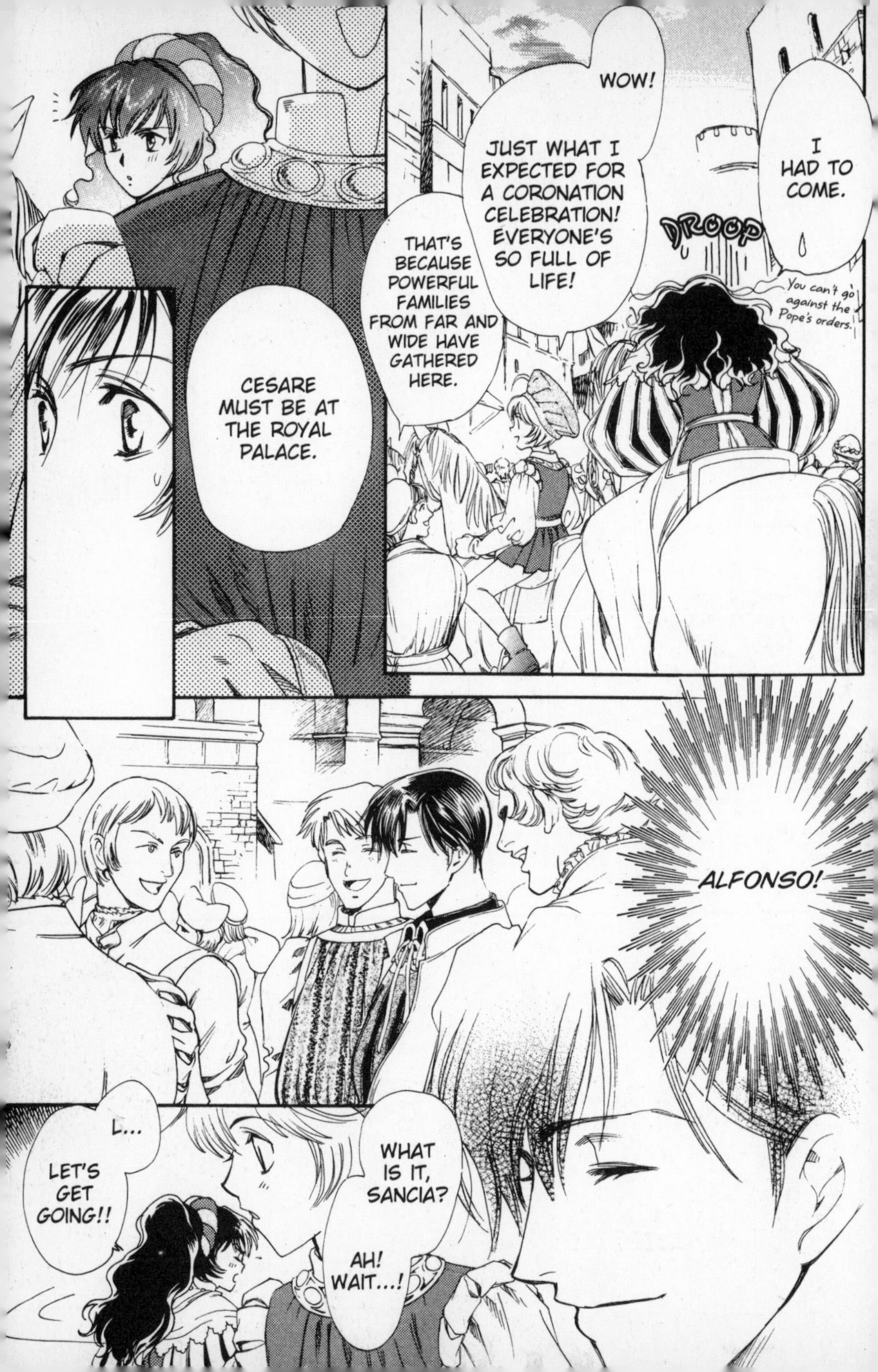
I HAD TO COME.
DROOP
You can't go against the Pope's orders.
WOW!
JUST WHAT I EXPECTED FOR A CORONATION CELEBRATION! EVERYONE'S SO FULL OF LIFE!
THAT'S BECAUSE POWERFUL FAMILIES FROM FAR AND WIDE HAVE GATHERED HERE.
CESARE MUST BE AT THE ROYAL PALACE.
ALFONSO!
WHAT IS IT, SANCIA?
L...
LET'S GET GOING!!
AH! WAIT...!

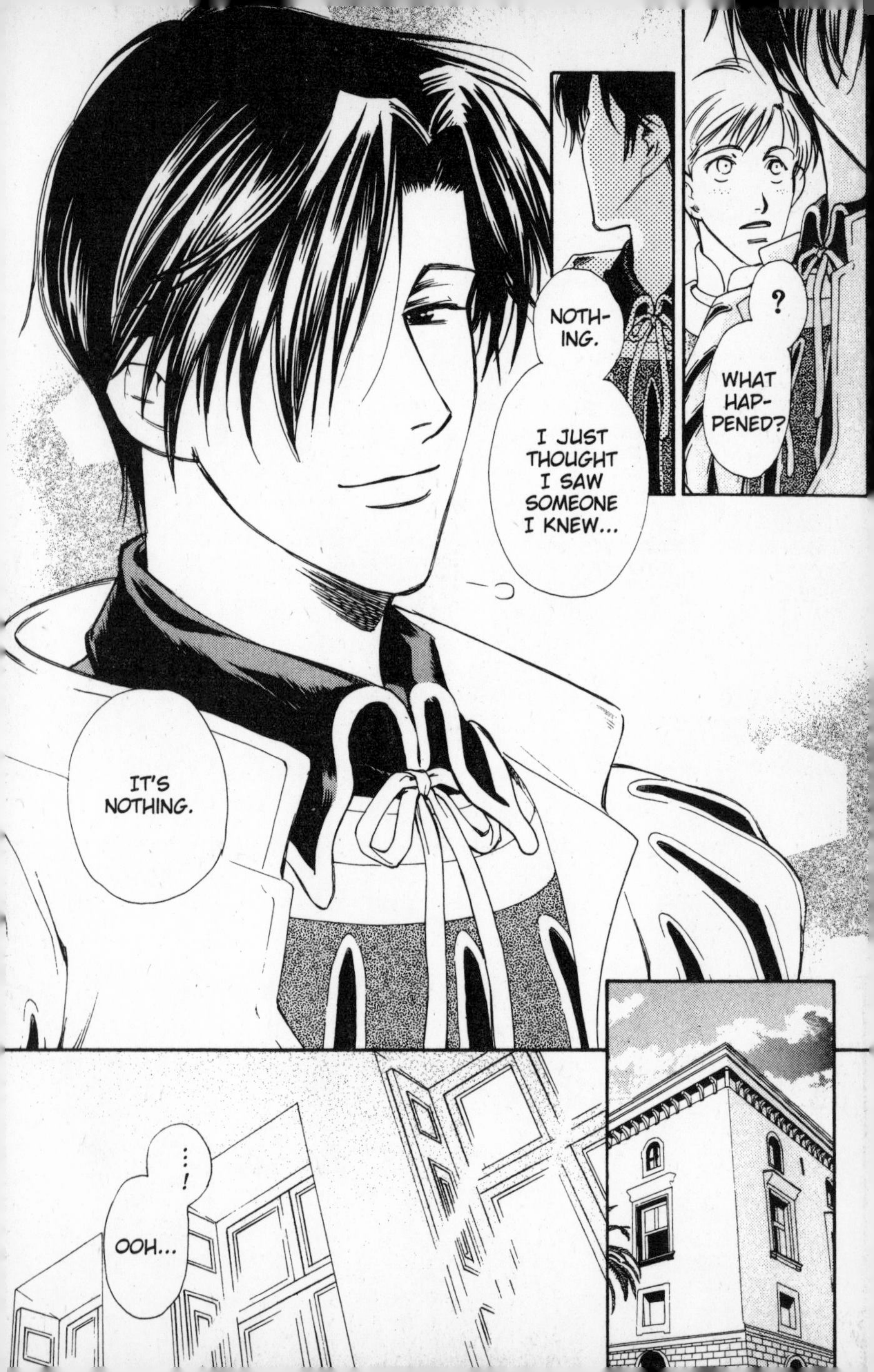
?
WHAT HAP-PENED?
NOTH-ING.
I JUST THOUGHT I SAW SOMEONE I KNEW...
IT'S NOTHING.
...!
OOH...

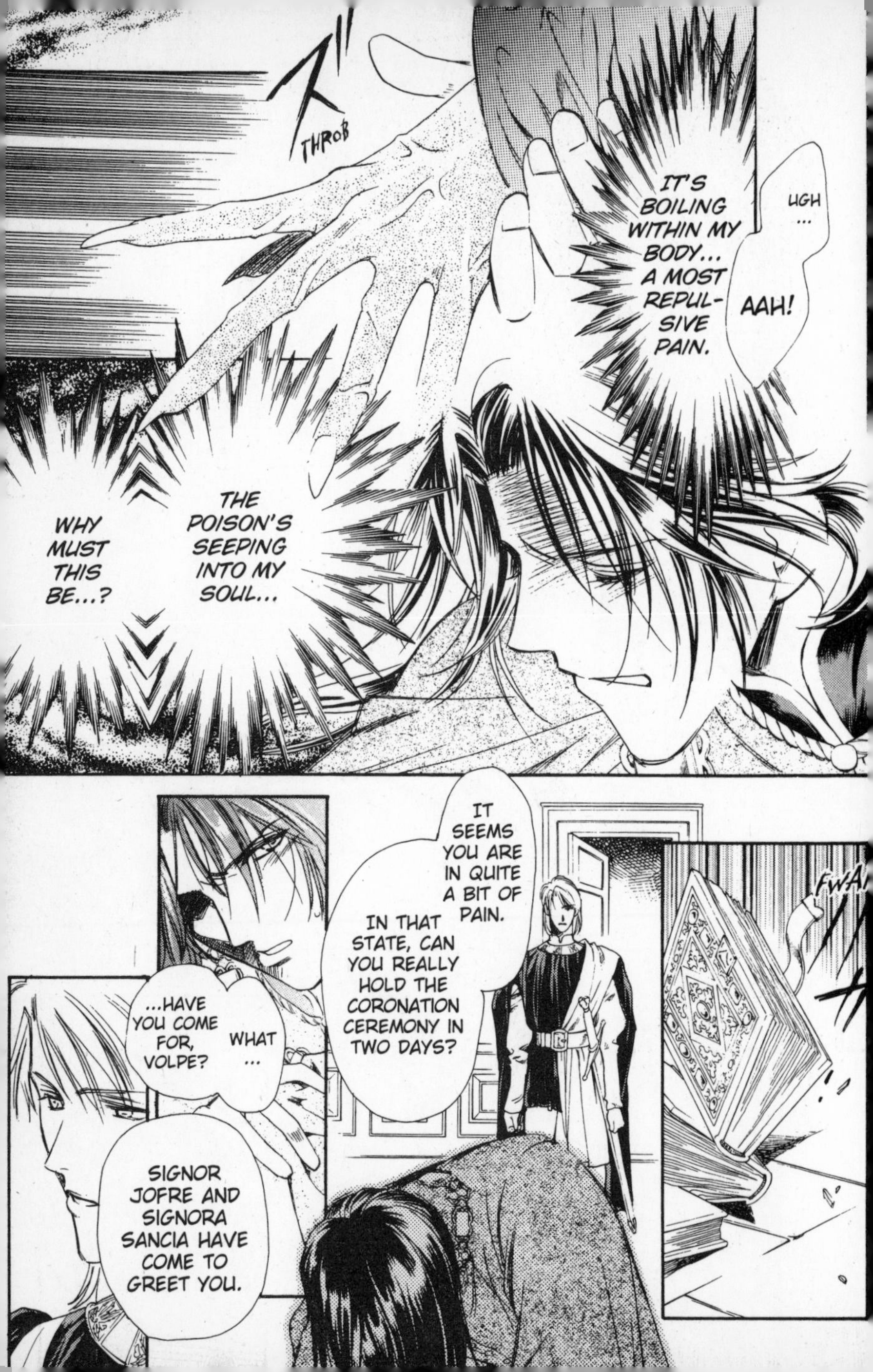
THROB
UGH... AAH!
IT'S BOILING WITHIN MY BODY... A MOST REPULSIVE PAIN.
THE POISON'S SEEPING INTO MY SOUL...
WHY MUST THIS BE...?
IT SEEMS YOU ARE IN QUITE A BIT OF PAIN.
IN THAT STATE, CAN YOU REALLY HOLD THE CORONATION CEREMONY IN TWO DAYS?
WHAT...
...HAVE YOU COME FOR, VOLPE?
SIGNOR JOFRE AND SIGNORA SANCIA HAVE COME TO GREET YOU.

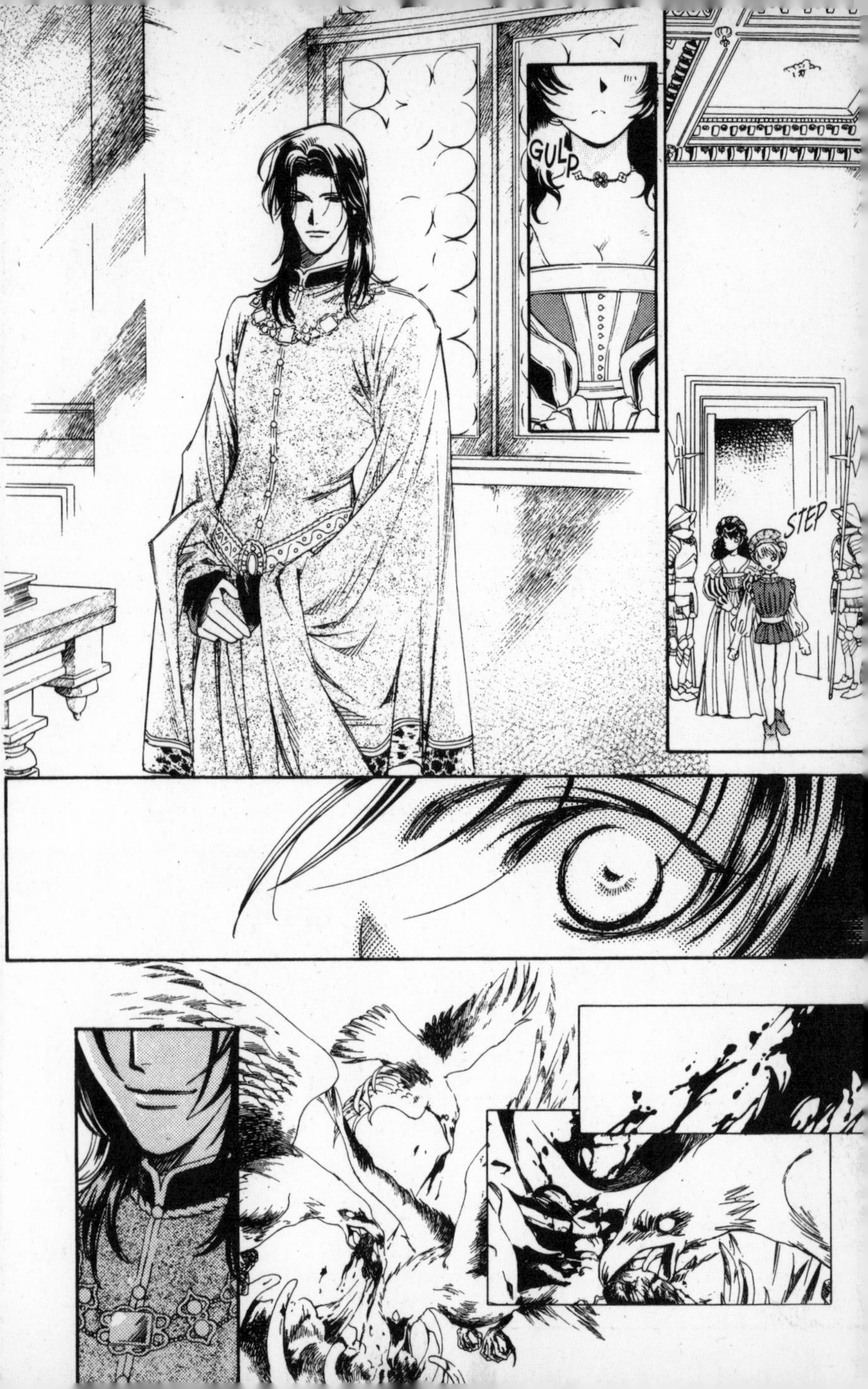
STEP
GULP

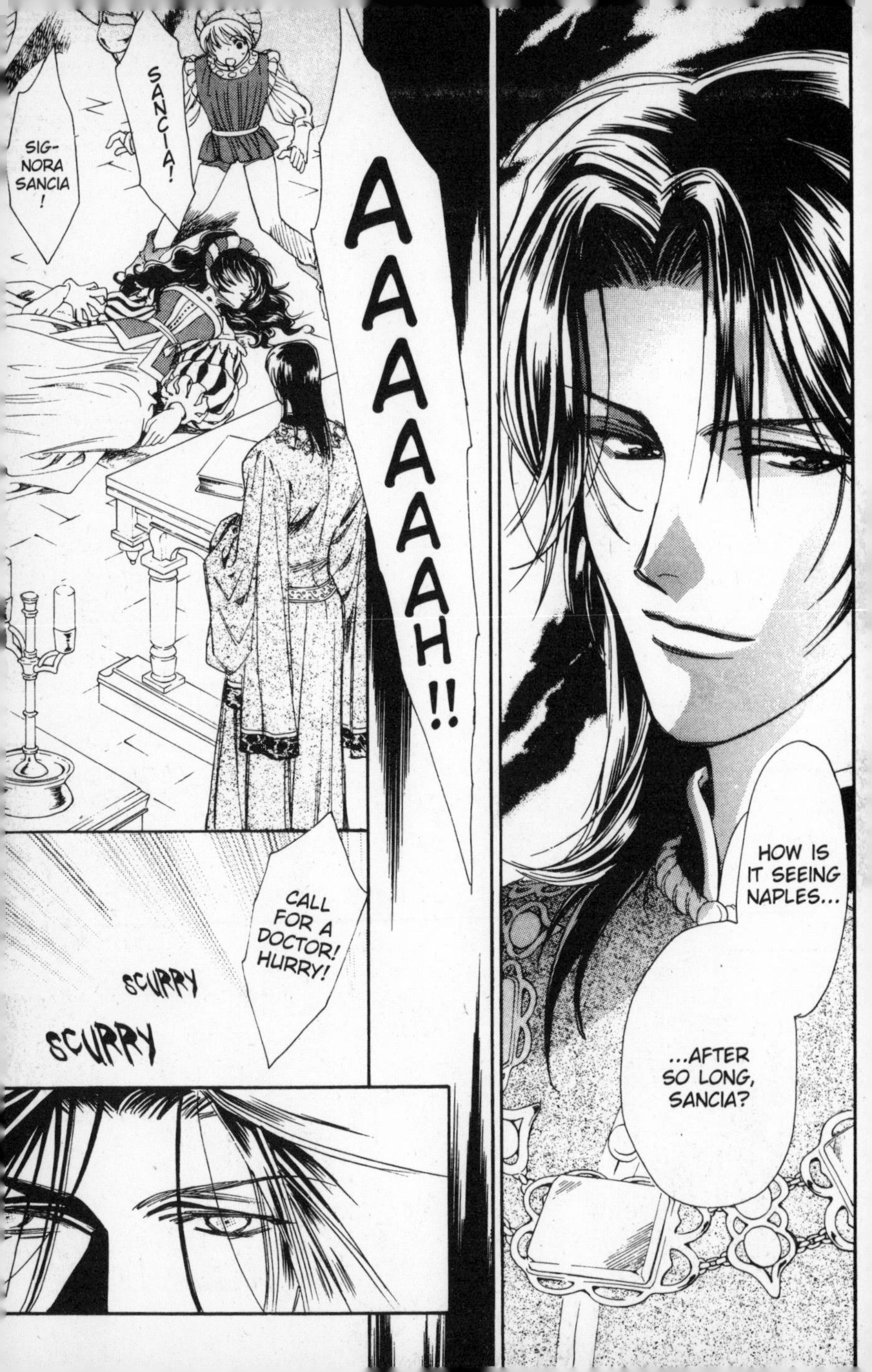
HOW IS IT SEEING NAPLES...
...AFTER SO LONG, SANCIA?
AAAAAAH!!
SANCIA!
SIG-NORA SANCIA!
CALL FOR A DOCTOR! HURRY!
SCURRY
SCURRY

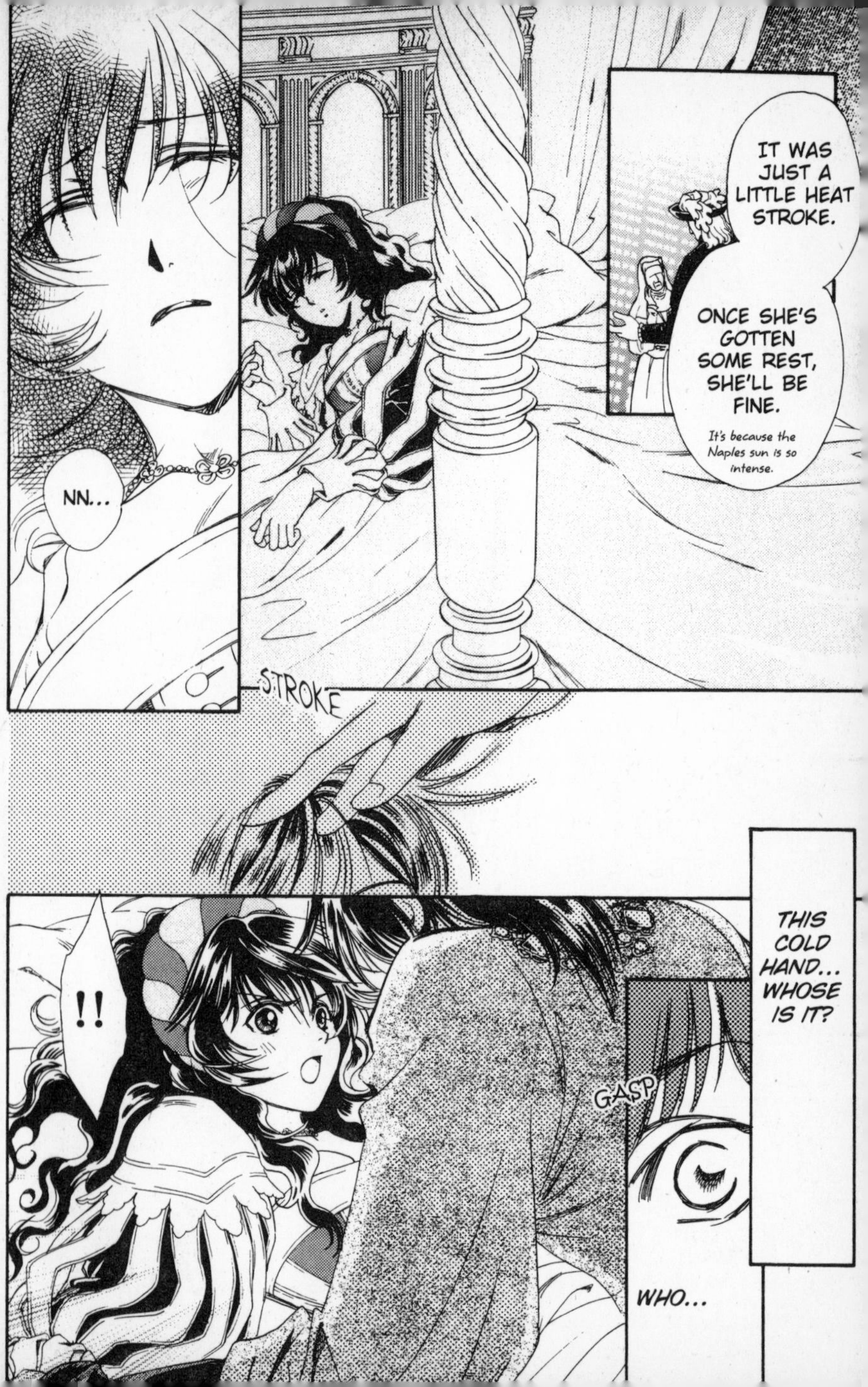
IT WAS JUST A LITTLE HEAT STROKE.
ONCE SHE'S GOTTEN SOME REST, SHE'LL BE FINE.
It's because the Naples sun is so intense.
NN...
STROKE
THIS COLD HAND... WHOSE IS IT?
!!
GASP
WHO...

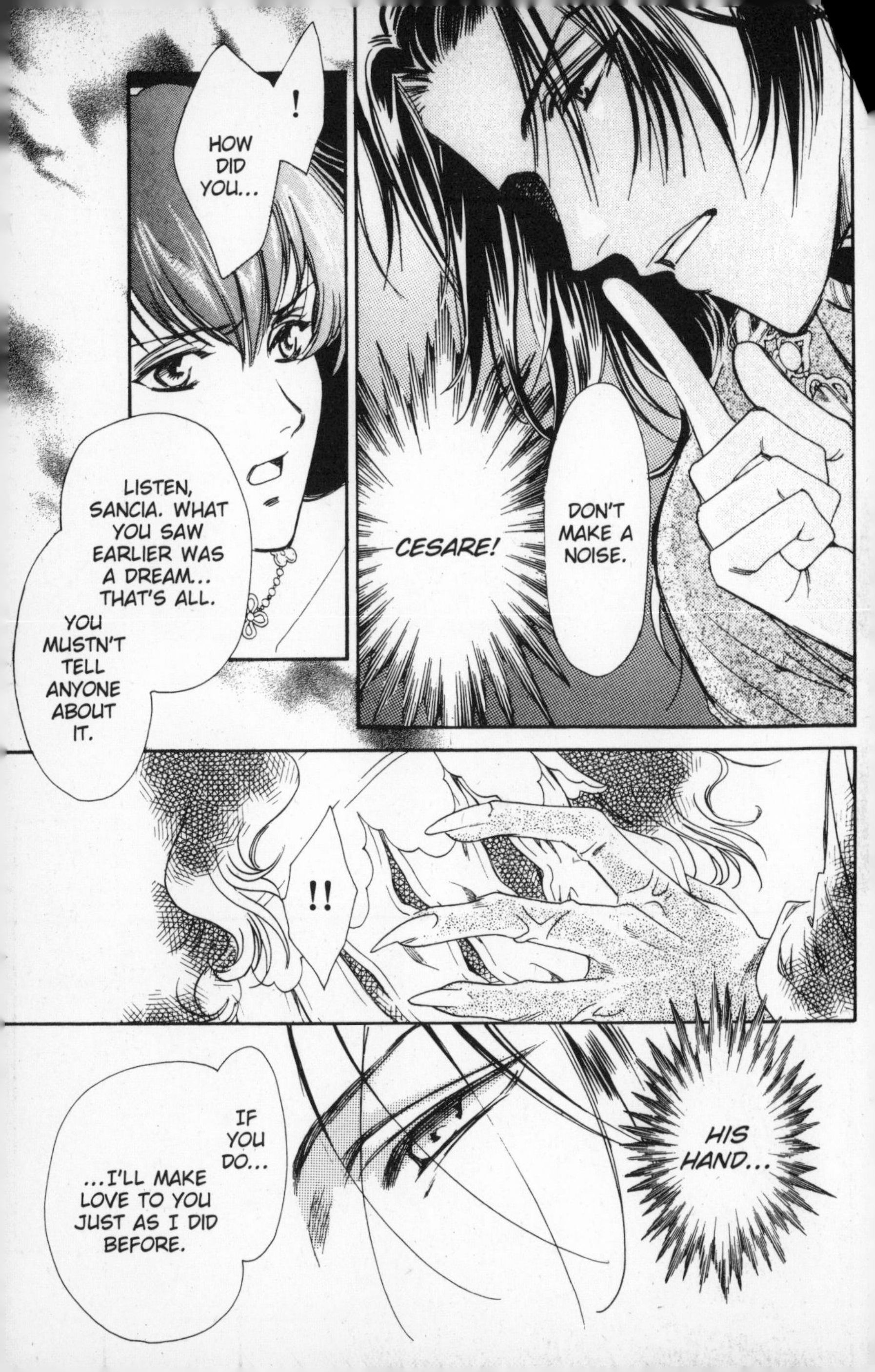

DON'T MAKE A NOISE.
CESARE!
!
HOW DID YOU...
LISTEN, SANCIA. WHAT YOU SAW EARLIER WAS A DREAM... THAT'S ALL.
YOU MUSTN'T TELL ANYONE ABOUT IT.
!!
HIS HAND...
IF YOU DO...
...I'LL MAKE LOVE TO YOU JUST AS I DID BEFORE.

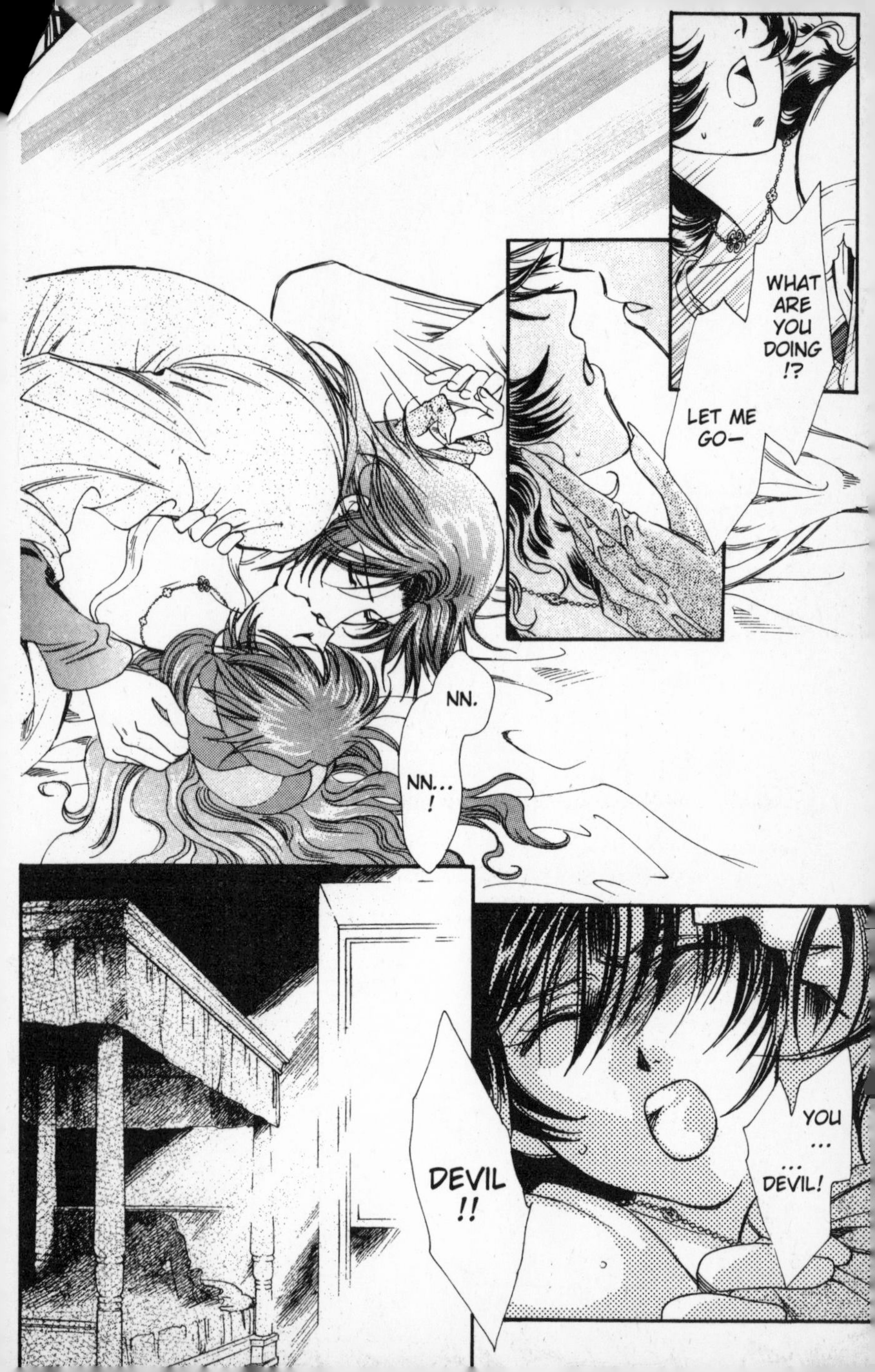
WHAT ARE YOU DOING !?
LET ME GO—
NN.
NN... !
YOU ... ... DEVIL!
DEVIL !!

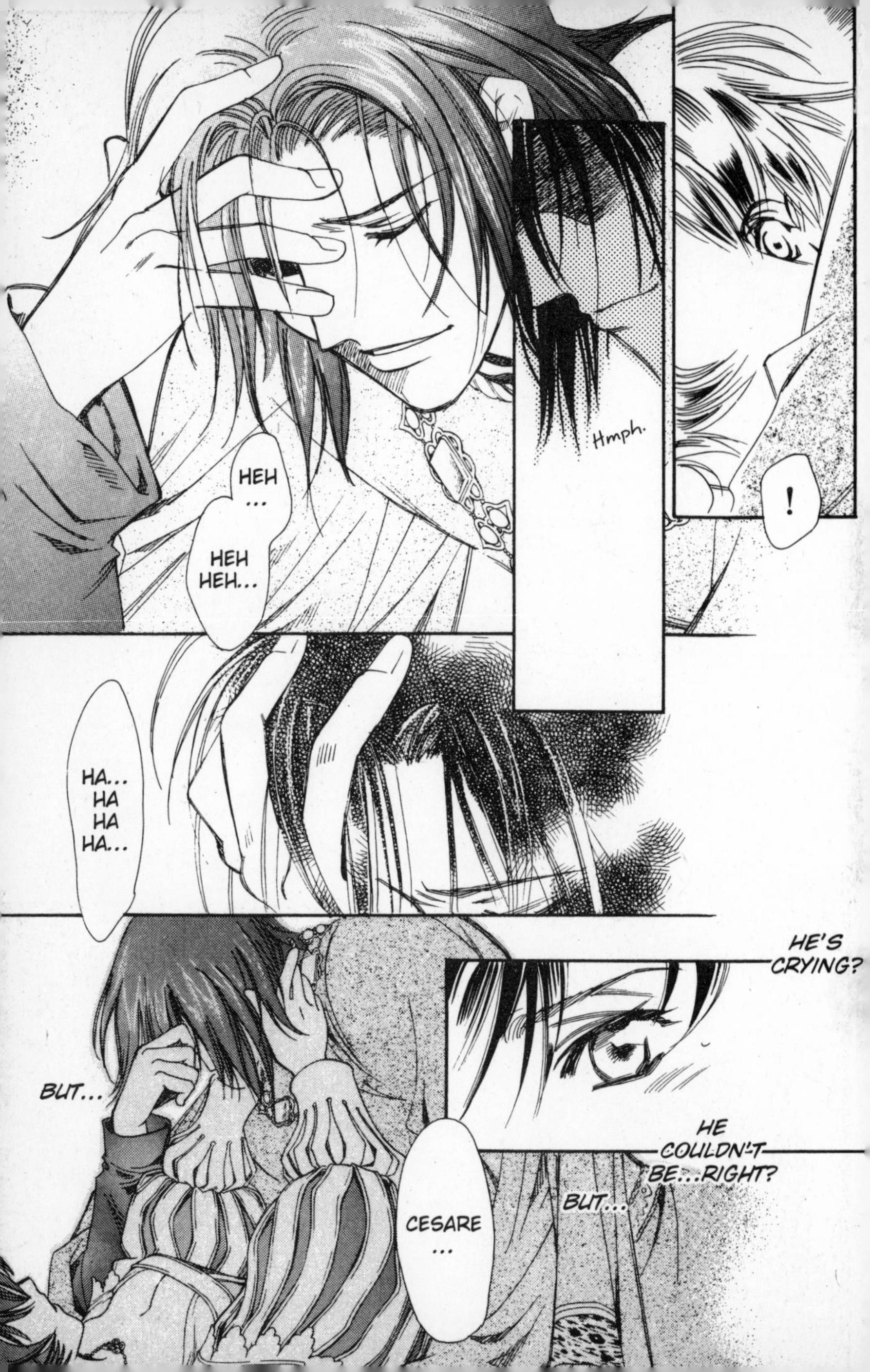
!
Hmph.
HEH ... HEH HEH...
HA... HA HA HA...
HE'S CRYING?
HE COULDN'T BE...RIGHT?
BUT...
CESARE ...
BUT...

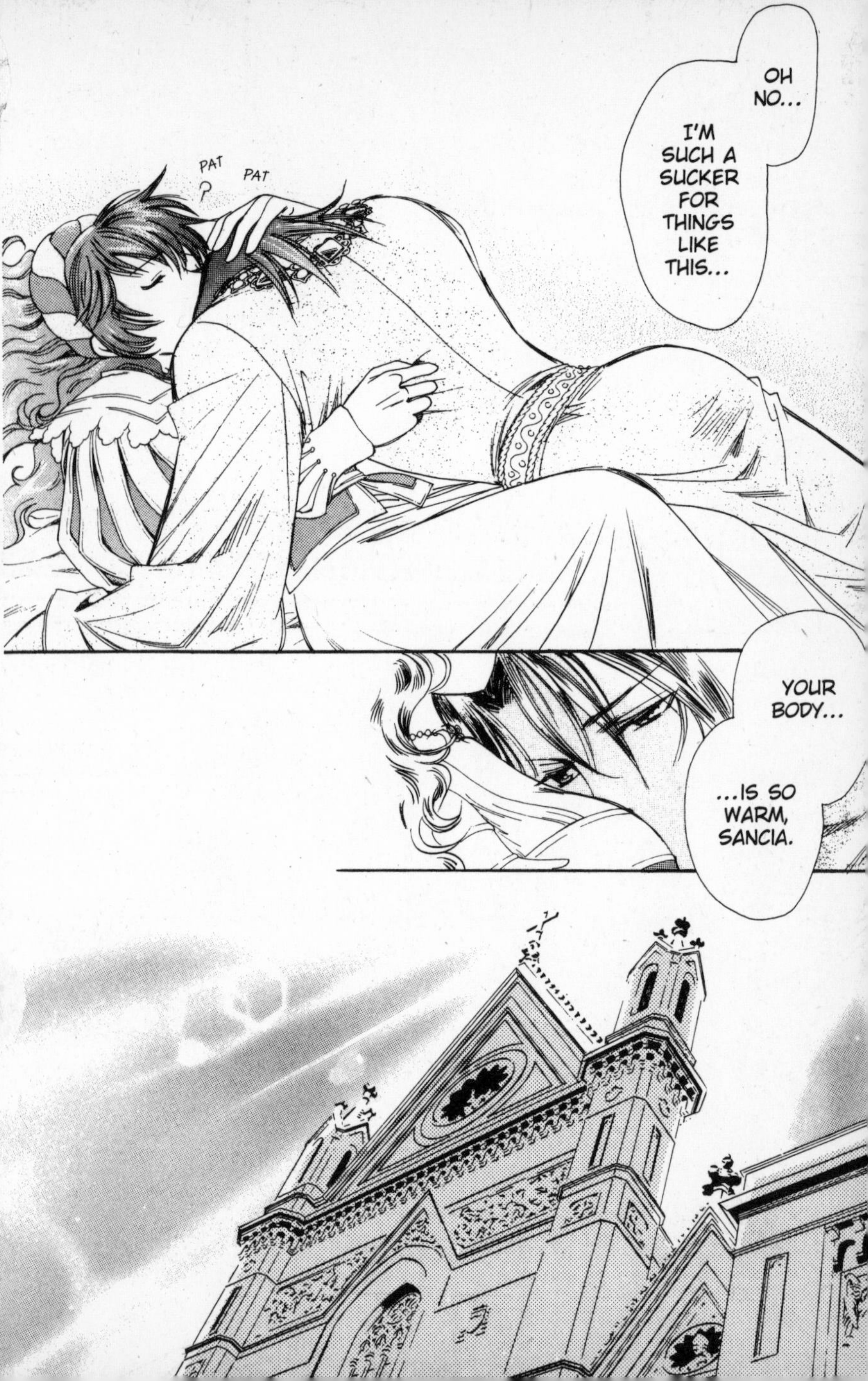
OH NO...
I'M SUCH A SUCKER FOR THINGS LIKE THIS...
PAT PAT
?
YOUR BODY...
...IS SO WARM, SANCIA.

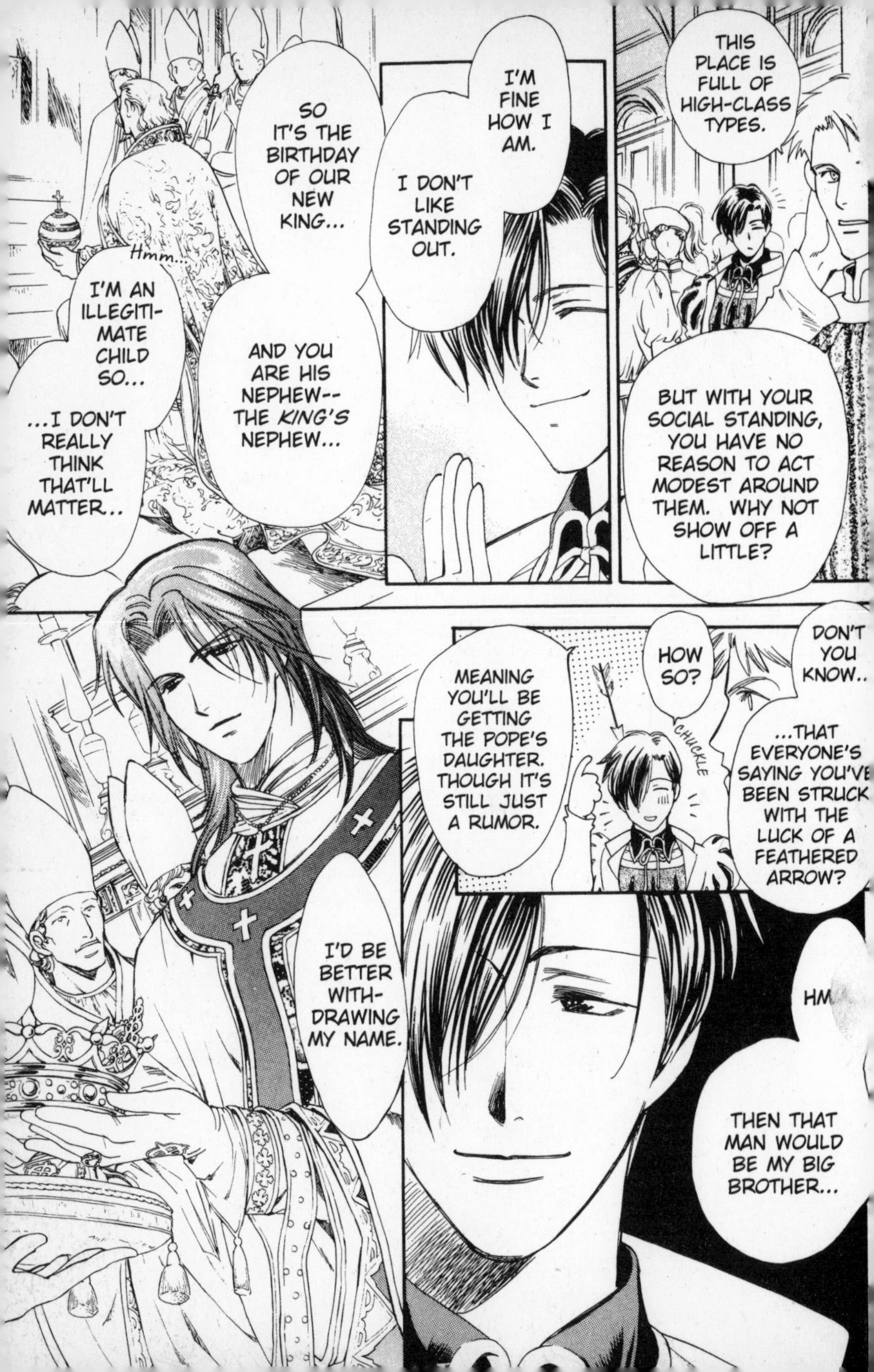
THIS PLACE IS FULL OF HIGH-CLASS TYPES.
BUT WITH YOUR SOCIAL STANDING, YOU HAVE NO REASON TO ACT MODEST AROUND THEM. WHY NOT SHOW OFF A LITTLE?
I'M FINE HOW I AM.
I DON'T LIKE STANDING OUT.
DON'T YOU KNOW..
...THAT EVERYONE'S SAYING YOU'VE BEEN STRUCK WITH THE LUCK OF A FEATHERED ARROW?
HOW SO?
CHUCKLE
MEANING YOU'LL BE GETTING THE POPE'S DAUGHTER. THOUGH IT'S STILL JUST A RUMOR.
HM
THEN THAT MAN WOULD BE MY BIG BROTHER...
SO IT'S THE BIRTHDAY OF OUR NEW KING...
AND YOU ARE HIS NEPHEW-- THE KING'S NEPHEW...
Hmm...
I'M AN ILLEGITI-MATE CHILD SO...
...I DON'T REALLY THINK THAT'LL MATTER...
I'D BE BETTER WITH-DRAWING MY NAME.

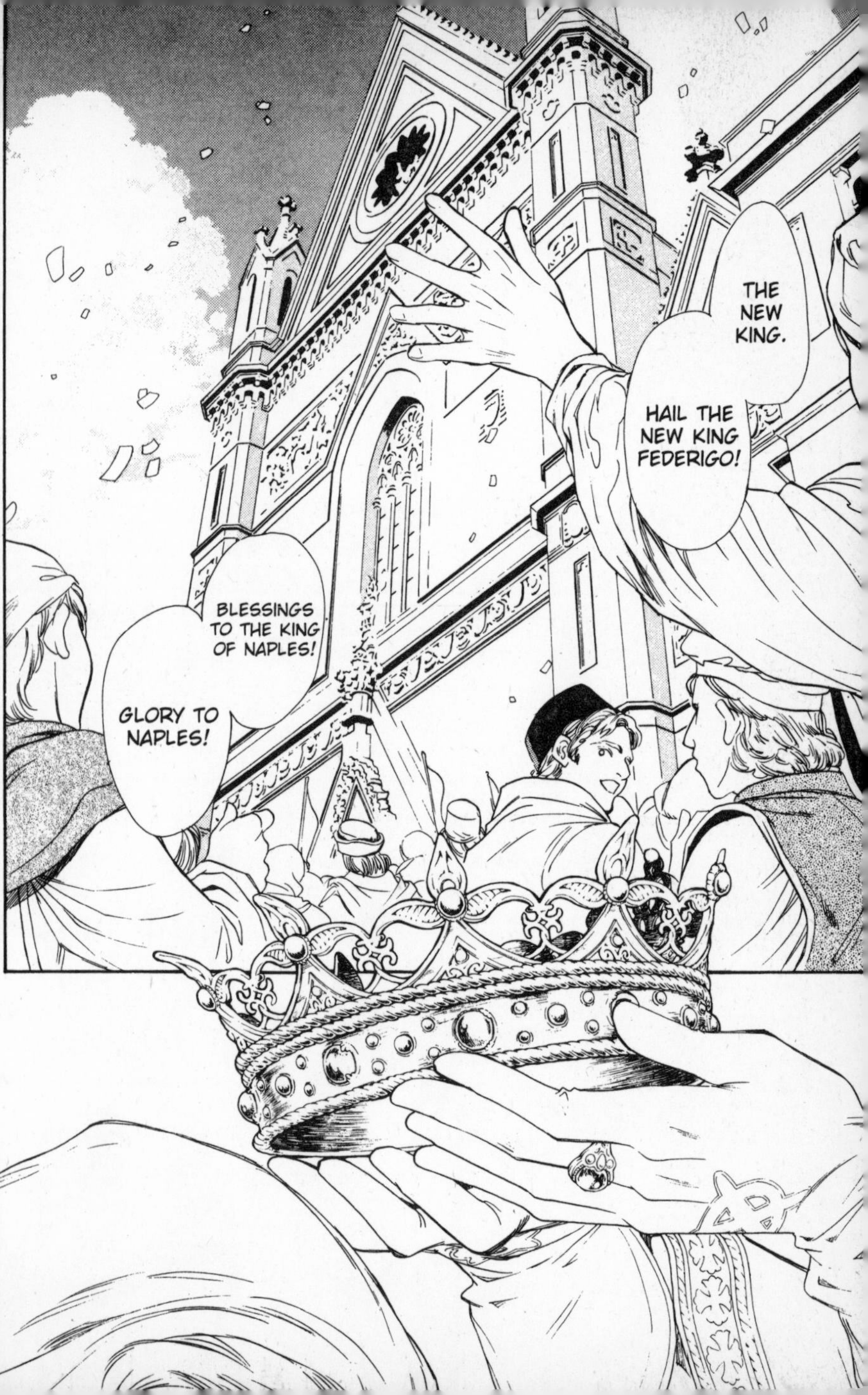
THE NEW KING.
HAIL THE NEW KING FEDERIGO!
BLESSINGS TO THE KING OF NAPLES!
GLORY TO NAPLES!

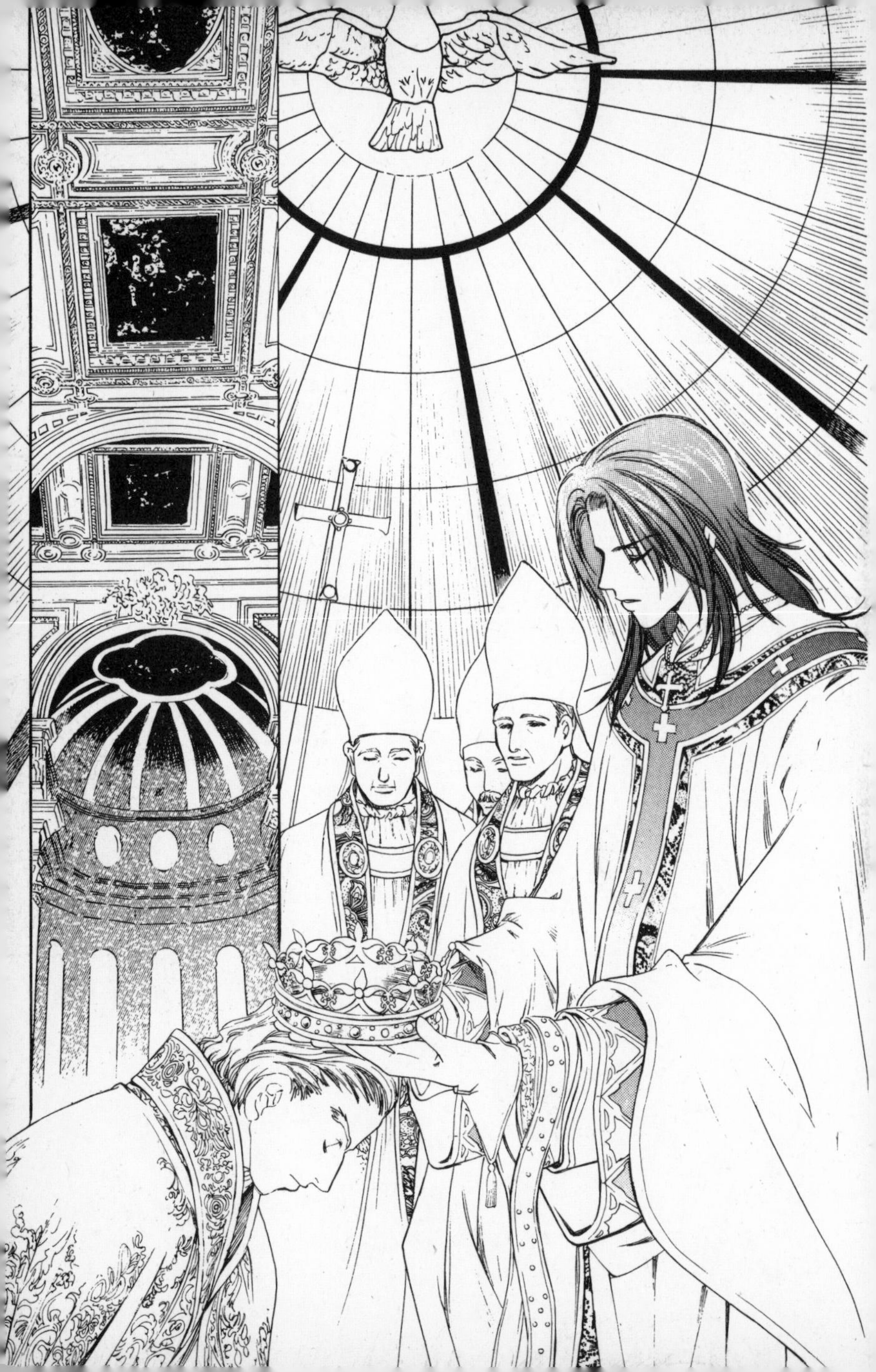

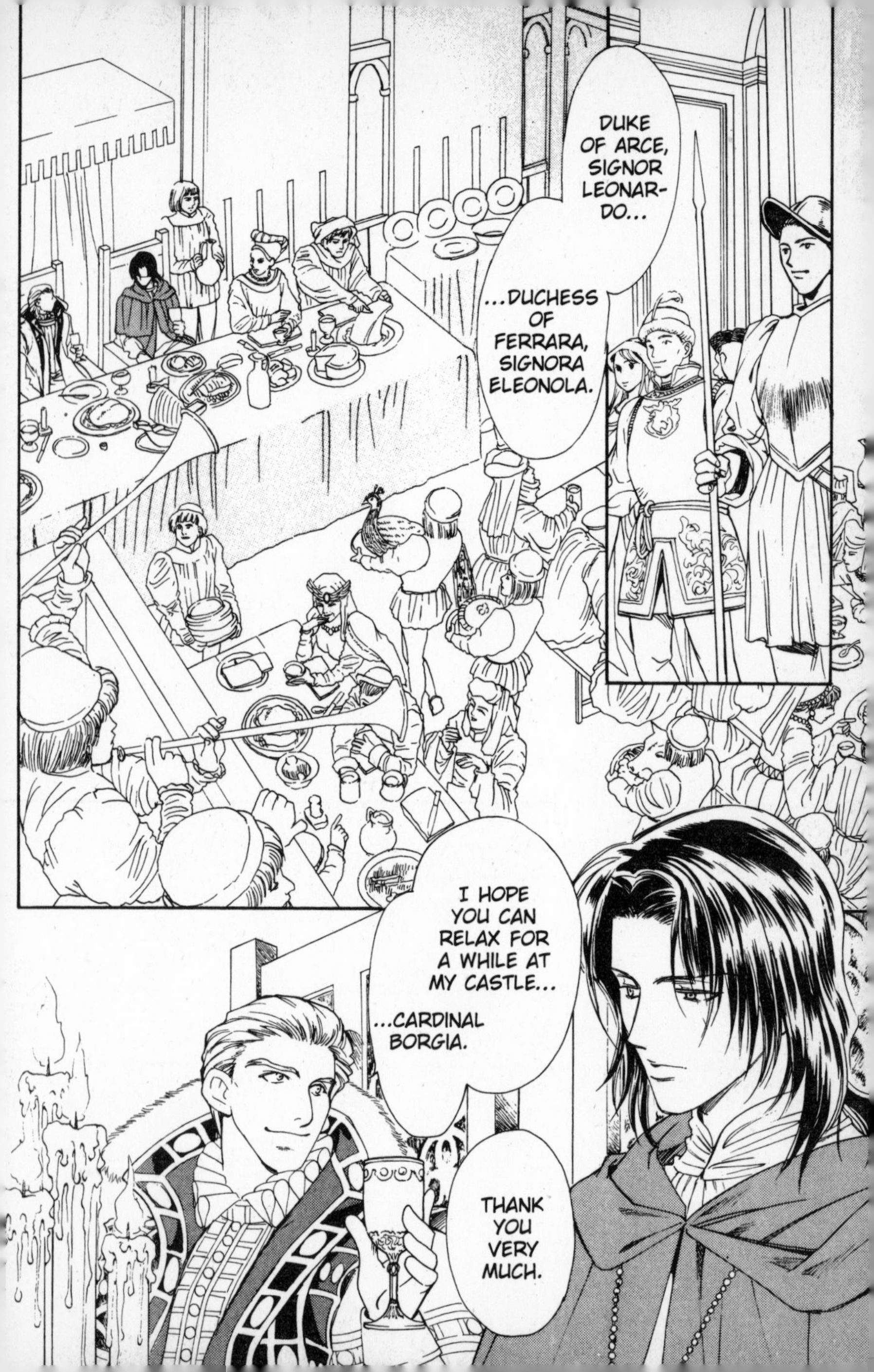
DUKE OF ARCE, SIGNOR LEONAR-DO...
...DUCHESS OF FERRARA, SIGNORA ELEONOLA.
I HOPE YOU CAN RELAX FOR A WHILE AT MY CASTLE...
...CARDINAL BORGIA.
THANK YOU VERY MUCH.

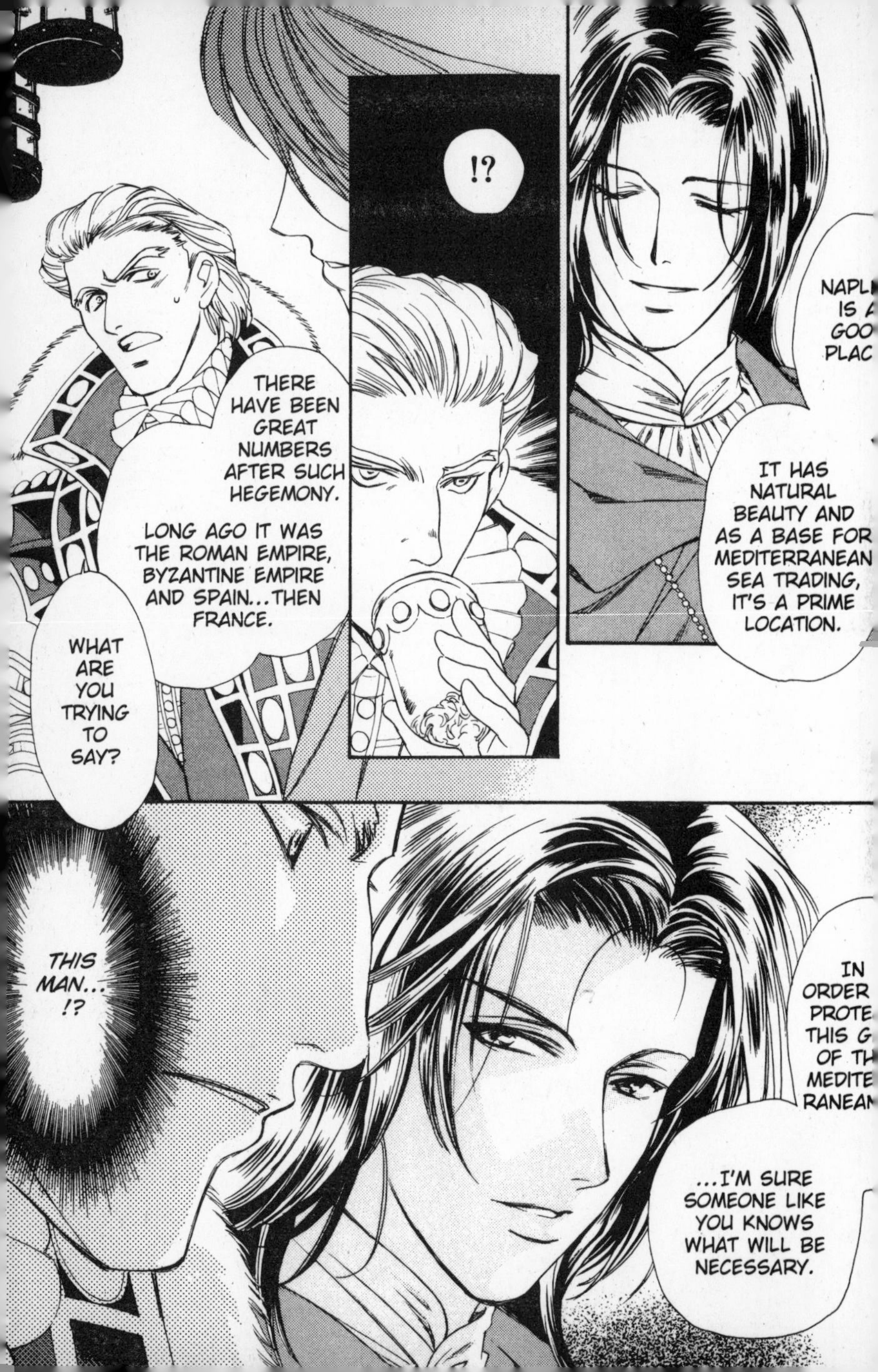
NAPL IS A GOO PLAC
IT HAS NATURAL BEAUTY AND AS A BASE FOR MEDITERRANEAN SEA TRADING, IT'S A PRIME LOCATION.
!?
THERE HAVE BEEN GREAT NUMBERS AFTER SUCH HEGEMONY.
LONG AGO IT WAS THE ROMAN EMPIRE, BYZANTINE EMPIRE AND SPAIN...THEN FRANCE.
WHAT ARE YOU TRYING TO SAY?
IN ORDER PROTE THIS G OF TH MEDITE RANEAN
...I'M SURE SOMEONE LIKE YOU KNOWS WHAT WILL BE NECESSARY.
THIS MAN... !?

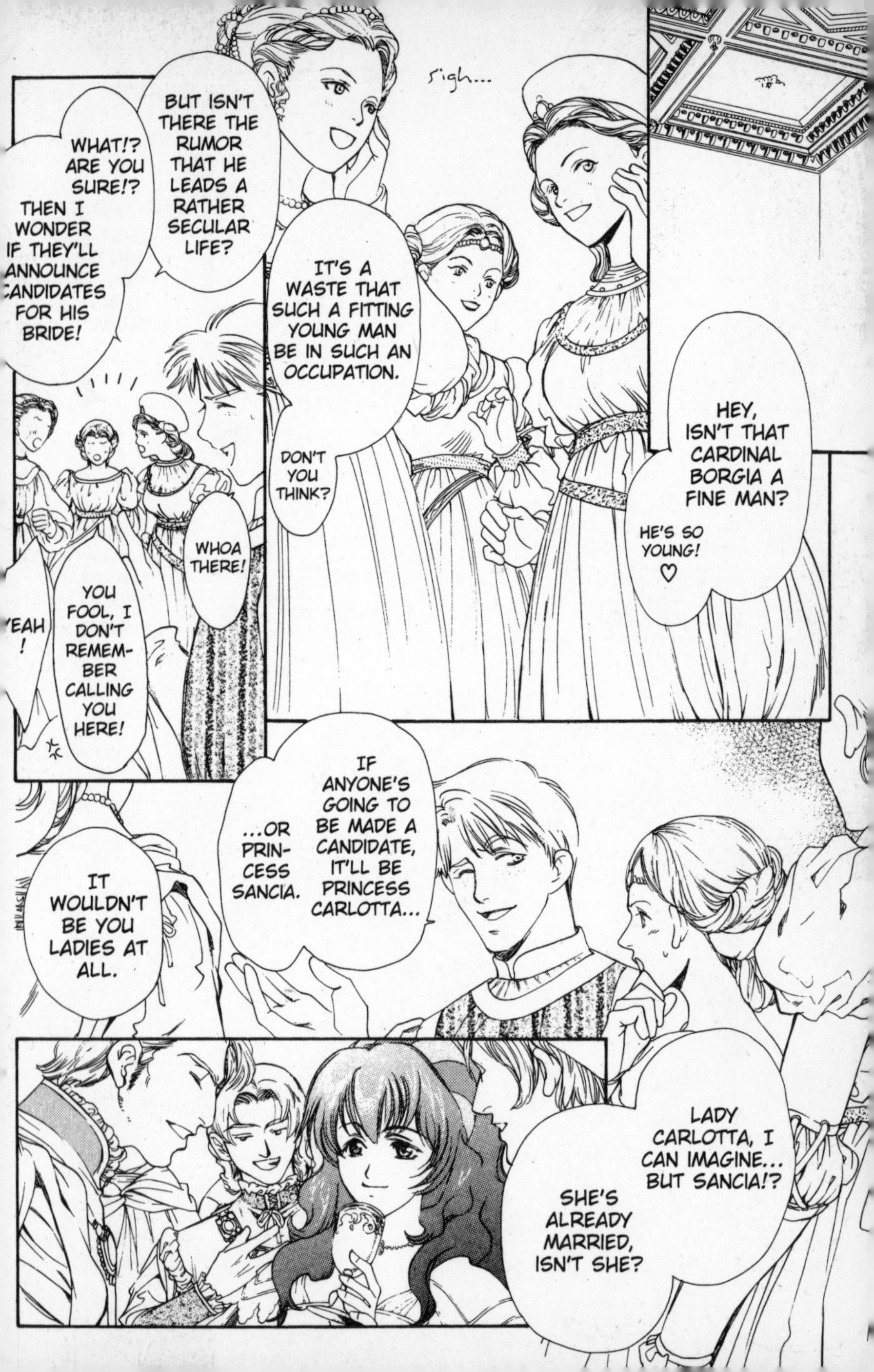
HEY, ISN'T THAT CARDINAL BORGIA A FINE MAN?
HE'S SO YOUNG! ♡
sigh...
IT'S A WASTE THAT SUCH A FITTING YOUNG MAN BE IN SUCH AN OCCUPATION.
DON'T YOU THINK?
BUT ISN'T THERE THE RUMOR THAT HE LEADS A RATHER SECULAR LIFE?
WHAT!? ARE YOU SURE!?
THEN I WONDER IF THEY'LL ANNOUNCE CANDIDATES FOR HIS BRIDE!
WHOA THERE!
YOU FOOL, I DON'T REMEMBER CALLING YOU HERE!
EAH!
IF ANYONE'S GOING TO BE MADE A CANDIDATE, IT'LL BE PRINCESS CARLOTTA...
...OR PRINCESS SANCIA.
IT WOULDN'T BE YOU LADIES AT ALL.
LADY CARLOTTA, I CAN IMAGINE... BUT SANCIA!?
SHE'S ALREADY MARRIED, ISN'T SHE?

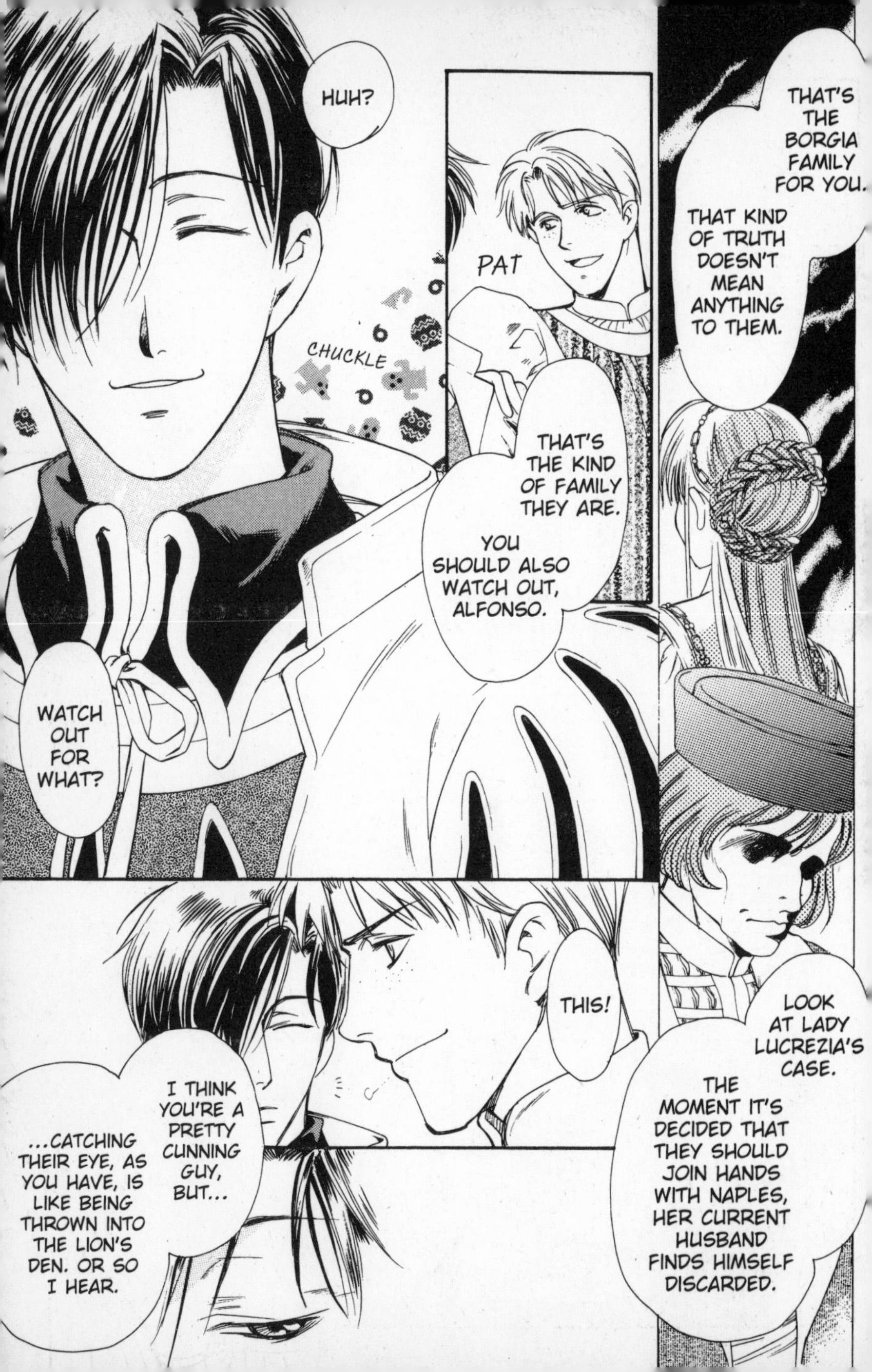
THAT'S THE BORGIA FAMILY FOR YOU.
THAT KIND OF TRUTH DOESN'T MEAN ANYTHING TO THEM.
LOOK AT LADY LUCREZIA'S CASE.
THE MOMENT IT'S DECIDED THAT THEY SHOULD JOIN HANDS WITH NAPLES, HER CURRENT HUSBAND FINDS HIMSELF DISCARDED.
PAT
THAT'S THE KIND OF FAMILY THEY ARE.
YOU SHOULD ALSO WATCH OUT, ALFONSO.
HUH?
CHUCKLE
WATCH OUT FOR WHAT?
THIS!
I THINK YOU'RE A PRETTY CUNNING GUY, BUT...
...CATCHING THEIR EYE, AS YOU HAVE, IS LIKE BEING THROWN INTO THE LION'S DEN. OR SO I HEAR.

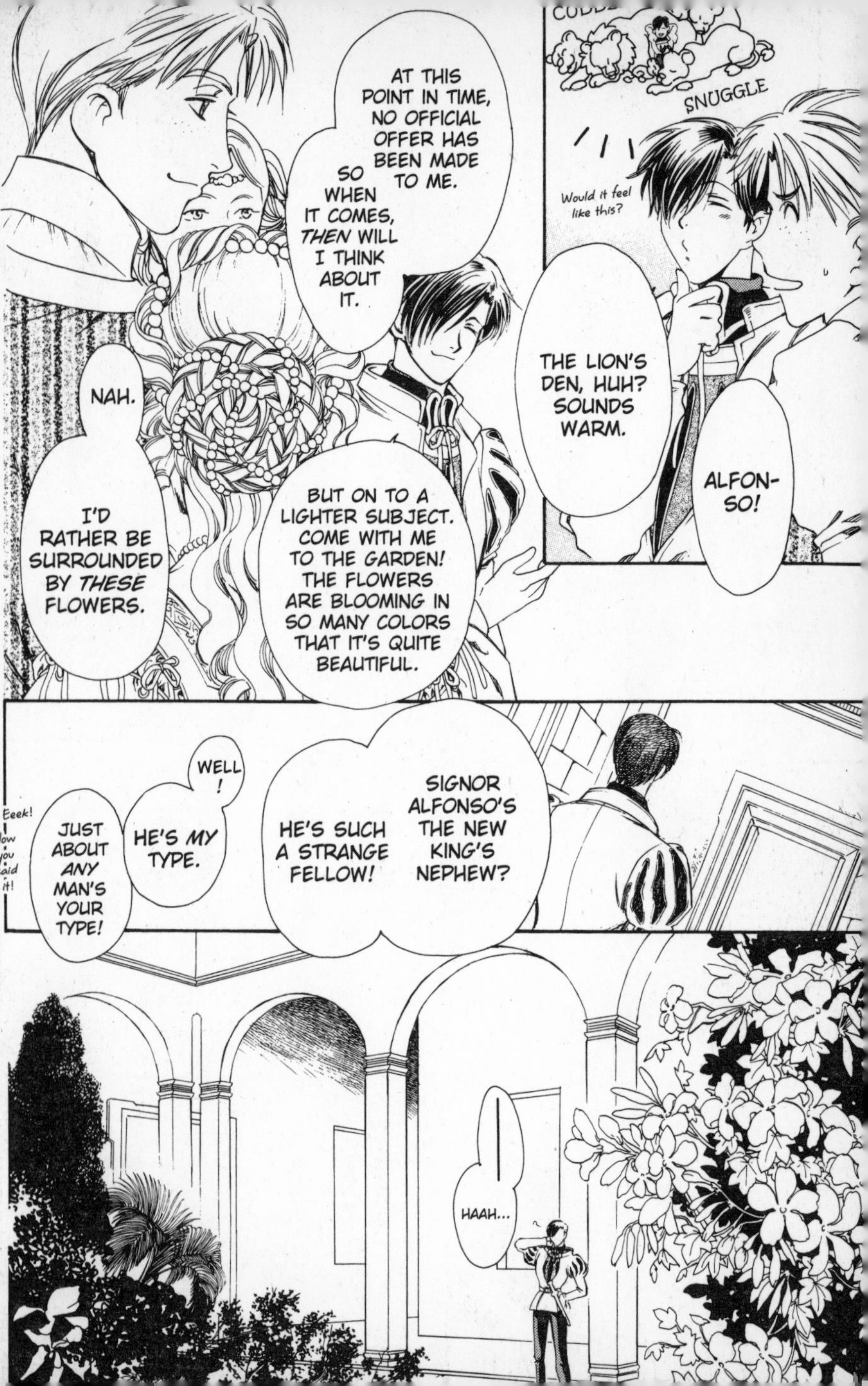
SNUGGLE
Would it feel like this?
THE LION'S DEN, HUH? SOUNDS WARM.
ALFON-SO!
AT THIS POINT IN TIME, NO OFFICIAL OFFER HAS BEEN MADE TO ME.
SO WHEN IT COMES, *THEN* WILL I THINK ABOUT IT.
BUT ON TO A LIGHTER SUBJECT. COME WITH ME TO THE GARDEN! THE FLOWERS ARE BLOOMING IN SO MANY COLORS THAT IT'S QUITE BEAUTIFUL.
NAH.
I'D RATHER BE SURROUNDED BY *THESE* FLOWERS.
SIGNOR ALFONSO'S THE NEW KING'S NEPHEW?
HE'S SUCH A STRANGE FELLOW!
WELL!
HE'S *MY* TYPE.
JUST ABOUT *ANY* MAN'S YOUR TYPE!
Eeek! Now you said it!
HAAH...

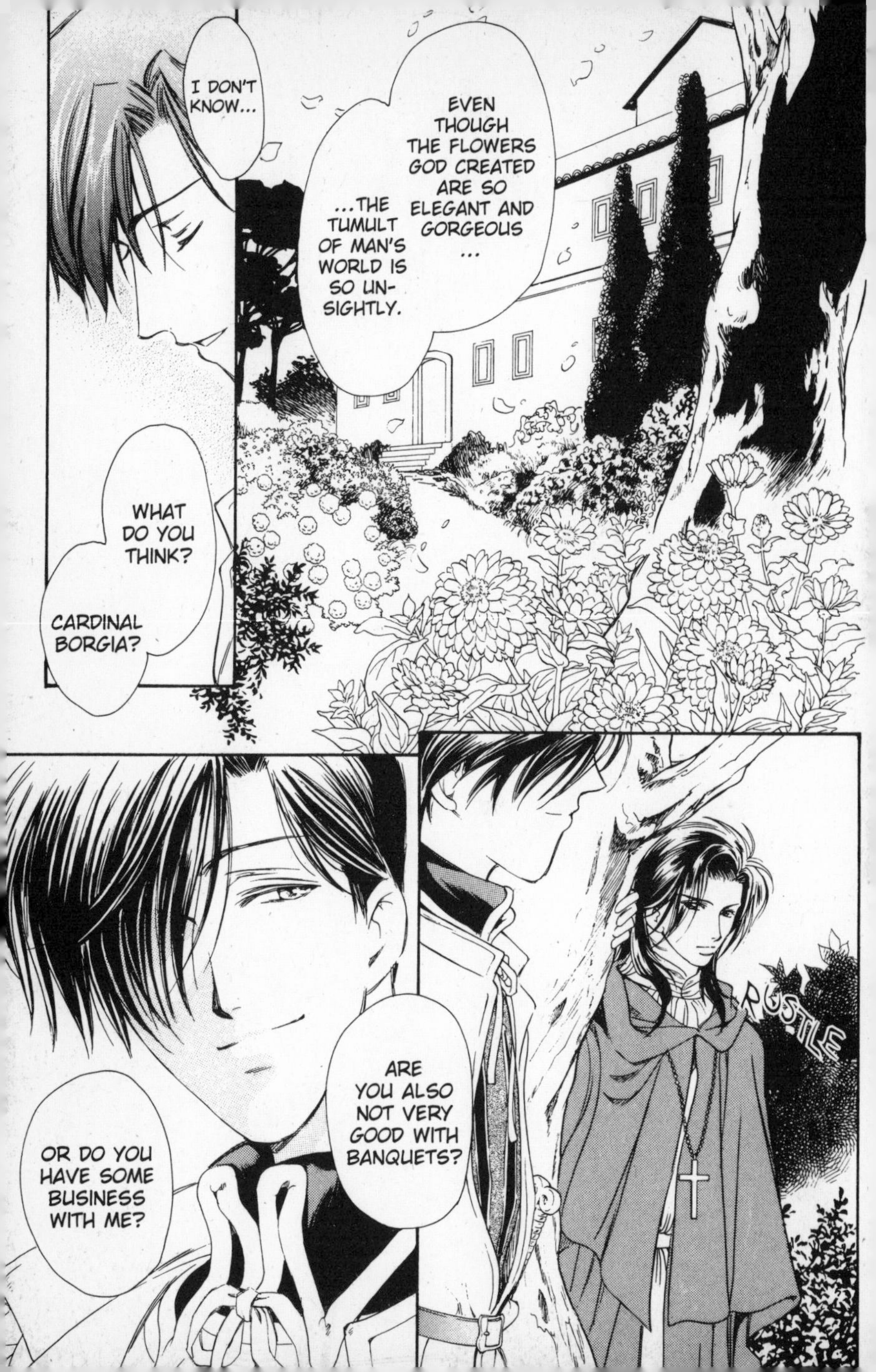
EVEN THOUGH THE FLOWERS GOD CREATED ARE SO ELEGANT AND GORGEOUS ...
...THE TUMULT OF MAN'S WORLD IS SO UN-SIGHTLY.
I DON'T KNOW...
WHAT DO YOU THINK?
CARDINAL BORGIA?
RUSTLE
ARE YOU ALSO NOT VERY GOOD WITH BANQUETS?
OR DO YOU HAVE SOME BUSINESS WITH ME?

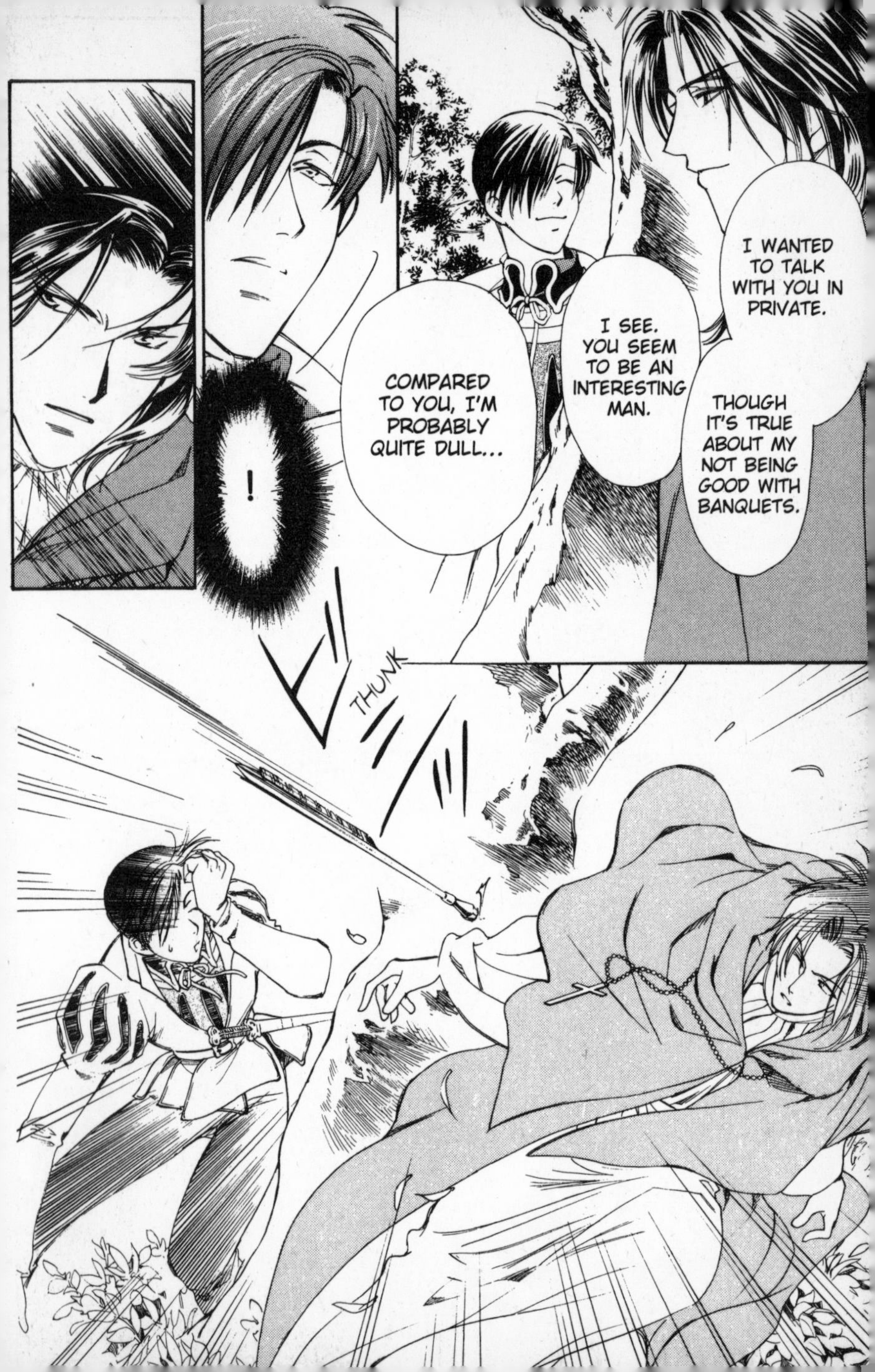
I WANTED TO TALK WITH YOU IN PRIVATE.
THOUGH IT'S TRUE ABOUT MY NOT BEING GOOD WITH BANQUETS.
I SEE. YOU SEEM TO BE AN INTERESTING MAN.
COMPARED TO YOU, I'M PROBABLY QUITE DULL...
!
THUNK

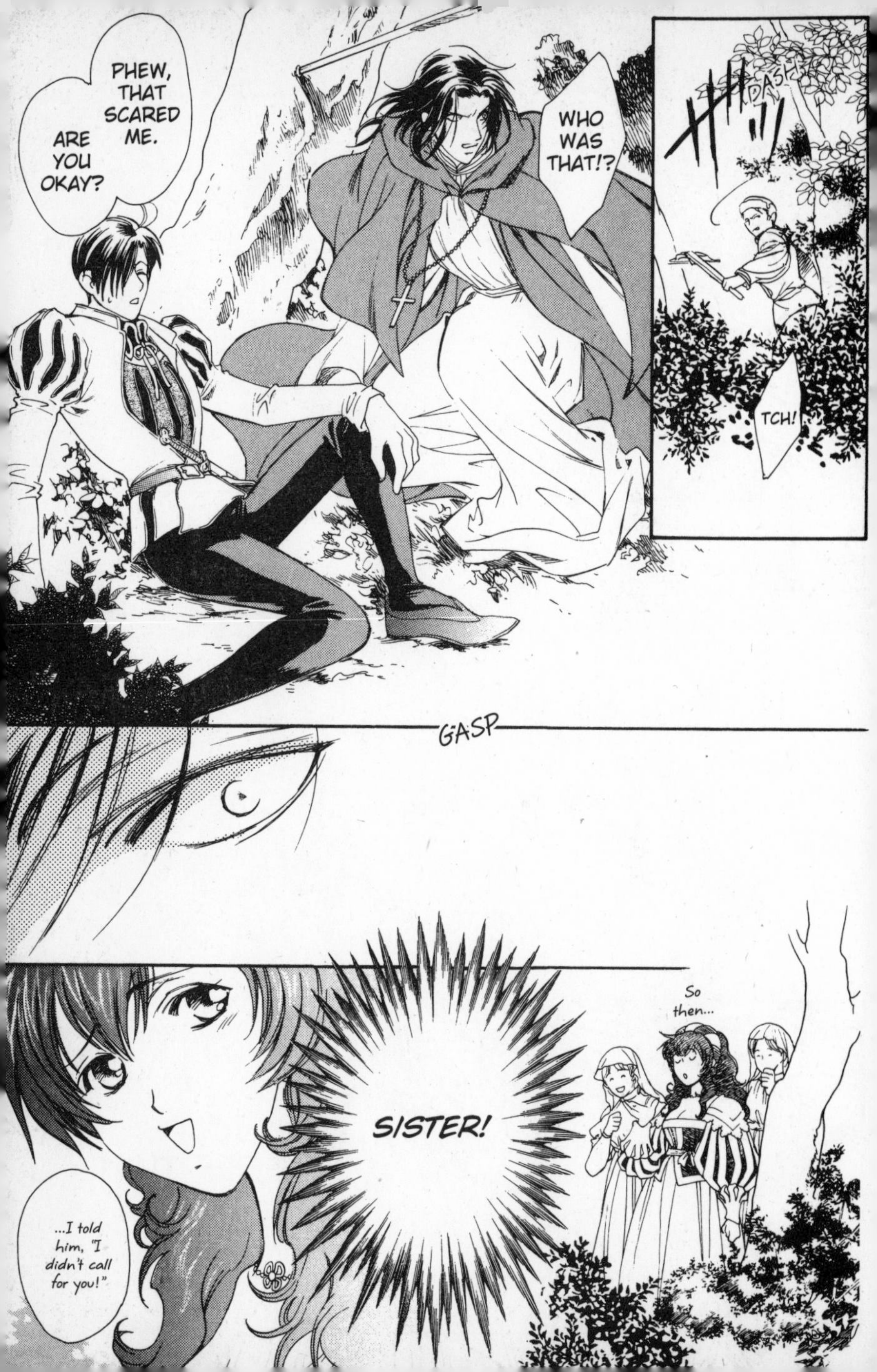
DASH
TCH!
WHO WAS THAT!?
PHEW, THAT SCARED ME.
ARE YOU OKAY?
GASP
So then...
SISTER!
...I told him, "I didn't call for you!"

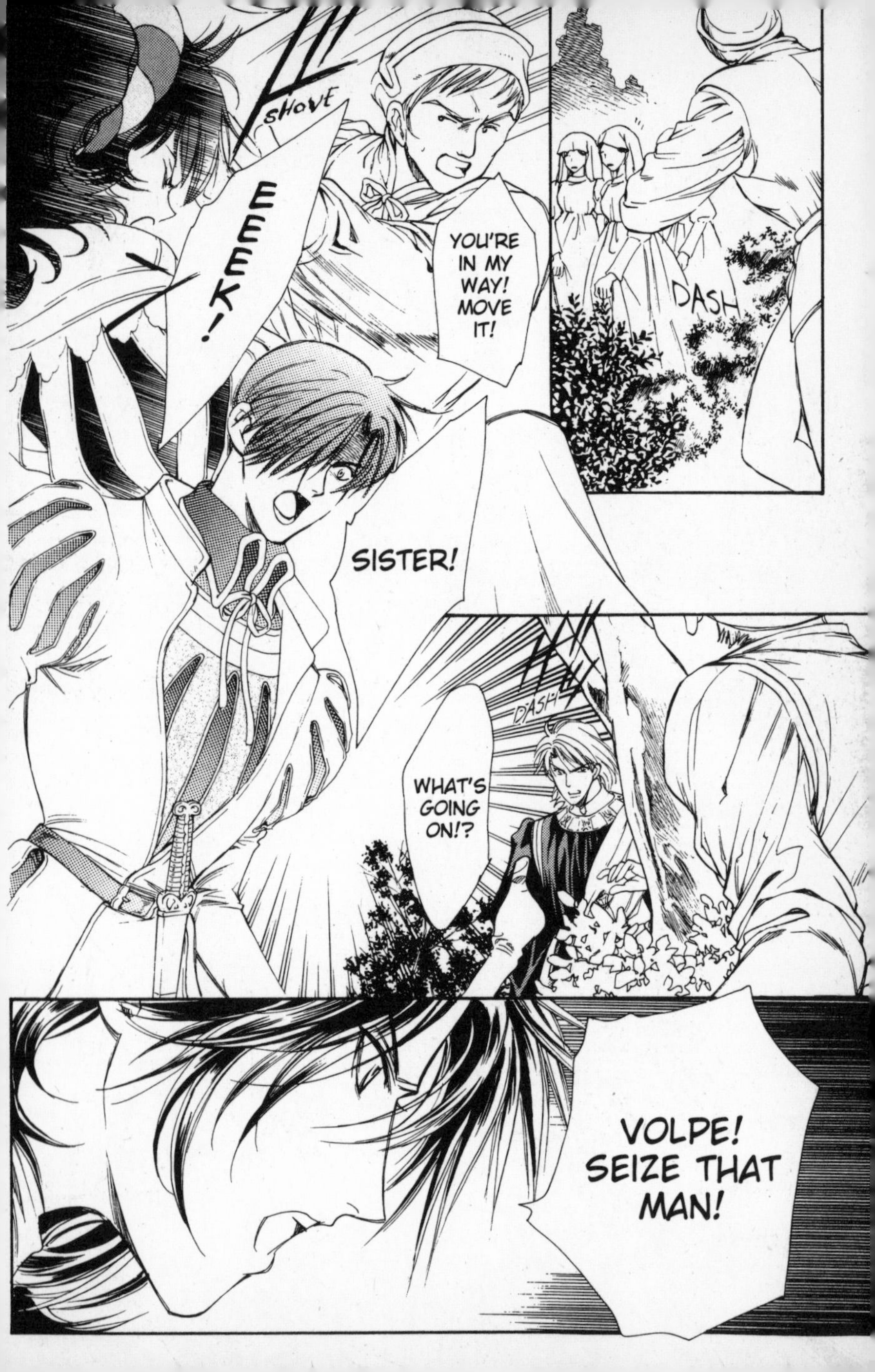
DASH
DASH
WHAT'S GOING ON!?
SHOVE
EEEEK!
YOU'RE IN MY WAY! MOVE IT!
SISTER!
VOLPE! SEIZE THAT MAN!

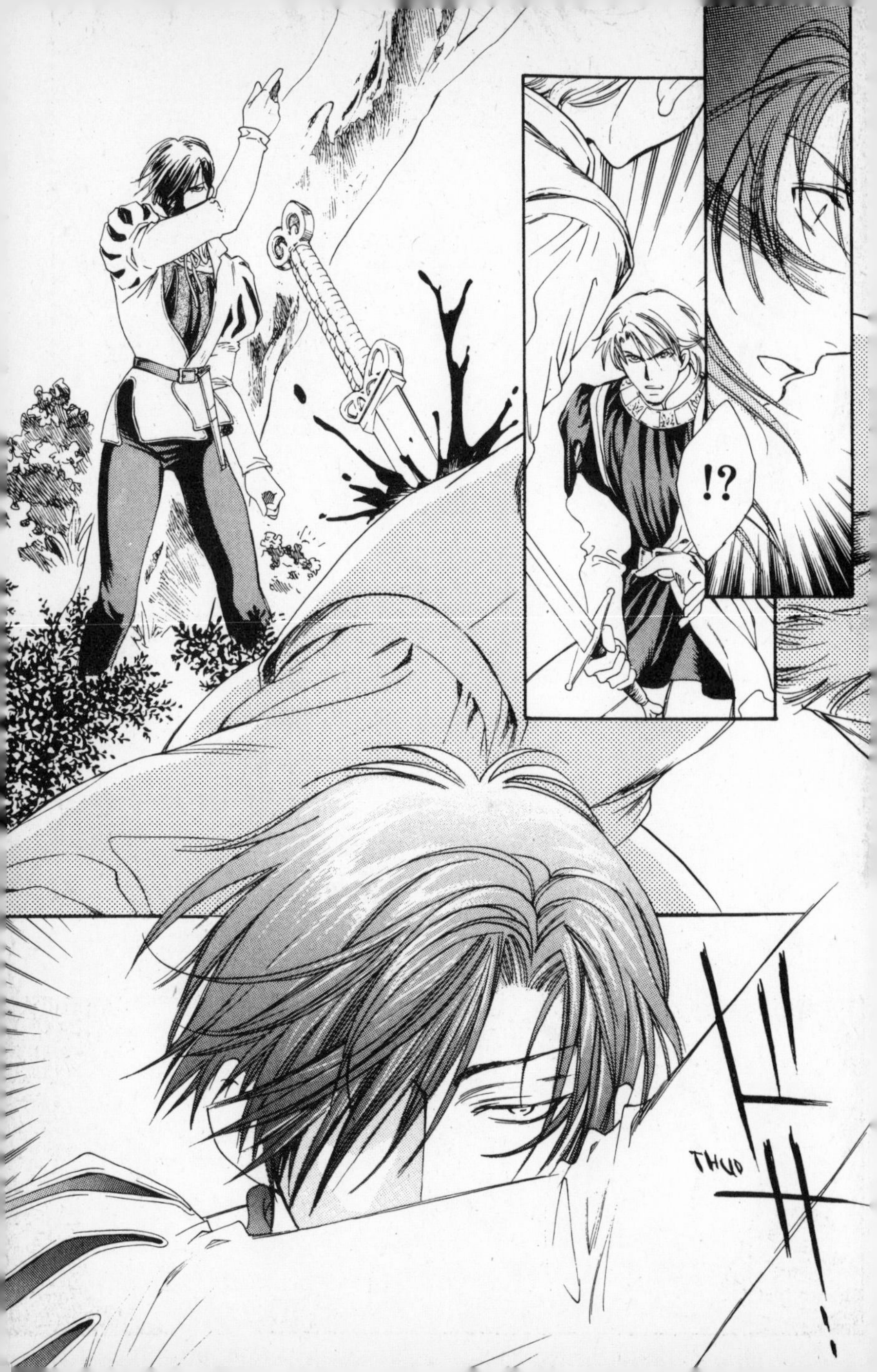
!?
THUD

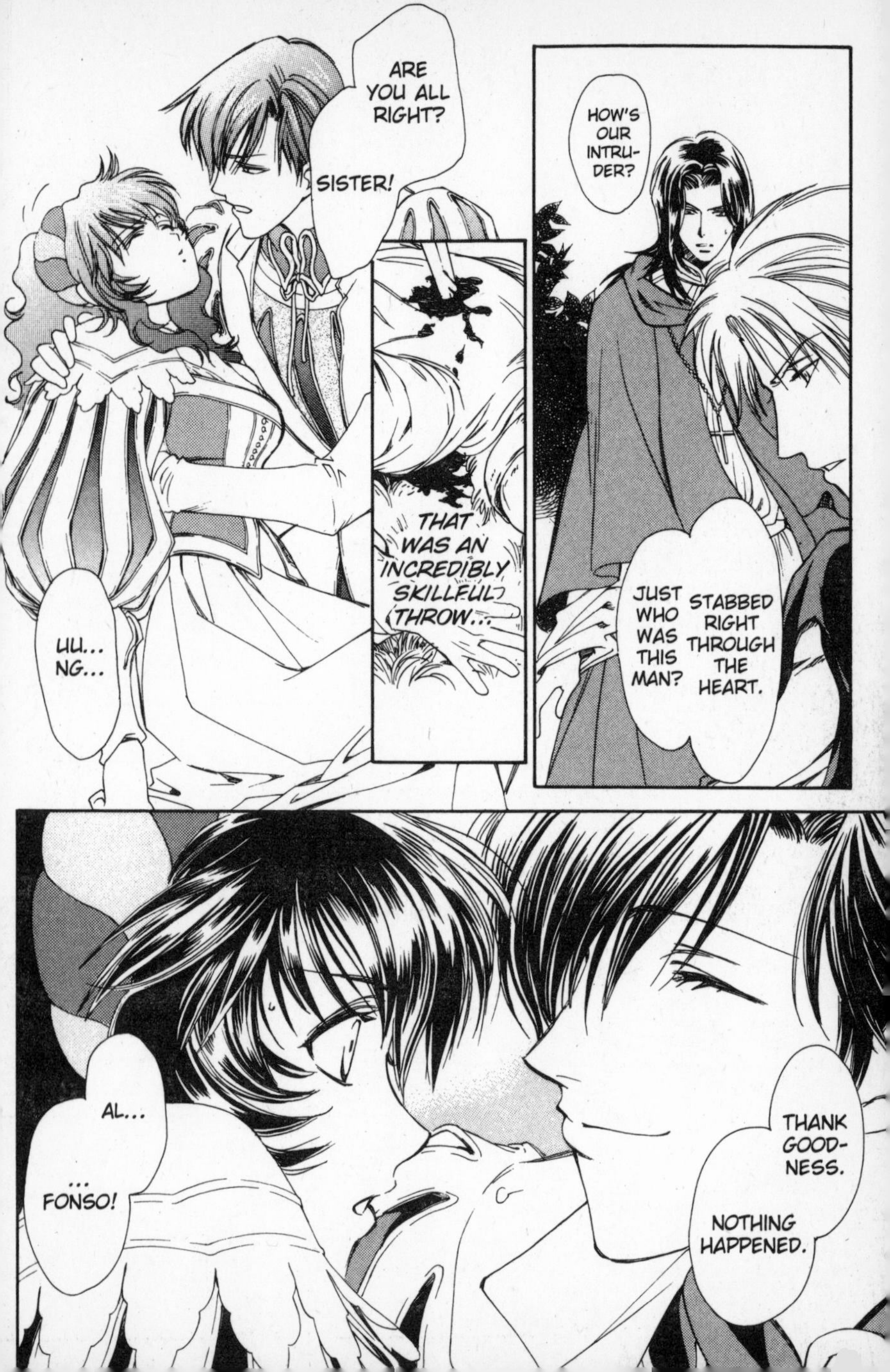
HOW'S OUR INTRU-DER?
STABBED RIGHT THROUGH THE HEART.
JUST WHO WAS THIS MAN?
THAT WAS AN INCREDIBLY SKILLFUL THROW...
ARE YOU ALL RIGHT?
SISTER!
UU... NG...
THANK GOOD-NESS.
NOTHING HAPPENED.
AL...
...FONSO!

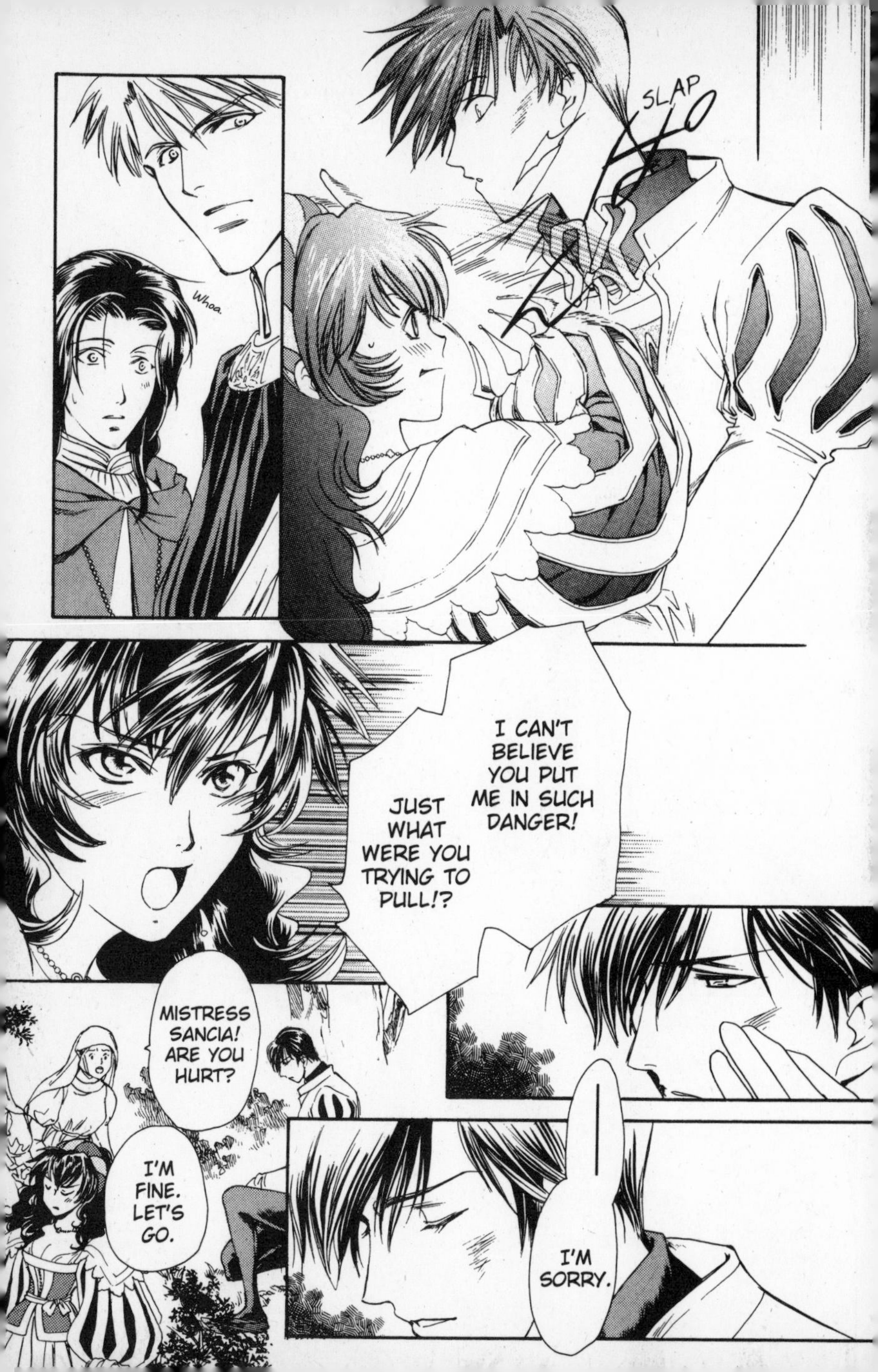
SLAP
Whoa.
I CAN'T BELIEVE YOU PUT ME IN SUCH DANGER!
JUST WHAT WERE YOU TRYING TO PULL!?
I'M SORRY.
MISTRESS SANCIA! ARE YOU HURT?
I'M FINE. LET'S GO.

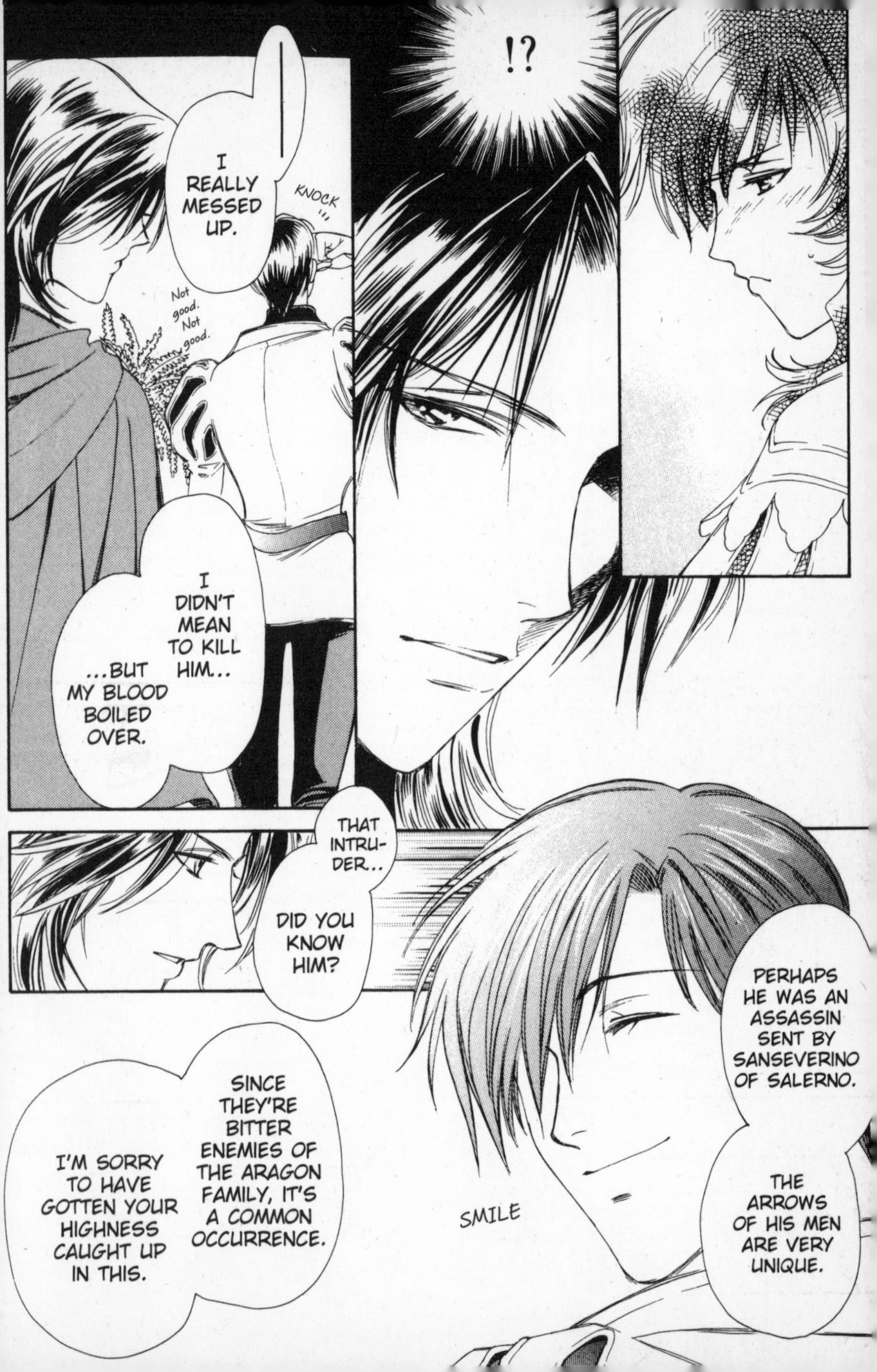

!?
—!
I REALLY MESSED UP.
KNOCK
Not good. Not good.
I DIDN'T MEAN TO KILL HIM...
...BUT MY BLOOD BOILED OVER.
THAT INTRUDER...
DID YOU KNOW HIM?
PERHAPS HE WAS AN ASSASSIN SENT BY SANSEVERINO OF SALERNO.
THE ARROWS OF HIS MEN ARE VERY UNIQUE.
SMILE
SINCE THEY'RE BITTER ENEMIES OF THE ARAGON FAMILY, IT'S A COMMON OCCURRENCE.
I'M SORRY TO HAVE GOTTEN YOUR HIGHNESS CAUGHT UP IN THIS.

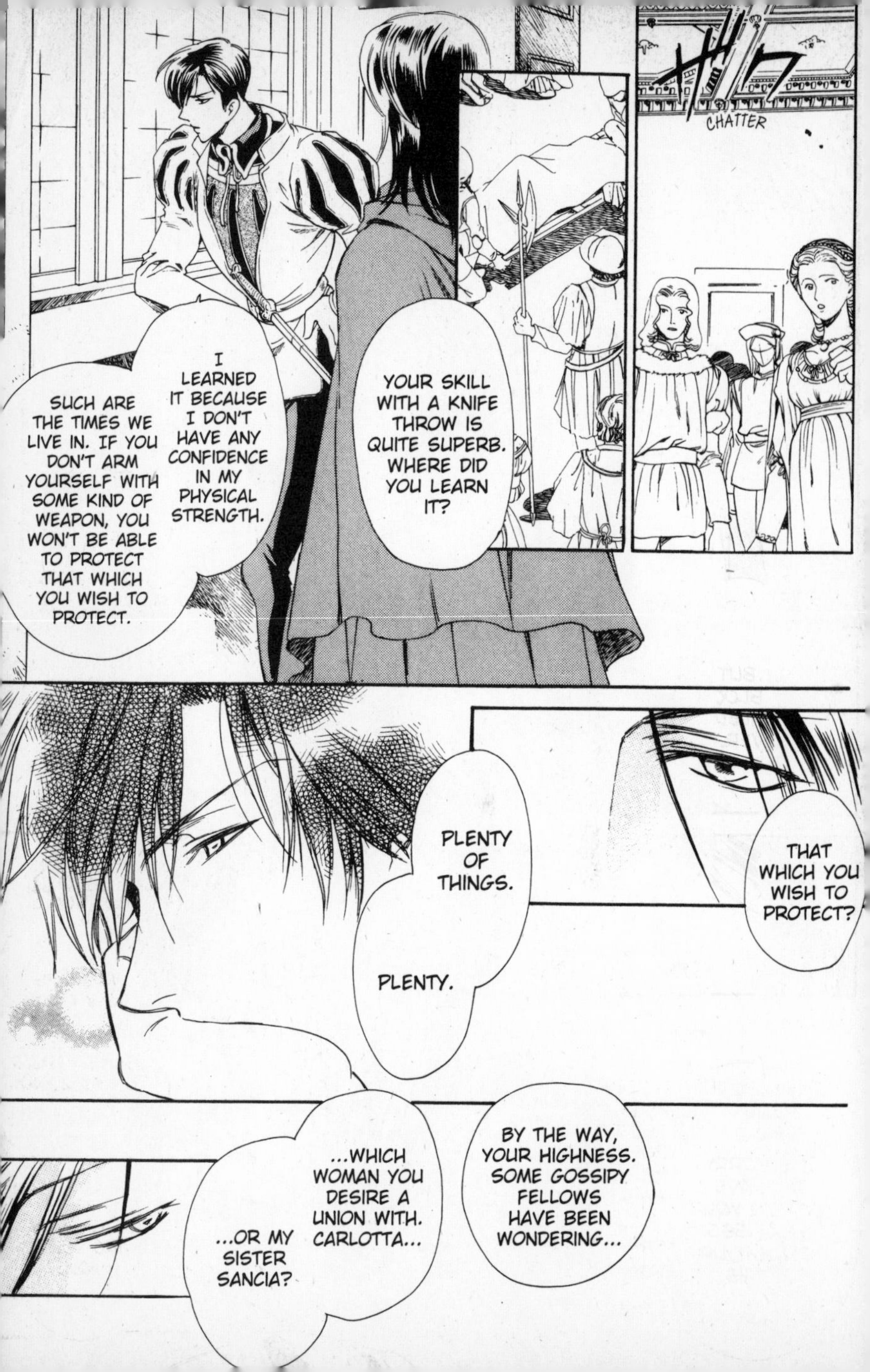
CHATTER
YOUR SKILL WITH A KNIFE THROW IS QUITE SUPERB. WHERE DID YOU LEARN IT?
I LEARNED IT BECAUSE I DON'T HAVE ANY CONFIDENCE IN MY PHYSICAL STRENGTH.
SUCH ARE THE TIMES WE LIVE IN. IF YOU DON'T ARM YOURSELF WITH SOME KIND OF WEAPON, YOU WON'T BE ABLE TO PROTECT THAT WHICH YOU WISH TO PROTECT.
THAT WHICH YOU WISH TO PROTECT?
PLENTY OF THINGS.
PLENTY.
BY THE WAY, YOUR HIGHNESS. SOME GOSSIPY FELLOWS HAVE BEEN WONDERING...
...WHICH WOMAN YOU DESIRE A UNION WITH. CARLOTTA...
...OR MY SISTER SANCIA?

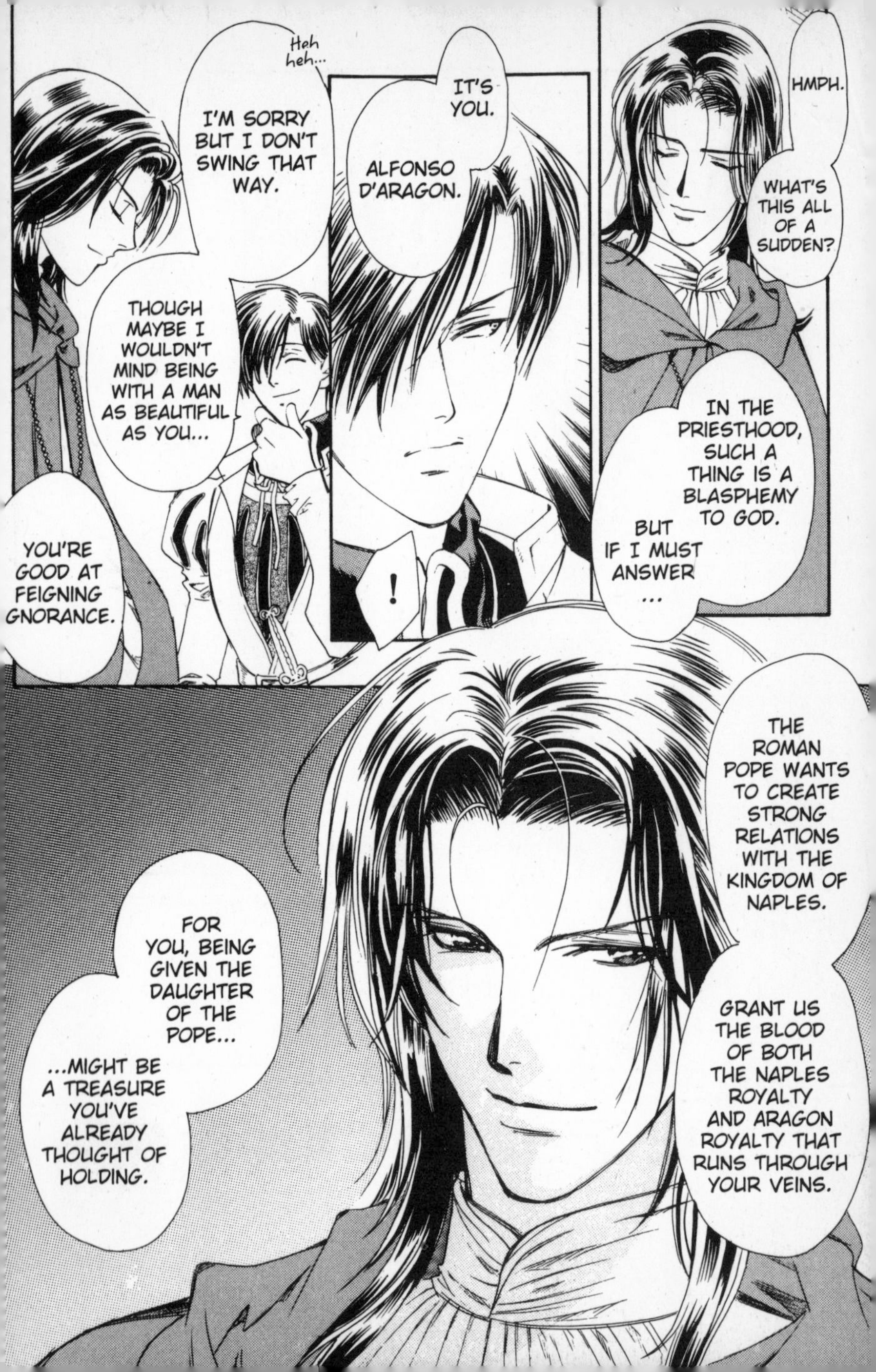
HMPH.
WHAT'S THIS ALL OF A SUDDEN?
IN THE PRIESTHOOD, SUCH A THING IS A BLASPHEMY TO GOD.
BUT IF I MUST ANSWER ...
IT'S YOU.
ALFONSO D'ARAGON.
!
Heh heh...
I'M SORRY BUT I DON'T SWING THAT WAY.
THOUGH MAYBE I WOULDN'T MIND BEING WITH A MAN AS BEAUTIFUL AS YOU...
YOU'RE GOOD AT FEIGNING GNORANCE.
THE ROMAN POPE WANTS TO CREATE STRONG RELATIONS WITH THE KINGDOM OF NAPLES.
GRANT US THE BLOOD OF BOTH THE NAPLES ROYALTY AND ARAGON ROYALTY THAT RUNS THROUGH YOUR VEINS.
FOR YOU, BEING GIVEN THE DAUGHTER OF THE POPE...
...MIGHT BE A TREASURE YOU'VE ALREADY THOUGHT OF HOLDING.

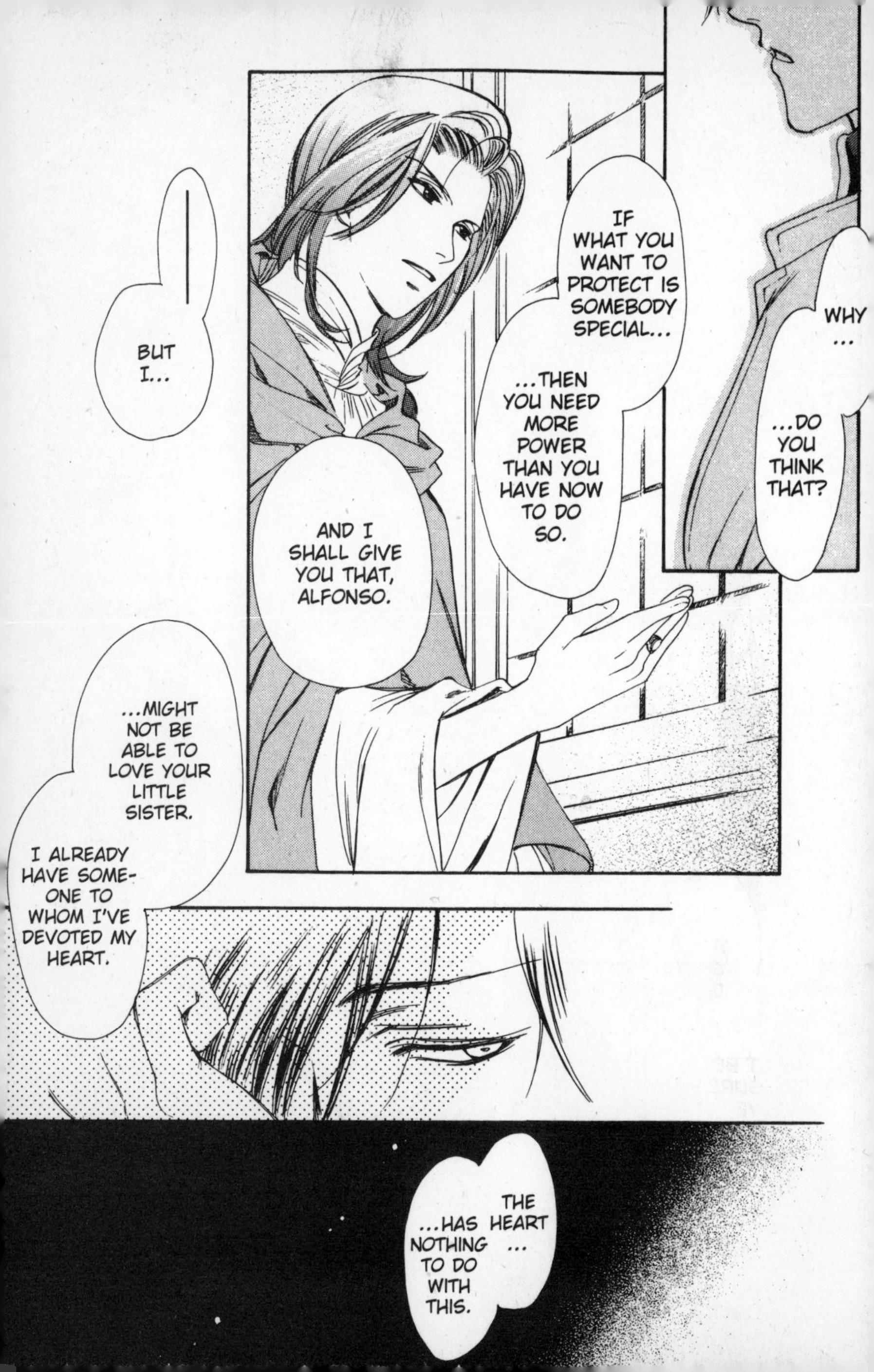
WHY ...
...DO YOU THINK THAT?
IF WHAT YOU WANT TO PROTECT IS SOMEBODY SPECIAL...
...THEN YOU NEED MORE POWER THAN YOU HAVE NOW TO DO SO.
AND I SHALL GIVE YOU THAT, ALFONSO.
BUT I...
...MIGHT NOT BE ABLE TO LOVE YOUR LITTLE SISTER.
I ALREADY HAVE SOME-ONE TO WHOM I'VE DEVOTED MY HEART.
THE HEART ...
...HAS NOTHING TO DO WITH THIS.

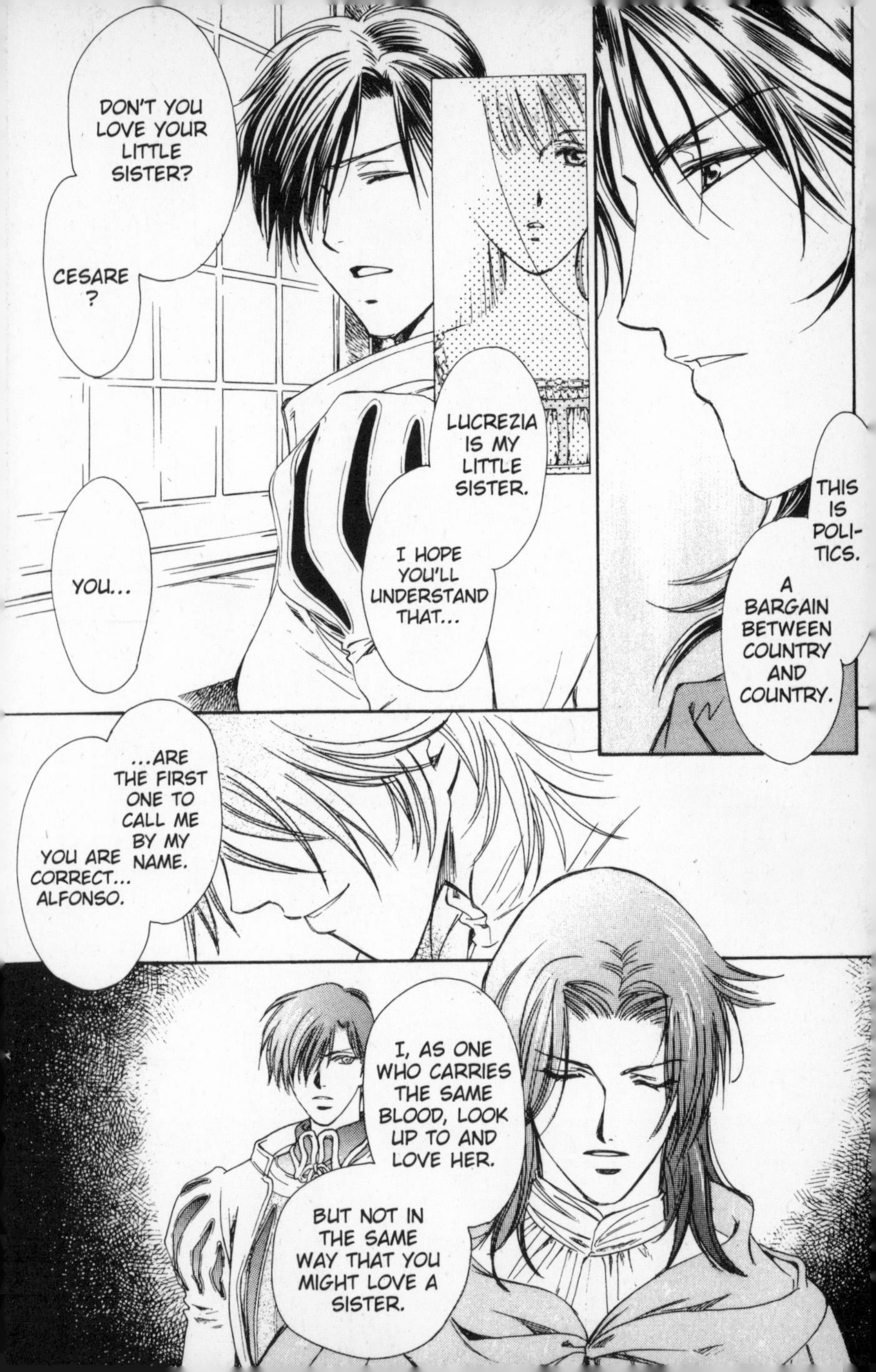
THIS IS POLITICS.
A BARGAIN BETWEEN COUNTRY AND COUNTRY.
LUCREZIA IS MY LITTLE SISTER.
I HOPE YOU'LL UNDERSTAND THAT...
DON'T YOU LOVE YOUR LITTLE SISTER?
CESARE ?
YOU...
...ARE THE FIRST ONE TO CALL ME BY MY NAME.
YOU ARE CORRECT... ALFONSO.
I, AS ONE WHO CARRIES THE SAME BLOOD, LOOK UP TO AND LOVE HER.
BUT NOT IN THE SAME WAY THAT YOU MIGHT LOVE A SISTER.

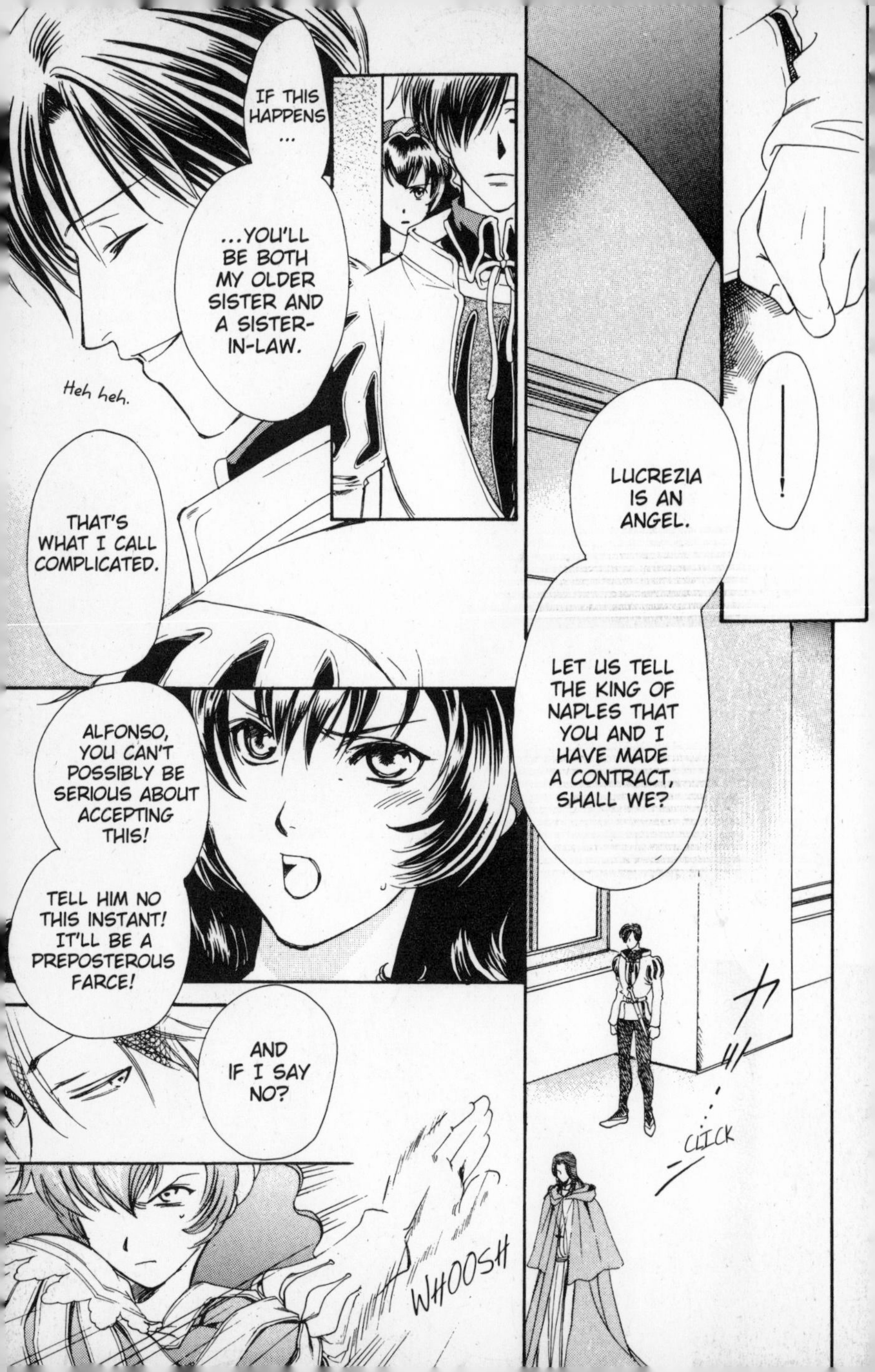

!
LUCREZIA IS AN ANGEL.
IF THIS HAPPENS...
...YOU'LL BE BOTH MY OLDER SISTER AND A SISTER-IN-LAW.
Heh heh.
THAT'S WHAT I CALL COMPLICATED.
LET US TELL THE KING OF NAPLES THAT YOU AND I HAVE MADE A CONTRACT, SHALL WE?
CLICK
ALFONSO, YOU CAN'T POSSIBLY BE SERIOUS ABOUT ACCEPTING THIS!
TELL HIM NO THIS INSTANT! IT'LL BE A PREPOSTEROUS FARCE!
AND IF I SAY NO?
WHOOSH

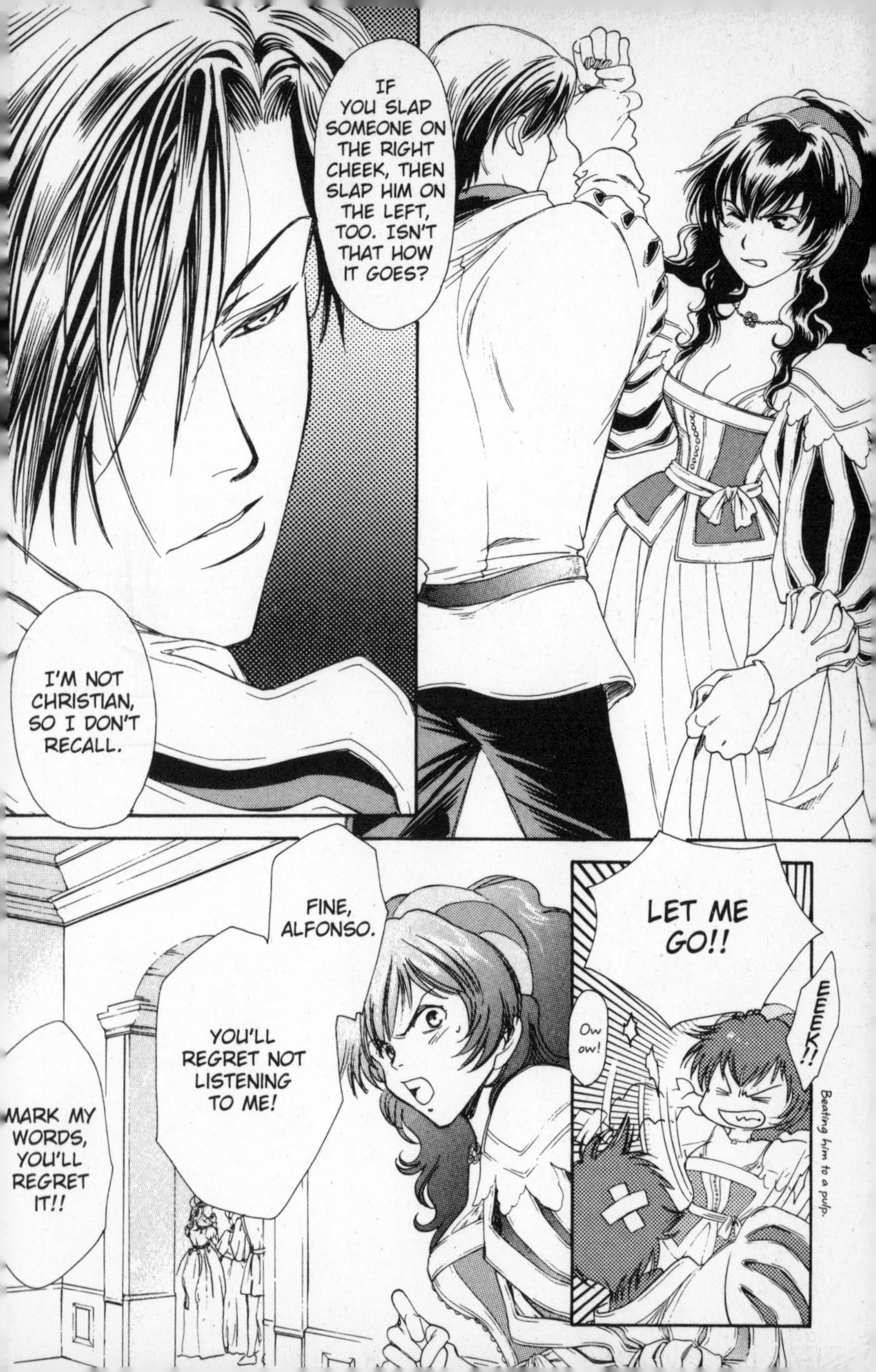
IF YOU SLAP SOMEONE ON THE RIGHT CHEEK, THEN SLAP HIM ON THE LEFT, TOO. ISN'T THAT HOW IT GOES?
I'M NOT CHRISTIAN, SO I DON'T RECALL.
LET ME GO!!
Beating him to a pulp.
EEEK!!
Ow ow!
FINE, ALFONSO.
YOU'LL REGRET NOT LISTENING TO ME!
MARK MY WORDS, YOU'LL REGRET IT!!

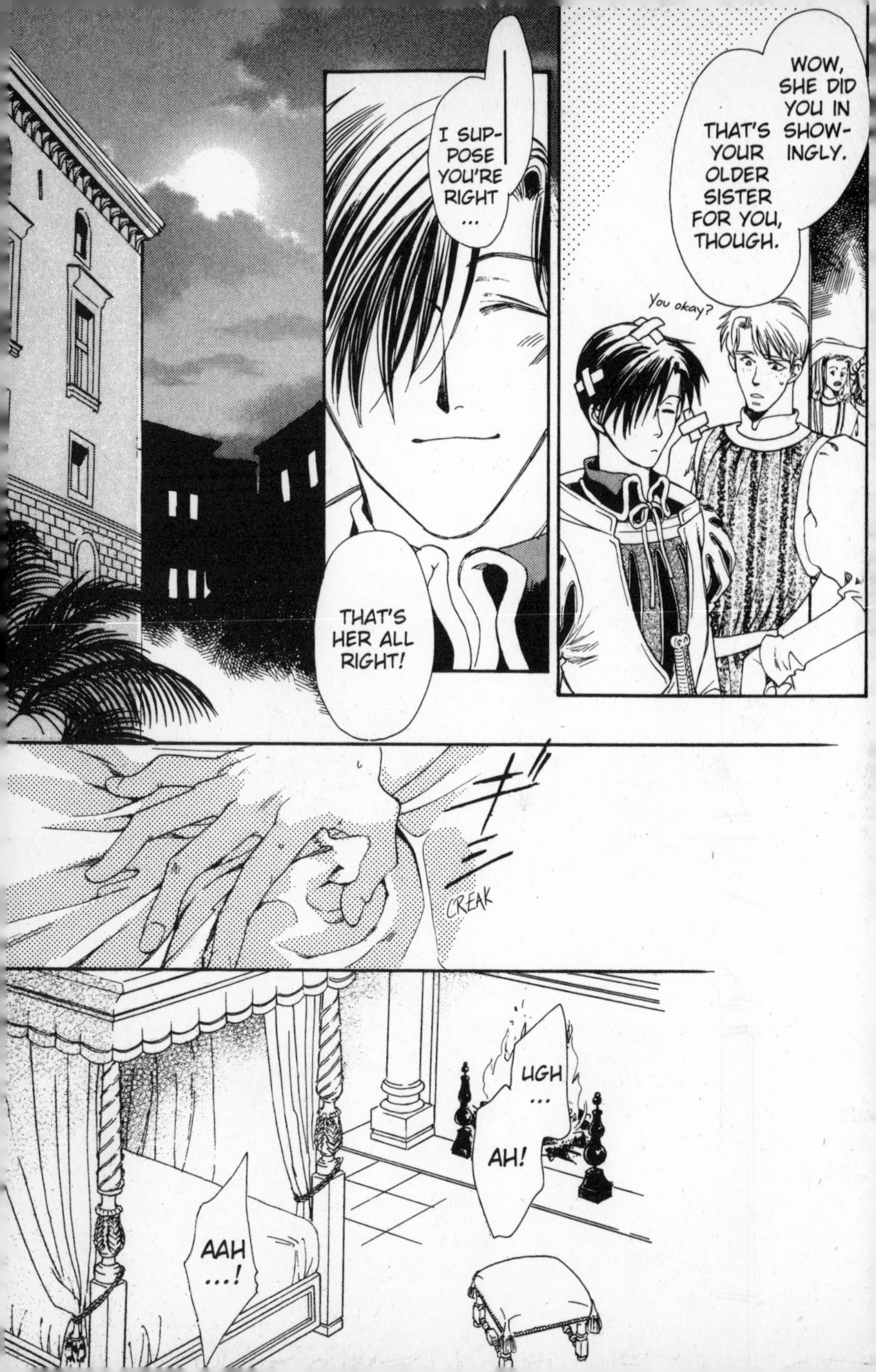
WOW, SHE DID YOU IN SHOW-INGLY.
THAT'S YOUR OLDER SISTER FOR YOU, THOUGH.
You okay?
I SUP-POSE YOU'RE RIGHT ...
THAT'S HER ALL RIGHT!
CREAK
UGH ...
AH!
AAH ...!

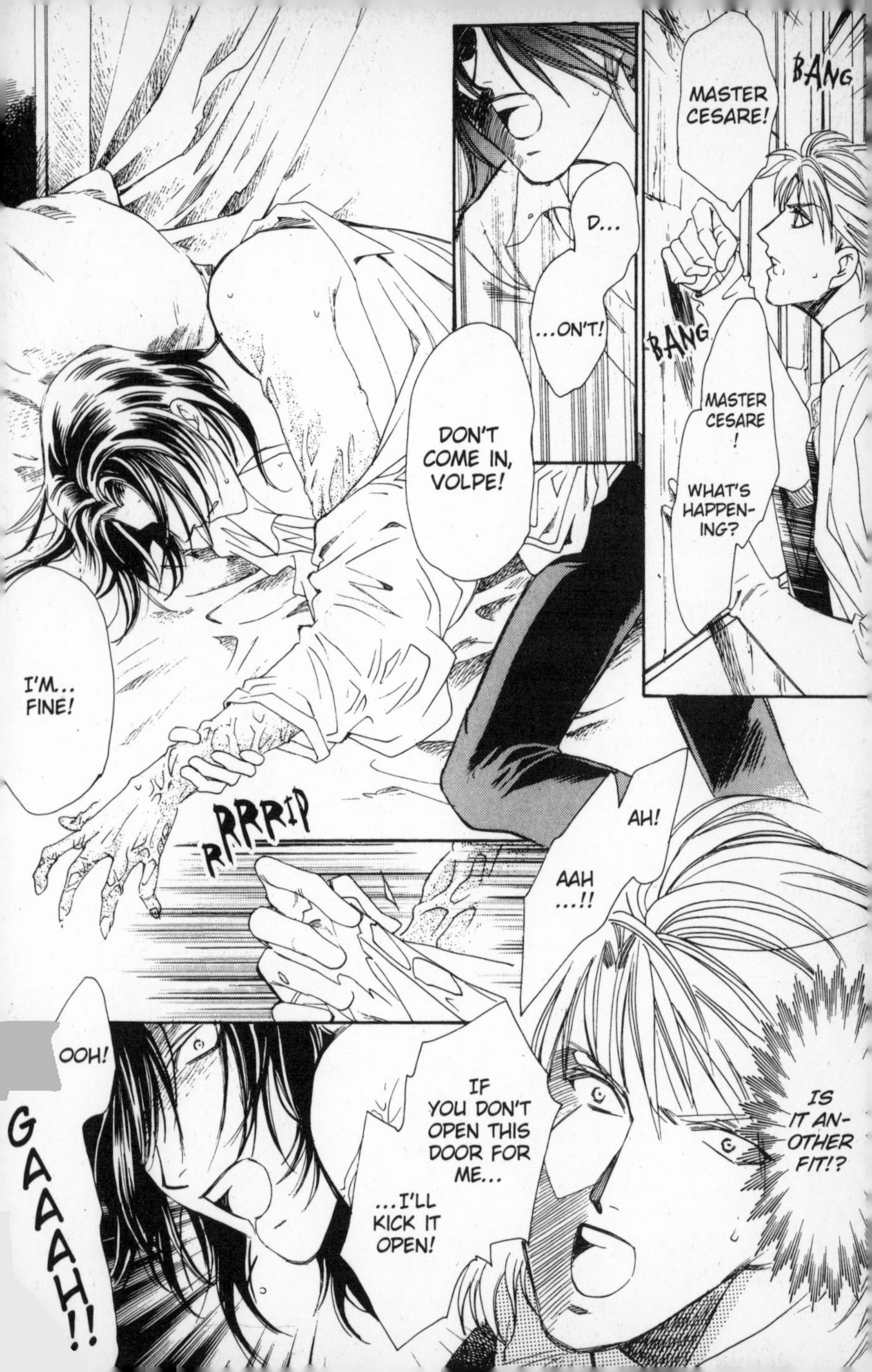
BANG
MASTER CESARE!
BANG
MASTER CESARE !
WHAT'S HAPPEN-ING?
D...
...ON'T!
DON'T COME IN, VOLPE!
I'M... FINE!
AH!
AAH ...!!
RRRRIP
IS IT AN-OTHER FIT!?
IF YOU DON'T OPEN THIS DOOR FOR ME...
...I'LL KICK IT OPEN!
OOH!
GAAAH!!

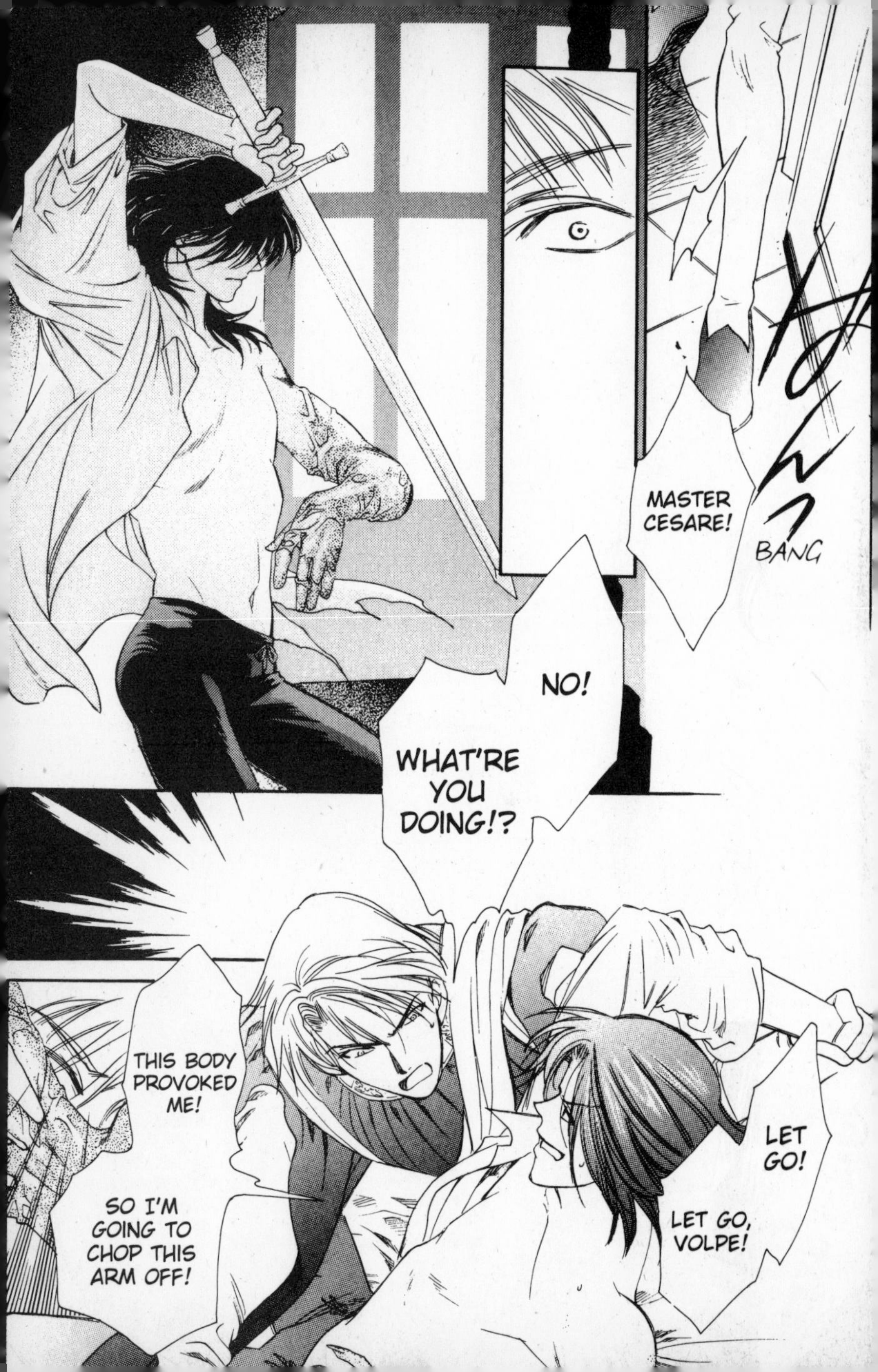
MASTER CESARE!
BANG
NO!
WHAT'RE YOU DOING!?
LET GO!
LET GO, VOLPE!
THIS BODY PROVOKED ME!
SO I'M GOING TO CHOP THIS ARM OFF!

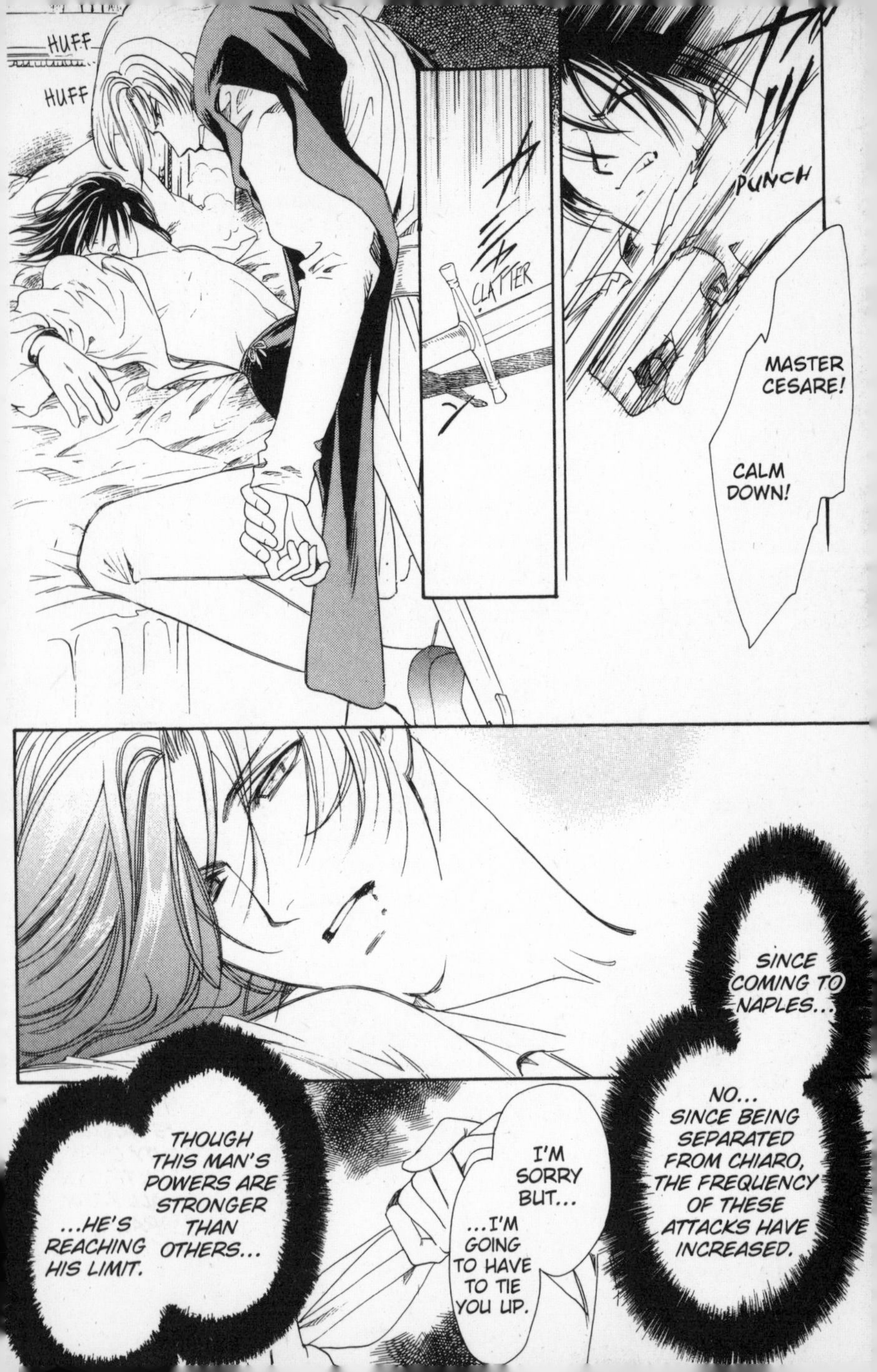
PUNCH
MASTER CESARE!
CALM DOWN!
CLATTER
HUFF
HUFF
SINCE COMING TO NAPLES...
NO... SINCE BEING SEPARATED FROM CHIARO, THE FREQUENCY OF THESE ATTACKS HAVE INCREASED.
I'M SORRY BUT...
...I'M GOING TO HAVE TO TIE YOU UP.
THOUGH THIS MAN'S POWERS ARE STRONGER THAN OTHERS...
...HE'S REACHING HIS LIMIT.

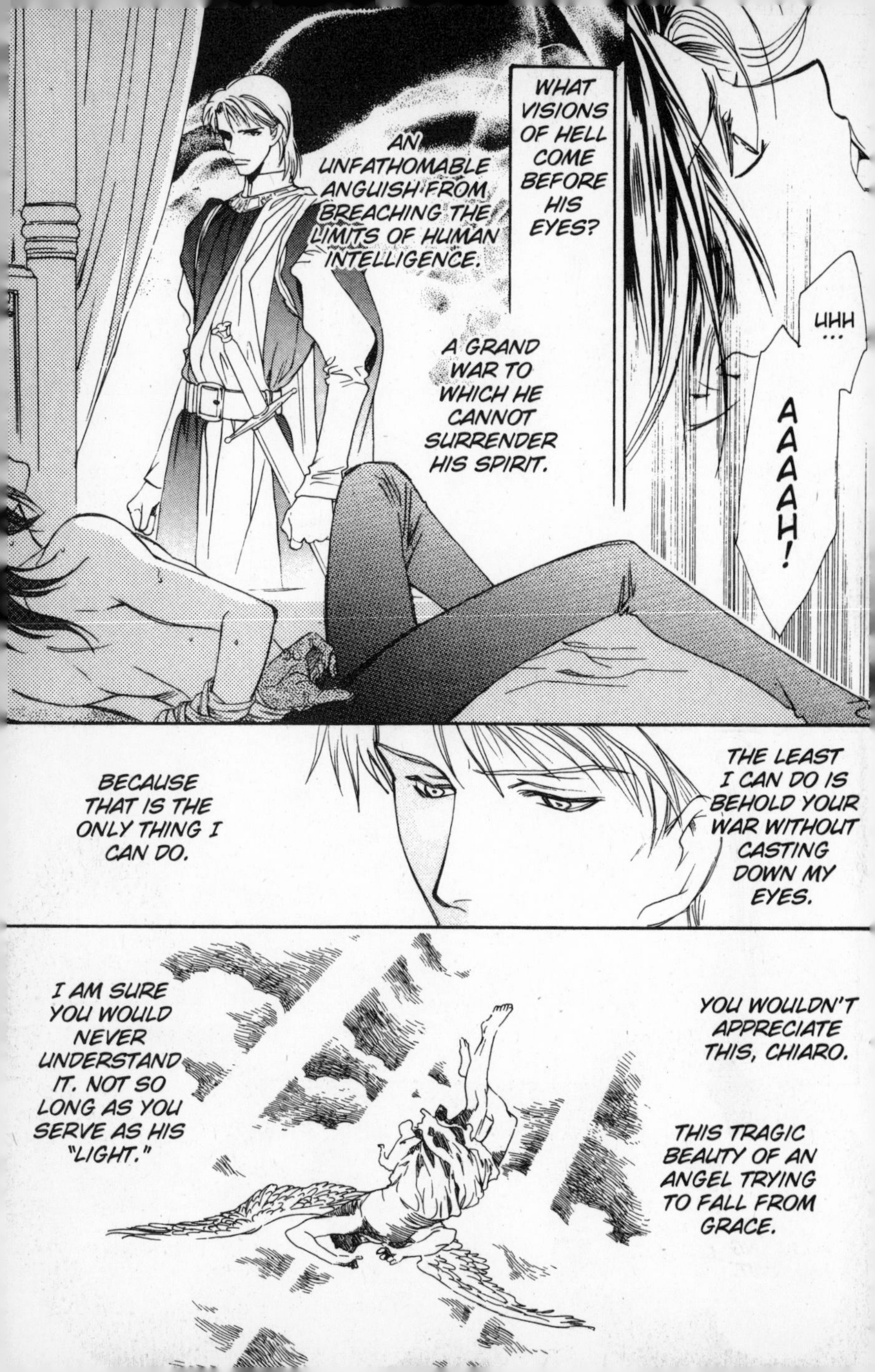
UHH...
AAAAH!
WHAT VISIONS OF HELL COME BEFORE HIS EYES?
AN UNFATHOMABLE ANGUISH FROM BREACHING THE LIMITS OF HUMAN INTELLIGENCE.
A GRAND WAR TO WHICH HE CANNOT SURRENDER HIS SPIRIT.
THE LEAST I CAN DO IS BEHOLD YOUR WAR WITHOUT CASTING DOWN MY EYES.
BECAUSE THAT IS THE ONLY THING I CAN DO.
YOU WOULDN'T APPRECIATE THIS, CHIARO.
THIS TRAGIC BEAUTY OF AN ANGEL TRYING TO FALL FROM GRACE.
I AM SURE YOU WOULD NEVER UNDERSTAND IT. NOT SO LONG AS YOU SERVE AS HIS "LIGHT."

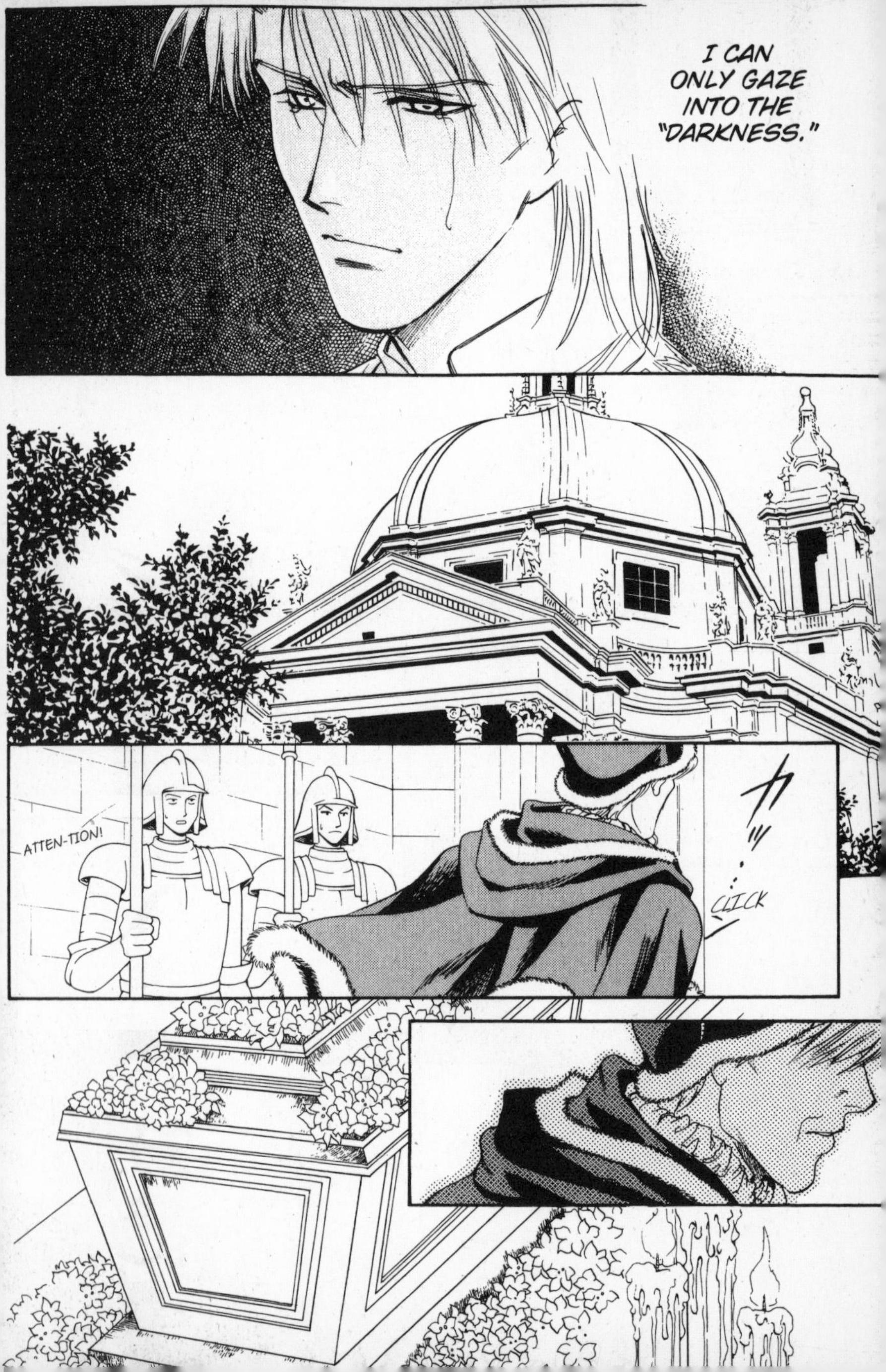
I CAN ONLY GAZE INTO THE "DARKNESS."
CLICK
ATTEN-TION!

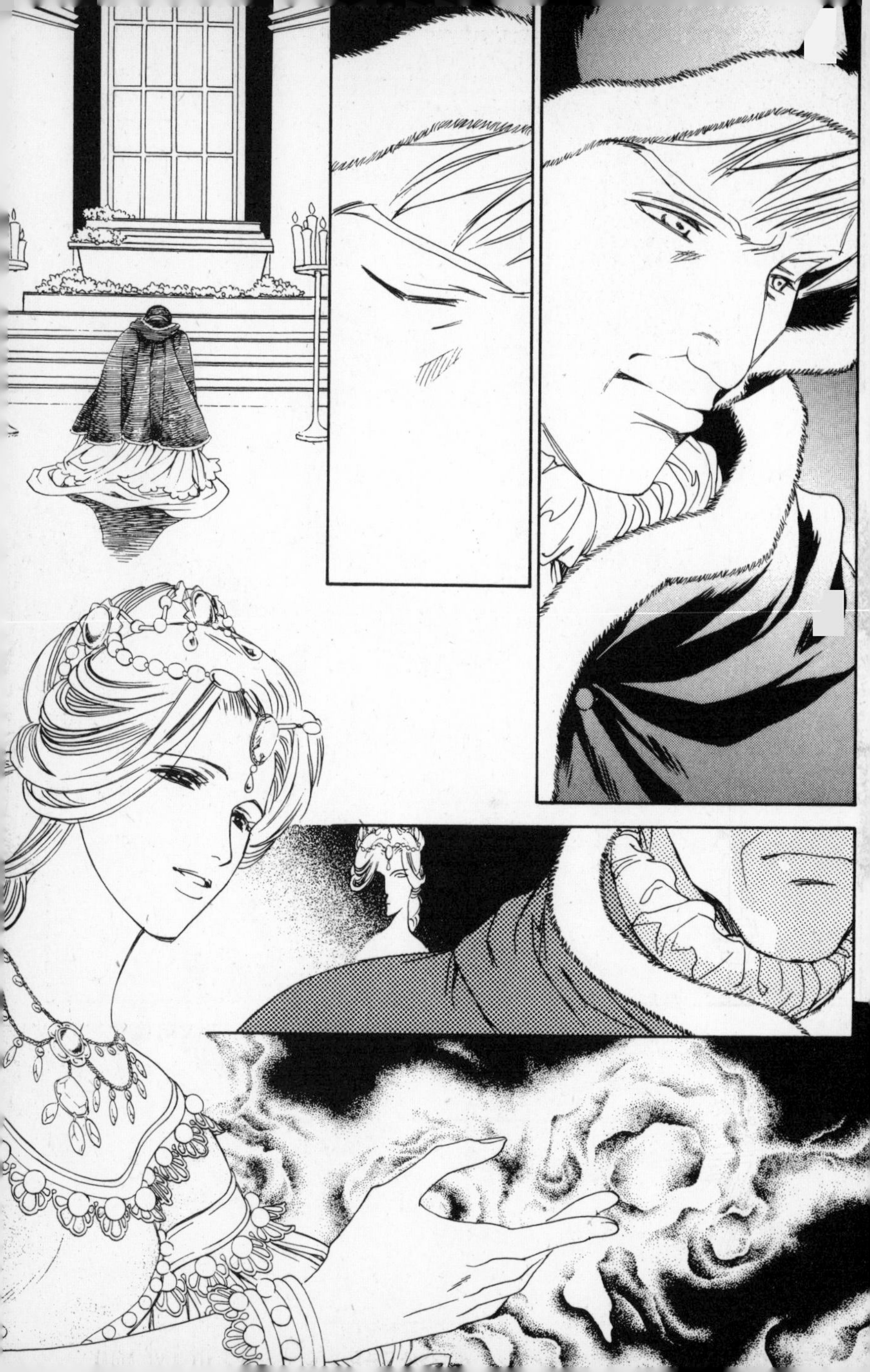

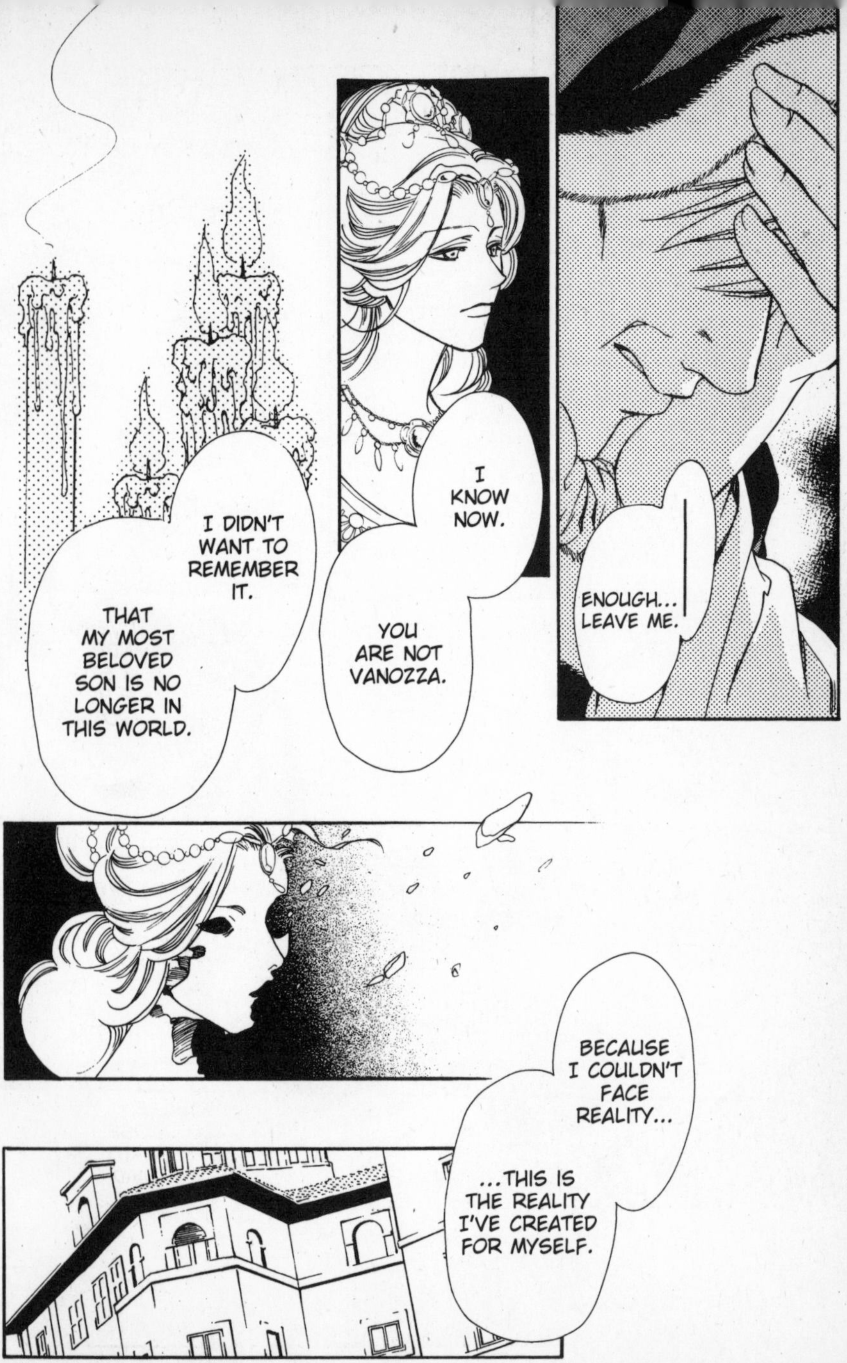
ENOUGH... LEAVE ME.
I KNOW NOW.
YOU ARE NOT VANOZZA.
I DIDN'T WANT TO REMEMBER IT.
THAT MY MOST BELOVED SON IS NO LONGER IN THIS WORLD.
BECAUSE I COULDN'T FACE REALITY...
...THIS IS THE REALITY I'VE CREATED FOR MYSELF.

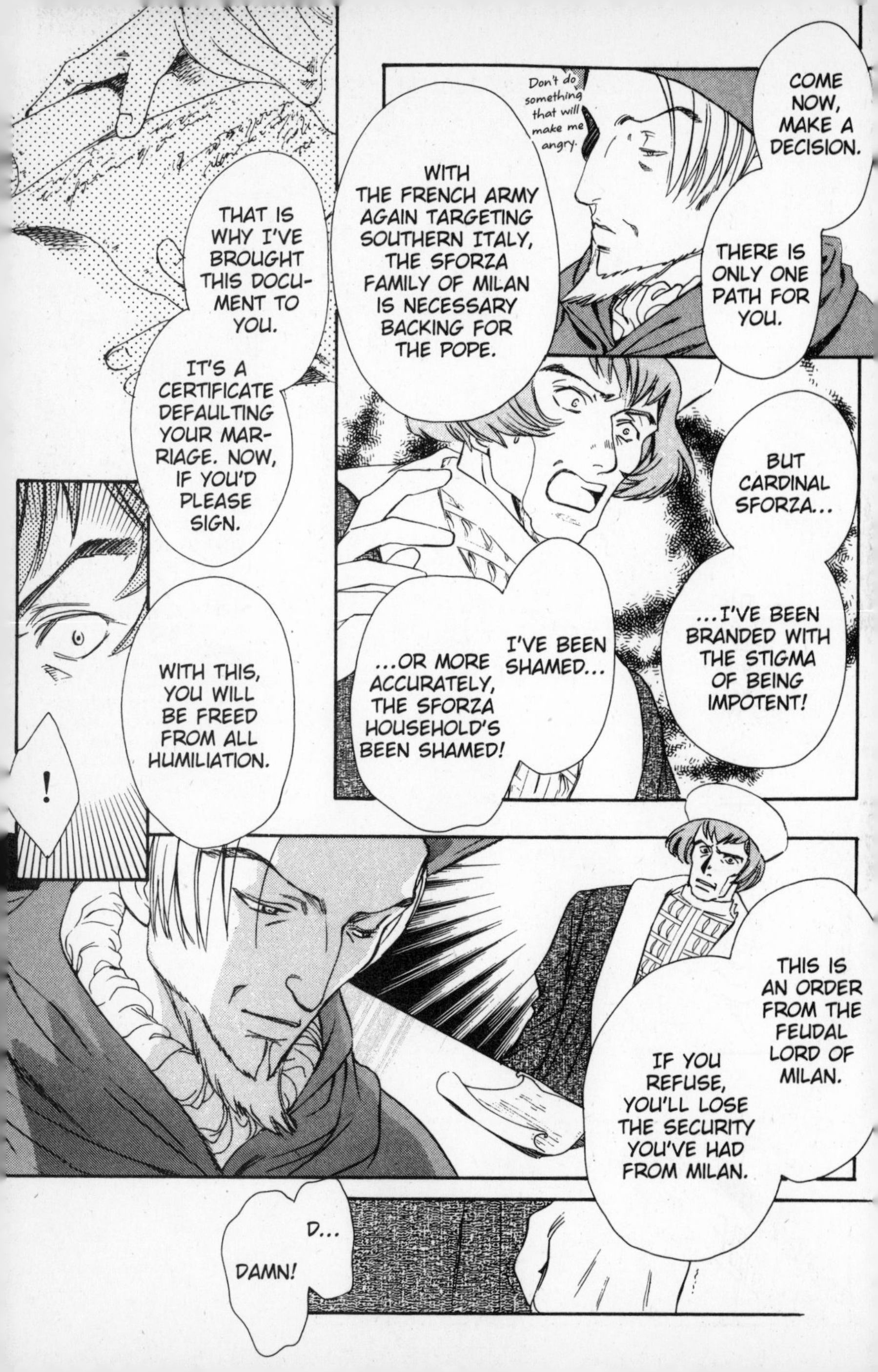
COME NOW, MAKE A DECISION.
Don't do something that will make me angry.
THERE IS ONLY ONE PATH FOR YOU.
WITH THE FRENCH ARMY AGAIN TARGETING SOUTHERN ITALY, THE SFORZA FAMILY OF MILAN IS NECESSARY BACKING FOR THE POPE.
THAT IS WHY I'VE BROUGHT THIS DOCU-MENT TO YOU.
IT'S A CERTIFICATE DEFAULTING YOUR MAR-RIAGE. NOW, IF YOU'D PLEASE SIGN.
BUT CARDINAL SFORZA...
...I'VE BEEN BRANDED WITH THE STIGMA OF BEING IMPOTENT!
I'VE BEEN SHAMED...
...OR MORE ACCURATELY, THE SFORZA HOUSEHOLD'S BEEN SHAMED!
WITH THIS, YOU WILL BE FREED FROM ALL HUMILIATION.
!
THIS IS AN ORDER FROM THE FEUDAL LORD OF MILAN.
IF YOU REFUSE, YOU'LL LOSE THE SECURITY YOU'VE HAD FROM MILAN.
D...
DAMN!

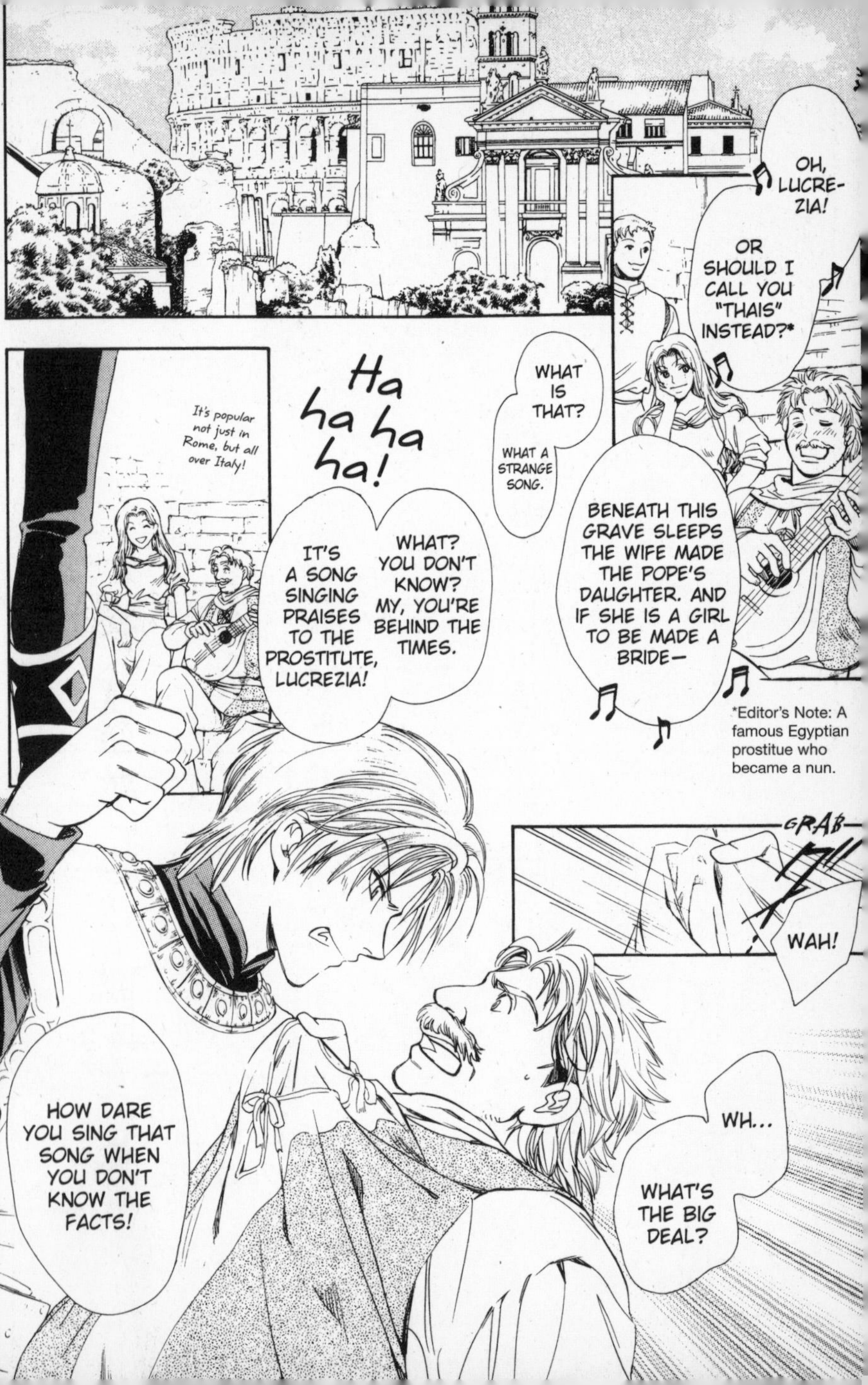
OH, LUCREZIA!
OR SHOULD I CALL YOU "THAIS" INSTEAD?*
BENEATH THIS GRAVE SLEEPS THE WIFE MADE THE POPE'S DAUGHTER. AND IF SHE IS A GIRL TO BE MADE A BRIDE—
WHAT IS THAT?
WHAT A STRANGE SONG.
Ha ha ha ha!
WHAT? YOU DON'T KNOW? MY, YOU'RE BEHIND THE TIMES.
IT'S A SONG SINGING PRAISES TO THE PROSTITUTE, LUCREZIA!
It's popular not just in Rome, but all over Italy!
GRAB
WAH!
WH...
WHAT'S THE BIG DEAL?
HOW DARE YOU SING THAT SONG WHEN YOU DON'T KNOW THE FACTS!
*Editor's Note: A famous Egyptian prostitue who became a nun.

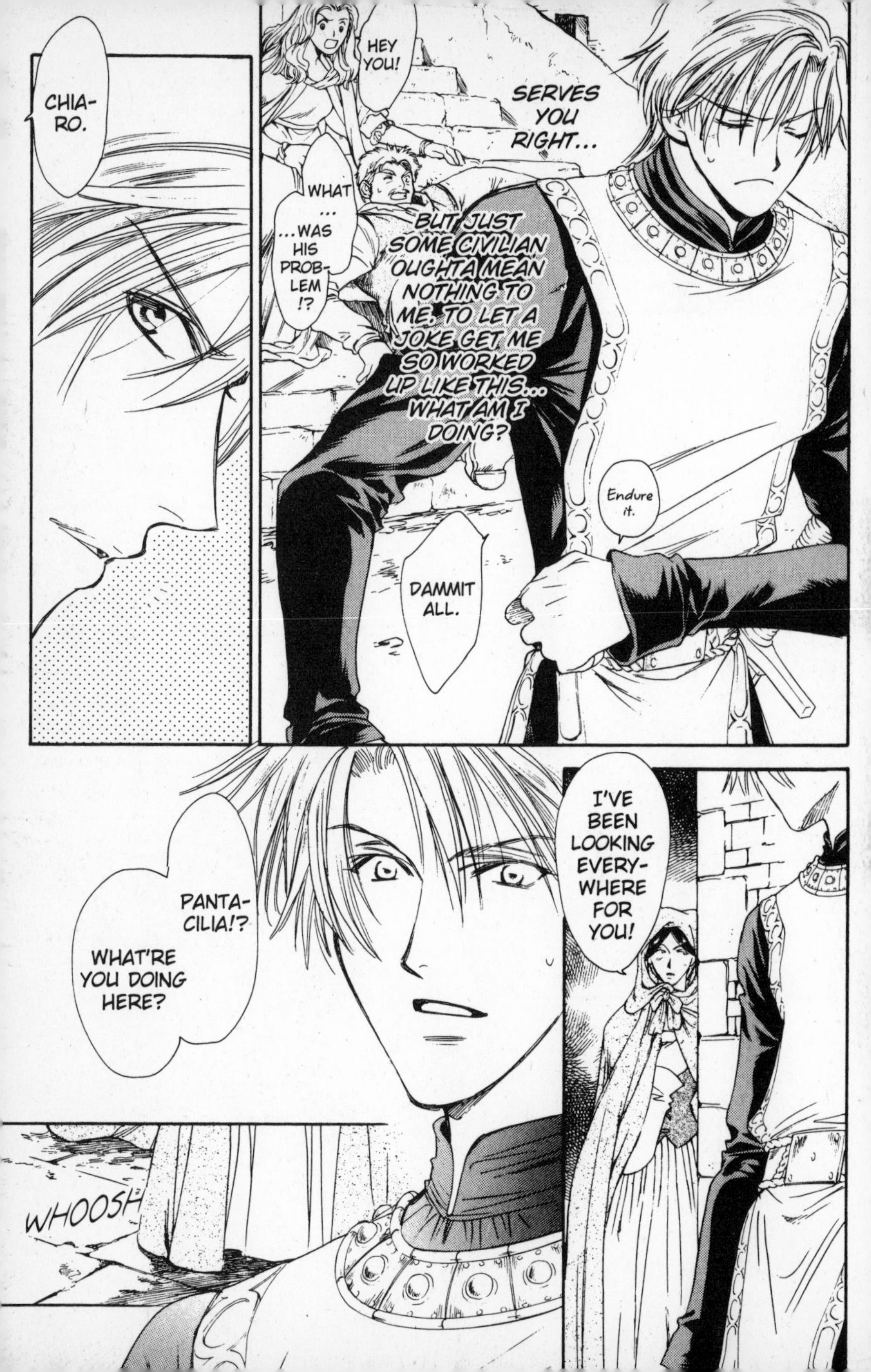
SERVES YOU RIGHT...
HEY YOU!
BUT JUST SOME CIVILIAN OUGHTA MEAN NOTHING TO ME. TO LET A JOKE GET ME SO WORKED UP LIKE THIS... WHAT AM I DOING?
WHAT ... ...WAS HIS PROB-LEM!?
Endure it.
DAMMIT ALL.
CHIA-RO.
I'VE BEEN LOOKING EVERY-WHERE FOR YOU!
PANTA-CILIA!?
WHAT'RE YOU DOING HERE?
WHOOSH

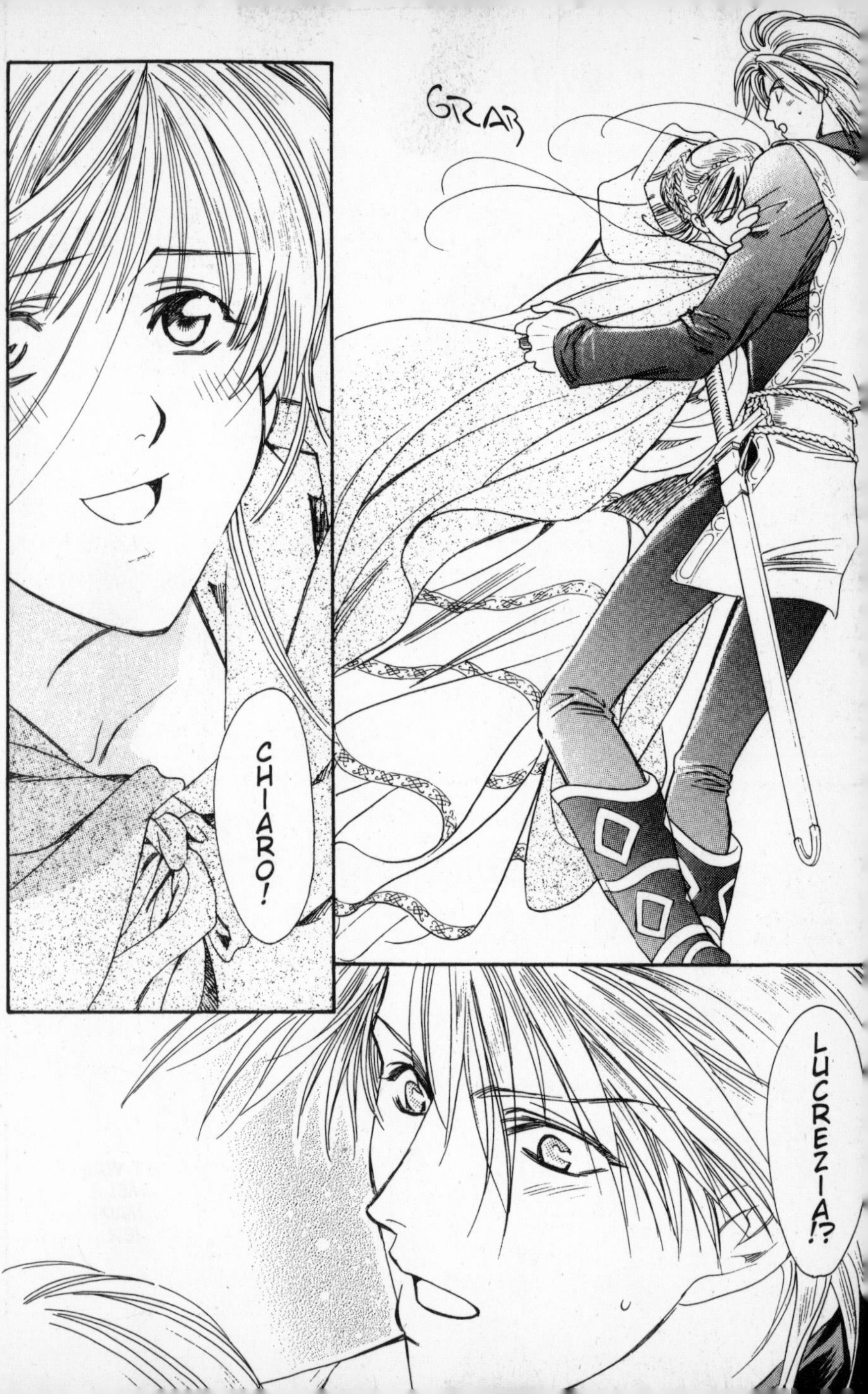
GRAB
CHIARO!
LUCREZIA!?

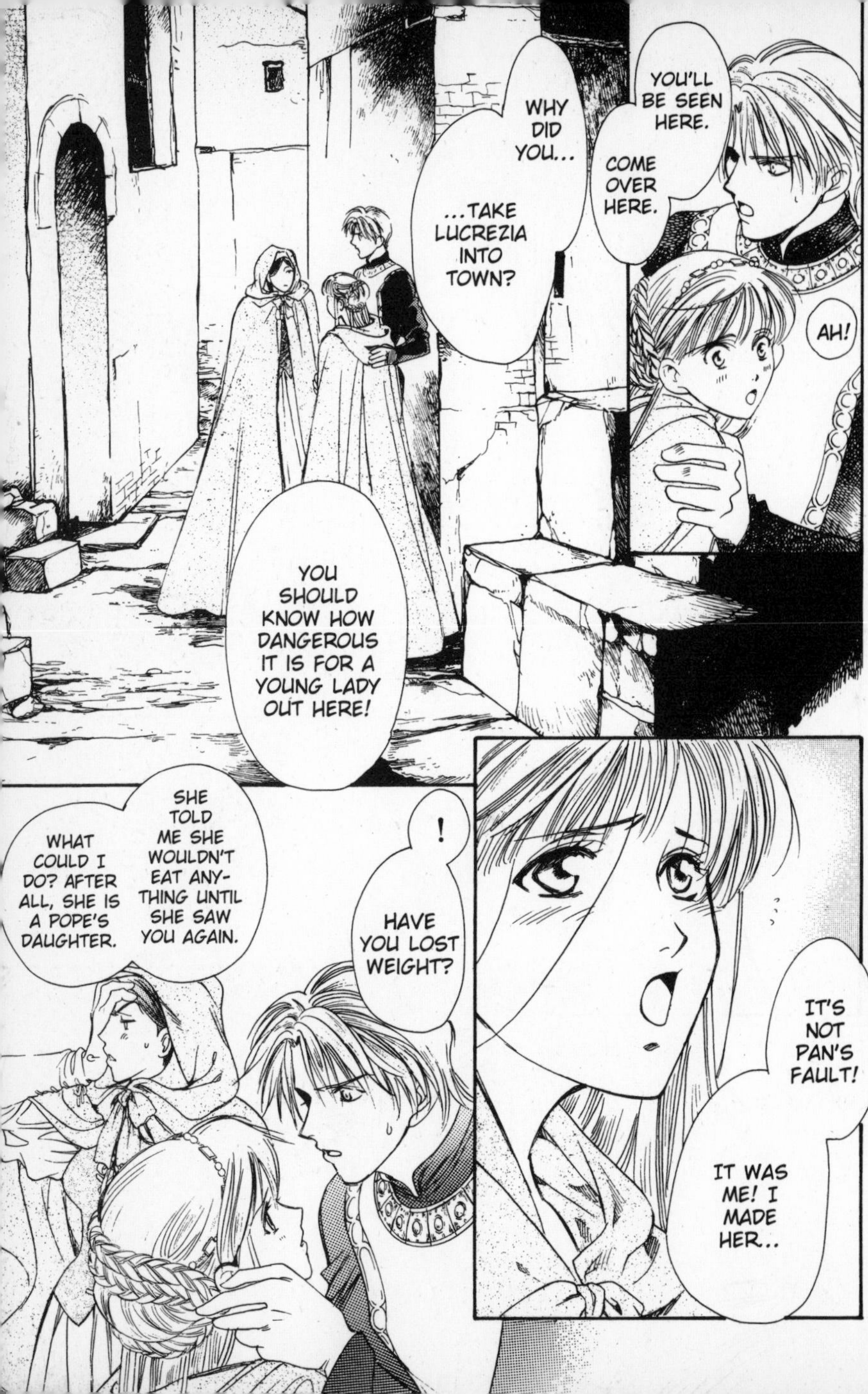
YOU'LL BE SEEN HERE.
COME OVER HERE.
AH!
WHY DID YOU...
...TAKE LUCREZIA INTO TOWN?
YOU SHOULD KNOW HOW DANGEROUS IT IS FOR A YOUNG LADY OUT HERE!
IT'S NOT PAN'S FAULT!
IT WAS ME! I MADE HER..
!
HAVE YOU LOST WEIGHT?
SHE TOLD ME SHE WOULDN'T EAT ANY-THING UNTIL SHE SAW YOU AGAIN.
WHAT COULD I DO? AFTER ALL, SHE IS A POPE'S DAUGHTER.

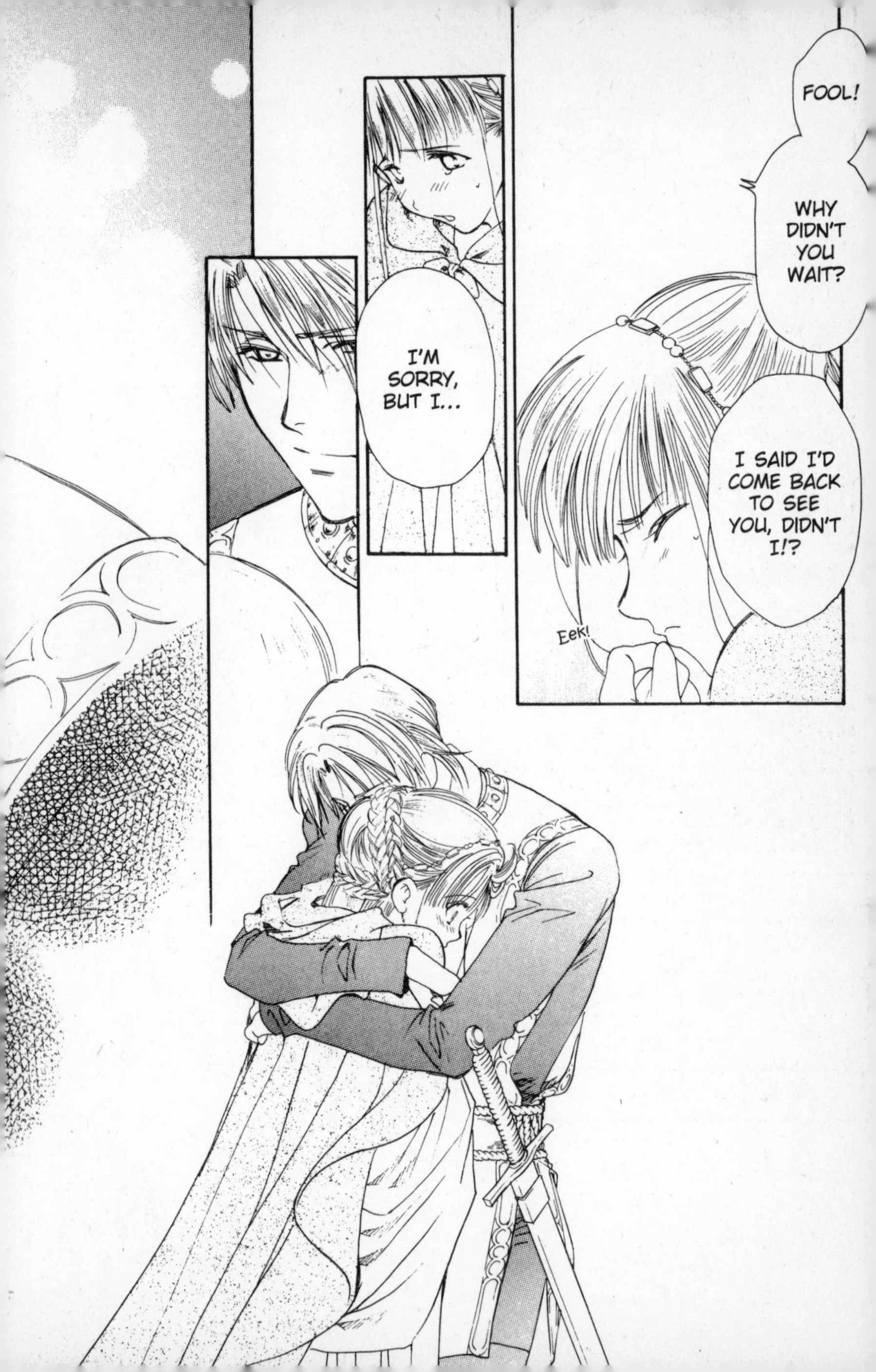
FOOL!
WHY DIDN'T YOU WAIT?
I SAID I'D COME BACK TO SEE YOU, DIDN'T I!?
Eek!
I'M SORRY, BUT I...

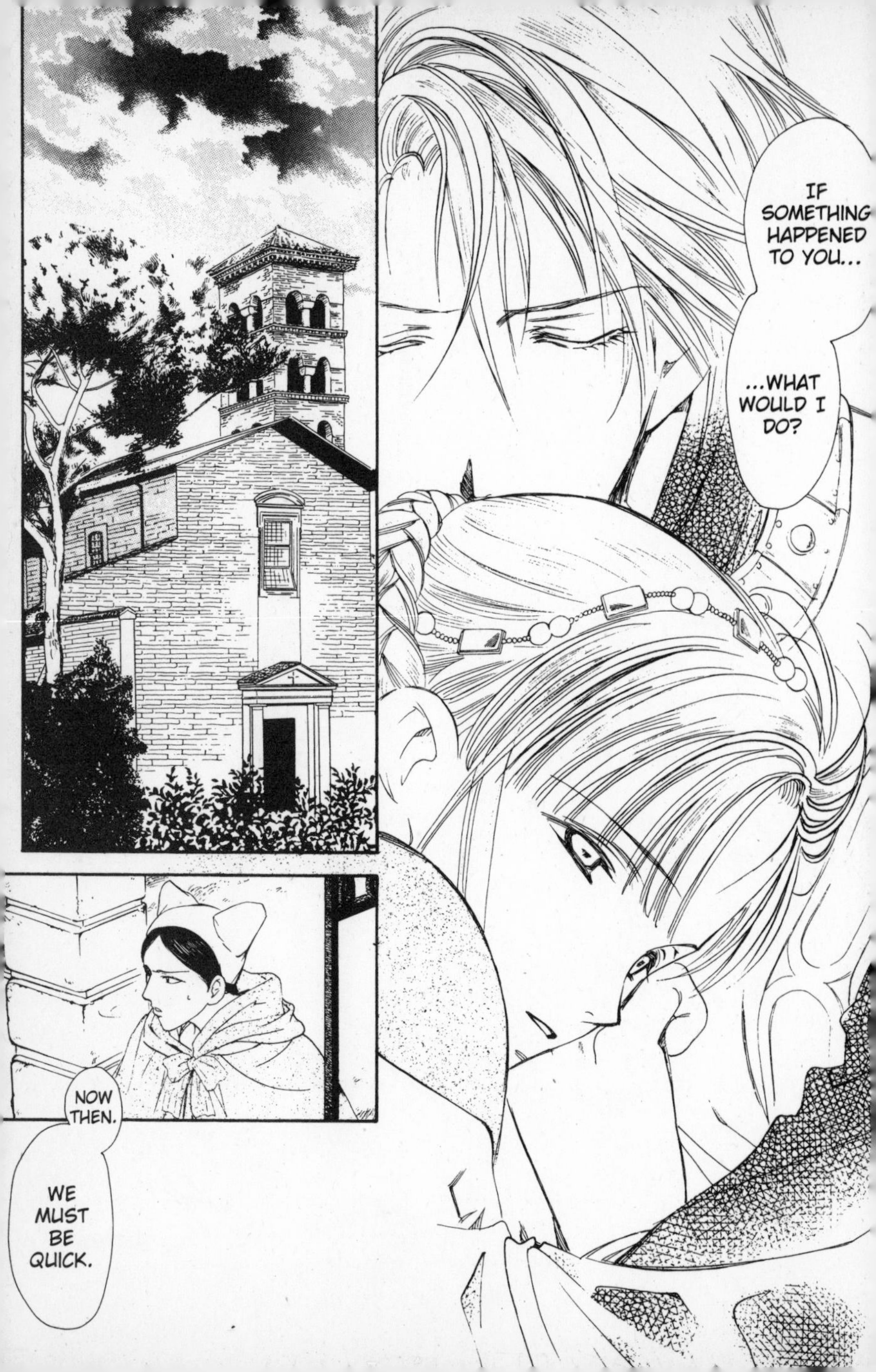
IF SOMETHING HAPPENED TO YOU...
...WHAT WOULD I DO?
NOW THEN.
WE MUST BE QUICK.

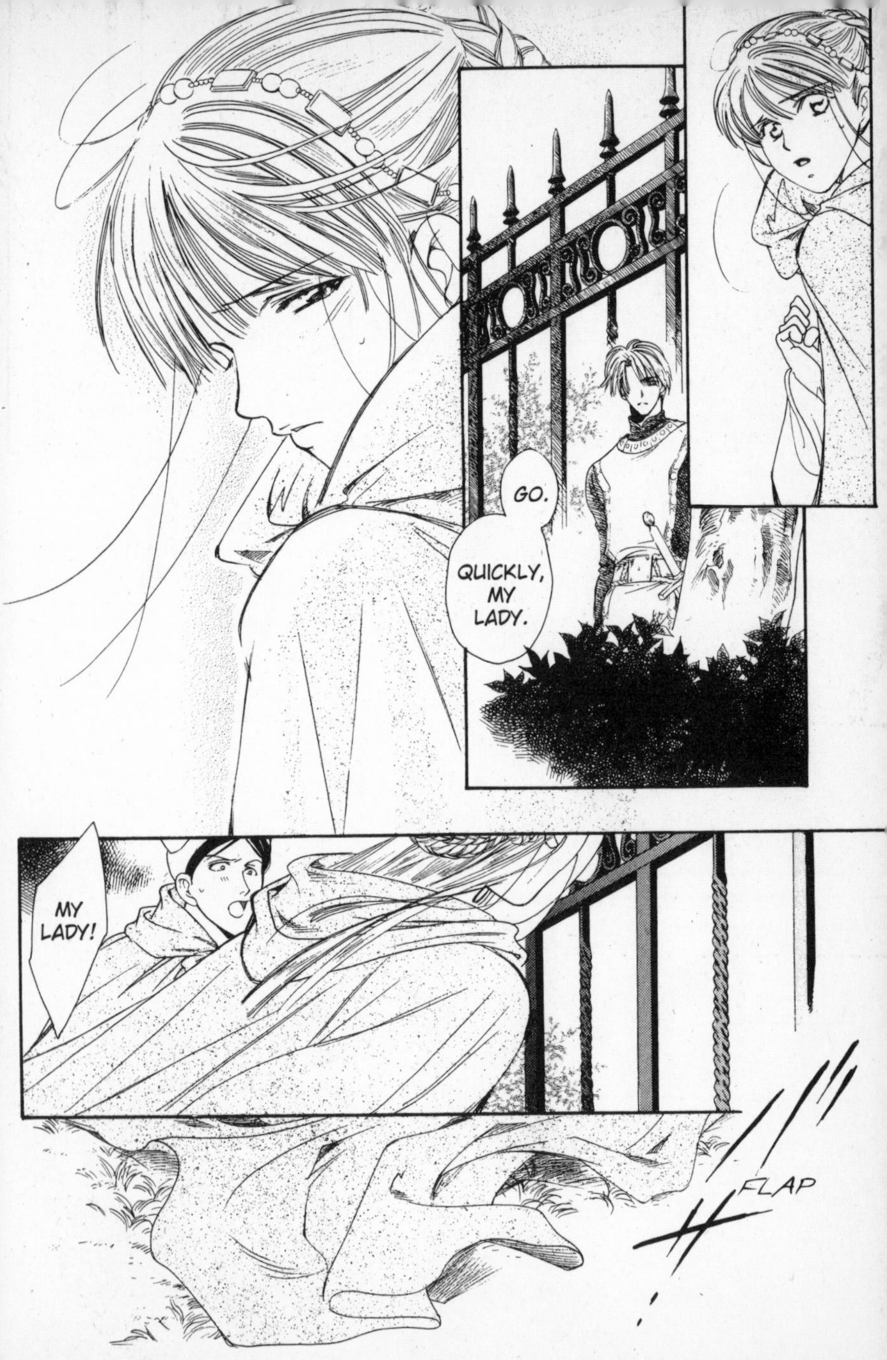
GO.
QUICKLY, MY LADY.
MY LADY!
FLAP

CLANG

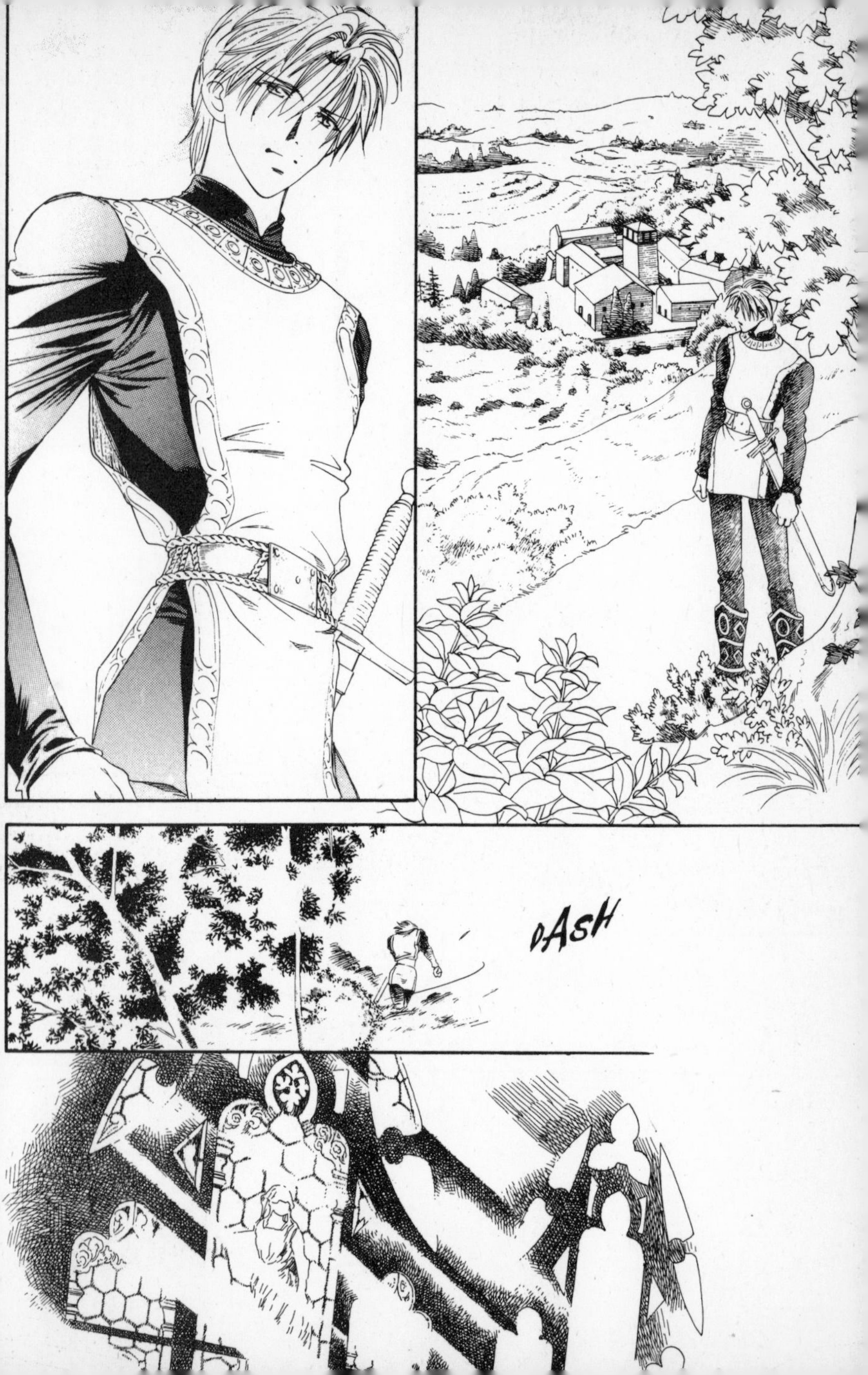
DASH

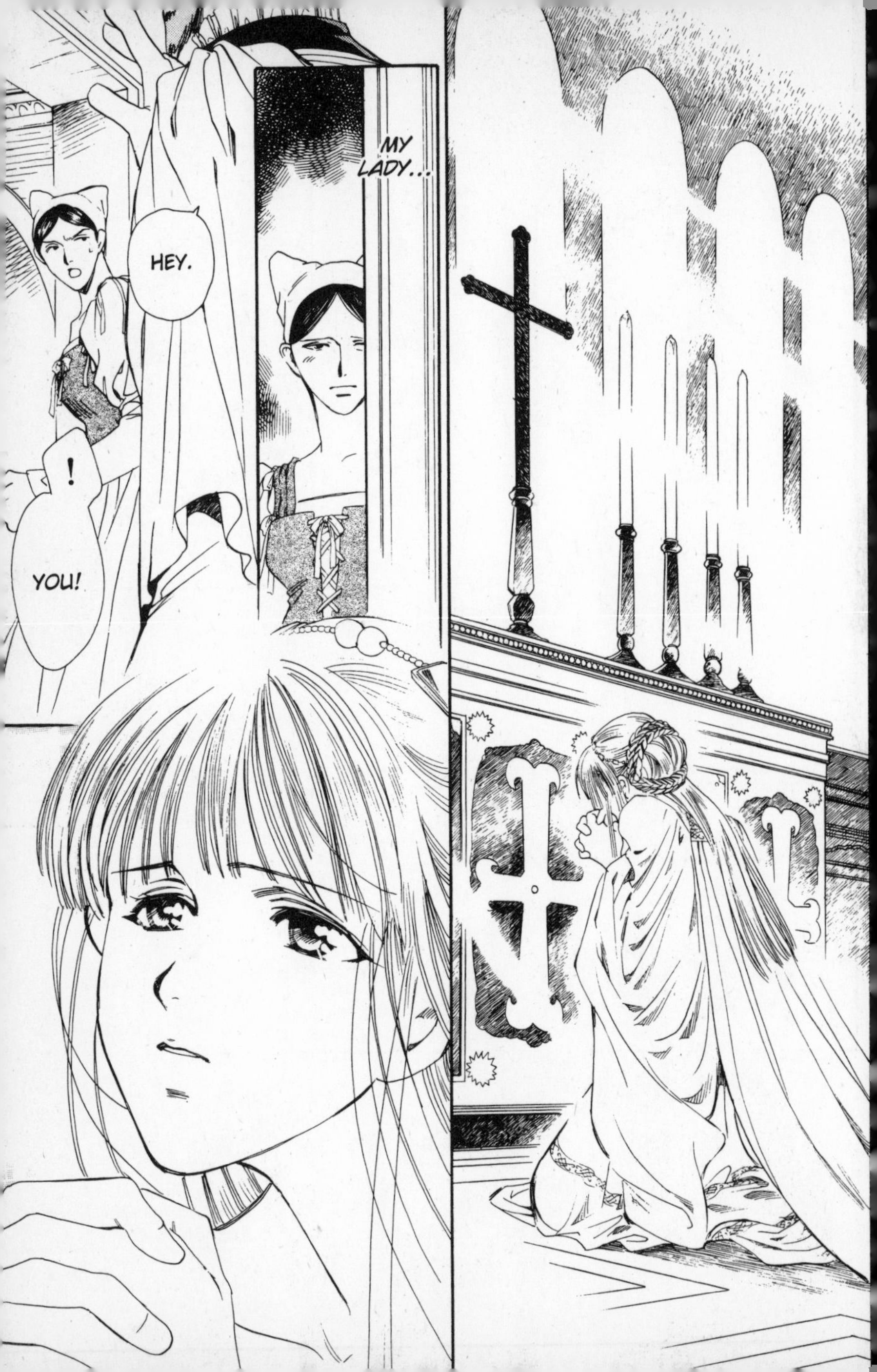
MY LADY...
HEY.
!
YOU!

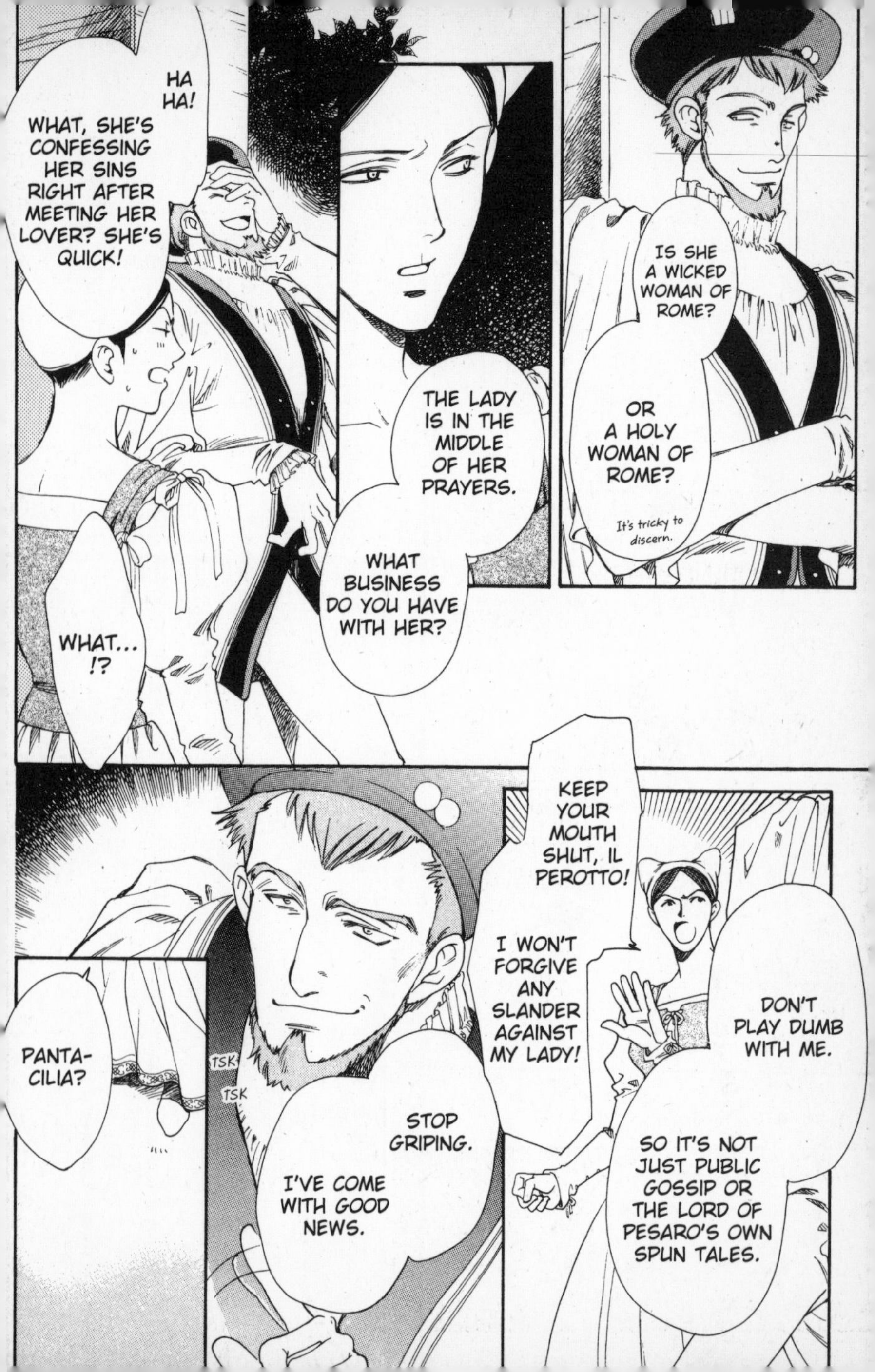
IS SHE A WICKED WOMAN OF ROME?
OR A HOLY WOMAN OF ROME?
It's tricky to discern.
THE LADY IS IN THE MIDDLE OF HER PRAYERS.
WHAT BUSINESS DO YOU HAVE WITH HER?
HA HA!
WHAT, SHE'S CONFESSING HER SINS RIGHT AFTER MEETING HER LOVER? SHE'S QUICK!
WHAT... !?
KEEP YOUR MOUTH SHUT, IL PEROTTO!
I WON'T FORGIVE ANY SLANDER AGAINST MY LADY!
DON'T PLAY DUMB WITH ME.
SO IT'S NOT JUST PUBLIC GOSSIP OR THE LORD OF PESARO'S OWN SPUN TALES.
TSK
TSK
STOP GRIPING.
I'VE COME WITH GOOD NEWS.
PANTA-CILIA?

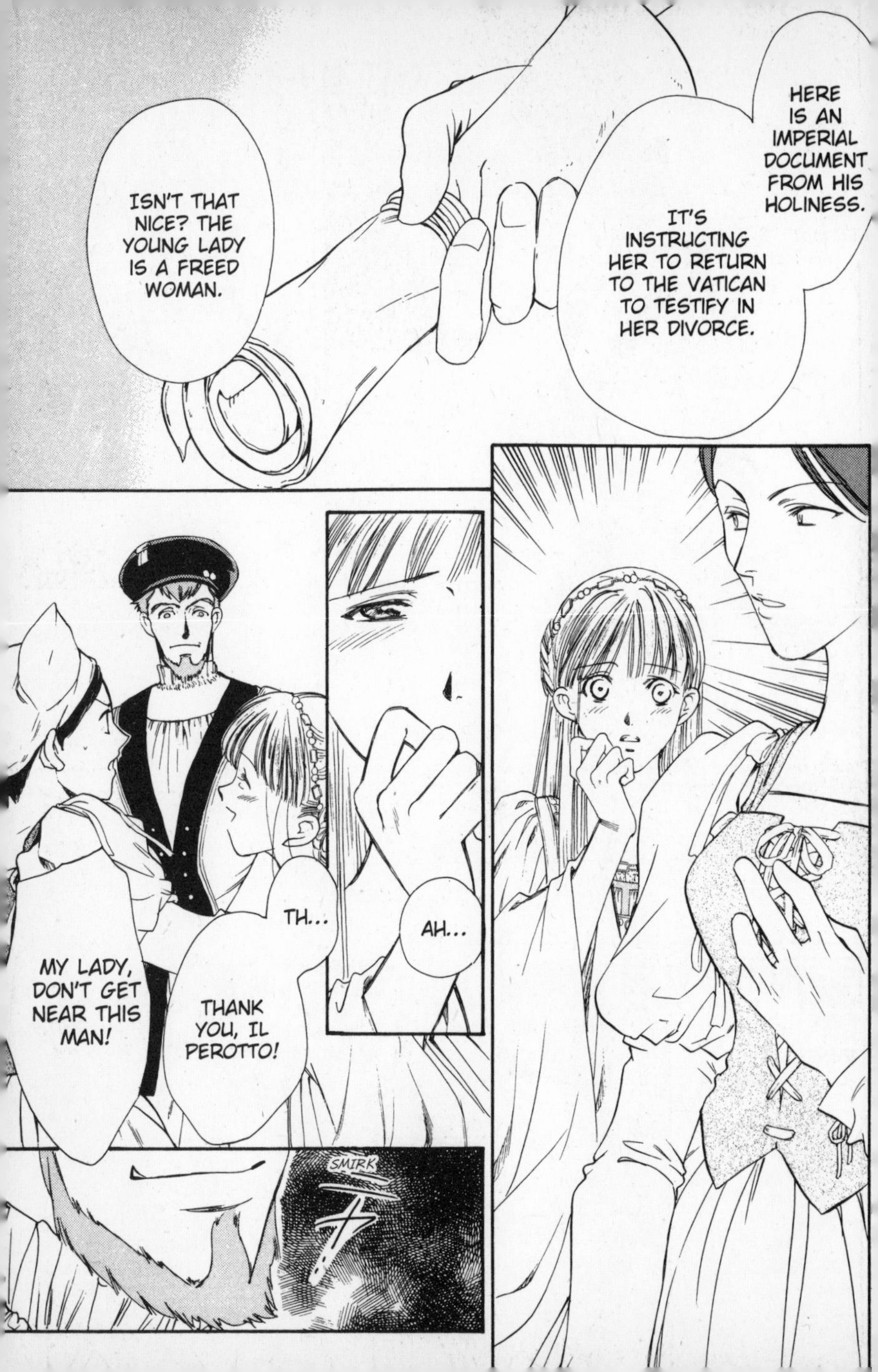
HERE IS AN IMPERIAL DOCUMENT FROM HIS HOLINESS.
IT'S INSTRUCTING HER TO RETURN TO THE VATICAN TO TESTIFY IN HER DIVORCE.
ISN'T THAT NICE? THE YOUNG LADY IS A FREED WOMAN.
AH...
TH...
THANK YOU, IL PEROTTO!
MY LADY, DON'T GET NEAR THIS MAN!
SMIRK

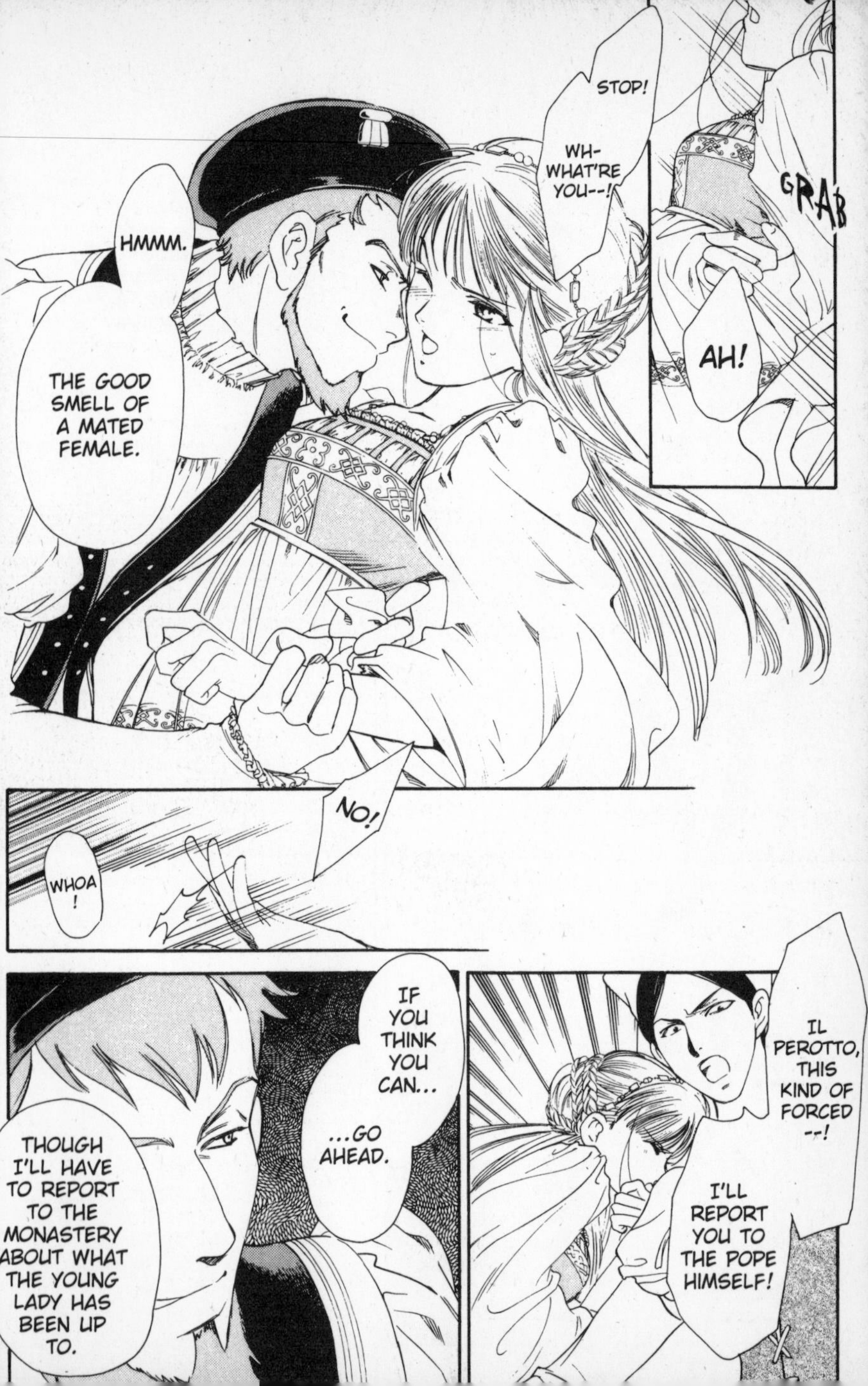
STOP!
WH- WHAT'RE YOU--!
GRAB
AH!
HMMM.
THE GOOD SMELL OF A MATED FEMALE.
NO!
WHOA!
IL PEROTTO, THIS KIND OF FORCED--!
I'LL REPORT YOU TO THE POPE HIMSELF!
IF YOU THINK YOU CAN...
...GO AHEAD.
THOUGH I'LL HAVE TO REPORT TO THE MONASTERY ABOUT WHAT THE YOUNG LADY HAS BEEN UP TO.

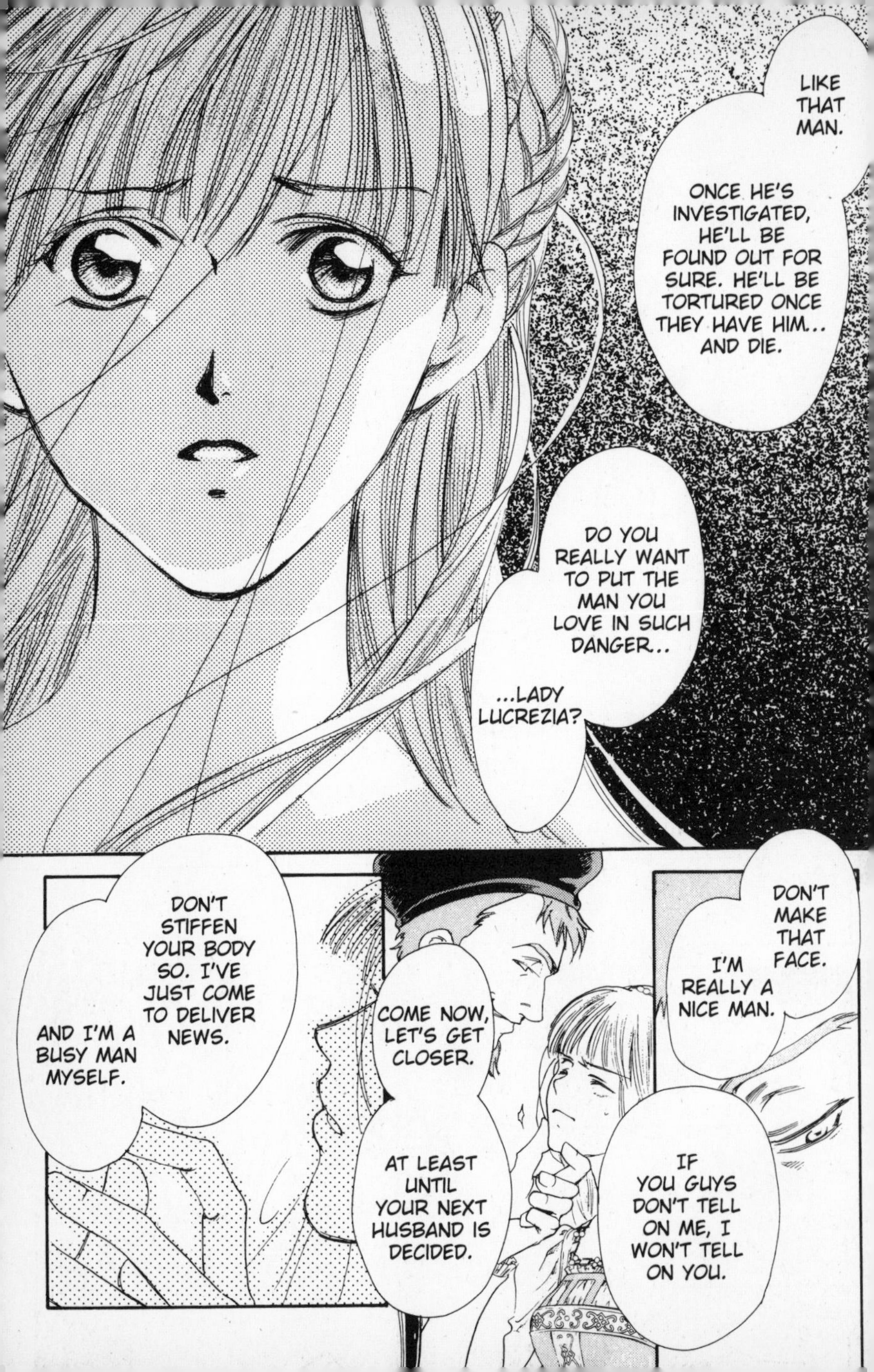
LIKE THAT MAN.
ONCE HE'S INVESTIGATED, HE'LL BE FOUND OUT FOR SURE. HE'LL BE TORTURED ONCE THEY HAVE HIM... AND DIE.
DO YOU REALLY WANT TO PUT THE MAN YOU LOVE IN SUCH DANGER..
...LADY LUCREZIA?
DON'T MAKE THAT FACE.
I'M REALLY A NICE MAN.
COME NOW, LET'S GET CLOSER.
DON'T STIFFEN YOUR BODY SO. I'VE JUST COME TO DELIVER NEWS.
AND I'M A BUSY MAN MYSELF.
IF YOU GUYS DON'T TELL ON ME, I WON'T TELL ON YOU.
AT LEAST UNTIL YOUR NEXT HUSBAND IS DECIDED.

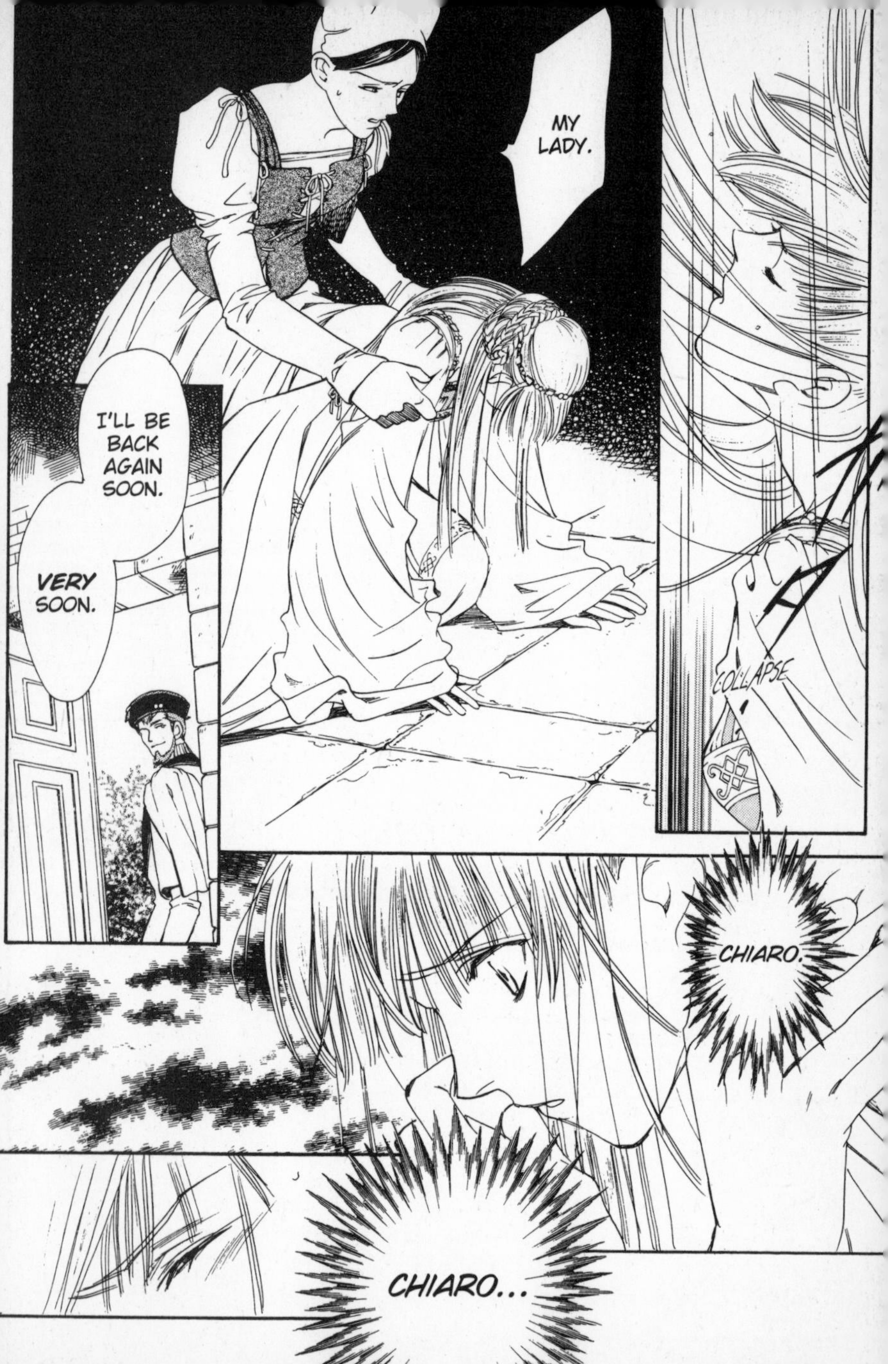
COLLAPSE
MY LADY.
I'LL BE BACK AGAIN SOON.
VERY SOON.
CHIARO.
CHIARO...

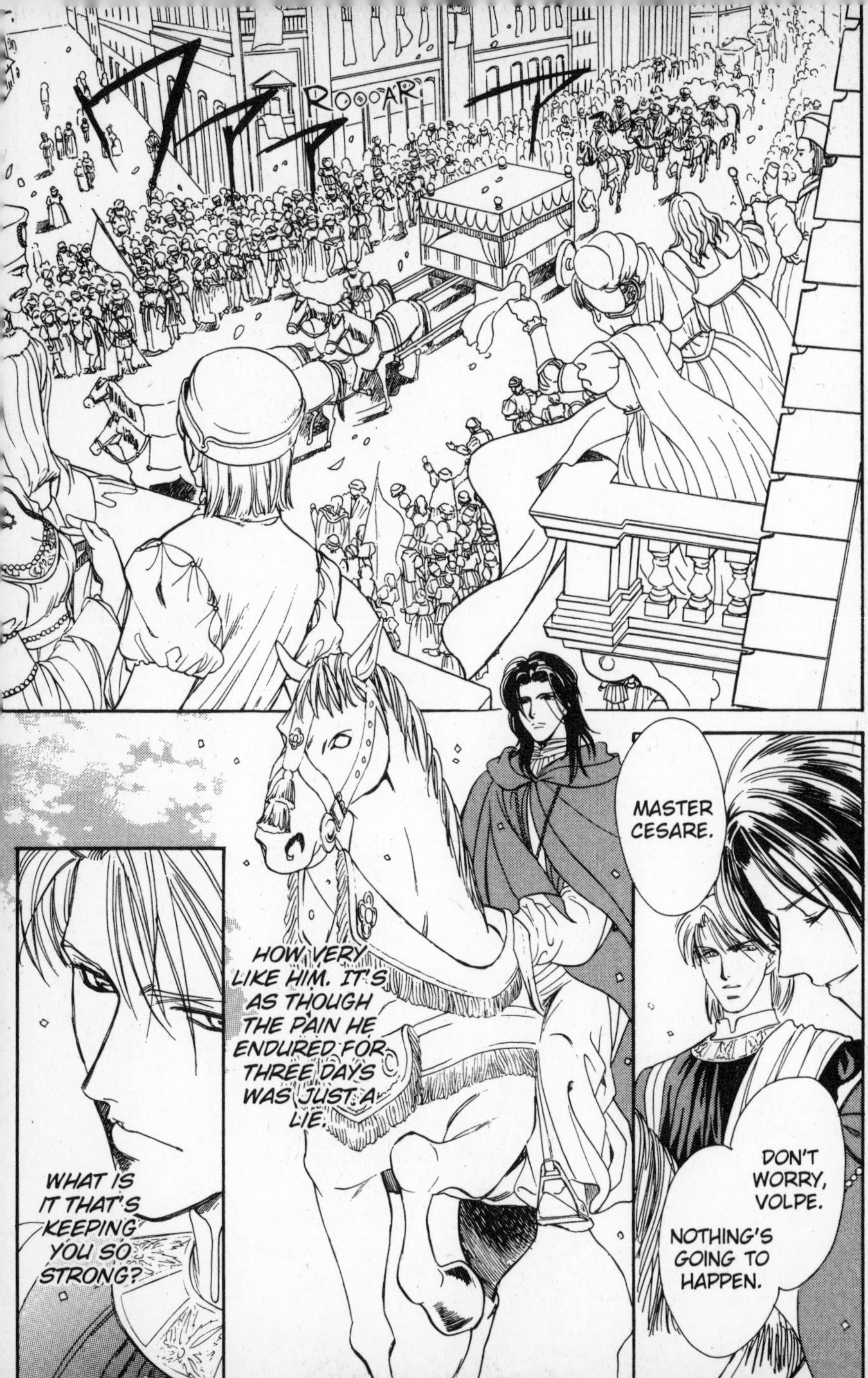
ROOOAR
MASTER CESARE.
DON'T WORRY, VOLPE.
NOTHING'S GOING TO HAPPEN.
HOW VERY LIKE HIM. IT'S AS THOUGH THE PAIN HE ENDURED FOR THREE DAYS WAS JUST A LIE.
WHAT IS IT THAT'S KEEPING YOU SO STRONG?

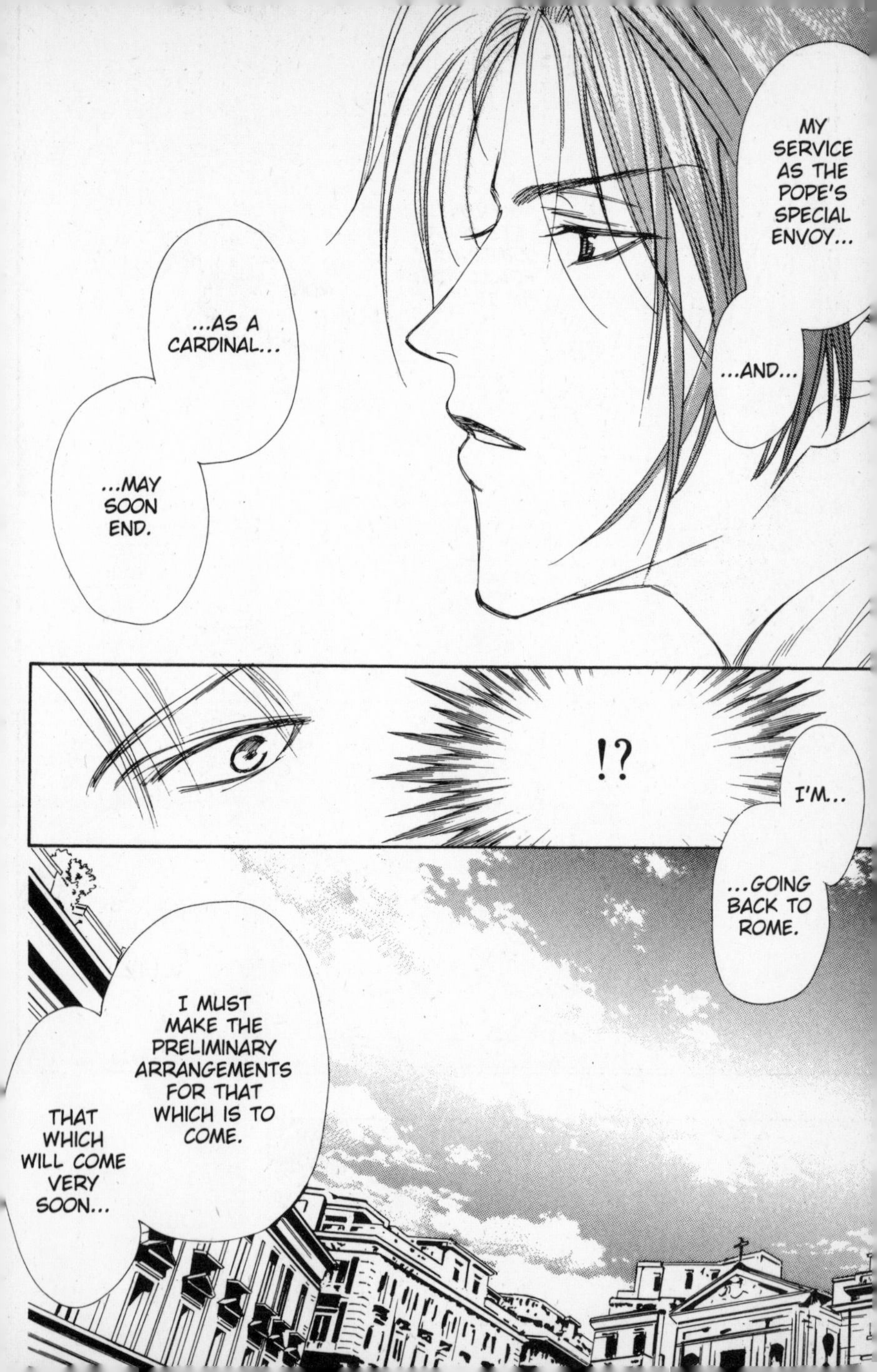
MY SERVICE AS THE POPE'S SPECIAL ENVOY...
...AND...
...AS A CARDINAL...
...MAY SOON END.
!?
I'M...
...GOING BACK TO ROME.
I MUST MAKE THE PRELIMINARY ARRANGEMENTS FOR THAT WHICH IS TO COME.
THAT WHICH WILL COME VERY SOON...

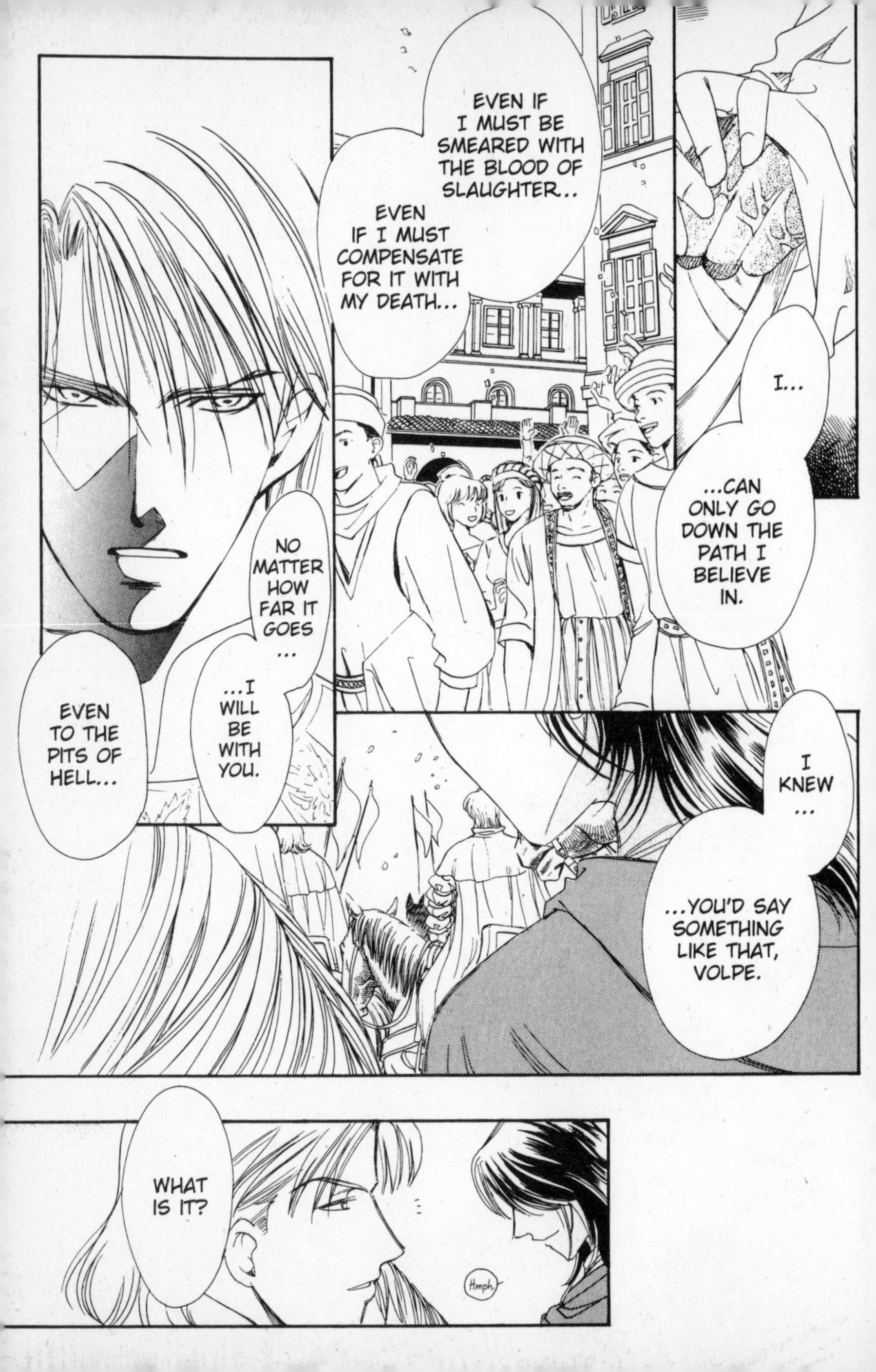
EVEN IF I MUST BE SMEARED WITH THE BLOOD OF SLAUGHTER..
EVEN IF I MUST COMPENSATE FOR IT WITH MY DEATH...
I...
...CAN ONLY GO DOWN THE PATH I BELIEVE IN.
NO MATTER HOW FAR IT GOES...
...I WILL BE WITH YOU.
EVEN TO THE PITS OF HELL...
I KNEW...
...YOU'D SAY SOMETHING LIKE THAT, VOLPE.
Hmph.
WHAT IS IT?

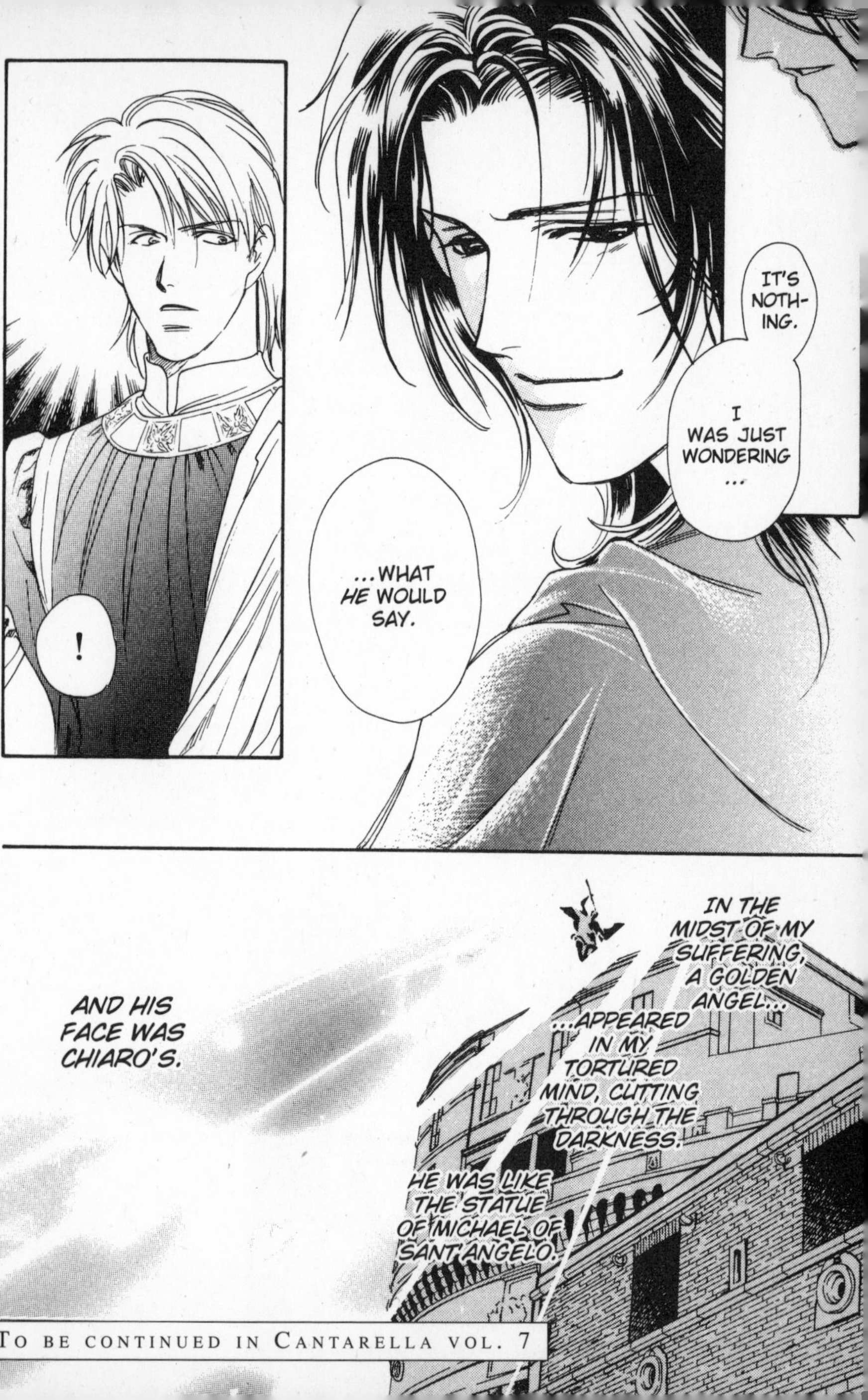
IT'S NOTHING.
I WAS JUST WONDERING...
...WHAT HE WOULD SAY.
!
IN THE MIDST OF MY SUFFERING, A GOLDEN ANGEL...
...APPEARED IN MY TORTURED MIND, CUTTING THROUGH THE DARKNESS.
HE WAS LIKE THE STATUE OF MICHAEL OF SANT'ANGELO.
AND HIS FACE WAS CHIARO'S.

To be continued in Cantarella vol. 7

チン・タレラ

"Cantarella" has already broken into its sixth volume! For a while, it was in battle-mode, but now it's gone into lovey-dovey mode, so I think it's turning into more of a shojo manga. (Or am I wrong? Hmm...) Alfonso d'Aragon-kun's entrance was brief, but since he's a fun character to draw, I'm looking forward to his next appearance.

Even though I went to Italy, my reference material is pathetic! The interiors are just too intense! And the garments--!! They're all separated parts joined together by strings. Because they're joined like that, the undershirt pokes through at times; that's actually a part of the design. What's even more strange is the intentionally made incisions. Please imagine, for a moment, the garments of the Swiss guards of the Vatican. There. See how the sleeves are all fluttery and look like decorations?

In old-school manga, the sleeves and bloomers of princes looked like 🦋. It looked this way because of the incisions that allowed for the material beneath to show through.

To draw this manga, I thoroughly examined all my research and finally understood all of it for the first time. I always would think of this while markering it all up with my assistant in charge of garments.

The thing that most confused everyone in the studio had to be the men's tights. The clothing crossed over in front and back and was also tied with string. Meaning that the middle was the only part you could flip up. It's soooo ugly. But I suppose it's practical. Or is it!?

So yeah, I could use this space for a dirty joke but instead shall move on to say thank you for picking up volume 6. Since I will be working even harder to up the tension even more, I look forward to seeing you in the next volume!

Topics of 2003:
• In September 2003, as a part of the Art Jeuness galleries of Tokyo and Osaka, I'm preparing to hold an art exhibit (I'll be selling pieces too).
• I've been put in charge of doing the character design and illustrations for the PS2 "Gakuen Heaven" to be coming out in September. I'd appreciate your support there too.*

*Editor's Note: "Gakuen Heaven" has since become a major hit, with an anime series, a game sequel, novels, and a manga series. Higuri-sensei has been involved in the production of all versions of it.

And to top it all off, to those who helped me in the drawing of this manga:
Izumi Hijiri-san, Naoko Nakatsuji-san, Wakusa Miyakoshi-san, Mitsuru Fuyutsuki-san, Akiyoshi-san, kiyo-chan, Akiko Tawara-san, Kou Ozawa-san, Eiko Sen-san, Eri Koizumi-san, my chief Ryoka Oda-san, chief princess 凸
sparkling Y-sama, my editor-in-chief, and everyone at the printing company…thank you!

Address for letters ♥:

Send fan mail to:
YOU HIGURI
c/o Audry Taylor
Go! Media Entertainment, LLC
5737 Kanan Rd. #591
Agoura Hills CA 91301

Or visit her official website in English at:
http://www.youhiguri.com

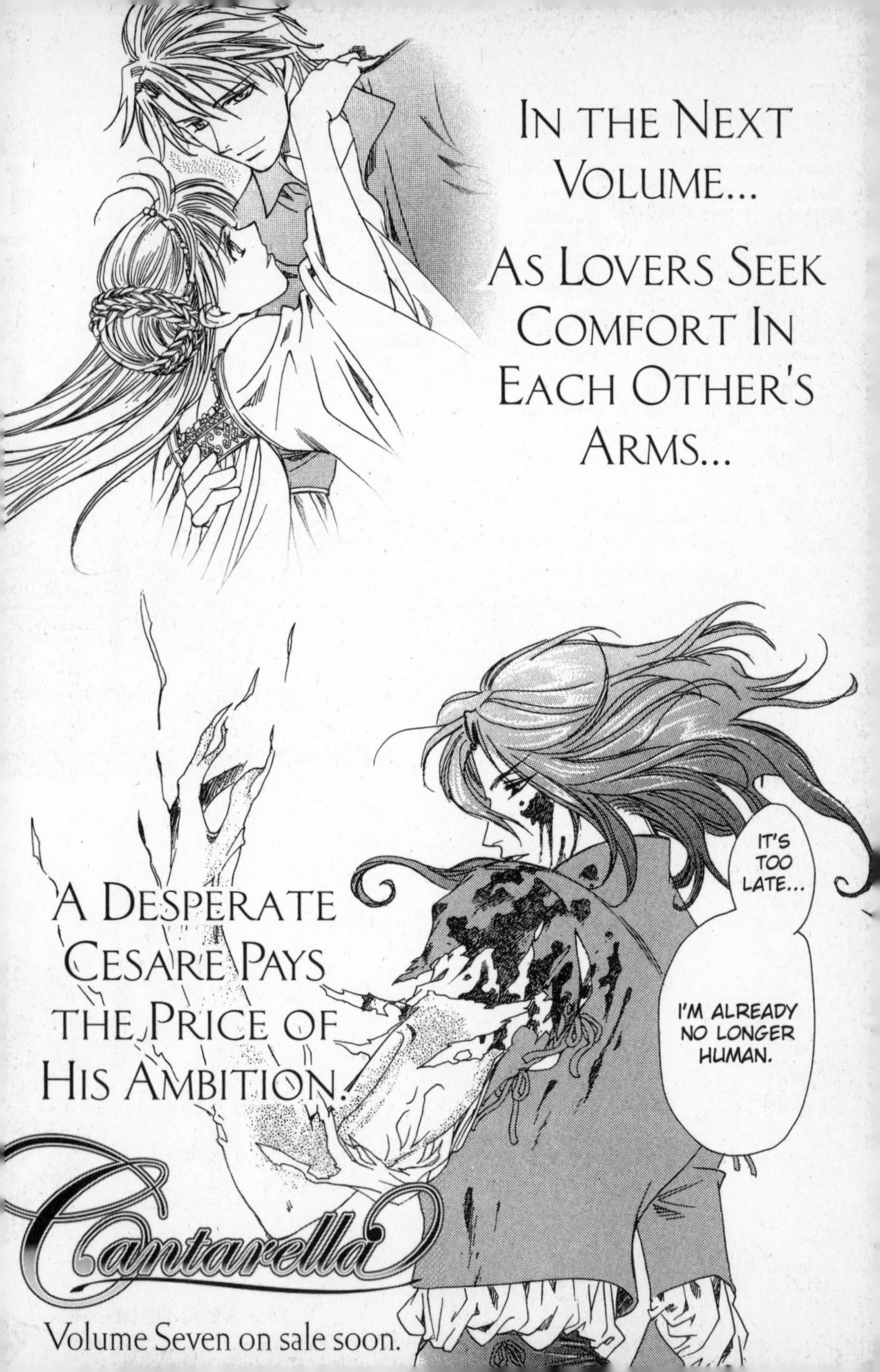
In the Next Volume...
As Lovers Seek Comfort In Each Other's Arms...
A Desperate Cesare Pays the Price of His Ambition.
IT'S TOO LATE...
I'M ALREADY NO LONGER HUMAN.
Cantarella
Volume Seven on sale soon.

BLACK SUN ● SILVER MOON

SAVING THE WORLD...
ONE ZOMBIE AT A TIME.

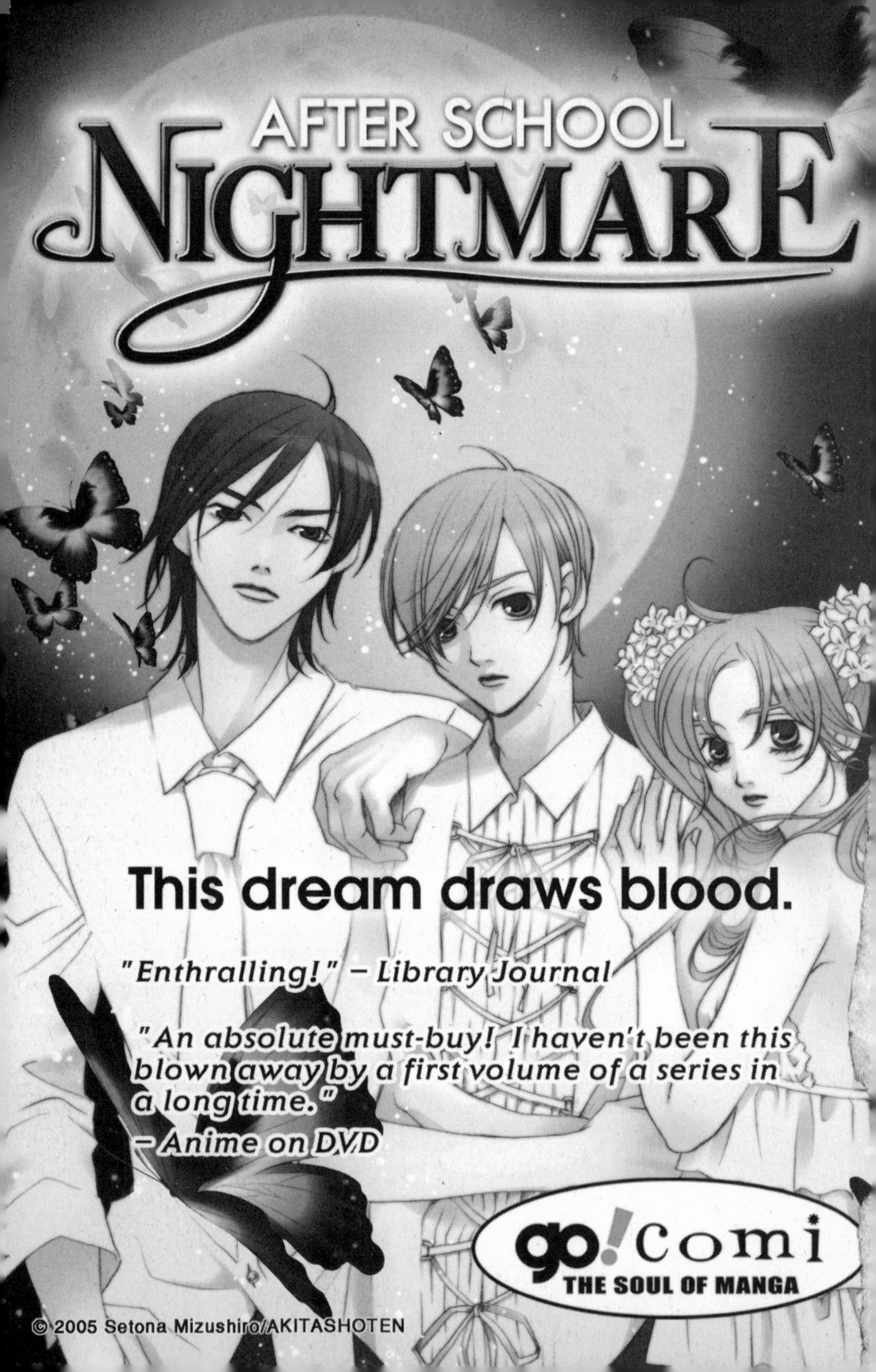
AFTER SCHOOL
NIGHTMARE
This dream draws blood.
"Enthralling!" – Library Journal
"An absolute must-buy! I haven't been this blown away by a first volume of a series in a long time."
– Anime on DVD
go!comi
THE SOUL OF MANGA
© 2005 Setona Mizushiro/AKITASHOTEN

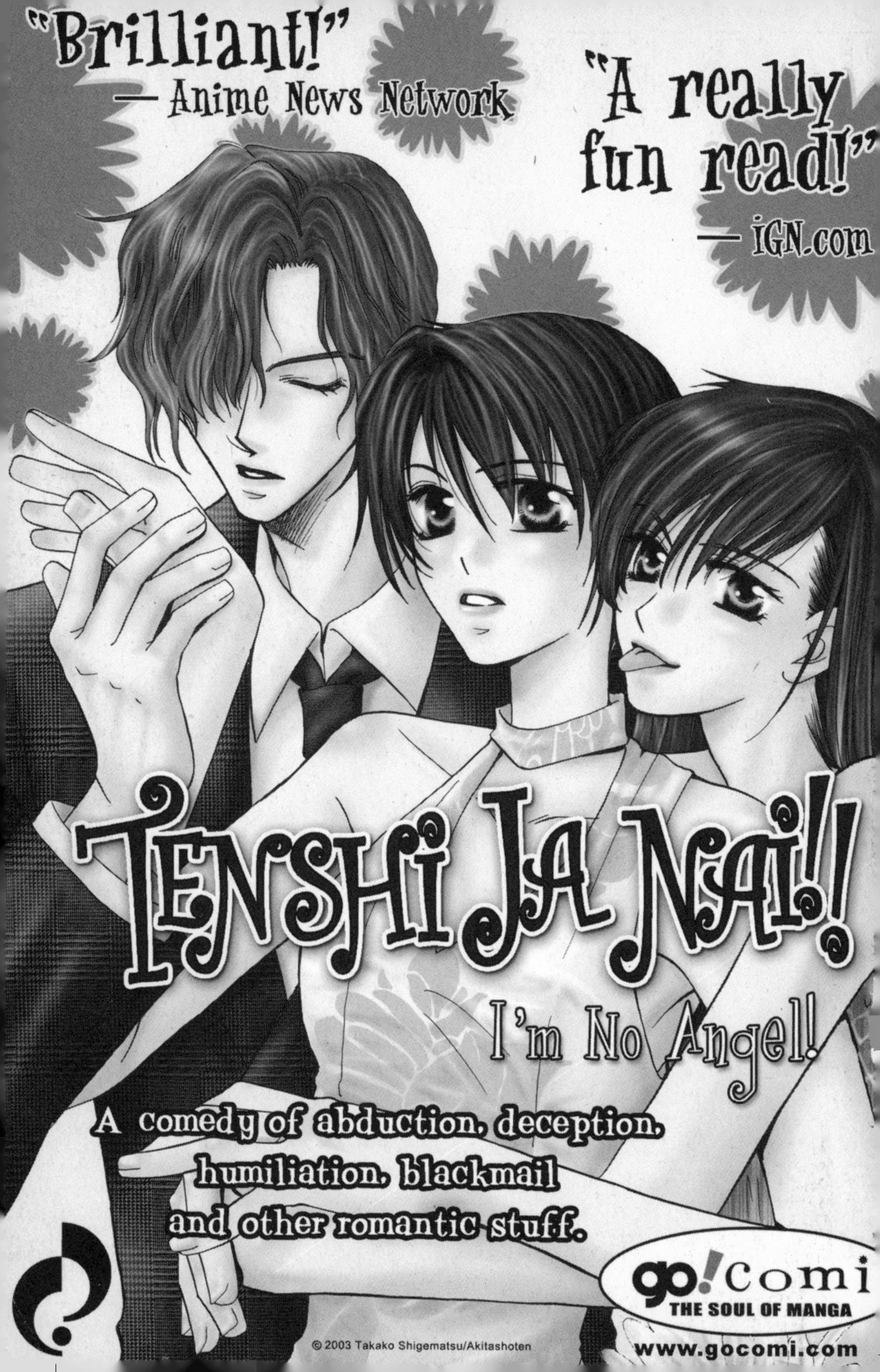
"Brilliant!"
— Anime News Network
"A really fun read!"
— IGN.com
TENSHI JA NAI!!
I'm No Angel!
A comedy of abduction, deception, humiliation, blackmail and other romantic stuff.
go!comi
THE SOUL OF MANGA
© 2003 Takako Shigematsu/Akitashoten
www.gocomi.com

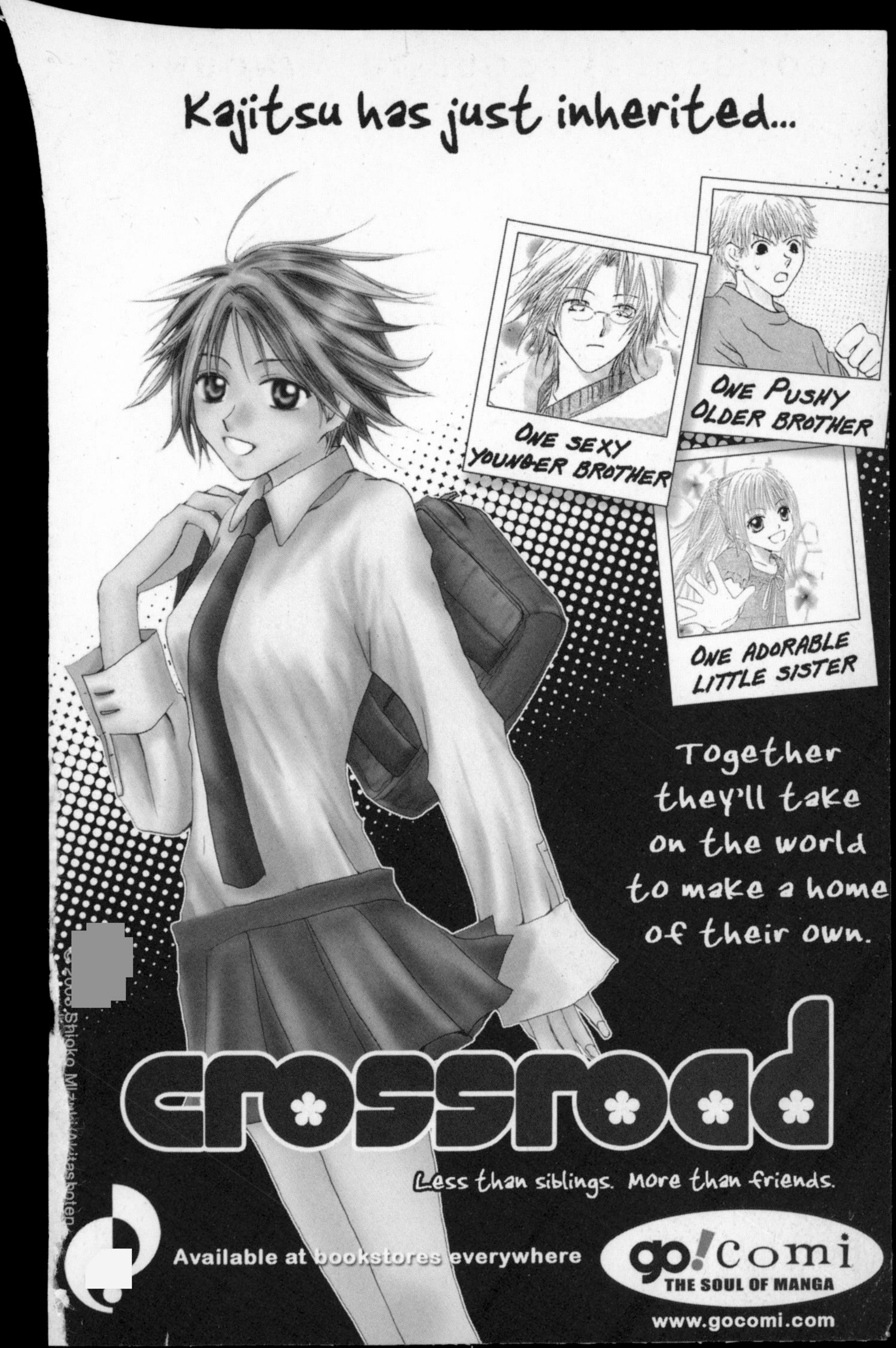

Kajitsu has just inherited...
ONE SEXY YOUNGER BROTHER
ONE PUSHY OLDER BROTHER
ONE ADORABLE LITTLE SISTER
Together they'll take on the world to make a home of their own.
crossroad
Less than siblings. More than friends.
Available at bookstores everywhere
go!comi
THE SOUL OF MANGA
www.gocomi.com

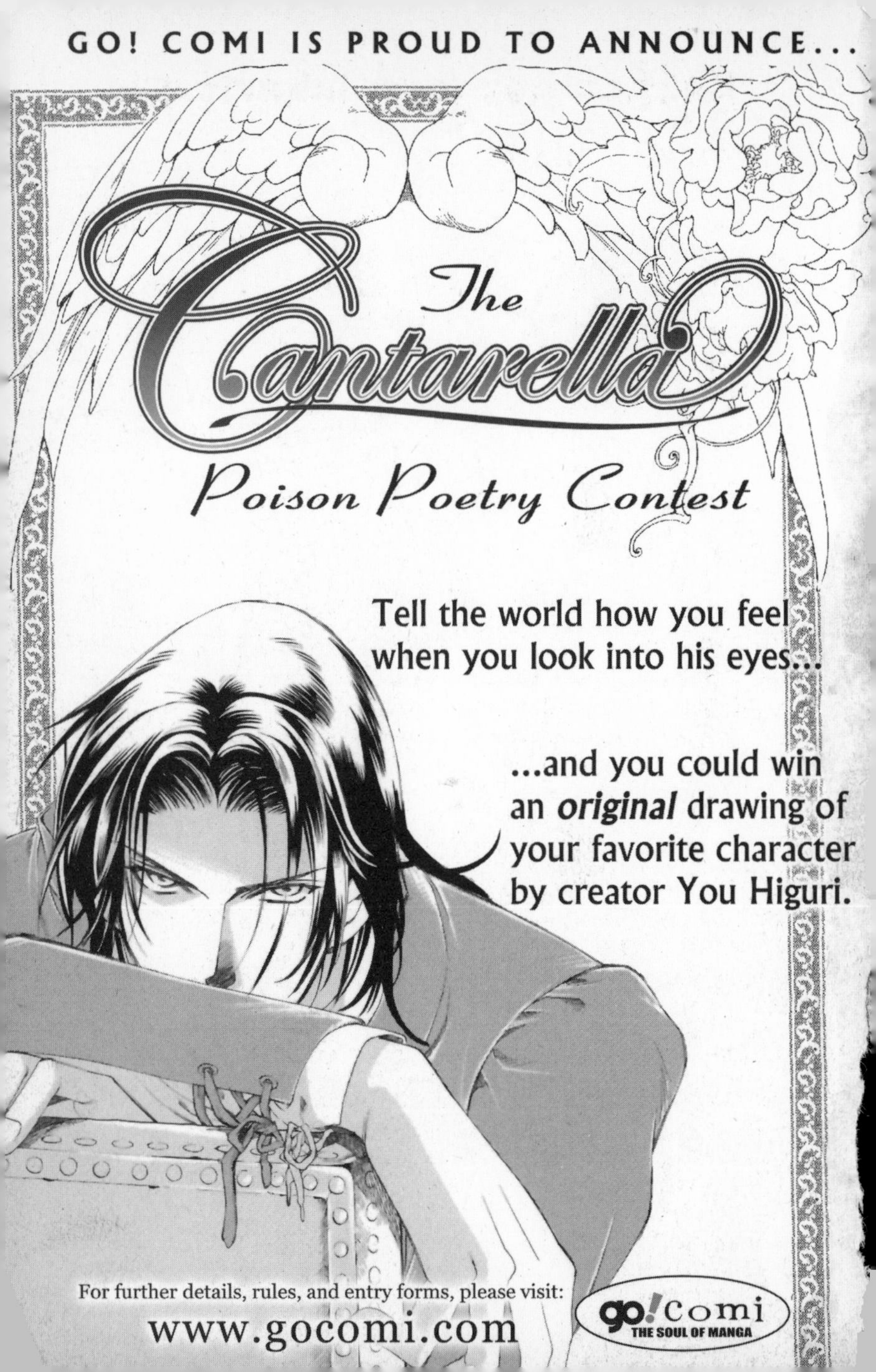
GO! COMI IS PROUD TO ANNOUNCE...
The Cantarella
Poison Poetry Contest
Tell the world how you feel when you look into his eyes...
...and you could win an *original* drawing of your favorite character by creator You Higuri.
For further details, rules, and entry forms, please visit:
www.gocomi.com
go!comi
THE SOUL OF MANGA

AUTHOR'S NOTE

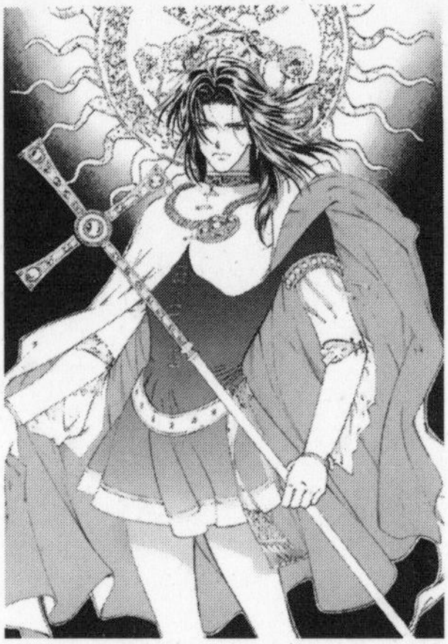

Seems the German version of "Cantarella" has been published. In such a Catholic country, is its material okay, I wonder!? Incidentally, the Chinese version of "Cantarella" was titled "禁断毒天使" (Prohibited Angel of Poison). Pretty cool, eh?

Visit You Higuri online at
www.youhiguri.com